Four
Horsemen

Four Horsemen

pollution
poverty
famine
violence

Esther Penchef

California State College, Los Angeles

 Canfield Press

San Francisco

A Department of Harper & Row, Publishers, Inc.
New York • Evanston • London

FOUR HORSEMEN: Pollution, Poverty, Famine, Violence

Copyright © 1971 by Esther Penchef

Standard Book Number: 06–386730–3

Library of Congress Catalog Card Number: 76–150864

Cover Design by Robert Bausch

Interior Book Design by Gracia A. Alkema

Contents

Preface ix

Introduction 1
Bibliography 9

Pollution 11
Man Against Nature: An Outmoded Concept 16
  Clarence J. Glacken

Our Vital Resources 28
  Jack Bregman and Sergel Lenormand

Genesis of a Nightmare 33
  George R. Stewart

It's Time to Turn Down All That Noise 39
  John M. Mecklin

What Needs to Be Done? 52
  Wheeler McMillen

Everyone Wants to Save the Environment 58
  Frank M. Potter, Jr.

The Chemistry and Cost 68
  R. Stephen Berry

Bibliography 83

Poverty 85
The Numbers of Poor 92
  Ben B. Seligman

The Sociology of Poverty 106
  Lewis A. Coser

The Poor Who Live Among Us 117
  Lee E. Dirks

Fifth Avenue, Uptown 127
  James Baldwin

The Culture of Poverty 135
  Oscar Lewis

The Invisible Land   142
Michael Harrington

Where the Real Poverty Is: Plight of American Indians   155
U.S. News & World Report

How Much Is Enough?   164
George Bernard Shaw

What Can Be Done?   167
Barbara Ritchie

Bibliography   176

Famine   179

The Population-Food Collision Is Inevitable   189
William Paddock and Paul Paddock

Hunger, U.S.A.   216
Citizen's Board of Inquiry

Population, Food, and Environment: Is the Battle Lost?   246
Paul R. Ehrlich

Birth Control Now: A Survey   257
U.S. News & World Report

The Right to Have Children   267
Marjory L. Bracher

School Lunch to Food Stamps: America Cares for Its
Hungry   274
Samuel C. Vannerman

The United States and World Hunger   280
Duncan Norton-Taylor

Bibliography   294

Violence   297

The Functions of Social Conflict   302
Lewis A. Coser

Historical Patterns of Violence in America   307
Richard Maxwell Brown

Violent Crime   342
National Commission

Response to Violence   350
W. Walter Menninger

Television and Violence   355
    James D. Halloran

When Does a Riot Become a Revolution?   365
    J. H. Plumb

Rioting, Insurrection, and Civil Disobedience   369
    Ralph W. Conant

Violent Men   380
    Hans Toch

Recommendations for the Prevention of Violence   404
    National Commission

Bibliography   412

Preface

Designed chiefly for courses in social problems and introductory sociology, this volume presents readings in four critical social areas —pollution, poverty, famine, and violence—that currently command the attention of most civilized societies. The worldwide scope of these problems demonstrates the extent to which conditions and processes in our environment interact and underlines the fact that they are not simply unrelated events or acute situations reported in the news media. For more than that, an analysis of these areas establishes that we must reorder our values so that our interrelatedness with all mankind, with all nature, will have top priority. Knowing the underlying, chronic conditions and their pervasiveness in our society will increase our overall perspective and help shape new directions in finding solutions.

Four Horsemen is not, of course, an encyclopedia of social problems or a compendium of knowledge in any of the four areas discussed. Hopefully, however, the book provides enough breadth and depth to stimulate awareness of each problem and to encourage further inquiry. Traditional areas of social problems are omitted, since many other books already give them excellent coverage. Theoretical elaborations have also been avoided in favor of discussions by qualified authorities of the specific ramifications of pollution, poverty, famine, and violence.

The generosity of the many authors who were willing to have their work included here is sincerely appreciated.

Esther Penchef

Four
Horsemen

Introduction

The Four Horsemen of the Apocalypse are allegorical figures in the Bible (Rev. 6:1–8) that symbolize the coming of calamities upon the earth. The first horseman rode on a white horse. He was carrying a bow and a crown was given to him. This figure represented a conquering invader, or Conquest. The second rider carried a great sword and rode on a red horse. The color red and the sword stood for the ravages of War. A black horse followed the first two, and its rider carried a scales for weighing grain that is understood to represent Famine. The last of the four appeared on a pale horse, and the name of the rider was Thanatos, which is translated sometimes as Death and sometimes as Pestilence.

Today's four horsemen, however, may be pollution, poverty, famine, and violence, for these are indeed among the most threatening and the most pervasive problems now confronting mankind.

Pollution is probably the most serious problem that human society faces today. It is not confined to specific geographical areas but is global in extent. In the last twenty-five years it has spread in one form or another over the whole planet and constitutes a genuine threat not only to the quality but to the very existence of life.

Poverty, like pollution, is global in range and involves all mankind. However, today a widening chasm separates rich and poor nations. The rich countries have benefited from the technological revolution by continuously improved standards of living.

The effect of the same phenomenon in the poor countries has been to multiply human misery, for the great technological advances have brought about a lower death rate so that the number of human beings is increasing at rates higher than ever before experienced.

The fact that an estimated two-thirds of the world's population live in countries in which the average diet is considerably below the minimum nutritional level required for normal health and activity indicates the extent and seriousness of the problem of famine. And even in America, where the food supply is more than adequate for the population, the incidence of malnutrition among the poor is shockingly high.

Capacity for violence is a part of human nature, and thus violence has plagued men and nations in one way or another over the centuries. In recent years an acute resurgence of violence in the United States has bewildered Americans and has put the problem emphatically in the foreground.

All of these problems are profound—both in the breadth of their effects on mankind and in the toll they are taking in our world. In sociology they are classified as social problems.

A *social problem* has four defining characteristics: it is (1) a condition affecting a significant, or large, number of people (2) in ways they consider undesirable, or in ways they see as threatening to an established social value; (3) there is a consensus that the condition can be eliminated or at least modified (4) through appropriate social, or collective, action. In other words, when conditions exist that do not conform to the real desires of a significant segment of the population and those members of the society are aware of the offending circumstances, there is a potential problem.

Social problems may issue from social disorganization or from deviant behavior. *Social disorganization* refers to inadequacies or breakdowns in a social system which result in the system not fulfilling its functions or purposes in some way. For example, when the economy failed to operate according to established principles in 1930, the country was overwhelmed by a great financial depression that was indeed a problem to millions of people. Deviant behavior refers to conduct that does not conform to the social norms or acceptable standards of society. When the behavior of any considerable number of people deviates unfavorably from what the majority holds to be good and proper, or when it deviates in a way that endangers social institutions—such as family, marriage, government—there is a potential social problem.

Behavior is structured around positions within the group. More or less specific patterns of behavior, called *roles,* are characteristically associated with given positions and society expects this behavior from those occupying the particular positions. For example, since a banker is expected to be trustworthy in handling the money of others, when he absconds with bank funds it is a greater shock to the community than when an ex-convict steals from the bank. The criminal is behaving according to his role and the banker is not.

The vast majority of people are highly conforming and they play their roles with integrity. Most students obey school rules, respect the relationship of teacher and student, acknowledge proper authority and meet the dictated requirements of their position. Teachers have expected this normative behavior from their students without significant disappointment for centuries; thus, when the recent demonstrations of protest, dissent, and defiance of authority were staged on college campuses, the shock was so extreme as to be paralyzing in some instances. The rejection of established procedures and the unpredictability of student behavior created serious problems of administration.

Deviant behavior is disruptive because it is a threat to the *status quo,* to convention and orthodoxy which depend upon a system of shared social values. The concept *social value* refers to the significance or meaning which is culturally attached to any given idea, object, process, or state of being. Values are the meanings, derived from culture and learned through social interaction, that each individual uses to interpret his environment. A dinner steak may be defined as a portion of the flesh of a beef cow or steer, prepared for human consumption by cooking. As such, in our culture it has a strong positive value, is considered highly desirable, and is socially approved. In India the definition would be similarly understood, but within large religious groups there, it would be given a negative value. Meat eating is disapproved and looked upon as immoral, so a dinner steak would call forth a different meaning or value than it does here. A concept takes on different meanings and significance according to the social values of the group involved.

Values cause one to have preferences. They are not to be confused with specific goals or objectives, but rather they are the general criteria by which goals are chosen. Values are at the root of what an individual or group wants and wants to become. They provide the framework for organizing behavior.

There are dominant and subordinate values. Strength or dominance depends on (1) what proportion of the population accepts the value; (2) how long it has persisted; (3) the intensity of the feeling toward maintaining it; and (4) the prestige of the persons, objects, or organizations that bear or uphold the value. Some of the traditional dominant values in American culture are: monogamous marriage, education, democracy, science, success, work, competition, and acquisitiveness.

Many different approaches are used in dealing with social problems. One popular tactic is to appeal to emotion, to arouse hostility, shame, or sympathy, and thereby encourage action. Some problems lend themselves to the idea of sin and guilt, in which case theologians and organized religious groups are often highly effective in influencing the people involved. Literary works many times have been influential in increasing public awareness of a problem and in motivating action by dramatizing the situation. If a problem persists, it is not uncommon for the group to resort to passing new laws designed to rectify the situation. All such reactions at best produce only temporary results unless they lead to changes in the circumstances that produce the difficulty.

There is great need for the scientific study of social problems. The sociologist, as a scientist, approaches problem behavior or problem situations in the same way he would approach normal or good behavior. He is concerned with factual information about what exists and how it came to be. Traditionally, his role has not been as an activist or ameliorator of problems, but as a supplier of the information and insights necessary in determining the most effective action for achieving a given goal.

Because of the need for scientific objectivity in relation to social problems, the sociologist has been expected to remain morally uncommitted as to problems and issues. Recently, however, more concern has been developing for the moral responsibility of scientists and the social usefulness of science. Many sociologists are taking a stand in favor of greater involvement in efforts to evaluate and resolve social problems.

The sociology of a social problem deals with (1) its epidemiology, that is, its incidence and distribution, and the nature of its effect upon people; (2) the genesis of the problem—whether it directly or indirectly issues from the value system, whether it is man initiated or a catastrophe of nature; and (3) what the solution will entail.

The disparity between social standards and actual conditions is the crux of a social problem. The extent of the discrepancy is usually not easy to ascertain. For example, there is great question as to the amount of delinquent behavior among juveniles. It is impossible to obtain an accurate count of offenses for many reasons. For one thing, what acts constitute delinquent behavior is vaguely defined. In addition, communities differ in their attitudes toward law enforcement in relation to juveniles, and record keeping and reporting are neither uniform nor mandatory. However, if numerical measurement were possible, the significance of such facts would still be a matter for evaluation by the members of the group concerned. If there is a high degree of consensus in regard to the social standards that are involved, a majority opinion as to the significance of the data provides a fair approximation of the seriousness of the disharmony between social standards and actual conditions. But there are difficulties in evaluating such data. Persons who have different positions and different vested interests hold dissimilar views toward many things. Furthermore, social standards are not applied equally to members of a society, and as a result similar behavior is variously evaluated. Finally, the judgment of an individual with great prestige and power has much influence in the definition of what is to be considered a problem, in which case the evaluation is not a valid expression of majority opinion. Nevertheless, as to amount and distribution, an approximation can be made on the basis of the factual data available, with due consideration given to all known variables.

Since values play an important part not only in a society's decision that some particular condition constitutes a problem, but also in the decision as to whether in a given situation the problem exists, the study of a social problem must include an analysis of the relation between behavior and values, between values and statuses and roles, and between various values within the system.

Values figure in the causality of social problems in many different ways. In a dynamic society the social situation may undergo such great change that previously held values are no longer appropriate and thus constitute a maladjustment. They may be unsuitable only for a certain segment of the population, in which case such severe stress and strain are produced that a subvalue system or subculture develops. Opposing values may exist within the same system and cause great personal and group conflict. The value system of a society may produce unforeseen and unintended consequences. For example, technological progress is given high priority in our society, and we have produced large, heavy, high-powered automobiles in such a way that they could be made available to great numbers of the population, with the overwhelming support and approval of the majority. "Two cars in every garage" is no longer seen as an unmixed blessing, however, since the cost has become apparent in the form of pollution, traffic congestion, and parking needs. But now the manufacturers of the automobiles and of the fuel for their operation are not eager to jeopardize their profitable production by supporting changes for the benefit of the total community. Some elements of a population have vested interests in statuses or roles founded on particular values that they will fight to preserve and perpetuate regardless of the broader effects.

It is helpful to know the derivation of the social value that is threatened. Some values arise spontaneously out of a social situation. For example, if every man were needed to help defend against an outside invader, the health and well-being of every man would be of prime importance as a matter of course. On the other hand, some values are superimposed by agencies for the purpose of facilitating control of one kind or another. They do not necessarily represent the attitude of the majority, but may represent merely its attitude toward the agency. Thus, virginity might not have been accorded great significance in our culture had the founders not been dedicated to the Christian faith.

Social problems are a relatively recent field of study. Earlier, less democratic societies were resigned to adversity because of their belief in predestination. They placed their hope for reform or relief in divine intervention. Inequalities and human misery and suffering were considered a part of the natural order on this earth. The realization that many of man's problems can be attacked by social action, that these efforts are appropriate in this world rather than the next, and that such activity is a worthy social value is peculiar to the democratic point of view. The acknowledgment of this value has been a long, slow process even within our own culture, and its limited and grudging acceptance adds to our difficulties when social reform is attempted.

The lack of accurate factual information about a problem situation and the varying interpretations applied to the inadequate data also are great obstacles to the efficient treatment of such conditions.

Competing theories as to how to solve a particular problem, or how to solve social problems in general, constitute another major handicap. The *laissez faire* philosophy is one of the oldest and most prevalent theories applied to economic systems. It opposes governmental regulation of the economic affairs of men. The contention is that men should be left to their own devices, in which case the law of supply and demand will control excesses and attempted exploitations, and the "right" and "natural" condition will evolve. The fallacy of this myth was demonstrated long ago, but the *laissez faire* doctrine still taints the thinking of many people. Most advocates of this idea wish to apply it only to their own advantage and are willing to support government intervention only when it will operate for their benefit. For example, many industrialists oppose government aid to agriculture but insist on protective tariffs for their own interests. *Laissez faire* principles do not support government assistance to the poor, to small business, or to any disadvantaged group for the purpose of alleviating a social problem. The doctrine is a kind of social Darwinism or "survival of the fittest" idea.

There is a wide range of opinion on the issue of whether efforts to solve social problems should be directed toward elimination or amelioration. To put an end to the problem may be highly desirable, but that requires correction at the source, which is usually very costly and sometimes impossible. It is argued that it is better merely to provide help that will enable the victims to cope with the effects. In other words, it is a matter of building a fence at the top of the cliff or stationing an ambulance at the bottom. Our population is divided today in respect to what is the proper direction of the attack on poverty, whether people should be educated and trained to be self-supporting or merely maintained at a subsistence level through handouts. The two points of view are not mutually exclusive, and it is likely that a combination of both is more practical than either one alone.

The question of whether to work at the correction of a problem piecemeal or *in toto* has support on both sides. The strongest argument is based on the high cost of widespread and all-inclusive reform of any kind. On the other hand, the use of superficial treatment or fragmental attacks only on the periphery may save initial dollars and cents but be far more costly in the waste and abuse of human resources in the long run. Moreover, many problems feed upon themselves, with consequent proliferation, so that the only way to stop the cycle is to completely uproot the source. Authorities tell us that the reconstruction of our environment requires a global approach if it is to succeed, although the present programs tend to concentrate on small areas.

From the beginning, our society has relied heavily on the effectiveness of "passing a law" to solve a problem. Coercion through legislation requires not only applicable laws, but also the enforcement of those measures. Laws are made to apply to all members of the society, and therefore to eliminate problem behavior through legislation may mean severe limitation on the freedom of everyone. Most people resent such restriction so much that they are apt to find the solution worse than the problem. In such instances the laws may become less effective and more difficult to enforce. It is probably true that police officers would be more successful in apprehending criminals if they were permitted to conduct searches without warrants and to eavesdrop by wiretapping, but allowing this procedure in the enforcement of law places every individual's right to privacy in jeopardy, and for most Americans protection against invasion of privacy represents a higher value than does the catching of criminals.

The alternative to such coercive measures is persuasion through education and enlightenment. Most situations are best dealt with by utilizing both approaches. It is unlikely that the Civil Rights Movement would have had any degree of success without the support of legislation. But education has made its enforcement much easier.

Those whose attitudes are ambiguous and whose values are inconsistent like to attribute causation of problems to factors that might be controlled or eliminated without treading on the toes of vested interests or prestigious institutions, or to factors that are conceded to be uncontrollable and therefore may be safely deplored. Our institutions, philosophies, and ideologies resist changes that threaten their own coherence.

These and many more circumstances tend to prevent penetrating analysis of social problems and impede their solution. Every choice of action or program has a cost, for in selecting one a hundred other possibilities are precluded.

From the many current social problems, four were selected for consideration in this book. They are large-scale problems in that they are global in character and cannot be dealt with effectively within the boundaries of any one nation. There are numerous other serious problems such as social injustice, divorce, drugs, and alcoholism, but they are not universal in their occurrence or in their effects. They are subject to local control according to varying norms. The ramifications of pollution, poverty, famine, and violence extend beyond national boundaries. The cooperative efforts of all nations in developing a world-wide strategy will be needed in order to cope successfully with these problem conditions.

The world has moved into a new era in which international cooperation on a level never before attempted must become a reality. Our value system must be reorganized to include a commitment to mankind that transcends personal and even national interests. If there is to be any kind of viable future, the human race must apply its full resources of knowledge and intelligence to directing the course of the vast, inevitable process of change. As a beginning, we must become acquainted with the needs of others as well as of ourselves, and we must see them in perspective as they interrelate. Some see the present as the period of cognitive dissonance that precedes change or restructuring. If this is true, then there must be an honest confrontation with our value system and a reordering of its hierarchy.

It is hoped that the study of the four problems treated in this volume may constitute a basis for wider and deeper reflection upon the dynamics of the world transformation through which we are now passing.

Bibliography

Cuber, John F., Kenkel, Wm. F., and Harper, Robert A. *Problems of American Society*. New York: Holt, Rinehart and Winston, 1964.

Frank, Lawrence K. "Social Problems." *American Journal of Sociology* 30 (1925): 463–473.

Fuller, Richard C., and Myers, Richard R. "The Natural History of a Social Problem." *American Sociological Review* 6 (1941): 320–328.

Gold, Harry, and Scarpitti, Frank R. *Combatting Social Problems*. New York: Holt, Rinehart and Winston, 1967.

Horton, Paul B., and Leslie, Gerald R. *The Sociology of Social Problems*. New York: Appleton-Century-Crofts, 1955.

Merrill, Francis E. "The Study of Social Problems." *American Sociological Review* 13 (1948): 251–259.

Merton, Robert K., and Nisbet, Robert A. *Contemporary Social Problems*. New York: Harcourt, Brace & World, 1961.

Vickers, Sir Geoffrey. *Value Systems and Social Process*. New York: Basic Books, 1968.

Photo by Richard F. Conrat, Photo Find, S.F.

Pollution

Pollution has been defined as "an undesirable change in the physical, chemical, or biological characteristics of our air, land, and water that may or will harmfully affect human life or that of any other desirable species, or industrial processes, living conditions, or cultural assets; or that may or will waste or deteriorate our raw material resources."[1] Today pollution is increasing at such a rate that the problem is no longer a question merely of harmful or unpleasant effects, but of how soon life itself will become impossible if the trend is not reversed. Our dedication to the futherance of technological achievement has produced remarkable accomplishments, but our failure or inability to foresee the ramifications of each advance has brought upon us unanticipated and unintended social problems. The unrestricted growth of the population and the concomitant increase of activity, coupled with unrestricted technology directed toward dominance of the environment, have produced a devastating by-product—an imbalance in the system of nature that makes life possible on this planet.

The balance of nature is dealt with in the field of *ecology*, which is the study of "the relation of organisms or groups of organisms to their environment." In ecology the world of living things is perceived as a system of dynamic interdependences. It is a great configuration in which all living things are interrelated and in continual interaction with the inorganic elements of the environ-

11

ment. Our universe is a field of variables so closely and mutually interrelated that any change, anywhere, will, in some degree, affect the whole. Charles Darwin used the metaphor "web of life" to describe the organism's struggle with both the organic and inorganic substance of its environment for its existence.

"Environment," as the term is used in ecology, refers to all the climatic and geographic factors, including plant and animal life, that exert influences upon an organism. The survival of an organism is determined by its environment; thus, life is a synthesis of organism and environment. The organism has the ability to manipulate factors in the external world and to seek combinations of factors congenial to its survival, but that ability is not always sufficient in the face of environmental change, which proceeds without regard for the welfare of the organism.

To illustrate the kind of network that binds different organisms together, Darwin described the relationship between the humblebees and red clover. Humblebees are the only insects that can pollinate red clover because they are the only ones that can penetrate to the nectar in the blossom. Field mice are enemies of humblebees. They rob the bees' nests of stored food, thereby decreasing the bee population. Cats destroy field mice. Thus, the fertilization of red clover is influenced by the number of cats available to control the field mice so that the propagation of humblebees can go on undisturbed.[2]

There is a mutual dependence between unlike organisms, the name for which is *symbiosis*. A symbiotic relationship is a kind of partnership in which each member has different needs; what constitutes waste for one is exactly what is needed by the other. Each is necessary to the other, and the destruction of one member leads to the death of the other.

Human beings are able to exist and enjoy life only because of the conditions produced on the earth's surface by the action of bacteria, plants, and animals. Any significant disturbance of the ecological equilibrium or the balance of nature is a threat to human life. Man has so altered the world environment that we are now confronted with the potential destruction of the balanced natural system that sustains life on this planet.

One of the elements of the environment that is affected most by the ongoing destructive processes is the air. Air over urban centers contains a conglomeration of metallic oxides, tar, stone, bits of metal, carbon, ash, aerosols, mists of oil, and soot. The sulphur dioxide that comes from the burning of fuel oil, coal, and coke literally eats into brick and metal; we can only assume that it leaves its mark on lung tissue, eyes, and skin. Photochemical smog, which is produced by the action of sunlight on the gases from automobile exhaust, as well as on other chemical fumes, carries within it hundreds of gases, some deadly. It is well known that polluted air can cause mass poisoning.

Crop sprays and DDT are carried by the air currents and are found at great distances from their source. Nuclear explosions have added radio-isotopes that are proving not to be as harmless as they were first thought to be. Some authorities have called attention to the problem of depletion of the oxygen content of the air. A jet plane, for example, burns thirty-five tons of oxygen in one trip across the Atlantic. There is the possibility that the consumption of oxygen may be greater than its production and replacement in the atmosphere.

Air pollution in the United States varies from city to city, being influenced by such things as wind currents, sunlight, number of automobiles and trucks in use, industries in the area, and the amount of coal and oil burned. The city said to have the most heavily polluted atmosphere is Anchorage, Alaska. Charleston, West Virginia, Chicago, and Los Angeles are not far behind.

Our need for water is constantly increasing, particularly our need for pure water. Rivers have become so polluted that they catch fire, and many lakes in all parts of the world no longer can sustain marine life. Regulation of the disposal of industrial waste and the discharge of sewage into bodies of water is still lagging.

The landscape has been attacked and irremediable damage inflicted through such things as strip mining, turning valleys into reservoirs, and dredging and bulldozing through forests and prairies with an arrogant singleness of purpose.

Another present-day impairment of the environment is noise pollution. The destructive effects of the excessive exposure of human beings to noise are only beginning to be recognized.

To cope with this gargantuan problem of pollution, a complete upheaval in our value system may be required. As new insights into the interdependence of species and the network of organic-inorganic relationships are gained, it may become desirable to phase out our competitive economic system in favor of a model based on cooperation. It may no longer be feasible to plan and program for states and nations, but rather for regions defined in terms of climate, topography, watershed, and similar factors. A more critical consideration of the potential of technology for solving the pollution problem may diminish our faith in the power of science. It may even be necessary to reverse our growth-and-progress orientation and to learn to care equally for all living things.

Many workable solutions to our environmental problems and many specific reforms are now being proposed. Some of the most frequently mentioned recommendations are:

1. Restrict the freedom of human reproduction so that we may preserve and nurture other and more precious freedoms.

2. Reduce consumption of natural energy sources, such as fossil fuels. Steps toward this objective include expansion of public transportation systems instead of highways; better railroad service for short trips; dis-

couraging the excessive use of electricity by increasing the rate charged as the quantity used increases.

3. Use the integrated control approach in controlling the pest problem, that is, the combination of chemical, cultural, biological, and physical techniques into a smoothly working system of pest management.

4. Develop game ranching, and make greater use of the wild ungulates as a source of animal products, because they have more potential for food production than domestic livestock with less stress on the environment.

5. Develop an engine that will power automobiles with nontoxic fuel cells or that will combust a much higher proportion of its fuel. In the meantime, for the second car, use a small electric cart.

6. Set up experimental colleges to counter the university's resistance to change, and work toward a balance between pure and applied research.

7. Study the relationship between some of our values, such as nationalistic vanity, pandering to corporate profit, and worship of technology, and our deteriorating environment.

8. Recycle waste material so that resources can be used over and over again instead of discarding material after one use. Discontinue planned obsolescence.

9. Organize collective action and pressure for legislation and favorable court decisions; bring actions against public officials who are guilty of nonfeasance; and bring nuisance, trespass, and negligence suits against polluters.

10. Change our concept of "man against nature" to one of balance and harmony of "man with nature."

If some of these proposals seem drastic, so are the problems they are designed to combat, as the articles that follow will establish. But these articles also make clear the obstacles to be encountered in attempts to resolve the pollution problem.

The author of the first article, Clarence J. Glacken, is a professor of geography at the University of California (Berkeley), and one of his chief interests is the history of cultural concepts of nature. He believes a change is necessary in our attitude toward nature, a change in our values. Glacken explains why man can no longer be against nature but must assume a stewardship of and responsibility for the protection of the natural environment.

The next four articles describe how contamination is affecting the environment. "Our Vital Resources" describes the existing threat to our supply of clean air and pure water. "Genesis of a Nightmare" deals with the cost of getting rid of the discarded and unwanted remains of our tremendous production system and describes the enormous proportions that the disposal problem in the United States is reaching. Noise has in the past been tolerated as an inevitable part of the environment, but it has so increased in volume and ubiquity that it is a threat to the mental and physical health of millions of people. "It's Time to Turn Down All That Noise" is especially informative regarding avenues to be pursued to bring about a reduction in this daily harassment. "What Needs to Be Done?" concentrates on the problem of pesticides. It does not minimize the problem, but it warns against following the suggestions of extremists who would ban pesticides without considering the problems that would arise from such action. The article illustrates the delicate balance that complicates programs designed to alleviate the present situation.

The last two articles present some of the major difficulties to be surmounted in any program for improvement and point out the direction that action should take. "Everyone Wants to Save the Environment" considers some of the reasons why efforts to do anything about pollution are usually thwarted. The article discusses the limitations of government and the bureaucracy and the necessity for collective action by concerned citizens. The author of "The Chemistry and the Cost," R. Stephen Berry, is a professor of chemistry at the University of Chicago and well qualified to present the specifics of air pollution. Berry offers concrete programs for action that he believes would prevent the otherwise inevitable crisis.

Notes

1. S. Fred Singer, "Global Effects of Environmental Pollution," *Science,* 162 (1968): 1308.

2. Charles Darwin, *Origin of Species,* 6th ed. (New York: Appleton and Company, 1904), p. 59.

The idea of man against nature has not been common to all peoples. Identification of man with nature is more typical of prehistoric and primitive peoples. In modern times Western man has directed his energies toward gaining dominion over nature as an essential element of the progress of civilization. The interrelationship of man and nature must be given greater recognition, and a reverence for nature must become one of our primary values if we are to prevent further deterioration of the environment.

Man Against Nature: An Outmoded Concept

Clarence J. Glacken

Outmoded means out of fashion or obsolete, no longer able to fulfill a proper function. I am not certain, therefore, that the title of this discussion is a precise one. For outmoded does not mean tired or lacking in energy or virility. The world is full of outmoded ideas which are still very strong and give no indication of dying off.

The topic of this lecture, including its subtitle, opens up themes so vast that their full analysis would carry us deeply into the history of thought, not only Western thought but all thought. The title, however, is much more than rhetorical, for some concept of the man-nature theme and the man-nature relationship is part of any philosophy of life or any world view.

"Man against nature." "Man's mastery over nature." These dichotomies are often thought to be the only important concepts in Western civilization expressing the relationship between the two. Frequently, the "Western" concept of dominance or opposition has been contrasted with "Eastern" concepts of harmony and union with nature, but I believe this contrast oversimplifies matters. Like all other great civilizations, Western civilization is not monolithic in its summations, and it has nourished all sorts of different ideas. There is no question, however, that the man-nature dichotomy has been and continues to be extremely important and, although challenged, it has held its own in popular thought and has, in addition, diffused to many parts of the non-Western world.

I have the impression, however, that the concept of man against nature is not typical of the history of thought as a whole, or of the ideas of prehistoric and so-called primitive peoples. And even if one has reservations about applying the I-Thou, I-It concepts of Martin Buber, as some have done, to the relation of prehistoric and primitive man to nature, I think it comes closer to the mark to say that these peoples thought of themselves more as identified with rather than pitted against nature. This was one of the conclusions of Henri Frankfort and his colleagues in their work, *Beyond Philosophy*[1]: in contrast to modern man, prehistoric peoples enjoyed a close, lively association and identification with nature—as if it were a "thou" instead of an "it." This is an interesting approach, but we still know too little about the matter to make distinctions. The area is still poorly explored, but the evidence seems to indicate a widespread feeling of closeness of human to other kinds of life; see, for example, Colin Turnbull's description in *The Forest People*[2] of the attitudes of the pygmies of the Congo toward the forest in which they lived. This probability is reinforced by recent ethnographic studies which emphasize the intimate knowledge that primitive peoples have of their environment.

The idea of man against nature is thus, in my opinion, more parochial than universal. Admittedly it has achieved great strength in Western thought, but we must recognize that it is parochial because, despite powerful influences toward uniformity of ideas through mass media, other non-Western cultures, with their own values, still exist. The recognition of such parochialism forces us to ask why and under what circumstances the idea of man against nature grew up and has prospered until this day.

One reason for the lasting strength of the idea has been that in modern times it became, in variant forms, the basis for a secular philosophy of history. In this philosophy the course of civilization was seen as a movement, an evolution from a time in which man was under the control of nature to a point at which the situation is reversed and man is in control of nature. The interpretation is closely tied up with the desire to ameliorate the human condition by cultivating the arts and sciences, an idea which gradually developed in the eighteenth and nineteenth centuries into the idea of progress, progress often but not always being seen in terms of both a divorcement from nature and a mastery over it. A primordial harmony was assumed before the coming of man, but man in his progress would gradually humanize the world, creating through technological inventions an even more exalted harmony through his struggles and labors.

I would distinguish between two traditions of the idea of man against nature in Western thought, the first being derived from the Old Testament, especially Genesis 1; the second, a product of modern times, for which I would cite the philosophy of Francis Bacon as a convenient marker without insisting that it is the actual place and time of origin.

The lines of Genesis are indeed striking. In Genesis 1:20–28 a distinction is made between the acts of God with relationship to all life except man and the acts of God with relationship to man. In the one case, all life is to increase and to multiply; in the other, man is not only to do the same, but also to "have dominion over the fish of the sea and over the birds of the air and over every living thing that moves upon the earth." This is reaffirmed by God after the flood and a new start for the human race with Noah, his three sons, and their wives.

These Genesis verses have taken on a new and ironical meaning in recent decades and in the immediate present because much has been learned in the last century about culture and environment, especially the effects of the former on the latter. The acts of man ranging from deforestation to air pollution and nuclear warfare and the multiplication of man have given dramatic proof of his obedience to the orders of God for all life to multiply and for human life, in addition to multiplying, to have dominion over the rest of the creation.

Observers, especially non-Western ones, have cited the Genesis passages as criticism of Western civilization and its great preoccupation with man and his struggle against nature. I think this analysis is in error because the matter is much more complex. Certainly this theme as it comes from Genesis and from other Old Testament texts continues to be important to the present. Pope Paul VI's Encyclical letter "On the Development of Peoples" (1967) reasserts the truth of the Genesis statements concerning the earth's creation by God for man in its statement that the earth's resources should be developed responsibly, intelligently, and justly. In a striking persistence of ideas, the condition of mankind today is thus linked closely to the Genesis doctrine.

In my opinion, however, the historic juxtaposition of man against nature depends much more on modern thought and on more secular ideas. Without ascribing origins to them (perhaps for these we should look to the history of alchemy) I would cite three thinkers of the sixteenth and seventeenth centuries who expressed this concept at a time when it was more creative than it is at present: Bacon, René Descartes, and Gottfried Wilhelm von Leibnitz.

One of the most famous apothegms of Bacon was that we cannot command nature except by obeying her, and perhaps here we should think of "obeying" as implying "knowing" also. There are many pertinent illustrations but I will confine myself to The New Atlantis, in which one sees a philosopher ambitious to reject the scholastic philosophy as a teaching of inactivity, to promote the arts and the sciences, encouraging invention in order to change nature and to adapt it for human uses. In The New Atlantis, Bacon compares the great voyages of discovery which have opened the horizons of man with the continued narrowness of man's intellectual vision. Thus, it is essentially a program for the control of nature by man, a creative broadening act comparable in spirit to what he saw in the voyages of discovery.

In that vividly autobiographical philosophical text, The Discourse of Method, Descartes tells how he meditated on the inadequacies of the scholastic philosophy. Like Bacon and Leibnitz, he saw knowledge as the key to human betterment. Notions of general physics are intertwined with the good of man. We must have practical knowledge in order to gain ascendancy over speculative philosophy; we must know the elements—fire, air, earth, and water—as well as we know the trades of our artisans and "thus make ourselves, as it were, the lords and masters of nature."

In Leibnitz the philosophy is even more explicit. This indefatigable, rich, and noble mind saw the earth as a divinely designed planet; he was untiring in his hopes for ameliorating the lot of mankind, and mastery over nature was beneficent, a mark of progress. His is one of the most exalted attempts to correlate the progress of civilization with earth's gradual development by human hands as a habitable planet. The advancement of mankind was intertwined with the cultivation of the earth, and it became a mirror of man's enterprising attitudes. In his work, the idea of progress is linked with the idea of control over nature: as man progresses, the earth under his guiding hand will become even more perfect.

If this admittedly incomplete analysis is correct, the early modern form of the contrast between man and nature was viewed less in terms of struggle, more in terms of creativity, and for two reasons:

1. The struggle with and the control over nature were ways of depicting the progress of civilization. In its material aspects, civilization meant this—the purposive changes in nature, the overcoming of natural obstacles by bridges, drainage, roads, and later by railroads and air and sea routes.

2. There was little awareness or study of the age-old cumulative but unnoticed effects of man's activities in changing the environment. There is ample evidence of local awareness but such knowledge was not widely diffused. Lacking is that crescendo of complaint, based on ecological theory, about destruction of the environment by man so characteristic of the last 100 years and now so common that it appears in articles in *Science* magazine, in Sunday supplements, and in presidential addresses.

By the nineteenth century some glaring inadequacies of this idea were apparent; they are still. We can regard one phase of the romantic movement, despite its complexity, as a rebellion against the dichotomy between man and nature. In the movement for the protection of nature, we owe much to romantic ideas of the beauties of untouched and remote wildernesses, and of the importance of being conscious of our attitudes to the natural world.

In the nineteenth century, the idea of man's control over nature or man against nature was closely linked with the idea of indefinite and inevitable progress. Even today its vitality, I think, is owing to its association with vague, popular, poorly examined notions of progress, even if this progress has no more meaning than that a statistic of the current year in some desirable category is greater than it was for the previous year. Technology and invention were grist to this mill because they represented clear and easily verified successes. Lines in Alfred Lord Tennyson's "Locksley Hall" (as John Bagnell Bury has pointed out in his *The Idea of Progress*[3]) expressed his faith in progress—in the control over nature—as colorfully as any. When Tennyson wrote about his trip in 1830 on the first train from Liverpool to Manchester, he said he thought the whole world ran in grooves: "Then I made this line: '[Forward, forward, let us range,] Let the great world spin for ever down the ringing grooves of change.' " The optimism was based on material progress, on the idea that this high rational civilization in its onward motion not only advanced itself but was producing humanized environments which went along with it. It is true that especially toward the end of the century a literature questioning technology and its effects began to take form but, on the whole one sees in Western civilization of the nineteenth century the apogee of faith in science and technology—under the rubric of "control over nature."

In the second half of the century, however, the seeds of alternate views were planted—and while these origins too are complex and, if pursued, would lead us far afield, I wish to discuss three works that are symptomatic of things to come: Charles Darwin's *The Origin of Species* (1859), George Perkins Marsh's *Man and Nature* (1864), and Charles Dickens' *Hard Times* (1854).

Before doing this, let us look a little farther into the inadequacies of the above detailed idea which were already apparent in the second half of the last century. If we grant that a world view in any culture must rest on some conception of the man-nature relationship, whether it is a religious, economic, or esthetic one, or a combination of these and others, then we can say that in the middle of the nineteenth century the concept revealed shortcomings as a unifier of a body of ideas and its concomitant knowledge.

These shortcomings have in the main survived to the present. What are they? First, the concept is narrow and restrictive—and subject to the same criticism of the conception of man in the earlier traditional concepts of design and teleology. To say of the earth that it has been designed by a Creator for the sake of all life is one thing; to say that it is made for man alone and to use as he sees fit is another. The anthropocentrism of the latter is narrow and crippling. In the secular versions, which follow, the narrow and crippling anthropocentrism continues in the assumption of universal utility for man. All nature becomes a resource.

Furthermore, the emphasis was on the dichotomy, on two worlds, the world of man and the world of nature. I believe also that the dichotomy encouraged the study of man within the framework of human institutions alone, his struggle with and his control over nature, being activities carried on within the purview of these human institutions. It tended to discourage an organic view; beauty, variety, plentitude could be celebrated in art, music, literature. It encouraged a utilitarian view of nature, not a preserving or conserving one; the former was progressive, the latter romantic, an incurable clinging to the past. But its most misleading aspect, especially when it was an indistinguishable element of the idea of progress, was the high plane on which it placed man and his institutions. He dominated nature by rationality and purpose.

Too much rationality was assumed in the changes that brought about this control over nature, this progress. Mastery was the mastery of intelligence and planning. One feels in reading the optimistic literature of the period that the rationality of civilization was taken for granted. The belief was widespread that a great gulf separated primitive peoples and the peoples of European cultures. We now know—it was known then too by many—that the assumption of rationality in civilization is very misleading. Today there is too much evidence to the contrary—so overwhelming that it requires little discussion. The assumption of rationality, that Western civilization was at the apex of civilizations in the march of progress, implied that mastery was rational mastery, that masters of nature were rational masters.

Let us now return to the three works I cited above. I admit my choices are capricious, but the trends they express are not, for they undermine correlations about the growth of civilization and the humanizing of the environment, the usefulness of the man-nature dichotomy, and they place esthetics and natural beauty in an entirely different context.

In the dreary argument over phylogeny, in the sharp debates over evolution and special creation, in the dramatic discussions of the struggle for existence, in the equally dreary and unimaginative attempts to transfer the struggle for existence to human society, what now stands out more boldly in *The Origin of Species* than when it was written is that the theory reasserted in modern evolutionary, not religious, terms the case for examining the interrelationships in nature. These were seen on the model of a web of life. The fact that such interrelations exist in the organic world did not have to await Darwin's exposition; they were part of the design argument, and at the basis of eighteenth-century observations in natural history. God in his wisdom had made the earth and all the living matter in it as a part of an overall rational design, and it was to be expected that everything would fit, that there would be intricate interrelationships in the natural world, replete with adaptations.

But Darwin saw balances and harmonies in nature, webs of life—today we call them ecosystems—as the result of evolutionary processes, products of time, circumstance, selection. This restatement of the concept of a unity and harmony of nature provided the basis for the building of modern ecological theory. In the cats-to-clover chain, the number of cats is related indirectly to the number of mice, bees, and clover, but it is also related to old maids, and the growth of Scotch fir is related to man's grazing animals and the building of fences. A fresh opportunity was created for reconsidering the question of man's place in nature—not vertically as was so popular at the time in the sense of his place in a hierarchy of being (T. H. Huxley's *Man's Place in Nature* is a good example) but horizontally, his activities as part of the organic world as well as of an economic, social, or political world.

The second work, Marsh's *Man and Nature,* was published five years after *The Origin of Species.* Marsh was one of the great American students of the natural environment. He was the first American Minister to Italy, appointed by President Lincoln, continuing in his diplomatic post from 1861 until his death in 1882. The Mediterranean and its adjacent lands were his great teachers—of the power of man to modify the natural world.

Marsh also used the idea of a balance or harmony of nature, not in the way that Darwin applied it (as a general concept bearing on a theory of evolution) but as a measuring device for gauging the force of human agency in modifying the environment. He was concerned with historical questions: the effects of domestication, deforestation, and the control of water and sand dunes. Many of the effects of human interference with the environment were unsuspected, and the vistas thus opened were far broader and deeper than the narrower confines of the idea of purposive control over nature.

Implicit in Marsh's work is the idea that earth history since the coming of man could be written in part as the history of cumulative change by human agency. In this view he had been anticipated by Count Buffon in the eighteenth century (in the seventh of his magnificent *Epochs of Nature*). Human history, observed Marsh, may be the history of man's gradual divorcement from nature; but it is also the history of displacements in the organic world, of the habitants of plants, animals and primitive peoples. Domestic plants and especially animals became extensions of human agency, of human will. The result was to suggest the poverty of history written within the human framework alone, the poverty of interpreting such changes as chapters in economic history. The great theme was that the cumulative force of human agency could be irreversible, could bring about such deterioration that the planet could become uninhabitable.

But why Dickens' *Hard Times?* Because of Chapter 5, which contains the famous description of Coketown—an ugly brick town, its canals black, its river purple with dye, its monotony of activity and appearance. Large streets were like one another; small streets were even more like one another. So were the jobs. Everything was "severely workful." Things were painted alike, people thought alike, everything was accepted as fact—the M'choakumchild school, the hospital, the cemetery. We see here a new type of life based on an industrial creation of brick, uniformity, conformity. Everything in the description of Coketown points to the imposition of values on an urban industrialized landscape, the creation of a new and unique way of living. Coketown is symbolic and symptomatic.

We can discern a similar viewpoint in the words of many other sensitive observers. To the French geographer Élisée Reclus, for example, the positivist tendencies of the day, the desire for progress and technological advance, were creating unique and ugly landscapes. The march of progress, the preservation of beauty were not the same. Is it any wonder, as Lewis Mumford has pointed out in his *City in History*, that such new landscapes produced their own reactions? How else can we read parts of Ruskin, the attempts by men like Augustus Pugin to idealize the medieval city? The cries for the preservation of beauty, for the old in the city, town, or village, were as strong as they are in many parts of the Western world today.

The Dickens description gives us a feeling for newly created and unique industrial landscapes and brings into entirely new perspective the esthetics of landscape. The web of life suggested by Darwin provided new opportunities for interpretations of the significance of the idea of balances and harmonies; it was the latest attempt to find a construct for the study of the natural world. Marsh made vivid and clear the strong interconnections between the nature of man and human culture and the environment; he showed that civilization inevitably has not created and will not create new and rational harmonies in the natural environment.

The web of life, Marsh's historical geography, Dickens' Coketown are hard to fit into concepts of man against nature or of man's control over nature. It is true that their insights could be ignored. The web of life could be relegated to science. Deforestation, erosion, drainage, river diversion could be referred to engineers. Canal blackness, the purple river, the chimneys, M'choakumchild school, and conformity could be dubbed nuisances that time and progress would correct.

In the latter part of the nineteenth century, the web of life, the realization of the historical depth of human agency in changing the environment, and the creation of unique industrial landscapes showed the need for a deeper, broader, more meaningful interpretation of man's place in nature—not, I repeat, his place in the hierarchy of life, but his place in a physical environment with its interrelating linkages much altered throughout the world, and altered for different reasons and in different cultural traditions.

I do not think these ideas were assimilated in the nineteenth century; in retrospect, however, the three examples exhibit tendencies toward undermining the comfortable idea of progress in terms of man's progressive control over nature. These tendencies also weaken the idea of progress as part of a broad teleological development in which civilization advances, the environment with its resources supporting it.

Thus, a gradually developing body of thought which recognizes that civilization might be progressing or at least changing while the environment might be deteriorating obviously confronts man with a new set of circumstances. Modern pessimism, alarm, and dissatisfaction with the concept of man against nature accompany a loss of faith in progress that has become widespread in this century. Too often civilization means a destruction and chaos of nature, not a softening and a rationalization of it. Today we do not need ideas or philosophies to tell us this. None of us would automatically embrace a declaration that environments become more beautiful as civilizations advance. Our eyes, our ears, and our noses tell us quite the contrary.

Two recent studies show the continuing pertinacity, strength, and allure of the idea of man against nature in contemporary thought. In an unpublished paper, "The Origins and Development of the Marxist Concept of Man-Nature Relationship," which Ladis Kristof prepared for the Far Western Slavic Conference at the University of California at Berkeley in 1966, he shows the decisive role of the idea of man's mastery over nature in Marxist thought from Marx himself to the present. The origin he traces to certain interpretations of the philosophy of Francis Bacon. He cites the relevance of G. W. F. Hegel's work on esthetics, especially his distaste for the view that works of nature are superior to those of man, for it is consistent with the view that man strives creatively through the mastery of nature to create a better society. Kristof continues the analysis from Bacon and Hegel to Nikolai Lenin, Joseph Stalin, and more recent contemporary rulers of the Soviet Union to show the importance of this philosophy in Soviet thought.

Equally striking is an article by Rhoads Murphey, "Man and Nature in China," published in the journal *Modern Asian Studies* I, (1967) 4. It is particularly interesting because it is pertinent to the history of this powerful group of ideas centering on the dichotomy of man and nature. In the following excerpt, Professor Murphey describes the extent to which the 1949 revolution has changed traditional Chinese attitudes toward nature:

> In at least one fundamental respect, however, the conquest of 1949 has, in the Communists' own phrase, turned on its head a set of assumptions and attitudes which were of basic importance in the traditional system and has replaced them with a reverse set which may be of equal importance in contemporary terms. This is the revolution in the conception of man's relation to his physical environment. The dialectical conflict and struggle of the 'permanent revolution' which is the touchstone to so much of contemporary China has replaced traditional notions of harmony and adjustment which underlay equally much of the traditional order. In no respect is this radical change more apparent than in the attitudes toward nature.

The Chinese example is particularly striking because of the age, cultural richness, and continuity of Chinese civilization. Chinese history, philosophy, and art afford many illustrations of ideas of a balance and harmony of man with nature, respect for nature, the role of nature in the life of man. The Chinese developed a nature philosophy, *feng-shui*—wind and water—in which there was a very close correspondence between the features of the landscape and cosmic influences, an amazingly intricate system of interrelationships which was the basis for the proper selection of house and grave sites. Recent reports from Hong Kong indicate that it is still important in regions of Chinese cultural influence. The strong place of nature studies and the love of nature in landscape painting, the long respect for tillage and the orderly conversion of the environment—all of these are a part of traditional Chinese attitudes toward nature, attitudes which Murphey's study shows are being consciously and purposefully changed in favor of the idea of struggle and mastery derived from Marxist thought.

It will be most interesting to see to what extent this restatement of the case for a philosophy of struggle against and mastery over nature, imported from the West, will succeed in competition with ancient and indigenous belief, because the traditional ideas and modern ecological concepts (despite their radically different origins and foundations) have a common foundation in a philosophy of interrelationships. In no respect is the radical change in the Chinese concept of the man-nature relationship more apparent than when it is contrasted, as Murphey does, with the traditional attitudes which have been so great a part, so great a force, in the history of China, for it would be impossible to write an adequate historical geography of that country without considering all these attitudes, *feng-shui* possibly foremost among them.

The concept of man against nature as a philosophy has lost whatever creative force it had in the past. Over the last 100 years the ideas of ecological interrelationships, of the web of life put forward by Darwin, of the biocenose of Möbius, the student of the oyster beds of Sylt, and of the contemporary ecosystem concept have been growing to challenge the traditional dichotomies such as man and nature, man versus nature, man against nature, man's control over nature, or progress as a divorcement from nature.

It is time to take what is creative in both ideas. Today, the idea of an ecosystem is the most acceptable construct that we have for envisaging the organization of nature. It is widely accepted as being fundamental to an understanding of world population growth, the effects of technological innovation, conservation, pollution, and nature protection. But one part of the idea of the man-nature dichotomy as it has developed historically should not be ignored, because it poses squarely the problem of the difference between human and other forms of life, especially as doers, as participating agents in their environment.

In the past, brave attempts have made to clarify the uniqueness of man and they continue but, unless I am grossly misinformed, we have not gone much beyond the first reassuring platitudes. We have no deep knowledge. We need also to have an understanding of the gulf between human and other life forms as it has developed in varying cultural traditions, and the implications of these findings for the preservation of the natural world, for the prevention of extinctions of threatened plants and animals even if human affairs retain—as indeed they inevitably will—a central position in the preoccupation of man.

Man's technological, innovative, conservative, conserving, humane role can be understood much better in an ecological setting than in one of contrast and antithesis. No good will come of reductionism, of denigrating the inspiring achievements and richness of human culture recorded in libraries, art galleries, museums, conservatories, and universities, especially in a tragic era like this. Man's place in nature, a venerable theme, must be the focus of a new synthesis.

For the most part we have no definitive history of the attitudes of our major civilizations toward nature; they are scattered about almost randomly in such repositories as philosophy, theology, poetry, science, and art history. We do not even have a definitive synthesis of this body of thought in Western civilization, nor of comprehensive national syntheses within it—to say nothing of the attitudes of primitive and preliterate civilizations toward nature.

Agglomerations of public and private decision-making bodies are, and no doubt will continue to be, powerful agents in the molding of our environment. Their decisions often are self-centered, utilitarian, or short-term in outlook. A discussion of a philosophy of man and nature or man in nature thus may seem remote, even disembodied, in such a world; but these decision-makers have their critics, eloquent, well informed and busy, and I will not compete with them. I am more worried about the continued force and influence of general ideas in the face of mindless, glacial power.

I hope, therefore, that there is room for humanistic participation in this broad area of ideas—ideas of different cultures and their histories—especially in the education of the young. We who are associated with universities know full well that our students are rebelling against poverty, racism, and war. Also evident is rebellion against blandness and an intense interest in environment because recognition of the importance of interrelationships needs no special apprenticeship. Fundamental to all these questions and interests, I believe, is the attitude toward life—all life—and the environs in which it exists that a culture or a civilization evolves. The genuine concern for the quality of environment, for the preservation of plants, animals, and human beings from extinction, and for the preservation of historical environments and wilderness is a hopeful sign; it mirrors a reaffirmation of life, its fullness, and beauty.

Single ideas, or groups of them, in the past have been remarkable organizing agents—the ideas of man against nature, Marxism, Darwinism, progress are examples—and other ideas will probably be so in the future. That is why attention should be given to their nature and their history. And the situation is particularly important in the man-nature theme because all signs point to an ever-increasing and intensified manipulation of the physical environment, but hopefully one in which the philosophies of interrelationships, rather than of dichotomies, will become increasingly important.

Conceptions of the interrelationship of man and nature historically have included esthetic, religious, philosophical, in addition to scientific components. In other words, they have included values. They have had to deal, especially in a secular world, with questions of man's stewardship of and responsibility, if any, to other forms of being; with anthropocentrism, the problem of extinction of nonhuman life and of human life by advanced civilizations. The concept of man against nature will become more and more unsatisfactory, if civilization survives, because it cannot accommodate the rich cultural variety of attitudes toward nature by the world's people over millennia, which is expressed in their myth, science, religion, art, and philosophy.

If the history of thought teaches us anything about culture and environment, it is the importance of the conceptions which people have of both—whether these conceptions are religious, philosophical, scientific, or utilitarian. It is a poor time in history to have a narrowness of vision and to continue to limit values to ideas of struggle and antithesis. The diversity of world cultures demands much more of us in understanding and imagination.

Notes

1. H. and H. A. Frankfort et al., *Beyond Philosophy, the Intellectual Adventure of Ancient Man: An Essay on Speculative Thought in the Ancient Near East* (Harmondsworth, Middlesex, Penguin Books, 1954).

2. Colin M. Turnbull, *The Forest People* (New York, Simon and Schuster, 1961).

3. John Bagnell Bury, *The Idea of Progress: An Inquiry into Its Origin and Growth* (London, Macmillan and Co., 1920).

The supply of fresh air is not unlimited, as is commonly believed. The continuous movement of air masses makes the contamination of air a national, not a local or regional, problem. Gradual suffocation of a population is a real possibility. There is also a critical shortage of pure water. The amount of water necessary to sustain our kind of culture is tremendous and is increasing. The amount remaining available in a pure condition is diminishing rapidly.

Our Vital Resources

Jack Bregman and Sergel Lenormand

Contrary to popular opinion, the supply of air and water is not endless, and if we do not begin to employ sound conservation practices now, the consequences could be more catastrophic than the dust bowls and river floods of the past five decades. Clean air and pure water—so often taken for granted —are essential to your welfare and your health every day of your life. If you are fairly normal in your personal consumption, you will have eaten about three pounds of food by the end of the day. In one way or another, you also will have consumed between four and five pounds of water. On any given day, of course, food is not essential, and for a while you can get along without water. To live through this day, however, you must breathe, and during any and every 24-hour period, you alone consume 30 pounds of air. While you often can detect and reject contaminated food and water by their odor, appearance, or taste, you cannot reject air. You must inhale it where you are, no matter how contaminated it is by dust, dirt, smoke, and gases.

Our vital personal need for air, however, is minute when compared with the enormous quantities essential to heating our homes, running our cars, and burning our wastes in a modern industrial society.

About one ton of air is required just to burn a tank full of gasoline in the normal American automobile. As some 80 million registered cars in the United States consume 70 billion gallons of fuel in one year, they use over four billion tons of air annually. At the same time, the human population inhales and expels three million tons.

The combustion of fuels, either for home heating or for industrial use, devours even more enormous quantities of air. One gallon of fuel oil consumes 90 pounds of air while a pound of natural gas uses 18 pounds of air. Burning a pound of coal requires 14 pounds of air. When the total consumption is added up and the appropriate calculations are made, experts estimate that in the United States we use about 3,000 cubic miles—20 billion tons— of air every year for fossil fuel combustion alone.

From "Our Vital Resources" by Jack Bregman and Sergel Lenormand. Reprinted from *The Pollution Paradox* by Jack Bregman and Sergel Lenormand. New York, Spartan Books, © 1966.

If there were unlimited supplies of fresh air, as most people believe, there would be little need for concern, but the total quantity of air is fixed, and its quality is being degraded on a massive scale because of the increasing demand of a society whose population, urbanization and industrialization continue to expand. Just as water supplies are broken down into discrete units, such as rivers or lakes, so air supplies frequently tend to remain relatively fixed in large masses over locations called airsheds, which are defined by terrain such as mountains and hills. New air gradually arrives in these airsheds while used air is departing. The quantity of air in these airsheds is determined by atmospheric features. Its quality is determined by meteorological factors as well as the amount and character of pollutants spewed into it.

Most air pollutants require a certain amount of time to cause damage, and so the length of exposure in the airshed also determines the seriousness of the problem. Finally, the degree of purity or contamination of the air arriving at the airshed is relevant to its ability to absorb and harmlessly disperse pollutants. Obviously, the more contaminated the air becomes in its transit, the less pollution it is capable of absorbing before reaching toxic levels. Clean ocean air, for example, is contaminated with nitrogen oxides by power plants along the California coast. As the air mass drifts into the Los Angeles basin airshed, it accumulates the organic vapors of auto traffic. Sunshine then triggers an interaction of these pollutants, which form the infamous "photochemical" smog that is now a West Coast tradition. Technically called synergism, this process also takes place along the Delaware River where power plants spew nitrogen oxides at the "accredited clouds of the sky." These react with the pollutants discharged by various cities and highway traffic in the valley's airshed. It is obvious that the movement of air masses and their quality, especially where there are numerous industrial clusters, is a national rather than a community problem.

Regarding the atmosphere's capacity to absorb toxic pollutants, Dr. Morris Neiburger, professor of meteorology at UCLA, recently made the dire prediction that "All civilization will pass away, not from a sudden cataclysm like a nuclear war, but from gradual suffocation in its own wastes." He believes the villain is the internal combustion engine, that "Mankind will sink to its smoggy doom through inertia and irresponsibility," and that our species will end "not with a bang, but a whimper." Although Professor Neiburger's gloomy forecast is conceivable, the authors of this book cannot image such prolonged, gross apathy. The meteorologist, however, raises a valid and crucial question: How much longer can we afford to overload the air with pollutants?

Unfortunately, this is merely one aspect of the contamination of our vital resources. Pure water is as essential as clean air, and in many ways the maintenance of water integrity is even more difficult than preserving the quality of our air. Harmful pollution by man and nature is even more universally pervasive in water than in air. Furthermore, the distribution of water is highly erratic. Anyone who remembers his geography lessons realizes that large portions of the earth's land mass are unsuitable for either industry or agriculture because of insufficient rainfall.

Unlike air, water resources are not easily tapped, especially in this age of pollution megatonnage. Even getting water from your faucet, which involves considerable investment in plumbing and treatment, requires more effort than inhaling. The effort and expense of producing clean water, however, does not mean we are short; we have an abundant supply of water. The average annual rainfall in the United States is about thirty inches, five billion acre feet that falls on two billion acres of land surface. In a single day our country is showered by 4,300 billion gallons of water, indicating how America became rich and resplendent with forests, game, rivers, fish, and a sea of grass before the meddling of man. Seventy percent of our moisture, however, is evaporated by the sun or transpired by plants and animals. This means 3,000 billion gallons are lost to the atmosphere each day, leaving 1,300 billion gallons for ground water, stream flow, or other forms of runoff. Of this, we are managing or controlling less than 400 billion gallons. Over half of this available water—drawn from streams and lakes or pumped out of the earth—is used by industry. Most of the remainder is consumed by agriculture and municipalities.

Overlooking the role of air, for the moment, industry's most important raw material is water. It is a source of power, a coolant, a transportation vehicle, an ingredient in processing thousands of products and materials, and a cleansing agent. Factories consume water in astonishing quantities— 1,400 gallons for a dollar's worth of steel, nearly 200 gallons for a dollar's worth of paper. This means that 65,000 gallons of water are required to produce a ton of steel and 39,000 gallons are needed for a ton of paper. A barrel of gasoline or oil involves 357 and 770 gallons of water respectively. Even the production of a gallon of whiskey requires 80 gallons of water. And a ton of soda?—85,000 gallons! These industrial uses of water understandably degrade its quality, sometimes making it as unfit for reuse as residential sewage.

While agriculture requires less water than industry, it "consumes" more. Many industries recover and reuse their water, but 60 percent of the water employed for irrigation is lost. Furthermore, the water returned to rivers and streams is often laden with salts, minerals, and agricultural chemicals which are difficult to remove by conventional waste treatment methods.

At the same time, better standards of living and sanitation—laundries, garbage grinders, air conditioners, multiple bathrooms, lawn sprinklers— increase our direct per capita use of municipal water. For these reasons, as well as population growth, many cities must draw their water from greater and greater distances or build expensive treatment plants.

Indirect human consumption, although rarely considered, is also relevant to our water resources. According to Professor Charles Bradley, a permanent water shortage affecting our standard of living will occur before the year 2000. In an article published in *Science,* he pointed out that the wheat used to make two and one-half pounds of bread transpires 300 gallons of water. In other words, if we lived by bread alone, we would each need more than 300 gallons of water daily. Obviously our lives are not so simple. The automobile you drive involved thousands of gallons of water for the production of steel, aluminum, rubber, and various synthetic materials. Just the paper for the book you're reading consumed two gallons of water. This is minute when compared to eating a one-pound steak. Each day a two-year-old steer weighing 700 pounds drinks 12 gallons of water and eats 30 pounds of alfalfa which transpired 24,000 pounds of water. In water terms, just getting your steak to the table required at least 2,900 gallons of water!

Higher incomes, better transportation, and more leisure have resulted in a national preoccupation with recreation as well as with good steaks. Much of this activity is related to swimming, fishing, and boating. Although recreational use of water cannot be measured in gallons, the growing danger to clean sandy beaches, expanses of blue water, and crystal mountain brooks—which yearly diminish in quality—is highlighted by other kinds of statistics. From 1920 to 1959, for example, the Department of Health, Education, and Welfare (HEW) estimates that the number of American swimmers doubled, rising to 60 million people. The number of fishing licenses sold in this period increased from 3 to 20 million. The greatest growth, by far, came in boating; in 1920, less than 20,000 boats of all types were sold, but by 1959, the annual sale had reached 550,000, a whopping 2,750 percent increase.

The changing character of our society is reflected in the changing demands for water by municipalities, agriculture, and industry. Today, municipal use is about nine times greater than in 1900, rising from 3 to almost 27 billion gallons daily while municipal populations grew five times from 30 to 150 million persons. In the same period, agricultural use—most of it for irrigation in the western states—increased from 22.2 to 140 billion gallons each day. At the beginning of the century, industry used less water than agriculture—15 billion gallons daily. In the following six decades, however, industrial consumption rose almost thirteenfold, and it now uses 190 billion gallons every day. This is not surprising when you realize that it takes more water to manufacture a yard of rayon than to grow, process, and weave a yard of cotton, silk, linen, or wool.

Do these figures indicate that we are running out of air and water? Of course not! But what is the appearance of the lake or the river you use for boating? What does it smell like? What kinds of beaches are available to the residents along the shores of Lake Erie? How was the view of the city you approached on your way to work? And did you close your car windows to avoid gagging on the fumes of trucks and buses?

Nationally, we are short of neither air nor water. The northeastern states get a generous 40 inches of rain annually—30 inches during recent drought years—yet New York City, which is surrounded by water, is having still another water crisis. While water officials have nightmares on the East Coast, residents of Los Angeles—where the annual rainfall is less than 14 inches—are watering lush green lawns and lolling in thousands of backyard pools. The problem in New York is not a shortage of water; the problem is a shortage of pure water. The problem in Los Angeles, smog capital of the world, is not an inadequate supply of air; the problem is an inadequate supply of clean air. The water crisis in New York City, the air pollution crisis in Los Angeles, the silent assaults on cities from sea to shining sea, will batter us senseless—as Professor Neiburger predicts—if we persist in corrupting our vital resources.

The environment, including the atmosphere, is fixed in size, while its content
is free to grow and expand. Not only has the population multiplied many times,
but the rate of consumption of material goods and the resultant waste products have increased per individual. Much of the waste is from man-made products
and will not decompose naturally. Thus the problem of disposal of unwanted
material may soon become a desperate one.

Genesis of a Nightmare

George R. Stewart

However subtly the enormity of the disposal problem may have encroached
upon the United States, there is nothing mysterious or inexplicable about it.
The development has occurred in about a century—let us say, from 1870.
It may be attributed to four causes—increase of population, the growth of
cities, the development of the "affluent" society, the invention of synthetic
technology.

In 1870 the United States had fewer than forty million people; there
are now five times as many. Other things being equal, five times as many
people produce five times as much of a disposal problem. At the same time,
however, the argument may run that five times as many people are available
to care for the problem, so that it should be no worse.

There is, however, a fallacy in this argument. The people have increased, but the environment has not. Since 1870 only a few small areas,
such as Hawaii, have been added. Merely because of growth of population,
therefore, five times as much material must be dumped on the same land,
or run into the same streams, or spewed into the same atmosphere. Moreover, the land has not improved its capacity for absorbing effluvia, nor have
the streams grown more numerous or larger, nor has the atmosphere increased its size or speeded up its winds.

Merely because of more people, in the course of one century, the burden placed upon the environment has thus been multiplied approximately
by five.

Even so, the fivefold increase in population is probably the least among
the four reasons. Of much greater importance, certainly, is the concentration of people in cities.

In 1870 the census classified three-quarters of the persons in the
United States as "rural." By definition, being rural meant that these people
lived on farms or in villages or towns of fewer than 2,500 inhabitants. A

hundred years later the situation has more than reversed itself. Only about one person in ten is rural, and nine out of ten are urban.

On an old-fashioned American farm, and in the small town . . . people essentially took care of their own disposal problems. They did not find the labor excessive, and they did not, in the process and by their solution, either injure their own health appreciably or noticeably degrade their environment. Obviously they had the advantage that there was, so to speak, a lot of environment per person.

The modern city has gained a little by the elimination of most of the animals, though it still supports a flourishing and sometimes troublesome population of dogs and cats—to say nothing of such partially domesticated and digestively active creatures as pigeons.

Except for fewer animals, the disposal problem of the city is manyfold worse than that of the farm or small town. The slice of environment available for each person is simply too thin. The amount of discarded material per acre goes up approximately in proportion to the number of people per acre. It may thus increase by a hundred or more. Even with the best of will (and the best of will is rare), the city-dweller has no way of disposing of his own waste. His dog has no place to bury a bone, and the very dog-droppings become a matter of city ordinance. The thought of a row of privies behind each apartment house is only humorous. The renter in the apartment house cannot burn his trash in the backyard, because there is no backyard. Even if there were, he could not burn the trash, because of fire hazard, and smoke-and-smog regulations, and the necessities of his own nine-to-five day.

What happens is that the disposal of waste goes into the hands of specialists—all the way from garbage-men and street-cleaners to city engineers and smog-experts. The individual citizen pays, either through taxes or by special charge, to be relieved of the duty that he and his family would perform on the farm and even in the small town. The normal citizen pays unwillingly and with grumbles, and so he rarely pays enough.

As far as the urban individual is concerned, about all that he himself, or she herself, is willing to do is to put material into garbage cans. Even the idea that there should be more than one garbage can, for segregation of material, meets with general lack of cooperation. Hopefully, the individual uses the litter can on the street for the wrappings of a candy-bar and a pack of cigarettes, but the condition of the sidewalks suggests that even so much labor is resented. Aren't there people who are paid to sweep things up, or can't the merchants have it done in front of their shops?

The delegation of duties to paid workers is in harmony with the modern specialization of labor, and there is nothing wrong with it in theory. The trouble is that it costs money, and costs that money just to get rid of something that you have already used and had the fun out of. A species that still thinks, apparently, in terms of just dropping things out of the trees is not happy about thus spending money. Moreover, disposal by specialists can hardly begin until the original producer of the material has taken the first step.

Even worse, however, as far as the modern city is concerned, is the basically mathematical problem of the space-ratio. Land, water, and air simply cannot take the strain. In the more thickly inhabited regions, even now, city is beginning to merge with city, and the disposal problem pyramids. An isolated city still has a chance. Megalopolis is ready to founder under its load.

At the same time, let us remember, the city not only creates the problem but then also passes it on. Rivers that flow through a pleasant countryside may have been already polluted by the up-stream metropolis.

Schematically, to return to the idea of the conservation of matter, we may think of a city as a center into which civilization pours an appalling tonnage of material. Beneath the ground the unseen pipelines bring water, oil, and gas. On the ground, the all-too-visible railroads and highways contribute their endless freight trains and their innumerable trucks. By air, an ever-increasing load of freight arrives at the airports.

By the pipelines there is no outward movement at all, except insofar as sewers extend to disposal plants on the city's edge. By rail, road, and air, a comparatively small tonnage of manufactured goods is removed from the city, but most of this merely goes to some other city.

As anyone can see, this process tends to bury the city under the accumulation. The city, as the cheapest way possible, has been accustomed merely to dump its waste on the nearby ground or into the streams and the air. The concentration of materials in cities, under the present system, is simply not being deconcentrated.

The third reason for the problem of what to do with things that you no longer want is what we generally mention with pride as "the affluent society." Our campaigns to end poverty mean that we are trying to extend affluence to people who do not have it already, and so we can only expect this phase of the problem of disposal to become correspondingly greater.

The affluent society is based partly upon the discovery that it is cheaper to produce something in quantity than to repair it. If the automobile part and its installation cost $6.24, and the mechanic's time to repair it would cost $7.14, obviously you are better off to get a new part. There is a slight fallacy, in that no one considers what happens to the old part. It is dumped somewhere, of course, and these thousands and thousands of discarded gadgets come to form a part of the engulfing mass.

This is only one of a thousand ways in which the affluent society increases the disposal problem—without, as a rule, doing anything about it. Americans have developed a psychological state of mind in which anything to do with saving or reuse is opprobrious. One of the few ethnic references still allowable is to call a person "Scotch." Or a person may be a "string-saver," or "chintzy," or a dozen things else. To utilize anything fully has become almost unpatriotic, since we are persuaded that the affluent economy depends upon rapid turnover.

We are psychologically adapted to throw things away readily—anything from a cigarette butt to the three-year-old car. We are equally careless about where we throw them.

Everyone, I suppose, likes affluence. Everyone, I suppose, approves of the affluent society.

In this connection, however, more clearly even than elsewhere, . . . [my] central theme . . . is apparent. "You are not so rich as you think," because the American people are not taking care of the waste that they create, and it is catching up with them. Our civilization is going to have to come to a working agreement with the environment, or it is going to become such a disagreeable civilization as hardly to be worth living in—if, indeed, anyone can live in it at all. To come to some kind of balance with the environment is going to cost a great deal of money.

The situation appears strikingly if we again consider the hundred-year perspective. Affluence was scarcely yet apparent in 1870. As an example, take paper, which is now the symbol of a thing of no value—"A mere scrap of paper!" . . . . "Not worth the paper it's written on!"

A hundred years ago paper was produced in comparatively small quantities, and was largely reprocessed, so that its disposal offered little problem. Occasionally, among old letters one comes upon a notable indication of the value of writing-paper, at least as late as the middle of the nineteenth century. In those times people sometimes filled the sheet in ordinary fashion, and then wrote across it again at right angles, thus getting twice as much writing on the page. It was a vile practice, and such letters are highly difficult to read. But it shows how valuable the paper was, in a society that had not yet grown affluent. That society continued to treasure such proverbs as "A penny saved is a penny earned!" and "Waste not, want not!"

In contrast, the current production of paper is between twenty-five and thirty million tons per annum. Only a small percentage of this remains intact even at the end of a year—stored up in libraries, or otherwise useful or potentially useful. About a third of the total is salvaged and goes into making new paper. The rest—fifteen million tons, to use a conservative figure—has been flushed down the sewers into the streams or has added to the smoke problem, or has helped raise the dump heaps, or lies along the roadsides as litter.

The affluent society, as yet, cannot be bothered with the detail of waste paper, not even fifteen million tons of it a year.

Probably, the affluent society is more responsible for our troubles than is urbanization. Previous societies, even that of the United States a century ago, were not to be called affluent and at the same time they scarcely had a disposal problem. The same has been true of all the older societies, and it is still true of most of the world, where affluence has not yet raised its head.

Once I saw the contrast, with the sharpness of crossing a line. . . . I was driving south through the Imperial Valley in California during the season of picking cotton. Along the highway the cotton-bolls lay, literally as thick as snow. They had blown from the trucks that were taking the cotton from the fields to the gins. No one was making any effort to recover this cotton, though it was obviously as good as it ever was. Wages being what they were, the salvage of this escaped cotton simply did not pay. What became of this cotton? Probably it blew about, until it lodged against a fence or a rock, and eventually, after a winter or two and some rain, it went back into the soil. Doubtless it did no great harm, only producing an unaesthetic look in the countryside.

As we drove along, I made the obvious remark, "In any other country, someone would be out picking up this cotton."

An hour later we crossed into Mexico. There also the cotton lay by the road where it had blown from the trucks. But there the boys were walking along, each dragging a sack and picking up the cotton as he went.

The United States is affluent, and in many of the disturbing details of its current civilization it is paying the price of an easygoing affluence that has sprouted quickly, and has not yet learned to pick up behind itself.

A more subtle shift in modern civilization has been its synthesis and manufacture of useful and attractive materials that do not ordinarily exist in nature, and, once produced, are long-enduring or permanent within the human time-scale. They simply do not fit into any natural cycle of growth or decay.

Considered in terms of evolution, the situation becomes vivid. Throughout millions of years many creatures evolved with the specialty of what, from the human point of view, may be called "recycling." Termites reduced wood to powder. Many kinds of organisms, especially bacteria, served to expedite decay. Every process of nature thus had its counter-process.

But now some technologists produce a detergent or a plastic having a composition not known to nature. Unless we assume a conscious planning of the universe, we can hardly expect that through the ages some organism has been evolving with a digestive system adapted to the highly specialized new product—some organism, so to speak, that says, "Ha! This is just the food that I have been waiting for!"

The most widely publicized and the most spectacular of the new products are the atomic wastes. In one way we may consider it fortunate that the residues of fission are so deadly that they even become of international significance. Moreover, to date, their production has been limited to a few large operations. As a result, they hardly come into the ordinary problem of disposal, but are policed at a national level.

Much more involved with the ordinary person are such new synthetics as plastics, detergents, and insecticides. Commonplace and cheap, but long-lived and subtle, many such products linger on. They are not consumed by their use. They have been employed, and still are employed, without consideration of what becomes of them.

Scientists continue to discover new synthetics, and manufacturers continue enthusiastically to exploit them. A chemical company triumphantly proclaims in an advertisement that it will produce two hundred new products in a single year. The advertisement, however, gives no indication whether there has been any research as to how to get rid of these products after they have served their purpose.

Most of the new materials are produced in small quantities, and are inert, after use. Others, inevitably, create trouble.

The problem of what to do with the discarded synthetics is quantitatively a small one, but the resistance to decay and the virulence of some of the materials raise serious threats, and the possible long-range difficulties threaten the health of the human race and the beneficence of the environment. . . .

Thus arising, the whole situation of disposal seems so closely involved with civilization itself as to be automatically produced and essentially insolvable. The crisis appears to be desperate, and it may well be so.

There is even the possibility that civilization has already passed some point of no return. No one, indeed, knows what the effect upon the race may have been from the release of radioactive materials, and what the effect upon the environment may be from the accumulation of pesticides, carbon dioxide, and the constituents of smog.

No one knows, moreover, how great may have been the psychological effects upon the millions of individuals who constitute society. A majority of them may have become used to a regime of dirt and confusion, so that they merely consider it a normal way of life.

Even if the problem is considered to be basically nothing more than economic, it may be such a large one as to pass the limits of self-discipline which the present generation is willing to impose upon itself. We may flinch from the charges, and prefer to let those charges be absorbed by the cumulative degradation of the environment.

There are also, however, some reasons for optimism and hope. What man has done, that also, one would think, man can undo. At least, before surrendering we should look at the situation in more detail.

The optimist, moreover, need not be wholly beaten down. He may still quote, "The other side of a problem is an opportunity." Inherent in certain phases of the complicated processes of disposal—notably, in connection with sewage—are revolutionary new processes for the maintenance of civilization.

The din in our homes and streets is doubling every ten years. It is frazzling our nerves and endangering our health. The technical skill necessary to abate this insidious pollution is available, but it will be necessary for us to demand relief in meaningful ways before the problem will be remedied.

It's Time to Turn Down All That Noise

John M. Mecklin

In the Bronx borough of New York City one evening last spring, four boys were at play, shouting and racing in and out of an apartment building. Suddenly, from a second-floor window, came the crack of a pistol. One of the boys sprawled dead on the pavement. The victim happened to be Roy Innis Jr., thirteen, son of a prominent Negro leader, but there was no political implication in the tragedy. The killer, also a Negro, confessed to police that he was a nightworker who had lost control of himself because the noise from the boys prevented him from sleeping.

The incident was an extreme but valid example of a grim, and worsening, human problem. In communities all over the world, the daily harassment of needless noise provokes unknown millions to the verge of violence or emotional breakdown. There is growing evidence that it contributes to such physical ailments as heart trouble. Noise has become a scourge of our land, a form of environmental pollution no less dangerous and degrading than the poisons we dump into our air and water; it is one of the main causes of the exodus from our cities.

In many ways, noise is the most difficult form of pollution to combat. It has been recognized only recently as a major evil. It works so subtly on the human mind that it has gained a form of acceptance. Shouting over the din of an air compressor in New York recently, a newsman asked a construction foreman what he thought about the noise problem. "What are you," the foreman shouted back, "some kind of a Communist?"

Noise pollution is hardly a new evil. The word itself derives from the same Latin root as nausea. Noise bothered Julius Caesar so much that he banned chariot driving at night. In 1851, Arthur Schopenhauer wrote about the "disgraceful . . . truly infernal" cracking of whips in German streets. In a study published in October, 1955, *Fortune* reported "a rising tide of noise [in] U.S. streets, factories, homes, and skies" and asserted that Americans "have decided that noise should be abated." The optimism was un-

From "It's Time to Turn Down All That Noise" by John M. Mecklin, *Fortune*, October 1969. Reprinted by permission of *Fortune*.

warranted. Today the level of everyday noise to which the average urban American is exposed is more than *twice* what it was in 1955, and the cacophony continues to mount: the crash of jackhammers, whirring air conditioners, snarling lawn mowers, family arguments penetrating the paper-thin walls of homes and apartment houses, and the blast of traffic on freeways. Everyday noise is assaulting American ears at an intensity approaching the level of permanent hearing damage, if indeed the danger point has not already been passed.

A Zone of "Unacceptable Annoyance"

As often happens with a slowly encroaching evil, it has taken a major outrage to stir up public concern. This is being provided spectacularly by the jet aircraft now bombarding some 20 million Americans every few minutes with a thunderous roar around our major airports. In the area of New York's John F. Kennedy Airport alone about one million people (including the students in about ninety schools) live within a zone of "unacceptable annoyance," as an official of the Federal Aviation Administration describes it. At Shea Stadium baseball games, the racket regularly drowns out not only the national anthem but also the players calling for fly balls. In Washington, jet noise so disrupted a ceremony attended by President Johnson at the Lincoln Memorial in 1967 that he ordered an aide to call the airport and stop it. In Los Angeles, concerts at the Hollywood Bowl have become virtually inaudible, and residents of nearby Inglewood have filed lawsuits that could total as much as $3 billion against the city.

The federal government is beginning belatedly to recognize that it has a problem—an awakening that may be partly due to the fact that approach paths to Washington National Airport pass directly over the homes of numerous top government officials. Congress last year voted to give the Federal Aviation Administration authority for the first time to fix aircraft noise limits, and the agency's initial order is expected momentarily. Though the effort may result in higher fares for air travelers, there is reason to hope that jet noise may be rolled back almost to the level of propeller planes within a few years.

But the same cannot be said for noise pollution in general. With a few exceptions, the steps taken so far have been palliatives. Memphis, for example, has enforced a ban on automobile horn blowing (instigated by an angry newspaper editor) since the 1930's. In New York in 1948 a landmark court decision upheld for the first time an award of compensation to an industrial worker who had suffered gradual hearing loss without losing work time. This type of claim is now recognized in some thirty states. Studies indicate, however, that only a small percentage of workers with legitimate claims have gone to court.

In Washington, at least a dozen federal agencies have become involved in the noise problem, and there has been one action of significance. That was the promulgation of a series of new regulations last spring under the Walsh-Healey Public Contracts Act of 1938, which limit industrial noise levels in most plants doing business with the government. The new regulations were initiated by the Johnson Administration, however, and were watered down by the Nixon Administration. Elsewhere a handful of unofficial organizations are agitating for noise abatement, notably in New York City.

Multitudes of special interests are arrayed against anti-noise measures whenever they are contemplated. When a state law was proposed to ban playing transistor radios in public vehicles, Buffalo radio-TV station WGR editorialized against such "inanities." Of about 125 industry representatives who testified last winter at Labor Department hearings leading to the new industrial noise standards, more than 90 percent were opposed to regulation. Sample argument: "It is unrealistic and literally impossible to comply with." The cause of noise abatement wasn't helped any when the *Journal of the American Medical Association* argued in an editorial earlier this year that "some noise must be tolerated as an unavoidable concomitant of the blessings of civilization."

Quiet Doesn't Cost Much

To permit this kind of thinking to prevail is the true inanity. Virtually all man-made noise, whatever its source, can be suppressed. While some major problems, such as thin apartment walls and the roar of New York City's subway, would cost large sums of money to correct, many of the most irritating noises could be reduced at negligible cost. The screech of truck tires on pavement, for example, can be reduced at no extra cost or efficiency loss by redesigning the tread, and a quiet home lawn mower costs only about $15 more than the usual ear-jarring model. Some other examples of added costs: a garbage truck $2,400 (on top of an original cost of $15,600), a small air compressor $500 ($5,300), and on most machinery an additional 5 percent atop the original cost. In some cases there is also a relatively small cost in reduced efficiency. Mass production of silenced equipment would lower costs still more.

The expense becomes even less formidable when measured against the savings from noise suppression. The World Health Organization estimates that industrial noise alone costs the U.S. today more than $14 billion annually—in accidents, absenteeism, inefficiency, and compensation claims. The human costs in sleepless nights, family squabbles, and mental illness are beyond measure, but they surely must be enormous.

In the cases of air and water pollution, one of the main obstacles to corrective action is the large governmental outlay required—e.g., for nonpolluting municipal incinerators and sewage-treatment plants. But society's noisemakers are predominantly privately owned machines, many of which wear out and must be replaced within a few years anyway. Moreover, noise is not a uniquely big-city problem of little interest to suburban or rural taxpayers who are not exposed to it. Modern technology, its root cause, is everywhere, from grinding dishwashing machines in farm kitchens to outlying airports and thundering throughways that can be heard for miles.

The first and perhaps the most important course of action is to generate all possible public pressure on governments. It is no coincidence that one of the world's most effective anti-noise programs emerged in West Germany after the leading political parties there began including it in their election platforms. Once it becomes clear to Americans that noise is not an inescapable fact of life, that something *can* be done about it, and at manageable cost, the support for real action could be overwhelming. Says Judge Theodore Kupferman, a former Congressman from Manhattan and long-time anti-noise crusader: "In addition to the merits of the anti-noise cause, I don't see why more politicians don't take up the cudgel. Who's going to be in favor of noise?"

The most effective approach to governmental action probably lies in *federal* regulation. The legal authority already exists in the laws providing federal regulation of interstate commerce, health protection, and such specific functions as federal guarantees of housing loans, and there is a precedent for federal regulation of noise in the 1965 legislation empowering the Department of Health, Education, and Welfare to set limits on air pollutants emitted by moter vehicles. At the same time, state and local governmental action against noise, as well as support from enlightened businessmen, could go a long way toward reducing the problem, and perhaps in setting a trend—as a few localities have already demonstrated.

No Lids to Close

Noise—commonly defined as "unwanted sound"—works on humans in two ways. One, of course, is to cause deafness through deterioration of the microscopic hair cells that transmit sound from the ear to the brain. A single very loud blast, as from a cannon, can destroy the cells by the thousands and they never recover. (The Veterans Administration is spending about $8 million a year on the claims of some 5,000 servicemen whose hearing has been damaged by gunfire in training or combat.) Constant exposure to noises commonplace in our society can cause slower deterioration as the hair cells gradually rupture. There is a glimpse of the remarkable "redundancy" of the human body—in this case in spare hair cells—in the fact that all of us in modern communities have lost a substantial portion of our hearing mechanism without ever missing it. An experiment conducted by Dr. Samuel Rosen, a leading Manhattan otologist, has shown that aborigines living in the stillness of isolated African villages can easily hear each other talking in low conversational tones at distances as great as 100 yards, and that their hearing acuity diminishes little with age.

The second effect of noise upon humans is psychological and intensely personal. It relates not only to a lifetime of experience, but also to mood. Thus the scream of a siren at night may bring fright and anger to a thousand neighbors, but it means hope to a desperate accident victim. The human ear, unlike the eye, has no lids and cannot be turned off, not even in sleep. Nature's initial purpose in providing animals with hearing presumably was to alert them to enemies, with its function in communication coming at a later stage. Thus the instinctive human reaction to noise, especially unexpected noise, is fear and an impulse to flee. Children play games with this "startle effect," as psychologists call it. But to older people, just home from a hard day's work, for example, a sudden noise like the slam of a door or an automobile backfire or even the bell of an ice-cream vendor often can tip the balance of self-control and lead to an emotional eruption. Studies of sleep patterns have shown that people never "get used" to noise; on the contrary, the annoyance, and loss of sleep, worsen as the interruptions persist. This is the main reason why there is, rightly, such strong opposition to the use over populated areas of supersonic airliners whose sonic booms would cause psychic havoc among millions.

Hypertension and Hallucinations

Clinical evidence has established conclusively that excessive exposure to noise constricts the arteries, increases the heartbeat, and dilates the pupils of the eye. Sigmund Freud wrote that noise could create an anxiety neurosis "undoubtedly explicable on the basis of the close inborn connection between auditory impressions and fright." One recent French study goes so far as to suggest that noise is the cause of 70 percent of the neuroses in the Paris area, compared with only 50 percent four years ago, and it blames noise for three recent premeditated murders. John M. Handley, a New York authority on industrial acoustics, recently wrote that "symptoms of hypertension, vertigo, hallucination, paranoia and, on occasion, suicidal and homicidal impulses, have been blamed on excessive noise . . . . 'Noise pollution' may be one of the reasons why the incidence of heart disease and mental illness is so high in the United States." Other authorities have suggested that noise may be related to stomach ulcers, allergies, enuresis (involuntary urination), spinal meningitis, excessive cholesterol in the arteries, indigestion, loss of equilibrium, and impaired vision.

Tests of the effects of noise upon animals have produced dramatic results. Prolonged exposure has made rats lose their fertility, turn homosexual, and eat their young. If the noise is continued still longer, it eventually kills them through heart failure. There is clearly a limit to the amount of noise that any animal, including humans, can tolerate. But at what point does the noise in our daily lives begin to be dangerous? Dr. Vern O. Knudsen, former chancellor of the University of California at Los Angeles and a leading authority on noise pollution, believes we have already reached it. "Noise, like smog," he says, "is a slow agent of death."

Death by Decibels

There is no single universally accepted criterion of what constitutes excessive noise. The most common noise yardstick is the decibel (db) scale, which is an expression of the sound pressure that moves the ear. The scale begins at zero db, which is the weakest sound that can be picked up by the healthy ear. Thereafter, because of physical laws, the scale increases as the square of the change. Thus so soft a sound as human breathing is about ten times greater than zero db, while an artillery blast is one thousand trillion (1,000,000,000,000,000) times greater. To simplify things, the scale is in logarithmic form so that ten times the minimum is 10 db and one thousand trillion times the minimum is 150 db. The db scale does not, however, take account of the tones in the sound being registered—i.e., the frequencies of the sound waves being propagated. Scientists' attempts over the years to work out techniques to weight such factors for accurate registration of the ways that noise sounds to humans have led to a plethora of measuring scales.

There is agreement that high-pitched tones are more annoying and thus should be given more weight than low tones, but there the agreement ends. The most common weighting system is the "A" scale, written dbA, which gives less weight to low tones and thus more nearly matches the effect of sound on people. Beyond that the variations are myriad. For example: dbC ("C" scale), PNdb ("perceived noise"), EPNdb ("effective perceived noise"), SIL ("speech interference level"), and the "sone" and "phon" scales.

Some sample noise readings in the dbA scale at distances at which people are commonly exposed:

Rustling leaves	20 dbA
Window air conditioner	55
Conversational speech	60
(Beginning of hearing damage if prolonged	85)
Heavy city traffic	90
Home lawn mower	98
150-cubic-foot air compressor	100
Jet airliner (500 feet overhead)	115
(Human pain threshold	120)

In the case of the laboratory rats mentioned earlier, death occurred after prolonged exposure at 150 dbA, or the equivalent of continuous artillery fire at close range. The take-off blast of the Saturn V moon rocket, measured at the launching pad, is about 180 dbA.

Very roughly, the noise level in busy sections of American communities is doubling every ten years. It has reached the point today where it is often greater than industrial noise levels. The main cause of the trend is the constant growth of the use of power. To cite one of the main new offenders, air conditioners are now in use in some 32 million homes. The giant machines on the top of large buildings often spew out more than 100 dbA and bother people for blocks around. No fewer than 89 million cars (up to 70 dbA) and about 18 million trucks and buses (up to 95 dbA) are cluttering our roads and streets. Millions of them are operating with defective mufflers, which always wear out faster than the vehicle. The beauty of our winters has been defiled by the din of some 700,000 snowmobiles, and our buses, trains, parks, and streets by millions of transistor radios. The racket in a modern American kitchen rises as high as 90 dbA midst an ever expanding profusion of dishwashers, mixers, grinders, exhaust fans, disposers, and the like. The National Institute of Mental Health is considering a proposal to wire up a typical housewife with telemetry like a spacecraft to try to study the effects of the pandemonium on her nervous system.

On top of all that, architects, engineers, and contractors in the $90-billion U.S. construction industry behave, says one acoustical expert, "as though they were born without ears." Thousands of new apartment buildings and homes are being thrown together like cardboard dollhouses, creating multimillion-dollar "noise slums," as one occupant puts it. Privacy, so badly needed by city dwellers, vanishes among the sounds of flushing toilets, electric razors, and family intimacies penetrating the walls, inhibiting conversation, and worsening tensions. Air-conditioning, heating, and ventilation ducts are made smaller and smaller to save space and weight, with the result that machinery must be faster, and therefore noisier, to move the same amount of air. Outside, meanwhile, some three million construction workers all over the U.S. create daily bedlam with jackhammers, air compressors, earth-moving equipment, riveters, and similar mechanical monsters.

Americans often seem to react to noise as if it were a narcotic, as though nature were compelling us to accept it, even savor it, rather than engage in a hopeless struggle. Researchers have found, for example, that workers in noisy jobs often refuse to wear ear plugs because they are proud of their ability to "take it." In truth, this kind of tough-guy syndrome seems to be a subconscious device for sublimating discomfort. Psychologists think a similar narcotic effect may help explain why teen-agers sit for hours in rock joints, overwhelmed by "music" (as high as 130dbA) that blots out all else in the world and, like marijuana, enables them to escape temporarily from reality.

Muffling the Jumbo Jets

The first real test of the nation's capability to roll back the engulfing tide of noise will be the FAA regulations on aircraft. At this writing, the FAA is about to announce its plans. The agency reportedly will begin by fixing noise limits on the new generation of planes soon to go into service—such as the huge 325-passenger Boeing 747 due to begin operating early next year. The ruling probably will stipulate that such planes must generate the equivalent of no more than about 95 dbA at a point about four miles beyond the start of the take-off roll; today's big planes register as much as 105 dbA. An improvement of that magnitude is already being built into the 747's by Boeing engineers.

To supplement the new regulations, the National Aeronautics and Space Administration has launched a $50-million program to subsidize development of still another generation of even quieter engines through design and engineering innovations to slow engine fan-blade tips below supersonic speeds and thereby lessen the noise-making air turbulence. The agency hopes this will permit it a few years hence to begin further reducing the limit for new planes, perhaps to the equivalent of heavy city-traffic noise.

A third move, tentatively expected early in 1970, will apply noise limits to the 2,000 airliners now in service on the nation's airways. The problem is much tougher in this case and no decisions have yet been reached. There is a good chance, however, that there will be a dramatic program, to cost about $2 billion, to "retrofit" the whole airline fleet with engine silencers. How such a program would be financed remains to be worked out, but it seems likely that the government would require passengers to share in the added costs; a general fare increase of 5 percent has been suggested. A "retrofit" program might be accompanied by a change in flying procedures. Instead of a gradual three-degree approach to airports, aircraft would make a two-segment approach, first at six degrees, then at three degrees for the final segment. That would permit them to stay longer at higher, and thus quieter, altitudes than is possible today. Such changes in procedure would also involve design changes in the aircraft.

A Nixon Compromise

In the area of general noise pollution other than aircraft, the one step that Washington has taken—new regulations under the Walsh-Healey Act—has been a disappointment to anti-noise advocates. The regulations benefit some 27 million workers in about 70,000 plants, but exclude millions of others in plants with fewer than twenty workers and less than $10,000 in government contracts, thus omitting small businesses where abuses are no less deplorable. The Johnson Administration, which initiated the action, originally proposed to fix a noise limit of 85 dbA, with higher levels permitted for short periods. The proposal was so hotly opposed, however, especially by high-noise industries like textiles, that the Nixon Administration compromised on a maximum of 90 dbA—or 5 dbA more than the experts regard as safe. Even at 90 dbA, however, the new regulations will have a notable, indeed historic, impact if they are enforced. At least half of American industry today permits noise levels above 90 dbA. The American Petroleum Institute estimates the cost of compliance to the oil industry alone at $40 million to $50 million to modify its existing equipment.

Meanwhile, the federal government is acquiring a great deal of valuable expertise in studies ranging from apartment-house noise insulation to a computerized analysis of transportation noise. By far the most significant of the studies is an exhaustive document called "Noise—Sound Without Value," published last fall by a special ten-agency committee. The report asserted: "Increasing severity of the noise problem in our environment has reached a level of national importance and public concern." With notable political courage, it added that the solution "frequently will require actions that transcend political boundaries within the nation." I.e., it should not be left to the states. Not long afterward, the Johnson Administration, which had promoted the study, went out of business.

Which points directly to a central unknown today: what will the Nixon Administration do about noise? The top authority is the newly created Environmental Quality Council, headed by Nixon himself, which to date has made no decisions on noise. There is fear among anti-noise advocates that Nixon's strong feelings about state responsibilities may lead him to stay out of noise control except perhaps for voluntary—and therefore ineffective—guidelines. Such concern is one reason why the Senate recently passed a bill proposed by Washington's Democratic Senator Henry Jackson to create a prestigious, independent council to recommend policy on all forms of environmental control, including noise. A similar bill is pending in the House.

If the Administration should leave non-aircraft noise pollution to the states, the outlook could be gloomy; few states have taken actions of any consequence. California has a law limiting the vehicle noise on freeways to 88 dbA, and a noise abatement commission will soon begin hearings aimed at producing recommendations by 1971. The law is so loosely enforced, however, that a Los Angeles police official confessed he did not know it existed. In New York State, indignant citizens along the roaring New England Thruway, where some 10,000 trucks create a steady din around the clock, persuaded the state legislature to fix a limit of 88 dbA on each vehicle. There have been only sixty-three arrests since 1965—and the maximum fine is only $10 anyway. Connecticut also plans to introduce a noise-abatement program soon.

In the long-suffering core cities, where noise works its greatest evil, the record is spotty. Several cities have anti-noise ordinances, e.g., Dayton,

Dallas, Chicago, and Minneapolis. In San Francisco the Bay Area Rapid Transit System now under construction is spending $1,250,000 (only one tenth of 1 percent of the total cost) on noise suppression; it is expected to be the quietest subway in the country—85 dbA on the platforms versus New York's numbing average of 102 dbA. Milwaukee attempted to reduce truck noise by a city ordinance, only to have it overturned by the courts on grounds that it invaded state jurisdiction; the effort was laughed into obscurity anyway when a newsman discovered that the city's own vehicles were violating the ordinance.

The Man Who Moved a City

Despite its multitudes of other problems, New York City probably has tried harder than any other big community to mount a really effective anti-noise campaign. Much of the initiative came from a group of volunteers called Citizens for a Quieter City, Inc., headed by Robert Alex Baron, forty-nine, who was so incensed by the din of a construction project outside his Manhattan apartment that he quit his career as a Broadway play manager in 1966 to do something about it. His efforts helped coax Mayor John V. Lindsay to appoint, in 1967, a special anti-noise task force of technical experts and public-spirited citizens. These and other pressures combined to persuade the city council last year to pass the first building code of any major U.S. city with an anti-noise provision. It requires that new residential buildings must be constructed to cut noise penetration by about 45 dbA, which is appreciably less strict than the codes of several European countries but nevertheless a major stride forward.

To prove that Americans do not have to live with noise, Baron arranged for a public demonstration of silenced machinery in New York's Lincoln Center one day in 1967.

Among other items, he displayed a quiet air compressor imported from Britain. Within a few months, at least one major American manufacturer, Ingersoll-Rand, began actively promoting a similar machine. The city is running a test of the feasibility of using paper bags for garbage instead of cans, and it has contracted with General Motors to develop quiet garbage trucks to replace the present fleet of "mechanized cockroaches," as Baron calls them.

In a report to be published this month, the New York task force has also recommended an extraordinarily ambitious program for further steps, ranging from new zoning rules to creation of a corps of noise inspectors, with the objective of reducing the noise level in busy areas to 85 dbA and the residential level to 40 dbA in daytime and 30 dbA at night. The New York initiative is attracting considerable local attention. On N.B.C.'s Johnny Carson TV show recently, Baron appealed for people annoyed by noise to write him; the result was some 2,500 letters, most of them venting long-pent-up anger and frustration.

But the effort has a very long way to go. The anti-noise forces to date have failed even to persuade the New York Police Department to try to enforce the ordinance against needless horn blowing. The problem is compounded by the fact that the city has no direct authority to act against noisy vehicle engines (which are the state's responsibility), or noisy aircraft (the FAA's), or even the New York subway system (the Transit Authority's).

Even the French Don't Blow Their Horns

There is no mystery about how to control noise. At least sixteen European countries have building codes with anti-noise provisions, many of them tougher than anything even contemplated in the U.S. The Soviet Union, which began a "struggle against noise" in 1960, says it has banned factory noise above 85 dbA and limited the level in residential areas to 30 dbA. The West Germans, among other actions, have set up no fewer than eight categories of noise limits; they offer tax concessions and easy credit to manufacturers willing to silence machinery acquired before the limits were established; and they stamp the maximum noise permitted each vehicle on the owner's driver's license. In France, needless horn blowing has been successfully outlawed—much to the surprise of the French themselves—and other noise regulations are so well enforced that a peasant recently was fined $50 for a noisy cowbell.

Unlike other forms of pollution, noise comes from an infinite number of sources and cannot be cut off simply by cleaning up a few big operations such as garbage dumps. The answer, however, does not lie in brave new proclamations. Ways must be found to get at the problem through appeals to the self-interest of business and community leaders and through governmental regulations that are realistic and easily policed.

Two further federal moves are needed now to provide a legal framework for minimum national standards. One is to broaden the recent anti-noise regulations to protect workers in all factories engaged in interstate commerce. The second is to invoke the interstate commerce principle to permit the fixing of limitations on the noise created by the machines that industry produces. The objective of such a move would be to oblige manufacturers to design noise suppression right into their goods, and its national application would guarantee that no company would be hurt competitively. Says Leo L. Beranek of Cambridge, Massachusetts, chief scientist for the nation's largest acoustical consulting firm: "We have got to have noise regulation at the federal level. Controls in only a few scattered cities won't work; quiet products must have a national market."

A proposal for federal action on such a broad scale obviously invites innumerable problems. For one thing, it would require congressional action. It would compound the infighting already under way among the several federal agencies competing for anti-noise responsibility. Whatever the bureaucratic machinery, however, the approach probably should be to seek a broad mandate from Congress, and then to begin application of specific controls on a progressive basis, beginning with the most urgent problems —e.g., highway vehicle noise and outrageously noisy machines like air compressors.

The Diverse Opportunities

Federal laws, of course, are no panacea. At best they can be expected only to provide minimum standards that could then be reinforced through state and local action. In some cases such action can be carried out most easily through local regulation—e.g., anti-noise insulation of residential buildings, which can be enforced with relative ease through existing building inspectors. The mere existence of federal anti-noise laws would create strong psychological pressures on local governments and industry to act.

Apart from legislation, there are innumerable other opportunities for action. The federal government buys something like 35,000 vehicles annually. To require such vehicles, especially trucks, to be fitted with good mufflers, quiet tire treads, and other noise-suppressing equipment would go a long way toward encouraging manufacturers to make such items standard equipment. State and local governments could easily do the same. Procurement policy can be similarly useful across a broad spectrum of other items that are purchased by both consumers and government agencies— e.g., garbage cans, which can be quieted for about $1.50 apiece. The Federal Housing Authority and other national and local agencies have the power now to make compliance with noise standards a condition for publicly backed loans. The National Park Service has the same kind of authority now to bar noisy vehicles, transistors, and the like from our national parks. It should also be feasible for the federal and local governments to grant tax concessions to encourage industry to suppress noise. By relatively simple fiddling with electronic circuits, buses and trains could be fitted with jamming devices to discourage transistor addicts. And automobiles could be equipped with two horns, one for highways and a quieter beeper for city streets, as is widely done in Europe. The Federal Highway Safety Bureau recently revealed that it is already considering a requirement of this sort.

Contrary to the view among some industrialists that noise control is an expensive luxury, it is in fact good business; the lack of effective noise control at the source, moreover, is bad for business. In the case of aircraft, anti-noise flight procedures—e.g., disuse of some runways—are further reducing the capacity of our congested airports, while popular reaction against aircraft noise is making it increasingly difficult to find sites for new airports. Cities like New York are losing tens of millions of dollars in traffic diverted elsewhere.

For industry in general, the mounting cost of hearing-loss compensation claims could easily become astronomic if workers began going to the courts in large numbers. In view of the growing evidence that noise is a significant health hazard, it would make eminent sense for insurance companies and labor unions to add their considerable weight to the battle. With a few exceptions, businessmen have been surprisingly slow to recognize that noise prevention can be marketed; for example, in advertising for quiet apartments or noiseless kitchen equipment. There is also a major public-relations consideration in the growing feeling among environmentalists that corporations have no more right to dump noise on communities than air and water pollutants.

"Let avoidable noise be avoided," said the late Pope Pius XII in a 1956 appeal from the Vatican. "Silence is beneficial not only to sanity, nervous equilibrium, and intellectual labor, but also helps man live a life that reaches to the depths and to the heights. . . . It is in silence that God's mysterious voice is best heard."

The dangers arising out of the use of pesticides are alarming large numbers of the population, but the conditions that would follow the restricted use of such materials would be even more frightening. Consequently, the threats presented by pesticides call for a rational and less hysterical evaluation and response.

What Needs to Be Done?

Wheeler McMillen

What, regarding pests and pesticides, should "we, the people" concern ourselves about in this second decade of the second half of the twentieth century? Anything?

We should, indeed! Mainly we should be demanding prodigious amounts of research; demanding it from government, expecting it from industry, encouraging and supporting it in universities and institutions. So long as pests subtract from our economy huge agricultural and forest losses, obviously we do not have enough effective control over them. We should proceed to master our environment.

Despite the unprecedented progress in recent decades, the control yet to be desired can be measured only in figures of impressive magnitude:

More than three thousand different major insect species still damage crop plants to the extent of $4 billion or more each year.

The crop loss caused by several thousand fungal diseases stands around $3 billion a year.

Weeds that compete with crops mean a $5 billion loss.

Rats, mice, and other rodents do $2 billion worth of damage.

Nematodes probably reduce production by $1 billion a year.

Add to this $15 billion total the illness and injury among animals, plus the billion farmers and others have to spend for pesticides and their application, and we arrive at a staggering $17 billion estimate.

These are not just wild figures; nor can they ever be exact; they are careful estimates over which scientists and economists would not greatly disagree; some may say that they are too conservative. This is not so much as the national debt, but it is two-thirds the amount of the FBI's $27 billion estimate of the nation's crime bill. It is considerably more than the $12 billion net income of farmers. And it represents more than a fifth of what consumers pay ($82 billion government estimate for 1965) for their food —a 20 per cent plus food tax—which no one gets!

To combat these enormous losses, science has provided a mounting store of knowledge and some biological controls; chemical research has developed about three hundred basic molecular compounds which, in many variations, are our pesticides. (While thousands of pesticides are registered, all stem from the relatively few basic ones. Malathion, for example, has 137 registrations for various labels, formulations and purposes.)

Fully or partially successful though these instruments have been for many specific pests, they have served only to begin a brobdingnagian task, and to foreshadow much of it that may in time be accomplished.

Can man anticipate a pest-free world? Can an American look forward to a pest-free nation here?

Probably not, ever.

Agriculture might possibly become free from weeds. They are not so mobile as insects. Rats conceivably could be exterminated if every town, city, community, and farmer determined to get rid of them. The means exist if the human will could be organized.

But few scientists would venture to predict the extinction of pest insects, fungal diseases or nematodes. They might look forward to very great advances in domestic animal health.

An unceasing probe to extract the innermost secrets of bugs and plants nevertheless goes on. Reinforcements in the forms of greater funds, new kinds of tools, and bolder ideas join and strengthen the attack. The insect has six legs instead of two, and must therefore have six Achilles' heels. Scientific arrows will find those vulnerable openings. The years ahead should disclose ways to deal with pests as new and revolutionary as was DDT in 1942.

The chemical poisons are likely for a long time to be the basic weapons in the endless antipest war. Today we use better ones than yesterday. Undoubtedly tomorrow will bring others more effective and more selective.

New techniques, moreover, in all likelihood will change some of the chemical approaches. Combinations of chemical and biological methods promise conspicuous advances.

For example, the synthesis of "gyplure" presages one such new shape of progress. The female gypsy moth was found to possess a substance that attracted—almost as if she were equipped with a magnet—the males of her species. The material was isolated, its chemical structure determined, and then successfully duplicated by synthesis of a related chemical structure. Traps baited with this chemical attractant quickly disclose whether the moths are in an area. Incipient outbreaks can be squelched before they spread far, or the male population destroyed as it concentrates around the lure.

The ladies of a dozen other destructive insect species are known to possess such natural sex attractants. As the chemical structure of these individual substances is disclosed, men will attempt to synthesize, and with that the possibilities for control or eradication brighten.

Some plant species, also, are already known to contain substances that lure insects to them. These substances, as well as the sex attractants, may eventually be synthesized and made into effective weapons.

Wherever an insect builds up large numbers, as many species do periodically, the present and future chemical controls will knock off the worst of an outbreak. Then, as the species population becomes considerably reduced, chemical attractants and sterilants may combine with smaller quantities of the poisons to attain a high degree of control. Eradications may more often be accomplished in situations where an exotic pest has not had time to spread too widely. Attraction by light and sound also are under study.

The prospect that natural populations may be sterilized chemically has gained acceptance from researches so far. Radiation sterility accomplished the screwworm eradication, but rearing the vast numbers required was expensive. Chemical sterilization is viewed as a much simpler process which, ideally, could lead to depletion or elimination of an objectionable species without using poisons.

Incidentally, the chemical manufacturers are not disturbed by nor do they oppose the study of biological controls. They do not expect that advances in this direction will put them out of a business that already is subject to frequent change; and they anticipate that in sterilants, attractants, or other devices they will find new opportunities. The prospects for greater successes as research receives more adequate support are encouraging on many fronts. The kinds of to-be-desired research are many.

More competent study in the broad field is going on today than ever at one time before. While Congress is seldom overgenerous to research, except for health, military purposes, or space spectaculars, for decades it has consistently provided moderate funds for pest control studies. These have lately been increased and the objectives broadened. Not only government, but industries, universities, and some private institutions are exploring and probing for new facts; new fundamental studies are getting under way that will eventually pay off in profitable new applications.

Fundamental research and applied research are distinct, but the distinction is not always understood. If a scientist takes five different insecticides, and tries them on potato bugs at five different dosages each, he is doing applied research. He is taking a fundamental fact and finding out how to use it. He is working with already known facts, materials and techniques. But, a scientist may study the potato plant to find out why it attracts that kind of bugs, or study the potato beetles to find out why they prefer potato plants; if he does find out, he will have discovered a new item of knowledge—this is called fundamental research. Other scientists will likely find a score of ways to *apply* that knowledge, not only to potatoes but to other problems.

High urgency demands that much more knowledge than we yet possess shall disclose what eventually becomes of pesticides. Where do they go in the air, soil and water, and what do they do there? Exactly what happens as they enter into insects, plants and animals, or as their fragmentary molecules rise into the air? What is their long-run destiny and effect?

This area has deeply concerned the earnest people who fear that pesticides are contaminating our environment to a dangerous or, at least, needless degree, with occasional lethal consequences to wildlife and conceivable or imaginary near- or long-time hazards to human health.

One may easily enough dismiss some of these fears by restating the well-attested fact that after a hundred years (and more than a score since DDT) no known illness, much less no human death, has been recorded that could be attributed to any properly used pesticide. The concern about wildlife is a little less easily dismissable, because fewer positive facts exist, and no one wants to see avoidable fatalities or needless reduction of any species.

With respect to human hazard, regardless of the millions of lives *saved* by pesticides and regardless of the wonderfully excellent record of safe usage, some types of people perhaps will never be freed from their apprehensions. Even though humans for three generations have been exposed and rats for fifteen or twenty, they will not be convinced that after fifteen generations people will not also be adversely affected. Even so, more research can and will diminish the numbers of the fearful.

Many phases of controversy about pesticide usages have emerged because research had not yet fully elucidated definite essential facts. The ablest controversialists, however, of whom we shall always have a number, are not always to be satisfied by facts, however obvious or definite. Some persons are still maintaining that no one can eat meat and remain healthy. A skilled controversialist can always ignore facts, divert attention from them, or twist them to his purpose. He can prove to his own satisfactions that if overdoses of DDT on Michigan State's elms killed robins, or overdoses of heptachlor killed snakes and quail in the early fire-ant campaign, pesticides ought not to be permitted anywhere at any time. Nevertheless, the higher the accumulation of incontrovertible facts, the less virulent will be the controversies and fewer misunderstandings will remain.

Merely to adduce an array of new facts to add to the vast store already available will not, however, be enough. We do have . . . a degree of danger from unwisely restrictive legislation that could greatly exceed any present or probable peril from pesticides. The danger here is that impossibly costly requirements, requirements that are not actually significant in relation to a pesticide's usefulness, effectiveness, or safety, may be imposed upon manufacturers and discourage or terminate their research progress. Public information and understanding can help to maintain correct and reasonable governmental attitudes.

The scientist who produces a new fact promptly announces it in his favorite professional magazine, which reaches perhaps three or ten thousand of his fellow specialists. He proclaims his fact in a polysyllabic technical vocabulary, which conceals it perfectly from comprehension by any of us who read only ordinary English. By chance some science popularizer may discover and translate the discoverer's report in a newspaper column or magazine article. Then, and then only, does there begin to be an informed public; and only an informed public can effectively resist or help to resist hysterical pressures upon equally hysterical politicians (of whom happily not too many exist unless their majorities are threatened) to impose legislation that can restrict the orderly progress of science and industry toward still safer and still more effective ways of pest control.

New trails have been blazed in the direction of biological controls. Obviously these should be pursued by vigorous research efforts. The new USDA laboratory at Columbia, Missouri, will concentrate in this field, extending old work and developing new directions. No longer is this aspect limited to the introduction of predators or parasites. These had their limitations. When an introduction that fed only on one pest species reduced that creature's numbers to a minimum, it naturally itself began to run out of food and failed to reproduce in numbers. Birds are valuable predators upon insects, but if all the insects were eaten up how then would the birds live? In contrast, some of the new biological techniques lack those disadvantages.

Across the years the relationship between private and public research has been mutually advantageous, and profitable also to the public. When the industrial chemist brings out a new material from the laboratory and test fields, the federal and state experimenters frequently find new ways to use it and new ways to make it applicable. An outstanding example appeared when USDA scientists studied how to get the best use out of DDT and certain other insecticides early in World War II, when so many American soldiers were stationed in tropical and other infected areas. They came up with the aerosol "bomb," the device that in a few short years became a common household tool for scores of purposes.

The pesticide makers will be first to say that more research ought to be conducted on the application of their materials. They recognize that both aerial and ground applications by prevailing methods are imperfect. The drift of materials over to adjacent crops or waters where they are not desired still presents problems. Helicopters for some jobs have been found to be more exact and satisfactory than other aircraft. Precision of application assures better results and economy of materials. Where large areas are to be treated, such as the public forests, protective strips near streams and lakes are usually skipped to avoid water contamination; yet these strips then remain as sources for reinfestation. More research is needed to devise suitable formulations where extremely small dosages are sufficient for spreading over large areas.

As research expands a new problem arises—that of finding sufficient trained and capable personnel. Entomologists, pharmacologists, biologists, toxicologists and chemists of varied specialties will be increasingly in demand. Young people whose interest lies in the natural sciences will find ample opportunities for careers in some of these fields.

Long years ago a commissioner of patents advised Congress that a plan to erect a new building to house the patent office was superfluous. No need to spend the public's money, he said: the cotton gin, steamboat, railroad, and reaper had already been invented, it was unlikely that progress could advance further.

Today's amazing chemical aids to food production and health, like those inventions, represent but a fair beginning. Unfettered scientific enterprise will never be content with yesterdays nor even with todays. Better tomorrows are its unchanging goal.

The prospects for governmental help on environmental problems are limited. The pressure of collective action by large numbers of aroused citizens is necessary to motivate the bureaucracy and provide information for the decision makers. Self-interest, the congressional committee system, lack of technical knowledge, inertia, the tendency of elder statesmen to vote for the status quo— all operate against obtaining reform through legislative and judicial channels.

Everyone Wants to Save the Environment

Frank M. Potter, Jr.

It is difficult to find a newspaper today that doesn't have at least one story on environmental problems. People who read these stories react to them and, with increasing frequency, their reaction is sympathetic. Environmental concerns are no longer the private preserve of the birdwatchers: the same bell tolls for us all.

In 1969, the National Wildlife Federation commissioned two polling organizations to investigate American attitudes on environment. The polls reached the conclusion that most people are actively concerned about environmental problems and would prefer that a greater proportion of their taxes be devoted to the costs of solving them. The level of concern here rose with income and varied inversely with age. Over fifty per cent of those interviewed felt that the government was devoting insufficient attention to environmental problems and was providing insufficient funds to resolve them. Over eighty per cent felt a personal concern, and most of these registered "deep concern." What, then, keeps them from the barricades?

Apathy, one might think, but the surveys rule that out. The most significant inhibitor of action may be that we are too easily convinced of our own political impotence. The larger the grouping, the more difficult it is for any person to make a significant impact upon social decisions.

On the other hand, when they are really aroused, people can take and have taken effective action. For example, a coalition of citizens joined forces in 1969 to require a reluctant U.S. government to quadruple the amount of funds to be used for waste-water facilities. They did so by informing their elected representatives that this was a matter of specific, personal, and urgent priority; their representatives listened and responded.

From "Everyone Wants to Save the Environment But No One Knows Quite What to Do" by Frank M. Potter, Jr. Reprinted by permission from the March 1970 issue of *The Center Magazine,* Vol. III, No. 2, a publication of the Center for the Study of Democratic Institutions in Santa Barbara, California.

Again, a few years ago, a small group of citizens banded together against the largest utility in the United States, opposing plans to construct a major hydroelectric plant within fifty miles of New York City. They stopped the utility company in its tracks. That company was Consolidated Edison, the plant was the Storm King project. The Federal Power Commission, which must decide whether or not the plant should be built, has still not made its decision. The strong case made by the citizens depended in large measure on the fact that they were able to propose alternatives to the project and to support their case by a wealth of technical and engineering detail that showed New York's serious power problems could be met by less damaging methods. Although Con Edison has not yet given up the project, it has adopted the alternatives, and many sophisticated agency-watchers now consider it unlikely that the Storm King plant will ever be built.

Collective action, then, can make a difference. Individually or collectively, we are confronted with a clear option: Are we to live well only for a short period, or must we cut back economic growth in favor of long-term survival for the species? For the most part we appear to have adopted the former course of action, and it is by no means clear that we would act much differently if the choice were clearer. *"Après moi, le déluge"* is an attitude confined neither to France nor to the eighteenth century. As individuals, we tend to be somewhat ambivalent about the importance of what might be called an environmental conscience.

With very little effort, we could educate our children about the importance of environmental responsibility; yet it is the children who seem to be taking the lead in educating us. A national Environmental Teach-In is scheduled for April, 1970, in schools and colleges across the country, and there are signs that problems of pollution are occupying a rapidly increasing portion of the attention of young people.

It is important to distinguish between the actions and attitudes of individuals and those of the citizen groups organized to consider environmental problems. The biggest problem faced by such groups is seldom a lack of motivation; it is financial. It is still rare for anyone whose economic interests are involved to oppose a polluter; this means that concerned citizens must themselves assume these costs, although the financial burdens of speaking out and working against a powerful and well-financed industry or government agency may be great. The costs of carrying on a major controversy may exceed five thousand dollars. We cannot reasonably expect any private group to bear such a burden, nor should we as long as the group is acting to protect assets that are common and valuable to all of us.

It is important to note, though, that even concerned citizens do not always organize themselves to protect the environmental system as a whole —one group may be interested only in visual pollution while another is interested in noise. It is an unfortunate fact of life that a normal resolution of a pollution problem often means pushing it into another area which may not be so vigorously defended. For example, the public concern with power-generation facilities producing air pollution in the form of coal dust, oil droplets, and increased sulphur dioxide emissions encouraged the building of nuclear plants, which involve none of these pollutants but may well present other problems in terms of radioactive and thermal pollution of cooling water.

To look to private business for solutions to pollution may be futile. Its horizons are deliberately limited to those factors which are considered to be of immediate importance, principally economic, and the hidden costs to the society at large tend to be ignored. These costs still exist, however, and they must be borne by everyone if not by the industry which creates them. A classic example would be a pulp processing plant which emits fumes of hydrogen sulphide, causing foul air and peeling paint for miles downwind. The resulting inconvenience, possible health hazards, and certain increases in maintenance costs have not traditionally been imposed upon the agency which created them. Instead, they have been borne by our whole society, regardless of the capability or willingness of individual members to bear them.

To be sure, some private companies have taken steps to limit the antisocial consequences of their operations and have done so at considerable cost, quite beyond what they have been required to assume by law. But a voluntary approach to reducing environmental problems, it is clear, is just not good enough. For one thing, the forces of competition tend to minimize such voluntary efforts. Few men or companies, however public-spirited they may be, are prepared to expend large sums on the internalization of indirect costs. Nor can they do so without incurring the wrath of profit-seeking stockholders, who are even further removed from the environmental mischief they have indirectly created.

Polluting industries have most often resisted pressure to clean up their operations by claiming that the measures proposed are unduly prohibitive or confiscatory. Their chief means of resistance has usually involved threats to pull up stakes and move elsewhere. This last resort has been adopted infrequently, if at all, and is only likely to occur where a producer has found himself impossibly squeezed between falling profits and rising costs. It has also been alleged that these are the marginal producers whom the next strong wind will blow away in any case, so that little lasting economic damage to the area ever occurs.

The mechanics for balancing social costs against economic values, then, must be found outside the private institutions themselves, and they are—this is a major function of government. The laissez-faire philosophy which at one time characterized the attitude of American government toward American industry won't work today. It is also apparent that the government is likely to expand its program in this area. Public attention has already been focused on air and water pollution. But there are other areas in which governmental action must be anticipated—among them, noise, solid-waste disposal, and the by-products of energy transfer are mentioned with increasing frequency.

Governmental over-view, if impartially and reasonably imposed, need not be hostile to the private sector; it may even be in its interest, both short-termed and long-termed. The National Association of Manufacturers has never been known as a hotbed of social activists, yet members of N.A.M. operating committees have endorsed proposals for a strong federal body to oversee environmental issues. Businessmen have to breathe, too, and most of them are prepared to accommodate themselves to the ecological imperative—as long as their competitors are subject to the same rules. We cannot assume, however, that increased governmental concern will take place without some economic disruption. Marginal producers will feel the pinch most strongly, and some may not survive. Nevertheless, the important consideration is that the rules must be enforced fairly and impartially upon all parties.

It is important to bear in mind that the mass of government workers— the *Lumpenbürokratie*—marches to a drumbeat that only it can hear. Higher levels of government, presumably more responsive to broad social needs, generally find their choices so circumscribed by business-as-usual decisions farther down the line that their options are dissipated by the inertia of the machinery. This is by no means peculiar to the solution of environmental problems, though these tend to be somewhat more acute because of the high stakes involved and because the new issues do not fit easily into the existing bureaucratic patterns.

In practically every agency of government, at almost every level, strong pressures to maintain the status quo are built up. As one progresses from local to national bureaucracy the inertia increases. A random example: early in the nineteen-fifties the Eisenhower Administration stated a strong preference for private power development as against public power, but it was not until the Kennedy Administration took office eight years later that the direction of bureaucratic thinking had changed enough to give effective support to the idea of private power. Nor could the Democrats reverse the trend.

There are also powerful personal influences that, in current bureaucratese, are "counter-productive." As one observer put it, "the paramount objective of the permanent bureaucracy is permanence." This contributes directly to the institutional resistance to change. Agency employees tend to react self-protectively. This was probably the principal roadblock encountered by Ralph Nader's "Raiders" in their government agency investigations during the past two summers. They often ran up against a bureaucratic wall which blocked the publication of several unfavorable agency reports on the controversial supersonic transport until the reports were wrenched from unwilling bureaucratic hands by actively concerned congressmen. To combat this reaction Congress passed the Freedom of Information Act, requiring disclosure of all but certain specified documents —a public law which has been honored far more in the breach than in the observance.

This problem is compounded by a frequent lack of clear policy guidance from the upper levels of government to the lower. New policies may be found in new regulations and pronunciamentos which either go unheeded or trickle down by word of mouth. This communications system serves as an efficient filter for any content that may fortuitously have crept into the public statements of the man or men at the top.

Such difficulties should not be ascribed solely to bureaucracy. The problem for bureaucrats is essentially the same as that of the private citizen: they are unable to relate everyday decisions to any specific action of the government machinery. Moreover, the results of yesterday's decisions are rarely communicated to the decision-makers as a corrective for tomorrow's programs. To be sure, there is enough feedback for everyone to know when a dam doesn't hold water (which happens), but when a dam destroys a delicate ecological balance and wreaks havoc in the local community, the mischief is rarely perceived as a genuine problem.

Still another troublesome aspect is that government agencies compete with one another. For decades, to cite an example, the Departments of the Interior and Agriculture have carried on a polite war; its prime casualties have frequently turned out to be considerations of the environment. Countless examples of this competition have been observed: timber-cutting practices on public lands and in national forests, pesticide regulation (if that is the correct term for it), dam building, and soil conservation are just a few. The same kind of competition may occasionally be found between the public and private sectors of the economy; once again, concern for the environment usually loses out.

In some respects, such competition is healthy. Occasionally, the public may even benefit from it. Several years ago, for instance, the Army Corps of Engineers conceived a plan to build a high dam on Alaska's Yukon River which would flood hundreds of thousands of acres of land in the process. The dam was successfully opposed by the Fish and Wildlife Service of the Interior Department on the ground that it would do untold damage to the wildlife in the region. The operative word here is "untold"; no one knew just how much damage would have been done and the Corps was not really interested in finding out.

There are other consequences of governmental competition. Although they operate with public funds, governmental agencies are under pressure to make the most of the funds they expend. The budgetary restrictions placed upon the head of a large operating government agency are no less severe than those upon the directors of a large corporation, and the body to which they report is no more aware of the importance of environmental factors than the average stockholder of American Telephone & Telegraph. This comparison ought not to be pressed, however, since while it will be difficult to improve the ecological understanding of the average citizen, it is not beyond our grasp to educate Congress.

The essential function of the Legislative Branch of government is to formulate and to review policy. In so doing, it operates under constitutional or other social restraints, and it must of necessity paint with a broad brush. Translating basic policy decisions into specific go and no-go decisions, never an easy task, is often complicated by pressures within the Executive Branch to change the policy decisions themselves. More important, policy is only as good as the information upon which it is based, and this information tends to be biased, conflicting, fragmentary, and/or out-of-date.

Consider the effect of the following factors upon the theoretical non-bias with which a congressional policy decision is supposed to be approached:

The nature of the proposal. Most legislation enacted by the Congress is originally proposed by agencies in the Executive Branch. (This, incidentally, may not be quite so common today; the legislative proposals of the present Administration have been criticized as somewhat sporadic. Many of the bills now before the Congress, however, are holdovers from earlier years, and the basic pattern seems to have changed very little.) Support for these measures tends to be channeled well in advance of their consideration—facts are marshaled, charts are drawn up, witnesses are prepared. A frequent result of this process is that the Congress may focus on the wrong issues.

The congressional committee structure. Committees of the Congress, and especially their ranking members, are among the principal focal points of power in Washington. This apparatus determines which bills are considered, whether testimony in opposition will be considered, and if so, how it will be rebutted. Unless the issue is getting the attention of the press and the public, or unless a maverick congressman digs in his heels, those controlling the committee have a relatively free hand in developing the arguments for and against the bill; hence they control its future.

The bias of congressional leaders. The environmental crisis is a relatively new phenomenon, and the young are more concerned with the problems than their elders. This is as true in the Congress as elsewhere. The result is that many of the older members, who exercise greater control over legislative action than their younger colleagues, are less inclined to meet the new challenge. Exceptions can easily be found, but the general truth of this observation is not seriously questioned. There is, then, a bias favoring inaction. It ought not to be discounted.

The adequacy of the testimony itself. Assuming that the measure is reasonable and that the controlling committee is interested in developing the real issues, the witnesses called to testify may nonetheless not be the best available. Witnesses on environmental issues have tended to be the elder statesmen—established scientists and professionals whose views on new problems and on the need for new approaches have been colored by their own studies and viewpoints, which are frequently considerably out-of-date. A review of non-governmental scientific testimony over the past few years shows that several names pop up again and again; these individuals (who may be spectacularly well qualified in their own areas of competence) occasionally edge into areas in which they are not well qualified to speak, and they often seem to be responding to the unspoken needs of some committee members to be reassured that things are not all that bad, and somehow technology will find a way. Although not every expert witness falls into this category, it happens often enough to constitute a real problem. There is, consequently, a need to develop a base of scientific testimony available to the Congress on environmental issues and to see that younger scientists, whose factual knowledge is more current, are heard.

The context of the legislative decision. Another conflict, not at all restricted to environmental issues, faces the legislator who must decide whether to favor the good of his own constituency over national interests. Thus congressmen and senators from the West are generally inclined to favor legislative proposals to open public lands for development (mining, grazing, lumbering, oil exploration, etc.), whereas the interests of the entire country might seem to favor retaining these lands in a less exploited condition. How to measure the interests of local areas against those of society is a serious question. Resolving the conflict may be one of the most significant functions of government.

The broad nature of the authority and responsibility of the legislature may prevent it from exercising effective control over the actions of the organizations theoretically under its direction. The policies the legislators are called upon to define are so broad they cannot possibly be spelled out in detail, and yet it is in such details that the actions of government become manifest.

The legislative mechanism may also be criticized for its slow reaction time. The Congress is a highly conservative body—deliberate in adopting new courses of action, and slower to change them once they are adopted. This is, of course, a source of strength, preventing today's fad from becoming tomorrow's straitjacket. But it is also a real source of danger to the system. Science and technology have transformed the world of the mid-twentieth century into something that was quite unimaginable fifty years ago. The rate of change is accelerating, and it is a brave man who will claim that he can predict the state of the world in the year 2000. Shrill voices may decry technology and demand that there be a halt to new technological development; they are no more likely to be heeded than were the machinery-wrecking Luddites of nineteenth-century England. Whether they are right or wrong is quite beside the point; barring massive catastrophe, technology will not be significantly curbed and the rate of technological change will almost certainly continue to speed up.

New technology creates new social conventions, which in turn affect legislative policy. Yet the mechanisms for determining that policy are keyed to technological considerations that may have already been out-of-date in 1800, and to decision-making processes that have remained essentially unchanged since the days of Roger Bacon.

Consider massive changes in climate. Scientists tell us that urban development and energy transfer now have a significant effect upon global weather patterns. We hear on the one hand of the "greenhouse effect," which tends to raise atmospheric temperature as a function of increased carbon dioxide production, and on the other of increased amounts of pollution in the air, which tend to lower atmospheric temperature by decreasing the amount of solar radiation reaching the earth's surface. Some scientists, extrapolating present activities, speculate that it would take ten years to decide which is the more powerful effect, and that by then large-scale climatic changes may be irreversible. This view is by no means commonly held, but it is under serious consideration by men whose voices ought to be heard. They are not given a hearing before Congress; if they were, they might well be outnumbered ten to one by men saying, "We are not certain, we do not know, and we should take no action until we do."

Our ecological problems, then, are not the exclusive province of the Congress; they are those of the scientific community and of all of us who have an interest in human survival. There seems as yet no way to force these problems to the forefront, conjoined as they are with an historically validated precedent for doing nothing—at least not yet.

Legislators tend to focus upon institutions rather than individuals—to see the needs of the larger groups whose existence depends upon traditional thought patterns and legal fictions. A water pollution problem is perceived as that of a municipality or an oil company, an air pollution problem as that of a manufacturer. Yet it is individual citizens whose favor the legislator must seek if he is to survive. This suggests in turn that if individuals can organize themselves to be heard as an institution concerned with environmental survival the legislators will respond. This has not yet happened generally. No significant environmental lobby has yet made its voice heard on the national level.

The courts exist to see that the written and unwritten rules of society are followed; that the policies formed by the people and their elected representatives are observed. Within narrow limits, the courts have been successful in this function. As a means of achieving rational decisions on environmental issues, however, the courts are usually ineffective. Their influence could increase, but this would require a significant departure from the usual legalistic approach. It would involve the recognition of a basic and inalienable human right to a livable environment. Such a decision appears to be a remote possibility. Without this new constitutional approach, the courts will almost certainly be hamstrung by inadequate policies adopted by the legislature and by common-law rights which were defined centuries before the current environmental problems appeared.

Only in rare instances can the courts make decisions with more than local force and effect. The U.S. Court in southern New York may properly hold that the federal Department of Transportation must observe certain procedures specified by statute that may have escaped the Department's notice, and for this reason a highway shall not be built over the Hudson River. At the same time, the same Department favors the construction of longer runways into the Columbia River. Technically, the decision of the New York court is not binding in Oregon; the Oregon courts are free to disagree with their East Coast brethren and such disagreements are in no way uncommon. A means does exist for resolving interjudicial disputes— the Supreme Court of the United States. The Court, however, is already operating under a fearful load and can devote only a limited amount of its energies to environmental questions, however important they may appear to be.

The courts also lack the information upon which to base their decisions. The common-law system is grounded upon the adversary system, the theory being that each side will present the most favorable case it can and that the court will then resolve the dispute on the basis of the evidence before it. The environmental problems arising today are very complex— very different from the land disputes and tort actions of centuries ago. In theory, expert testimony ought to be available to both sides to support their cases; in practice, this simply does not work. Even if environmentalists can afford to hire experts (and often they cannot), experts cannot always be found. It is a rare electrical engineer who will agree to take the witness stand on behalf of opponents to a power plant or transmission line; he knows that other utilities may thereafter hesitate to contract with him for services even in circumstances that may be wholly unrelated to the present controversy. Conscientious men do exist and some may be found to testify, but it is not easy to find them. Cases have been lost and will continue to be lost for this reason alone. Without that interplay of expert testimony, the court is at a major disadvantage.

Even if experts can be found by all parties, the court's information problems are not thereby solved. Technical questions are already difficult, and they are growing more complex every day. Judges spring from different backgrounds, but the law operates according to the theory that their experience is essentially irrelevant to the issues that they must decide. Historically, ignorance has been a prime virtue, the court acting as the *tabula rasa* upon which the cases of the opposing parties may be written. This is a manifest absurdity, but it is the way the law grew, and it is a fact that lawyers with weak technical cases prefer judges with little technical competence.

Another weakness built into the judicial system is its tendency to delay decision. Combined judicial and administrative delays have postponed the Storm King decision by five years already. If the parties fight down to the wire, a longer delay is likely. In many respects this delay has worked in favor of the conservation group, but this happy state of affairs is not the rule. Citizens opposed to a particular proposal or project are usually forced to seek injunctive relief from the courts; they may and often do find that this relief cannot be obtained without their posting a substantial bond which is quite beyond their means. The result is that while they work their way through the courts, the opposition is busily building or digging or chopping down. By the time that the court is ready to decide, the essential question has become moot. Injunctive relief is typically the only possible hope for environmentalists, since the alternative is a damage suit, and it is a basic tenet of such organizations that money cannot replace what is threatened.

Constitutional revision has been proposed as a means of providing a clearer and more enforceable definition of our rights to a satisfactory environment. New York State has adopted such a program, and similar efforts have been mounted on a national level. An Environmental Bill of Rights would indeed be a valuable tool, but no such proposal has a chance of even being seriously considered without vastly increased pressure upon the Congress and upon the legislatures of the several states.

Pollution will be inevitable until we can develop adequate tools for dealing with it. The government will never do the job by itself. The solution seems to lie, rather, in putting stronger weapons into the hands of the public—helping it to bring about the necessary reforms through legislative and judicial channels.

The problem of pollution abatement is not solely technological. Economics and politics play a large part in any program for this purpose. Public attitude has shifted toward greater resentment and intolerance. There are some specific programs of action that, if adopted promptly, may hold off the almost inevitable catastrophe looming in the future.

The Chemistry and Cost

R. Stephen Berry

We are making a fast transition into a society in which many people recognize the environment as the finite medium in which we live, and not as a limitless source and sink.

Let me summarize the present state—the physical, biological and legal aspects of the pollution problem—and point out a few examples.

Sources of air pollution can be classified expeditiously as (1) power and heat generation, (2) industrial processes, (3) waste incineration and other waste disposal processes, and (4) transportation. The first and last of these sources have characteristic and moderately well-studied patterns of emission. Power and heat generation is still primarily achieved by burning coal, oil or gas. The best-identified pollutant from this class of sources is of course sulfur dioxide; others from the same sources include solid particulate and nitrogen oxides. Transportation, meaning automobiles and trucks and jet airplanes burning hydrocarbon fuels, is responsible for carbon monoxide, hydrocarbons and their oxidation products, nitrogen oxides and solid particulate, especially lead. Waste incineration produces particulate and nitrogen oxides under any circumstance, and carbon monoxide if it is improperly done. Each type of industrial processing source has its own pattern of pollutants, almost as characteristic as a fingerprint.

The prospect for the next few years is an increasing flood of air pollution from all these sources. The world's annual sulfur dioxide production doubled between 1940 and 1965 and will more than double between 1970 and 1990. The number of automobiles is increasing fast enough that by 1980 the trend toward lower pollution (from the use of control devices) will be reversed. Per capita solid wastes are increasing two to four per cent each year, and if present policy is not changed, part of this waste will appear as air pollution.

From "The Chemistry and Cost" by R. Stephen Berry. Reprinted by permission of *Science and Public Affairs, the Bulletin of the Atomic Scientists*. Copyright © 1970 by the Educational Foundation for Nuclear Science.

Brown and Gray Cities

The pollution patterns of various cities and even neighborhoods differ considerably. Some cities, like Eugene, Oregon, with its kraft paper plant, or Gary, Indiana, the victim of steel mills and coking ovens, derive most of their pollutants from a single industry. Larger cities, however, generally fall into one of two basic classes, which I call the brown air cities and the gray air cities. Brown air cities derive a very high proportion of their pollution from automobiles. In relatively young cities, such as Los Angeles or Denver, the morning air is visibly brown from nitrogen dioxide, produced in the early traffic rush. The older, gray air cities, such as New York or Chicago, depend heavily on the burning of coal or oil for space heating, and derive their electric power largely from the same fuels burned in generating stations in or near the cities. This burning produces vast quantities of particulate. So much particulate is produced each morning from coal or oil burning that the air has a gray color, rather than the brown of nitrogen dioxide. These two types of cities have to be dealt with somewhat differently.

Pollutants can be classified usefully in several ways other than by source. For purposes of analyzing the problem, we may categorize pollutants according to how well they are now monitored. Moderately reliable methods are available for measuring sulfur dioxide concentrations continuously; it has recently become possible to monitor carbon monoxide on a continuous basis also. The technical difficulties associated with such monitoring are due primarily to the fact that the pollutants occur in very small quantities, one to 100 parts per million for carbon monoxide, and a hundredfold less for sulfur dioxide. Hence one needs methods of high sensitivity and high specificity to avoid interference. Nitrogen oxides and "total oxidant" levels can also be measured with moderate ease, but with some ambiguity about what one is measuring. Particulate is measured on an intermittent basis by filtering the material from large volumes of air, or continuously by an opacity method that is unfortunately influenced by particle size. The content of the particulate is rarely investigated systematically or regularly, except to determine the combustible fraction. More selective or convenient particulate monitors are appearing, but only a few laboratories, particularly of the U.S. Public Health Service, have done extended monitoring studies of individual hydrocarbons, of nitrogen oxide and nitrogen dioxide separately, and occasionally of other species such as hydrogen fluoride that tend to be associated with specific kinds of sources.

Electron Analyzer

All in all, we do now have effective continuous monitors for at least one characteristic substance from power and heat generation and from transportation. More general monitors, applicable to gaseous pollutants from a wide range of industrial processes, will probably appear on the commercial market within the next year or two. For example, an electron impact analyzer has been developed at the National Bureau of Standards and will probably be a prototype for a monitoring device. Particulates and droplets still require batch analyses, and normally are restricted to analyses for heavy elements and a few specific compounds. Hydrocarbons could be monitored automatically and frequently by gas chromatography. As yet, systematic hydrocarbon measurements have been carried out at the research level, rather than as routine monitoring.

In all probability, the course of pollution control has been influenced by the ease with which various species have been monitored. For example, systematic and automatic on-site analyses are not available for carcinogenic hydrocarbons such as a benzo-a-pyrene, or for phenols, or for lead. None of these pollutants has been the focus of a control campaign, or of extended low-level toxicological studies. Until recently, carbon monoxide analyses could not be done on a continuous automatic basis, especially in the road-level sites where they would be most useful. Now, with monitors available, standards for air quality are being established with regard to carbon monoxide. Sulfur dioxide, the easiest common pollutant gas to monitor, is the standard villain and the target for most grass roots antipollution campaigns, as well as the first gas for which regional air quality standards have now been proposed. Perhaps if the differential infra-red monitor for carbon monoxide now coming into use had been available a few years before the colorimetric sulfur dioxide monitor, automotive pollution would be a much smaller problem today.

Recognizing the dependence of control strategy on input data should prepare us for future surprises. The field is still young enough that significant new pollutants or components in pollutant-generating cycles continue to come to light. In photochemical smog, peroxyacetylnitrate (PAN) was discovered in 1960 and identified as a major irritant despite its very low ambient concentrations. Other peroxyalkylnitrates were recognized at the same time. Then, eight years later, the peroxyarylnitrates such as peroxybenzylnitrate turned up in smaller concentrations, but proved to be far more irritating.

Effects on Health

The relationship of air pollution to health is of course the nub of the problem and in some ways its most difficult aspect. Systematic public health studies of the effects of pollution are still rather rare, and, with a few important exceptions, the medical profession has not rushed to make these studies.

Several studies looked for correlations of cancer with air pollution. The case for such a correlation with cancer of the lung is not a strong one now. On the other hand, a recent study including several other types of cancer found significant correlations of mortality, particularly in gastrointestinal cancer, with chronic exposure to sulfur dioxide and nitrogen dioxide. I estimated from the results of this study that a fivefold reduction in Chicago's average annual sulfur dioxide concentration (with all other variables held constant) would reduce the number of deaths from cancer by about 800 per year.

Statistical studies and physicians' observations have coupled bronchitis and emphysema with pollution. Increases in the sulfur dioxide concentrations correlate well with increased degree of illness in cases of chronic bronchitis, when these increases are accompanied by increases in particulate levels. As yet, the acute effects on human health of atmospheric sulfur dioxide without particulate, at present ambient levels, are not known. However it is almost impossible to conceive of a realistic situation in which we would encounter sulfur dioxide without particulate pollutants. This point is currently important because studies of sulfur dioxide alone have sometimes been misinterpreted in the press. Evidence is growing that exposure for 24 hours to about 0.2 parts per million of sulfur dioxide, with particulate present, represents a recognizable danger to health.

Carbon monoxide levels are high and are overwhelmingly due to motor vehicles. Concentrations are of course highest along crowded arterial streets and highways, especially at times of day when cars accelerate and decelerate in the speed range up to 40 miles per hour. The monoxide levels now exceed 30 parts per million occasionally and exceed 15 parts per million (ppm) very often for periods of eight hours or more in heavy traffic areas. The toxicity and general health effects for such carbon monoxide levels are subject to some dispute. New York aims for no eight-hour averages as high as 30 ppm and no more than 15 per cent of the eight-hour averages to exceed 15 ppm. Some changes in judgmental abilities and motor control have been reported from carbon monoxide levels of 30 ppm. It has been suggested that four to six hours of exposure to this concentration is equivalent, in terms of the oxygen-carrying capacity of the blood, to being at an altitude of 6,000 feet, without acclimating.

High CO Level

Clearly the carbon monoxide levels are not so high that people collapse on city streets from lack of oxygen. However they are high enough in selected places—tunnels, for example—to worry seriously about direct toxic effects. And, apart from the direct effects, one presumes that driving an automobile requires some skill and alertness, particularly in traffic, but the monoxide levels suggest that this may not be the case. Apparently, there are no studies as yet of possible correlations of carbon monoxide levels and automobile accident rates.

Sometimes air pollution has been the clear cause of injury and death. Called by the sardonic euphemism of "episodes," documented examples of those shameful incidents have occurred in the United States, Mexico, France, England and Japan. The "episode" that occurred in November and December of 1962 was quite remarkable in that it was recognized in the United States, England, Holland, Germany and Japan. The worst in terms of demonstrated mortality was the London "killer smog" of 1952: a conservative estimate puts the number of excess deaths from this one "episode" at 3,500 to 4,000, due to the pollutants that accumulated during the four days of the incident. Other estimates run to 8,000 or more.

Focusing attention on "episodes" is useful both because it does arouse public sentiment, and because it can be the basis for a reasonable expedient control strategy. However men have literally made the atmosphere non-viable in at least one place. The industrial city of Yokkaichi, Japan, is so badly polluted that its inhabitants were officially urged to move elsewhere.

One naturally wonders whether places such as Los Angeles will become uninhabitable. At present, it appears that people do build up some resistance to exposure to ozone, one noxious component in the atmosphere of brown air cities. Perhaps we can adapt to the entire complex of pollutants of photochemical smog, so that people can continue to move to Los Angeles, provided they condition themselves. Unfortunately, there is no indication of a build-up of resistance to the sulfur oxides from coal burning. In fact, sulfur dioxide may be radio-mimetic, causing damage to nucleic acids.

Control Strategies

Pollution abatement and air management strategies differ, depending on what the pollutants are and on the time scale of the control program. The easiest program to implement is usually one designed to control "episodes" by reducing peak pollutant concentrations for a few hours or days. This kind of program obviously represents the smallest perturbation of the society. Reducing chronic pollutant levels is usually a slow and moderately costly process; even the conversion of a single large boiler from one fuel to another may require an entire season.

The health problems and control strategies for gray air cities, brown air cities and cities polluted by single industries obviously differ. As yet, no critical short-term incident has been identified in which large numbers of people died from the photochemical smog of brown air cities. Brown air is more a source of severe chronic discomfort than of acute incidents of increased mortality. By contrast, most of the severe "episodes" occurred in gray cities, at times when sulfur dioxide and particulate levels were high. Yet people have tolerated chronic gray air conditions for hundreds of years with little more than grumbling.

The obvious Machiavellian inference is that in gray air cities, the public would probably be mollified with abatement programs designed only to deal with incidents of dangerously high levels of sulfur dioxide and particulate. In brown air cities, we would have to reduce the chronic level of automobile pollutants below some intolerance level determined largely by our ability to adapt to these substances. In industrial areas, we would have to control odors and obnoxious visible stack products such as foams or sewage fumes. In fact, some major pollution control programs have in part taken this form. Such programs of expediency and minimum perturbation may be quite sinister, insofar as they sometimes pre-empt more fundamental approaches. But expedient programs may be necessary to save thousands of lives, because we may not get something better into effect before the next killer smog comes along.

A classic comedy situation arose when the New York City Council prohibited garbage burning—obviously a simple way to reduce air pollution quickly. Unfortunately no one had checked to see that other means were available for disposing of the garbage. Another example emphasizes the folly of the expedient approach. William Stanley, former Director of the Air Pollution Control Department of Chicago, often said: "Sure, I know how to get rid of air pollution from garbage-burning tomorrow; dump the garbage in the river."

What are the alternatives to the fast and expedient approach I have treated so cavalierly? We should examine these rather carefully; it may be that the cures are as bad as the disease or worse. In looking at ways to handle the air pollution problem, and some other problems too, we have to examine the effects of the cures and, eventually, the goals and values.

The complexities of trash and garbage disposal are easy to recognize as soon as one is sensitized to them. One quickly realizes that a reasonable control strategy must deal with collection and disposal problems of solid and liquid wastes, as well as with the incineration problem. Other areas of air pollution abatement may involve more subtle interactions, or sometimes interactions about which we can only speculate. It may be, for example, that sulfur dioxide from coal burning acts as an inhibitor for formation of photochemical smog from automotive pollutants. No one knows whether this actually occurs, but on chemical and observational grounds, it is a possibility we must examine. The answer may have a strong influence on the strategy of pollution control in gray air cities, at least for intermediate times of five to 20 years. This influence operates as follows: at the moment, it looks considerably easier to achieve control of the emission from coal (or oil) burning than of automotive emissions. If the two pollution systems, from coal burning and from automobiles, do not interact, then the strategy of choice is obviously to work in two stages, solving the easier problem first. This way we would get rid of the bulk of the sulfur dioxide and particulate from coal or oil as fast as possible. On the other hand, if sulfur dioxide were really helping to keep gray air cities free of photochemical smog, then the best strategy might be to reduce coal-burning and automotive pollutants together, even if this procedure meant removing sulfur dioxide slower than we would with a two-stage strategy.

No One Solution

The problems of pollution abatement are partly technological, partly economic and partly political. Let me explore one example in which engineering, economics and public pressure all have clear roles in determining the strategy, but for which there is no single clear solution. This is the problem of pollutants from coal-burning electric power plants. There are at least four possible directions for the electric power industry: improving the fuel quality, removing the pollutants (primarily sulfur dioxide and particulate), switching to gasified coal or re-siting the plants. Each has its own gains, its own alternative ways for implementation, and its own time scale.

Improving fuel quality normally means switching from coal containing about three per cent sulfur or more to coal with 1.5 per cent sulfur or less. This is probably the method most available. One can expect a 50 to 70 per cent reduction in sulfur dioxide this way. The low-sulfur coal costs two to six dollars per ton more than high-sulfur coal, and cannot be used in all furnaces. Presently, only dry-ash, and not "wet bottom" or slag-tap, furnaces are adapted for the high-melting ash of low-sulfur coal. Furthermore the amount of fly ash is approximately inversely proportional to the sulfur content in much coal, so that either greater precipitator capacity must be installed or more particulate will come out the stack. Partial desulfurization is another potential tool, but still presents formidable technical problems. With low-sulfur coal from either source, the net gain is a reduction by a factor of two or three in sulfur dioxide output, per ton of coal. However electric power requirements are predicted to increase by a factor of five by 1990, and 40 per cent of this power will be generated by coal burning. Hence the use of low-sulfur coal is at best a short-term expedient for badly polluted cities. Burning gas or low-sulfur oil is a possibility for short-term relief, but the supplies of both these fuels are limited.

Several chemical methods of removing sulfur dioxide from stack gas are either available or will become available in the near future. Most of these methods produce a by-product suitable for sale: sulfuric acid, elemental sulfur or ammonium sulfate, for example. The net cost to the company for the operation is estimated to be between $2.50 and $0.35 per ton of coal, and removes 90 per cent or more of the sulfur dioxide. One process with no by-product, based on reaction of sulfur dioxide with dolomite, has already been used at the Union Electric Company in St. Louis (with considerable problems) and in Lawrence, Kansas (with more success).

Any or all of these processes could almost surely be available very soon if a major engineering task force—a micro-NASA—were put to work on them. At the moment, effort is highly fragmented. The Electric Research Council is working at a leisurely pace on one, and industries in the gas-cleaning business are each trying to develop their own process with what in-house capability they may have. Two or three years ought to be a sufficient time for the development, engineering and installation of chemical controls, if the problem were treated as a national goal and the attack upon it were implemented accordingly.

Mine-mouth gasification is a possible direction but it will be at least another 18 months before the pilot plant stage is complete. It will probably be at least three to five years before even the best-situated coal mines could start supplying gas to electric power plants. Much of the technology is known already in Europe but to be competitive with American coal, the developers would have to develop designs and methods of their own.

Still further in the future is plant re-siting and power transmission by super-conducting transmission lines. Generating stations have lifetimes of 40 years or more; many large operating plants still have long useful lives. However the projected demand for electric power means we need many new plants. Presumably some of the new plants will replace existing facilities in polluted cities, and not merely supplement them. Moreover, in terms of use of natural resources, it may be sensible for many of the new power stations to burn high-sulfur coal, collect the sulfur oxides and convert them to salable by-products. The only serious limitation on this strategy will be the problem of the carbon dioxide that will be produced.

Other, still more exotic, methods to generate electric power also lie on the horizon as possibilities. Probably they will eventually be needed, but until there is strong motivation to work them out, they will remain exotic.

Let us assume that electric power companies will eventually reduce their pollution. Which course they choose will be a function of costs and of public pressure, as it appears in public policy. If public pressure is great enough, they may have to commit themselves to a mixed strategy, with short-term, intermediate, and long-term abatement measures. For example, a relatively inexpensive short-term approach is complete or partial conversion from coal or high-sulfur oil to low-sulfur oil or coal—or, where it is available in sufficient quantity, to gas. The intermediate time range might be handled by chemical recovery of sulfur oxides from the flues, with high-sulfur fuel as the principal fuel. The long-term part of the solution might be construction of power plants at the mine sites, with all the technology for sulfur oxide and carbon dioxide collection built into the new plants.

Strategies

Whatever changes we choose to make, somebody has to pay. A basic problem with direct implications for our strategy of implementation is simply "Who should pay?" I shall put off the question of punitive actions for the moment, because pollution is an area where punishment is only part of a strategy to achieve an end, and is never defensible for vengeance, that is, as an end in itself.

Who should pay? Who can be made to pay? The general public, which we can equate with those who presumably benefit from a clean environment, is one group. In many cases, probably in most cases, the "customers" of the polluter may be made to bear the costs. This includes the tenants of an apartment converting its furnace from coal to gas, as well as the buyers of steel from a company that installs precipitators. Utilities can, under existing law, pass the costs of capital equipment directly on to their customers; in fact they are entitled to obtain profit on this equipment. Hence the electric power rates will presumably go up as power companies install pollution control equipment. Operating costs cannot as readily be passed on as higher rates; there is a time lag because of the regulatory process for utility rates and the problem of determining what may be a fair profit. Another important situation, in which the polluter could be expected to bear part of the cost rather than pass it on to his customers, is the case of one polluting industry in a field in which the other competitors are under no pressure to spend money on pollution control. The polluter, forced to control emission, must raise prices, cut other costs or work on a smaller profit margin until he has paid for his control measures. This case is probably more the exception than the rule. A third situation where the polluter could be made to pay for the privilege of polluting or for the cost of pollution control is the case of the private automobile.

Until last year's change in attitude, it was ridiculous to think a polluting industry would voluntarily control its pollution and bear the costs. Now that pollution control is becoming socially acceptable or even desirable, voluntary and self-supported abatement begins to look less like a laughably naive policy. However, no one has yet polled a company's stockholders to see whether they would let the cost of pollution control be absorbed in their dividends. It would be amusing to try.

Essentially, then, we can expect the costs of pollution control to be borne by the public or by the customers. A strict theory of benefits would say, in most cases, that the general public is the principal recipient of the benefits, so that public money should pay the costs. This could take the form of fast tax write-offs (which now operate), direct subsidies, or low-cost loans underwritten by the government; the form is not particularly relevant here. A theory based on harm, which seems to be the choice of some of the recent entrants to the anti-pollution campaign, would put the costs on the polluter. However, I hope the foregoing argument makes it clear that this would usually amount to passing the costs on to the polluter's customers. If expedience and speed, rather than benefits or harm, were the prime consideration, public financing would probably be the method of choice. Theories based on costs, especially in the broad sense used by most economists in this field, are roughly equivalent to a theory of harm. Cost theories have the difficulty that the inferences one draws are terribly sensitive to how broadly one defines costs, and how one deals with the valuation problems of health and aesthetics. At the present time there is another difficulty; the society is, in effect, trying to develop pollution management programs while it is changing its entire assessment of harm, costs and values. What still seems like a small cost to one part of American society has been re-evaluated now by another segment as a high cost, or a severe harm.

Polluters Pay

One other basis of judgment, my own current favorite, is one of negligence. This view, like the cost theory, has the danger of being all things for all men, when applied to pollution. However I see it as putting part of the responsibility for improvement on the negligent polluter, and part on the public for tolerating the muck we live in. Furthermore I see strong reason to use methods that get things done as soon as possible, especially when these things involve major research and development. The implication of this view is that we should spend substantial amounts of public money for air pollution control, but it also implies that each polluter should carry a significant share of the effort and costs of solving his own specific problems. We simply cannot wait for the coal industry to find economic ways of desulfurizing or gasifying coal, or for the steel industry to take voluntary initiative in developing effective controls for coking operations.

Let us grant that there is finally some public sentiment for change; how might governments and polluters now deal most effectively with the problems of abatement? Pollution problems will not go away spontaneously; we have some 800 years of historical precedent to make this assumption.

For the short term, roughly the next 20 years, we can afford to treat pollution problems as if they were primarily technical and administrative. We need new ways, far faster and more effective than those we have, to develop pollution control technology. We must develop and implement programs of pollution management to reduce the hazards of the environment that we are so rapidly making hostile. But it is terribly important to recognize and accept that the problem of environmental pollution is fundamentally neither technical nor administrative. The problem is far deeper and more difficult; it is really a problem of the goals and aspirations, of the manner of life of the human species. We shall return to this aspect in the final section.

Let us examine the administrative problems first. Several viewpoints which suggest themselves are based on whether one considers pollution and its control a matter of benefit, of blame, or of negligence. In effect, these different views imply different relative amounts of carrot and stick. To analyze the abatement problem, we also must consider the secondary effects of any pressure we apply, the public's degree of impatience, the inertia of polluters and the technological time scale. Whatever the approach, it is important to keep in mind that the goal is pollution abatement, or better, rebalancing technological benefits against the quality of our environment.

Interpreting pollution problems in terms of blame implies that the pressures for change should be more punitive than persuasive. Fines, taxes, jail and injunctive closure of plant operations have all been suggested or used. The concept of a pollution tax is popular in some quarters, particularly in connection with theories based on cost. Unfortunately, if my analysis is correct, in most cases where a pollution tax would be applied, the cost would be passed on to the polluter's customers who would have to pay this cost. In other words, the poor customer would pay for the privilege of letting his vendor pollute. The pollution tax would only be effective in situations where the polluter could not or would not pass the tax on to his customers. It is not at all clear that enough examples of this kind exist to make a general pollution tax effective or desirable. An exception is the private automobile; one could tax effluent from automobiles by taxing the fuel or, with inspections, the vehicles, and then use this money to pay for the development of lead-free gasoline refineries and catalytic muffler reactors, for example.

Pollution taxes are an indirect way of achieving an end. Proponents of such taxes have argued largely by showing how they would work successfully, without examining the alternative ways they might operate. In particular, the assumption is usually made that the effluent fee will drive the polluter into reducing his effluent. The obvious alternative is that he will pay the fee and pass it on to his customers, or simply absorb the fee. The closest thing to evidence on this in America comes from fines for pollution. Here, the chronic problem has been the difficulty of making the fines large enough to be punitive. In general, pollution fines have been notoriously ineffective as a device to reduce pollution; they are simply absorbed in operating costs. The landlord raises rents a little to pay the fines for a dirty coal furnace, rather than raising them enough to pay for conversion to oil or gas. I fear that effluent taxes would operate the same way.

In terms of real remedies, injunctive closure has been a much more effective force than a fine, particularly with industrial processes. Personal penalties, such as jail sentences, are another possibility. Thus far, we cannot judge their effectiveness. At one time, incidentally, air pollution in London was a capital crime.

If taxes, fines and jail sentences are the sticks, then subsidies, low-interest loans, tax benefits and technical assistance are the carrots that we could offer. A benefit theory makes these all reasonable possibilities: the public wants to get rid of pollution, so the public is the customer that should pay. This approach certainly appears at first sight to be the most efficient, in terms of overcoming the inertia of the polluters. It has not really been tried on a large scale, except in London. There, it was very effective recently in implementing a smoke control program.

Cost-benefit analysis, at least in its more simplistic forms, seems inappropriate and possibly dangerous now for pollution and environmental problems. Apart from the usual difficulties of valuation, it may be too early. At this time, many harmful effects of pollution are just being demonstrated; we can expect to learn much more about effects of pollution on health in the next few years. It would be judicious to act now from a medically conservative position, using correlation studies, such as those of sulfur dioxide and particulate matter with morbidity and mortality, to define the strictest standards and goals, both long- and short-term, that our technology allows. In time, when we have a clearer understanding of the medical picture, we should consider a cost-benefit approach and a revision of the standards.

Now let us examine the technological aspect. One approach opened by the Air Quality Act of 1967, but not yet exploited widely, is the use of federal mission-oriented research and development money. True, the National Air Pollution Control Administration (NAPCA) has started in this direction by awarding money for research and development of air management methods: some 350 grants will be awarded in 1970 for these purposes. The NAPCA budget, however, is modest. A typical program within NAPCA, that of the Process Control Engineering Division, is doing some in-house research on one method of sulfur oxide removal, cooperates with other groups to study several other specific control methods, and is beginning to study the pollution problem more broadly, by trying to determine where research is needed.

Task Forces Needed

A different and more vigorous tack is available, and has been suggested in various forms. I shall state it in the way I like best: we could create strong, well-funded and highly directed task forces to solve specific technological problems of environmental management. These micro-NASA projects would be natural devices to move much faster than we now do with the development of chemical methods for removing pollutants from stack gases, with coal gasification, with developing automobiles and other, perhaps radically different transportation systems that produce far less pollution per passenger-mile or per passenger-trip. Industrial participation in these projects is clearly very desirable; once developed, the new technologies have to be produced and supplied to society. However we can expect, judging from the situation with which we are now wrestling, that industry alone will not ordinarily support major programs to do this engineering, at least not at a sufficiently rapid pace. We learned from NASA how fast a whole new technology can be created, developed, engineered and applied. We could use the space program as our model, learning from it what to do and what not to do, to solve many of the specific technical problems of environmental management that we can now define as precisely as John Kennedy defined the goal of putting men on the moon.

The National Laboratories have been suggested as natural locations for these task forces. This seems eminently reasonable to me. Programs could be developed in which in-house teams of broadly trained scientists and engineers could work with larger groups of specialists on loan or leave from industries. Presumably the success of each task force would destroy the need for its existence. Moreover it looks as if we have enough major problems of research, development and engineering in environmental control to justify long-term support for continuing versatile in-house groups that would give the generalist's viewpoint in each new task force. University programs are starting to appear, from which these "environmentalists" can hopefully be drawn.

Clear solutions to some of the immediate outstanding technical problems would do much to resolve our critical pollution problems, at least on an intermediate time scale. Financial inducements in the form of tax credit or direct subsidies would equally well induce major polluters to develop and install the devices, and adopt the control methods that our task forces would presumably produce. This is admittedly the approach of an impatient man, and I concede to being guilty of impatience. I would like to persuade many others to be as impatient as I am.

At the same time that we try to solve well-defined technical problems, we can look at the harder, more ill-defined problems of consumption of raw materials, goods and energy, the problems of environmental management that we are learning to recognize. These are problems that deserve careful, scholarly investigation. We cannot expect to achieve a basic solution of the solid waste problem, or the urban transportation problem, or the problem of restoring a dead lake to some still-undefined "healthy" state, by a crash program. They are the long-term problems that require that we consider the effects of each proposed solution. Recognition of these as deep-seated problems is symptomatic of a technological society just realizing that it must pay the piper. Programs in universities and national laboratories have started to appear with advertised intentions to deal with these grand-scale problems, and a little federal money may be available, even in these times, to support them.

At this time, the most hopeful possibilities for relief seem to lie in the Federal Air Quality Act of 1967. The definition of Air Quality Control

Regions, with precisely defined standards of air quality, in terms of specific ambient pollutant levels and time-schedules, represents a broader, clearer and more direct approach to air quality management than any this country has ever seen before. Taking these steps was extremely important, but the most critical step of all is the one we now confront: adopting implementation procedures. Here is where the aroused and—presumably—informed public, with its newly awakened concern for the environment, can help determine the quality of the air it breathes.

Ultimate Catastrophes

Let me move on to an apocalyptic note. We almost surely can manage the environment, and maybe clean it, for another 20, perhaps even 50 years. It is virtually certain that we cannot do this indefinitely, the way we now live. All sorts of cataclysms await us. In air pollution, the increasing concentration of carbon dioxide is a popular favorite. There is a reasonable possibility that there will be enough carbon dioxide in the atmosphere in 2020 to create a greenhouse effect, melt the polar icecaps and inundate the coastal cities. Certainly the carbon dioxide concentration is rising just a bit less than one ppm per year, or about 0.3 per cent per year. Not surprisingly, opposed to the hot-world people (those who believe that carbon dioxide will warm up the earth) is a group of cold-world people, who believe that the increasing opacity of the upper atmosphere, due to particulate matter, will reduce the amount of sunlight absorbed by the earth and ultimately cause a new ice age. It has even been suggested that we use the opposing effects and balance the carbon dioxide and particulate in the atmosphere to keep our climate temperate.

I myself have tried my hand at the game of cataclysms by examining the rate at which we consume energy, and comparing this rate to the rate at which we absorb energy from the sun. If we are successful in developing the underdeveloped nations and in maintaining the growth of the developed nations, then in two or three hundred years, we will be spending energy as fast as we absorb it. One rather clear conclusion of this estimate, albeit a far-reaching one, is that we can look forward to our grandchildren and great-grandchildren living with some sort of energy rationing.

Another favorite apocalypse of my own is due to the world-wide appearance of lead in the atmosphere. Present levels are supposedly well below industrial toxic levels, but only by about a factor of three. However statements to this point are usually carefully worded to say that the chronic effects of very low doses are not known. One of the effects of chronic lead poisoning is to make its victims stupid. I sometimes think we have passed that critical threshold.

At the risk of repeating the most popular platitude of 1969, I want to point out again that we must understand and select a balance between the benefits of our technology and the benefits of a clean environment. We can have both, at least for a time, but we must recognize the costs. For the next 50 years or so, we can afford the price of clean air and water. Public sentiment at the moment even suggests that perhaps we shall soon be willing to pay it. Until 1969, just the opposite seemed the case. We can see this by comparing the death rate from the worst air pollution "episodes" with an excess death rate (i.e., available by existing means) that we know American society has tolerated. The death rate in Vietnam has been between 20 and 40 per 100,000 per week. This is just about the death rate in the London smog of 1952, and is roughly 10 times that of November 5 to 11, 1969, in Chicago. In plain words, we have been killing ourselves with air pollution, but only at a rate that society seems willing to sustain. The new concern has come well before pollution-caused mortality has reached a disaster level. Let us take sensible advantage of this period of grace.

Bibliography

Bregman, Jack, and Lenormand, Sergel. *The Pollution Paradox.* New York: Spartan Books, 1966.

DeBell, Garrett, ed. *The Environmental Handbook.* New York: Ballantine Books, 1970.

Helfrick, Harold, Jr., ed. *The Environmental Crisis.* New Haven: Yale University Press, 1970.

Laycock, George. *The Diligent Destroyers.* New York: Doubleday and Co., 1970.

Rienow, Robert, and Rienow, Leona. *Moment in the Sun.* New York: Ballantine Books, 1967.

Steward, George R., *Not So Rich As You Think.* Boston: Houghton Mifflin Co., 1968.

Still, Henry. *The Dirty Animal.* New York: Hawthorn Books, 1967.

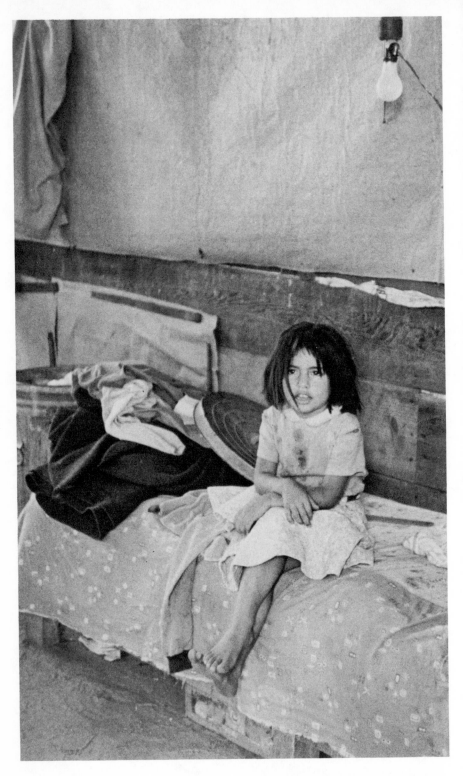

Poverty

Poverty cannot be defined simply. First, there are many approaches to the subject, and each has its own definition. Economists, sociologists, social reformers, politicians, and statisticians all consider the concept from dissimilar frames of reference. Then, too, poverty means something quite different in the United States than it does in the underdeveloped countries of Asia, for example. Finally, what is looked upon as poverty in any place from whatever point of view is relative to the level of man's total achievement at the time.

Pauperism is a term rarely used today, but is perhaps more comprehensible than poverty. It at once conjures up the image of people barely maintaining life. Historically, it has referred to a category of the population that lacks the capacity to subsist without assistance from agencies outside the kinship group. In preindustrial society it was considered an abnormal condition that called for remedial action. Pauperization as a consequence of catastrophes such as flood and famine was dealt with by the whole society by means of public measures adapted to the situation, but under normal circumstances the local community was expected to make provision for its members who were unable to maintain themselves. This policy of local responsibility for poor relief prevailed until the twentieth century. By relief is meant aid other than voluntary that is provided formally by agencies to those whose inadequacies make them unable to support themselves. This "policy of provision" is the forerunner of modern welfare programs.

The attitude toward paupers and the duty owed them changed as social and economic conditions evolved toward the industrial state. When the pauper was an able-bodied adult, the community was reluctant to encourage dependence by donating means of survival. Beggars and vagrants came not to be considered bona fide members of the community. Compulsory labor became a condition of relief, and penal sanctions were applied against the able unemployed.

This change in attitude was a manifestation of the changes that took place in the value systems of societies as they underwent industrialization. In preindustrial societies, poverty was an understandable ideal for saints, holy men, and the like, but as economic development more and more came to be the impelling force, the idea was less tolerable. The nonacquisitiveness of those who provided social service for modest compensation—for instance, teachers, clergymen, and public servants—was approved, but inability to sustain oneself was not morally acceptable. The Protestant capitalist societies went so far as to equate poverty with personal sin or guilt.

With the rapid economic expansion in the developing countries, it seemed not unreasonable to expect that most cases of pauperism could be eliminated through employment, self-help and private charity. Public assistance, such as that provided for in the English Poor Law of 1834, was reserved primarily for the absolute unemployables—the irreducible residuum. The rationale of this theory was based on the *laissez faire* principles of the uninhibited operation of a free economy.

The idea of assuring all citizens at least a minimum standard of living came later, after there was some disenchantment with the self-regulating nature of a capitalist economy. This change in perspective was encouraged also by the increasing political influence of the poor, the establishment of labor unions for the protection and advancement of the working class, and the increasing significance of socialist ideologies.

The abolition of poverty is widely advocated today. Not all societies advocate unlimited enrichment, but the desirability of elevating the minimum standard of material life and eliminating social inequalities coincident with poverty is subscribed to by most societies.

Statistics purporting to show the extent of poverty must be viewed with regard for the various frames of reference set out at the beginning of this discussion. There are different versions of what constitutes poverty: social poverty, moral poverty, material and nonmaterial poverty. Material poverty is usually basic to poverty as a social problem.

In the United States major concentrations of poverty in metropolitan areas are referred to as poverty areas. These areas are made up of census tracts in which there is in evidence a relatively high frequency of five poverty-linked characteristics, namely:

1. Families with incomes below the poverty level, which represents a level of survival income sufficient to buy bare necessities. The poverty level

was set at $3,000 in 1964, and it rose to $3,410 in 1967 and $3,553 in 1968.

2. Children under eighteen years old not living with both parents.

3. Males twenty-five years old or over with seven years or less of school completed.

4. Unskilled males in the labor force.

5. Housing units lacking some or all plumbing facilities or in dilapidated condition.

The first characteristic, that of income below the poverty level, applied to approximately 40 million persons in 1959 and to about 25 million in 1968, which represents a decline from 22 percent of the population in this category to 13 percent.[1] The number of families below the poverty level declined by 3.3 million or 39 percent. This sharp decrease is misleading if it is taken to mean that poverty is being rapidly and steadily eliminated. The facts are that a period of sustained economic expansion from 1959 to 1968 benefited those who were able to take advantage of the increased need for labor.

The uneven distribution of the decline among population groups suggests that more and more the poor are those who gain least from economic growth. For example, the number of poor white males decreased from 22 million in 1959 to about 11 million in 1968, whereas the number of poor white females remained at about seven million and the number of poor females of other races increased from approximately three million to over four million. A breakdown of the 39 percent decline in the number of poor families during this nine-year period shows that the number of white families below the poverty level dropped 42 percent compared with a 27 percent decrease for Negro families. The number of poor families headed by men under sixty-five years of age decreased about 51 percent and, at the same time, the number headed by females remained almost the same overall but increased 12 percent among nonwhites.

Among poor families in general, 15 percent had five or more children under eighteen years of age, whereas only four percent of families above the poverty level had that many. About two-thirds of the poor families are headed by persons with less than an eighth grade education, few of whom have gone beyond the educational level of their fathers. Very little upward occupational mobility is noted from one generation to another. This factor alone contributes greatly to the perpetuation of poverty in families. To break this cycle many programs have been devised for exposing the children to other influences as early as possible.

Although statistics suggest that the number of poor has diminished, there has been no appreciable change in the United States since 1944 in the proportion of total national income received by the poorest 20 percent of families. In 1944, those families received five percent of the total national income, and this figure remained almost the same in 1960. On the other hand, the wealthiest five percent of all families has continued to receive from 18 to 20 percent of the total national income.

It is a fact that real incomes have risen for most of the population, and even those at the lower levels enjoy a far higher standard of living than most people in other parts of the world. But needs are not based entirely on what is lacked, but also on what the neighbors have. There is a real problem of rising expectations in our society as a result of the growing affluence in this country.

Very few Americans literally die in the streets of starvation, and our poorest are not poor at all by the standards of many other countries, but people's circumstances must be appraised in relation to their own milieu. A horseless carriage capable of traveling thirty-five miles per hour is like a racing car when compared with foot travel, but not many manufacturers would be content to make them in view of our greater technological ability. Our economy depends to some degree on the generation of new needs via television, movies, and other mass media, and thus the poor have new needs also.

The dollars and cents value of income is a narrow and inadequate measure of the degree of poverty represented. Income must be evaluated in relation to the cost of attaining the minimal levels of health, housing, nutrition, and education that our present stage of scientific and technological knowledge finds to be necessary for life as it is lived in the United States in 1971.

In the years of the Great Depression, there was a different attitude toward poverty. The poverty of the Depression was an emergency, a crisis, and was treated accordingly. It was looked upon as temporary, and all of the politicians were forced to be seriously concerned with the alleviation of what was a general, overall state. The need for relief measures was unquestionable. The problem had a dramatic quality and therefore aroused sympathy and understanding, which in turn produced a willingness to help. The poverty of today is not so widespread, but is instead more apt to be found in "poverty pockets" surrounded by opulence. It is chronic and congenital.

Poverty that is a temporary crisis, such as the poverty of the Depression or the poverty experienced by the frontiersmen, is unlike poverty that is a permanent state, concentrated and perpetuated among certain disadvantaged groups, such as that found today. Eradication, not amelioration, must be the objective of the programs dealing with this kind of problem. It is more difficult now than it was in the 1930s to arouse public interest or to get the attention of political groups, because today's poor do not have the unmitigated blessing of the affluent of the population. The poor are viewed with more impersonal detachment, and welfare proposals are not received with great enthusiasm.

The poor of the '70s are responding to urgings and encouragement from outside and are showing a restlessness and a defiance that are somewhat new features. New approaches are needed in attempting to resolve their problem.

The most plausible recommendations for the eradication of poverty in the United States can be classified under the following general approaches:

1. The new careers concept is based upon the premise that meaningful employment is essential for the growth and development of individuals handicapped by having been socialized in the world of the poor.

Automation, technical change and high educational requirements have reduced the number of employment opportunities open to unskilled, uneducated persons. The capacity of the national labor force to absorb such workers will undoubtedly continue to decline as private industry has less and less need of them. Most of the increases in employment in the past five years have been in the health, education, and welfare fields. In view of the continuous expansion of the population, the probability is great that the need for people to work in these and other types of public employment involving services to people and all areas of human relationships will not stop growing in the foreseeable future. But years of formal education are required for licensing in most jobs of this kind—they are the realm of the professional.

The new careers concept calls for opening up our opportunity structure so that everyone has maximal chances for upward mobility, maximal opportunities for psychological gratification, and maximal opportunity to make a good living. The problem is how to fit the people for the jobs that will be available.

It is suggested that the qualifications required for employment in these jobs be examined to determine their validity. Experiments have demonstrated that the uneducated can be trained for these fields by means other than years of formal college education. Our system of higher education is obsolete in many respects and could well be modified to permit persons to obtain credit for what they learn wherever they learn it, on the job or in the class. An individual might start as a teacher's aide, for example, and learn much of what constitutes the job of teaching by direct observation and participation, a kind of apprentice relationship. With this foundation, he might round out his preparation by taking pertinent college courses. Thus, parallel paths to becoming a teacher, a nurse, or a social worker can be developed that would allow for structuring jobs to fit the people who need the work.

2. The economists place their confidence in greater national economic growth, which in turn provides more employment opportunities. They hold that full employment is the way out of poverty. They point to the fact that many benefits now denied to the poor would accrue to them once they became employed. For example, the working man has the protection of unemployment insurance, social security, labor unions, and group health and hospitalization insurance plans. The poor have much greater need for these supportive measures than the middle class, yet they are largely excluded from their advantages.

This theory is based upon the inevitability of an ever-increasing number of jobs of the kind the unskilled can handle and the belief that those who need work will somehow find the right openings.

3. The negative income tax is considered by many to be a more effective device for providing for those below poverty level than the public assistance programs now in use. By this method, those whose incomes are below the taxable level would receive an amount sufficient to raise their income to the maximum amount exempt from taxation. The system is a kind of reverse income tax. One of the points in its favor is that it could be administered more easily than present systems of welfare payments. Also, much degradation, humiliation, and loss of self-esteem might be avoided for the recipients, and a greater freedom from anxiety might be afforded by the assurance of at least a subsistence income.

4. According to the views of Saul Alinsky, poverty means poverty of power. He contends that until the poor have gained collective power that enables them to exert some influence and control over their circumstances, there will be no great reduction in poverty. The poor must be enabled to seek objectives that they understand and desire, for only as they try to help themselves, and are permitted to do so, will they gain the self-esteem, self-confidence, motivation, and know-how that will impel them to persevere. They must be helped to become self-directive, and this goal requires their participation in decision making. They must have the opportunity to try and to fail and to try again until a new cycle is generated in the "Other America."

Alinsky has acted upon his conviction by responding to many groups who sought his help and by teaching them how to organize for the purpose of generating power and how to become involved in the activities of democratic citizenship.

The articles that follow should facilitate an assessment of the relative merits of these proposals. The first two articles deal with the definition of poverty. "The Numbers of Poor" explains how the poverty index is determined and indicates the complexity of the task. In "The Sociology of Poverty" Lewis A. Coser develops an idea suggested by Georg Simmel in which the critical factor in the problem of poverty is dependence.

The next three articles describe the reactions of the poor to their condition. "The Poor Who Live Among Us" gives many different points of view and evidences the many, many facets of the total problem. "Fifth Avenue, Uptown" describes what it is like to be black and poor. "The Culture of Poverty" focuses on the poor of a less-developed nation, Mexico. The article elaborates the author's concept of a "culture of poverty," a characteristic life style that evolves among those in poverty and whose traits can be found universally among the poor.

Michael Harrington's *Other America,* from which "The Invisible Land" is taken, is credited with being the catalyst of the social movement of the '60s in behalf of the poor. The selection presented here contains the thesis of Harrington's book, which is that the poor have been ignored because they have been kept invisible and isolated. "Where the Real Poverty Is" describes poverty among the American Indians and reinforces Harrington's thesis.

The last two articles point toward what is needed to bring about change. "How Much Is Enough?" suggests some of the consequences of further neglect of the poor. "What Can Be Done?" gives a brief statement of the many programs that have been developed under the aegis of the War on Poverty to cope with this serious condition in the United States.

Note

1. The statistics included here were taken from "Poverty in the U.S. 1959 to 1968," *Current Population Reports,* Series P-60, No. 68, December 31, 1969. U.S. Department of Commerce Publication, pp. 1–8.

Poverty is defined by what a society believes is essential for minimal living. An index developed from certain variables and characteristics is used to identify those who are in a state of poverty or deprivation.

The Numbers of Poor

Ben B. Seligman

Any social problem requires a definition of its boundaries. The limits of the condition presumably help to define the time and effort needed to work out a solution. When it comes to poverty, some definitions use consumption standards rather than money income. In other words, the limits of poverty are set by what a society believes is essential for minimal living. In effect, such a definition makes money income less significant, for it also includes non-money income, borrowing, gifts, and dissaving (using past savings for current consumption). A completely objective definition might begin with "disposable" or available personal income and then add or subtract, as the case may be, transfers of non-money income, public services, and the like. It is also possible, if one wishes, to add net assets to the definition, or to vary the standard of poverty by age, size of family, and type of head of family. To use all the variables involved in defining what poverty is becomes a highly statistical and complicated task.

Nevertheless, some sociologists and economists have deemed the effort worthwhile. Charles Booth, an English sociologist, defined poverty at the turn of the century as affecting those families with weekly incomes of less than 21 or 22 shillings a week. In essence, the definition depended on establishing some monetary dividing line. A similar procedure was employed by B. Seebohm Rowntree, who found in a classic study of York that some 28 per cent of the inhabitants were beneath the poverty line. Rowntree used budgetary and income concepts to establish his poverty line. In a similar manner, several University of Michigan economists, Morgan, David, Brazer, and Cohen, insist that income, need, and "income adequacy" are all significant elements in a definition of poverty.[1] To measure income, these analysts start with "gross disposable income" and then adjust that figure to show the total cash flow of the family. Additions are made for imputed or estimated rental income on a home, and subtractions are made for income tax liabilities. Need itself is measured by standard family budgets, a rather knotty problem. Morgan, David, et al., make use of the New York Community

From "Problems of American Society: Permanent Poverty" by Ben B. Seligman. Reprinted by permission of Quadrangle Books from *Permanent Poverty: An American Syndrome* by Ben B. Seligman. Copyright © 1968 by Ben B. Seligman.

Council budget for 1959 as a basis for estimating need; this budget analyzed various factors stemming from employment, the number of children and their ages, rental costs, and the like. For an employed head of family, housewife, and two children, aged eight and eleven, the Council budget was $4,330. Applying a variable income figure as a poverty line, based on the factors indicated, the authors estimated that the poor in the United States comprised a fifth of the nation's families.

This conclusion was confirmed two years later in the Report of the President's Council of Economic Advisers.[2] The War on Poverty had been declared in the State of the Union message in January 1964. The CEA then concluded that a fifth of the population of the United States was poor. It found that 22 per cent of the poor were Negroes, and that they comprised nearly half the Negro population of the country. Education was another significant factor in poverty: the heads of over 60 per cent of poor families had but a grade-school education; and of all Negro families headed by a person with eight years or less schooling, 57 per cent were poor. The CEA observed an inverse relationship between the extent of education of family heads and the incidence of poverty.

Discrimination was a powerful conditioning force, too, said the Council: a comparison of Negro and white families whose heads had similar educational attainments revealed that Negroes were likely to be poor about twice as often as whites. A third of poor families were headed by persons over the age of sixty-five; indeed, 50 per cent of such families could be classified as poor. The cities contained 54 per cent of the poor; 46 per cent could be found on farms. If a family lived in one of the southern states its chances of being poor were twice those of families living in other parts of the country. A fourth of poor families were headed by women; half of families headed by women were poor. In 1960 Texas had the largest number of poor; New York and California followed in close order. The facts were dreary and depressing.

How did the Council arrive at these measurements? CEA suggested in its 1964 report that the concept of poverty should refer to those persons and families whose basic needs exceeded the means to satisfy them. Presumably this would allow for such factors as size of family, age of its members, housing, and health requirements. The problem was to define the standard for basic needs: by present American levels of living, the rest of the world is clearly poor; by the same criteria, most Americans 150 years ago were poor. Yet such statistical difficulties did not prevent the Council from specifying 20 per cent of American families as poor—9.3 million families out of a total of approximately 43 million families. Included were eleven million children, or about one-sixth of all youth. The numbers had been derived by using a $3,000 yearly income cut-off.

Furthermore, said the Council, 5.4 million families had incomes of less than $2,000 a year. What of those persons who were living alone? The

Council found that 45 per cent of such "unrelated" persons had incomes of less than $1,500 a year. The final estimate was that 33 to 35 million Americans were living at the poverty level, and the likelihood was that almost five million poor families would make no progress by 1980, even though the economy might continue its rapid expansion. Poverty had become endemic.

The poor were ubiquitous. They could be found in all parts of the population, in all sections of the nation, in all age groups. They were not necessarily unemployed; striking was the fact that almost 13 per cent of all families with an employed head were poor. Poverty was not merely a Negro problem, for 78 per cent of all poor families were white. Poverty, said the Council, could be traced to low earnings, low productivity, discrimination, low bargaining power, lack of mobility, and inadequate minimum wage protection.

Savings were not always available to help a poor family, and even if there were savings, they would not help very much to relieve the situation. On the average, the additional income that might accrue from savings on an annuity basis to a family with a head over age sixty-five would amount to about $135 a year.[3] An annuity of $1,500 a year would require a capital sum of $19,000 at age sixty-five; the average net worth for spending or consumption "units" with aged heads was $8,000, and most of this was frozen in home ownership. Thus property was not protection against poverty.

Yet the Council's estimates were considered by many economists and sociologists as either too conservative or too crude. Herman P. Miller, the Census Bureau's expert on income analysis, argued that the CEA choice of a $3,000 poverty cut-off line was much too arbitrary, for it did not take account of family size, the age of the family head, or geography.[4] The Council, said Miller, had made a quick choice of a poverty definition to provide a rationale for an impending political decision. Miller argued that a single poverty line distorts the analysis of poverty, overstating poverty among certain groups and understating it for others. A variable standard, or a "band" of poverty, centered around a figure of $3,000 for a family of four, might range from $1,800 a year for a young couple to $4,200 for a family with four or more children. Had CEA used such a standard, said Miller, the percentage of urban poor would have been 11 per cent less than the estimate in the Council's 1964 report.

The idea of a poverty band was also employed by Oscar Ornati in a study that relied mainly on data for the five decades prior to 1961. Ornati established lines described by the expressions "minimum subsistence," "minimum adequacy," and "minimum comfort," so that income requirements defined by these lines set the limits of the poverty band over the years. In current dollars the band moved from $413 to $726 in 1905, and from $2,662 to $5,609 in 1960. Since these figures were based on workers' family budgets, there seemed to be a measure of circularity in their computation, for, as Ornati observed, the budgets specify what people ought to buy but are derived from data based on what they actually do buy.[5]

Miller, in contrast to the CEA, argued that a single line overstated the number of aged among the poor, since they have smaller than average families and lower than average earnings. Furthermore, a band would have revealed many more children in the poverty strata. In the last analysis, the probability was that variable lines would have counted more persons among the poor, for as the economy changes, new demands and expectations develop, shifting the boundaries of poverty. As S. M. Miller and Martin Rein have argued, "Those not poor today may be poor in tomorrow's circumstances, though they have not suffered any absolute decline in their conditions."[6]

The notion of a band seems a reasonable way to measure the extent of poverty, because it is difficult to say that a family with an income of $3,010 is not as poor as one with an income of $2,090. The issue can be further complicated when consumption standards are considered. Take the problem of housing. Adequate housing may be defined as an apartment with direct access, a kitchen, cooking equipment, and hot water. On this basis, only 5 per cent of white families and 10 per cent of Negro families can be said to have had poor housing in 1963. If housing standards were employed as the sole measure, very few families would be classified as poor. Even when income is used to define poverty, one finds relatively high ownership of television sets and automobiles among the poor.

Yet to associate ownership or lack of ownership of such material objects with poverty would be quite misleading. In many instances, a television or radio is a relic of former affluence; or it may be a hand-me-down gift; and in fact, as Herman Miller concedes, such items contribute to poverty because they are bought at the expense of an adequate diet or adequate medical care. Perhaps the most important element in poverty is psychological—what aspirations do poor people have, what hope is there for them to break out of the cycle of poverty? Most of the evidence suggests there is little hope indeed without massive public programs to break the cycle.

Hence, where one places the poverty line or band sets the dimensions of the problem. When John Kenneth Galbraith suggested that poverty had been virtually eliminated in the United States, he was using a $1,000-a-year yardstick as a poverty cut-off.[7] With a low cut-off the poverty population would be dominated by rural families, the aged, and families with female heads. While farm families have some recourse to income-in-kind, their overall needs for material things appear to be less than for urban families. When one moves the poverty line higher, more low-paid workers and unskilled workers fall into the class of the poor. Yet such a movement of the poverty line does introduce statistical distortions: the increase in the pro-

portion of aged among the poor from 1947 to 1962 may have been decep-
tive, for with an upward movement of the general income scale, a cut-off
figure of $3,000 per annum would really have moved downward in the total
scale. Such a poverty cut-off figure in 1947 was fairly close to the average
or median income figure, so that the proportion of the aged was smaller.
On the other hand, a definition of poverty in terms of the lower fifth of the
income scale does not reveal much change in the composition of the poor
over time.

Clearly, there is a measure of flexibility in defining poverty, especially
if needs are taken into account. With needs representing an expression of
social standards, poverty becomes an indication of the extent to which sectors of the population participate in the large society. Electricity, automobiles, and television may appear to some sociologists to be luxuries, but
today they do provide measures of involvement in the habits of Western
civilization. To that extent poverty definitions express subjective evaluations from which there is no escape if realistic appraisals are to be made.

Michael Harrington tells in his important book how he arrived at his
sizable estimate of fifty million poor.[8] He points out that in the late 1940's
several congressional investigations had suggested $2,000 as a dividing
line. Updating that figure to 1961 implied a line of $2,500 annual income.
Subsequently, Robert Lampman of the University of Wisconsin related income to family size and came up with a poverty definition set at $2,500 for
a family of four and $3,236 for a family of six. On this basis, 19 per cent
of the population, or 32 million persons, were deemed to be poor. In 1963
a Joint Economic Committee study set standards of $1,261 for a single
individual and $4,088 for a family of seven or more: this measure also in-
cluded 32 million persons. AFL-CIO economists then estimated that poverty afflicted 24 per cent of Americans or 41.5 million persons. But, argued
Harrington, if family budget data were taken into account, these estimates
would be understatements, for the budgetary standard for a family of four
in 1959 figures ranged from $5,370 in Houston to $6,567 in Chicago.
Hence if half the budgetary standard were taken as a poverty cut-off, or
around $3,500, then, Harrington estimated, a count of fifty million poor
would not be far off the mark.

Be that as it may, it was clear that consumption standards as well as
income had to be incorporated into the analysis of poverty criteria. As
Mollie Orshansky of the Department of Health, Education, and Welfare
has said, a poverty profile ought to be based on accepted standards of consumption and should allow for different needs of families with varying
numbers of adults and children.[9] Miss Orshansky developed a measure
based on the amount of income remaining after allowing for adequate diets
at minimum costs. She concluded that in 1963 there were 34.5 million poor
in the United States, including fifteen million children and 5.2 million aged
persons. These were the people who were compelled to choose between a

minimum diet and other material needs of life, because they simply did not have enough for both. But, she added, if we include the "hidden poor"— 2.8 million persons living with families—the total rises to 37.5 million. For the 34.5 million people there was a gap of some 40 per cent between what they had and what they required—in money, about $11.5 billion. "From data reported in the Bureau of the Census in March 1964, it can be inferred that one in seven of all families of two or more, and almost half of all persons living alone or with non-relatives, had incomes too low in 1963 to enable them to eat even the minimal diet that could be expected to provide adequate nutrition and still have enough left over to pay for all other living essentials."[10]

While Census data suggest that an income of $60 a week is characteristic of the poor, income, argued Miss Orshansky, cannot be considered as the sole factor. Food intake adequacy might be viewed as a supplementary guide in judging levels of living. Relying on the food plans devised by the Department of Agriculture, Miss Orshansky concluded that a poverty income cut-off would range from $1,580 for a single person in urban areas to $5,090 for a family of eight, with a pivot of $3,130 for a family of four. The food plans had long been used by welfare agencies to set public assistance budgets. The Department of Agriculture "economy" food plan provided 22 cents per meal per person in a four-person family. As of January 1964 the cost per person was $4.62 a week. It was obvious that a diet based on such estimates was extremely low and apt to be deficient in critical nutrients, such as calcium and proteins. After evaluating the relationship of income to the "economy" standard, Miss Orshansky suggested that poverty could be defined in terms of a family income less than three times the cost of an "economy" diet. This was applied to families of three or more persons. The income of families whose position in the economy was set in this manner was about 65 per cent of the required income necessary to remove them from poverty. The gap was quite substantial.

In a rapidly changing society, argued Miss Orshansky, there cannot be only one measure of poverty. A single line, such as advocated by the Council of Economic Advisers, and which in fact established public policy for many months, included some who did not belong in the poverty strata and excluded others who were decidedly poor. Any poverty measure ought to reflect at least rough equivalency in levels of living for individuals and families of different size. There might be an element of arbitrariness in the resulting count of the poor, but the standards would at least be more reasonable than a single income figure.

This line of thought underlay the "poverty index" of the Social Security Administration.[11] The intent was to create a sensitive measure of poverty, taking into account the different needs of different sorts of families. Following the Orshansky concept, the SSA Poverty Index specified the minimum money income required to support an average family of given size at the lowest level consistent with a decent standard of living. In essence, it specified an acceptable level of consumption, thereby providing broad limits to the relative incidence of poverty. A new poverty line was drawn separately for 124 different types of families. These were classified by sex of the head of family, number of other adults, farm versus urban, and number of children under the age of eighteen. Then the amount of income was determined that would buy an adequate diet based on Department of Agriculture criteria, and excess income over this amount was used to set the various poverty lines. While in the main the food bill was estimated at a third of total income requirements, different ratios were used for different sizes of families. The total sum necessary to meet the needs of a family headed by a man, based on the "economy" diet, was $3,220 a year; for a family headed by a woman, $2,960. The actual income medians were found to be $1,760 and $1,300 respectively. Again, the estimate of the number of poor persons came to 35 million for 1963.

A clearer picture may be given from the following tabulation of possible poverty lines:[12]

Number of Persons in the Family	Non-Farm		Farm	
	Male Head	Female Head	Male Head	Female Head
1 under 65 years of age	$1650	$1525	$ 990	$ 920
1 over 65	1480	1465	890	880
2 under 65	2065	1875	1240	1180
2 over 65	1855	1845	1110	1120
3	2455	2350	1410	1395
4	3130	3115	1925	1865
5	3685	3660	2210	2220
6	4135	4110	2495	2530
7 and more	5100	5000	3065	2985

These notions were also applied to counting the poor in specific areas. As a result, the Welfare Council of Chicago, for example, discovered in 1965 that the largest number of poor in its jurisdiction—more than 40 per cent—came from families of five or more persons. It found 55,600 children in families with annual incomes of less than $1,000, increasing its previous count of the poor by 62,000 to a new total of 762,000, one out of every eight persons in the Chicago metropolitan area. In fact, the sliding scale used, derived from the SSA Poverty Index, was low at all levels for families living in Chicago because the city was a high-cost living area, thus offsetting any improvements in economic conditions that had taken place since 1960. The new count underscored the fact that the special problems of large families had been receiving less attention than merited from poverty program officials.[13]

The significance of these figures was illustrated by Congress' attempt to employ poverty measures in various legislative programs. The major question was: should a family of four be considered poverty stricken, by federal standards, if its annual income falls below $3,130, the figure used by the Office of Economic Opportunity, or should the poverty cut-off be closer to $2,000, the figure used by the Office of Education in allocating aid to elementary and secondary schools? OEO was employing a flexible scale based on the Orshansky concept, but the Office of Education was bound by the school aid law passed in 1965, which defined families living in poverty as those with annual incomes of less than $2,000 a year or those receiving public assistance.

According to Leon Keyserling, all of the foregoing indices err grievously on the conservative side.[14] Using both single-line and "band" measurements, Keyserling came up with 38 million persons in poverty and 39 million in deprivation, a standard of living somewhat higher than poverty but still not affluent. The cut-off points for poverty were set at $4,000 a year for families and $2,000 a year for single persons. A range of $4,000 to $6,000 in income defined the "deprived" family, while a range of $2,000 to $3,000 was applied to single individuals. Why this seemingly more liberal definition? Keyserling relied on "modest but adequate" household budgets for 1959, then estimated the income required to sustain such budgets. Thus for large families the budgetary range was $6,216 to $9,607; for small families, $3,893 to $4,270; and for single individuals, $2,324 to $3,140. Nevertheless, continued Keyserling, such data failed to tell the whole story, for the average income of all families with incomes under $3,000 a year in 1962 was $1,778; and for all families with incomes under $2,000 the average was but $1,220.

Yet not all attempts to define the poverty spectrum were so liberal as Keyserling's. Some leaned quite the other way, seemingly anxious to dismiss the entire debate as irrelevant to the state of affluence in America. This point of view was stated most forcefully by Rose D. Friedman in a pamphlet written for the American Enterprise Institute.[15] According to Mrs. Friedman, the only objective basis for defining poverty is the nutritive sufficiency of the family's diet. With this standard, the cut-off point becomes $2,200 a year; the conclusion is that only 10 per cent of Americans may be said to live in a condition of poverty.

How was this calculation achieved? The simple fact is that Americans enjoy a diet substantially greater than what the rest of the world gets. Half the people of other lands must live on 2,250 calories a day, and another 20 per cent are able to obtain 2,750 calories a day. But Americans not only have a superior diet, they also have radios, television, electricity, and plumbing. The latter, however, are non-quantitative elements: they cannot be measured, argued Mrs. Friedman, leaving only the caloric content of a family's food intake as the sole objective factor. And it is demonstrable, she continued, that Americans suffer from overweight. Moreover, the caloric content for the diets of the lowest third in the income scale increased 13 per cent between 1955 and 1956, from 2,580 calories a day to 2,910 calories a day. As the notion of "adequate nutrition" cannot be established in any genuinely scientific fashion, the estimation by Mrs. Friedman of such matters as protein requirements is little more than guesswork. As one sociologist, Peter Townsend, remarked, defining what one needs for adequate nutrition is like trying to define adequate height.[16]

Income or educational attainments were said by Mrs. Friedman to be irrelevant. She insisted that it was not true that any large segment of the American people had been left behind and had failed to share in the country's economic progress.[17] (We shall see later how well this assertion applies to Negroes and the aged.) As income could not be used to measure poverty, neither could housing standards or clothing consumption. For how many square feet of floor space, asked Mrs. Friedman, constitute adequate housing? Any effort to measure housing or clothing would be subjective and therefore not meaningful. The only way to define a housing standard would be to speak of protection from the elements, a function no doubt performed equally well by a ten-room heated home in suburbia and a tar-papered shack in Appalachia. Finally, Mrs. Friedman assumed that anyone with adequate nutrition would also have adequate clothing and shelter, a gratuitous assumption at best.

Such an approach, of course, would equate poverty with hunger, and since no one in his right mind would assert that hunger is rampant in the United States, *ergo* there is little or no poverty to be observed. At any rate, conversion of the nutrition adequacy definition into income provides for a flexible standard ranging from $1,295 a year for a two-person family to $3,155 a year for a seven-person family. The average four-person family would require, on this basis, only $2,195 a year. Hence it is obvious to Mrs. Friedman, if not to many others, that grinding poverty in the United States does not exist, and in any case, only 4.8 million families in the country may be considered poor. Not unrelated to this view is that of the U.S. Chamber of Commerce, which defined poverty solely in case terms.[18] Since poverty involves only specific persons, families, and groups, it is not a serious issue, nor is it massive, said the Chamber. (To say that poverty affects only Negroes, families with female heads, or the uneducated, does not seem to make it less massive, however.)

A far more useful measure of poverty is the index developed by the Census Bureau, which combines five socioeconomic characteristics: low income, low education, unskilled men in the labor force, substandard housing, and children in broken homes. Such an index makes it possible to compare the characteristics of families residing in poverty areas with those living in non-poverty sections of metropolitan areas. Using this five-factor index, the Census Bureau discovered 193 poverty areas in the 101 Standard Metropolitan Statistical Areas (the official designation for large urban complexes). And within these 193 poverty areas were 57 per cent of urban and suburban Negro families, as compared to 10 per cent of white families. Moreover, Negro families comprised 42 per cent of all families in poverty areas and only 6 per cent of all families in non-poverty areas. In contrast to the latter, the poverty areas had twice the percentage of families headed by a woman; the ratio of unskilled workers was three times as great; they had double the percentage of families with unemployed heads; and almost twice the percentage of families with five or more children.

While it is true that the poor can be classified into specific groups, the number of families involved total in the millions. Thus, Morgan, David, and their associates found that poor families with an aged head numbered 2.8 million; Negro heads of families totaled 2.9 million; single women with children comprised 1.2 million families; unemployed heads were 1.1 million; and families with disabled heads were 1.7 million.[19] In many instances, multiple factors accounted for poverty: thus 22 per cent of Negro heads were also aged, 26 per cent were disabled, 29 per cent were unemployed, and 43 per cent were single with children. Expected earnings of those families with inadequate income were set at $2,204 for 1959; the *actual* earnings per family head were $900. For many persons, the condition of poverty has been a long-term affair: the average highest income ever earned was $4,143 for the self-employed poor. For Negro heads of families it was $2,490; for the aged, $2,230 a year.

Whatever assets the poor have are likely to be used up quickly. They have little protection against illness: a third of poor families have some health coverage for the head, while 60 per cent have no health protection at all. This situation contrasts to hospitalization coverage for 63 per cent of the general population. In most cases the poor lack any sort of rights to either public or private retirement; for persons fifty-five or older this can become a critical matter.

These characteristics, in effect, condition the transmission of poverty from one generation to the next. They are reinforced by a lack of education. The Morgan-David study revealed that heads of poor families do not have much more education than their fathers had. Less than 40 per cent of poor family heads did better in school than the older generation, while in the general population 60 per cent of family heads whose parents had less than nine years of schooling went beyond that level. The consequence was that heads of poor families had skill attainments about on a par with those of their fathers. Expectations among the poor are low: only about a third of poor families would like to see their sons attend college, as compared to two-thirds of all families that express such desires. Poverty by no means is a short-run phenomenon; it is no accident; it is produced rather by an unprotected and unrewarded relationship of the poor to the rest of society.

Much of the problem may be attributed to the pattern of income distribution. While there has been some improvement as contrasted to pre–

World War II periods, the fact remains that income distribution patterns are substantially unchanged since the mid-1940's. The lowest fifth of consumer units in 1965 had an average personal income of less than $2,900 and received only 4.6 per cent of total family personal income. In the main, reductions in income inequality have occurred only in the top half of the distribution scale; there are very few changes for families located in the lower half.[20] At the same time, the share of net worth that goes to the top 2 per cent of families increased (from 58 to 61 per cent between 1953 and 1962), while that going to the lowest fifth of income receivers fell from 11 to 7 per cent. Before 1950 Negroes had been closing the gap between themselves and whites, but in the mid-sixties that trend was reversed. And it was likely that the earnings of young men in the twenty to twenty-four age group were more unequally distributed in 1961 than in 1951. Superimposed on these factors is an overall tax system that is steadily losing its progressive character, placing a relatively heavier burden on low-income families. It seems that little can be done, for the poor are voiceless, without influence, and out of the mainstream of economic activity.

The poor consume very little and they produce very little. Lampman estimates that the poor account for about 3 per cent of the gross national product and consume about 5 per cent. The deficit is covered by transfer payments—social security, unemployment insurance, welfare payments— of which they obtain about 30 per cent. The total income of the lowest fifth in the distribution scale approximates $25 billion, including some $10 billion in transfer payments. Public assistance represents $4 billion of the latter, but half the poor receive no public aid at all. Those who argue that a more rapid rise in productivity would solve the problem forget that a third of poor families have no wage earners. To bring six million poor families and three million poor individuals just over a $3,000-a-year poverty line would cost about $10 billion. If this sum is to be in the form of wages, then GNP would have to be increased by $14 to $15 billion. Offsetting increased wages might be the loss of transfer payments, free public services, and high taxes for the poor. But against whatever net figure might result, there would be the qualitative gain of the involvement of the poor in the larger society, and it would be difficult to attach a price tag to that achievement.

Of course, the numbers of the poor vary with the vicissitudes of the business cycle. That is, there are exits from poverty as well as entrances. If one uses current standards measured in constant dollars, the conclusion is that poverty has dropped sharply. The Ornati "band" on this scale moves from a range of 39 to 88 million persons in 1941 to 20 to 71 million persons in 1960. However, an alternative calculation based on contemporary standards in current dollars—the actual situation in each year—shows much less "exiting" from poverty: the band in 1941 on this basis was 22 million to 63 million persons, compared with 20 million to 71 million in

1960.[21] Even if we focus only on the lower limit—minimum subsistence— the exits from poverty over a two-decade period appear to have been but two million persons (when contemporary standards are used).

In 1962, 9.3 million families were classified as poor; in 1963 the number had dropped to nine million families. But the outward movement is slow and may decelerate further, simply because the number of poor families with no head in the labor force increases proportionately. In 1950 such poor families represented 29 per cent of all poor families; by 1963 the ratio had increased to 48 per cent.[22] Not unexpectedly, the aged comprised the largest part of such families, but at 23 per cent Negro families were not far behind. In any case, the Johnson administration was elated at the outward movement of families from poverty: credit was given to "the general economic expansion and the anti-poverty, education, and health programs [which] had brought jobs, fuller work schedules, higher pay, job training, a lowering of the barriers of discrimination, and more adequate social insurance."[23] It was recognized, however, that much more had to be done for the aged, Negroes, rural areas, broken families, the uneducated, and the handicapped.

For it was evident that 70 per cent of poor families in 1962 were also poor in 1963. While 23 per cent moved up the income scale, to just above the poverty line, another 23 per cent dropped below that line. Whatever gains had been made seemed attributable to the dissolution of some 6 per cent of the poor families in excess of the creation of new poor families. Exits from poverty were highest for those families with a head of prime working age, but poverty persisted to a greater than average degree for Negroes, families headed by women, and the aged. Sometimes a family will climb out of the lowest income group when children come of working age and are able to add to its resources. The shifts do not take place evenly: demographic and geographic differences affect the changes. As the population grows older, there is an increase in aged poor; large families among the poor contribute to a further increase in the number of poor family units. And it is evident that richer states are able to reduce their poor more rapidly than poorer ones: in the decade from 1949 to 1959 Mississippi reduced the number of poor families within its borders from 70 per cent to 52 per cent, a one-fourth reduction, while Connecticut reduced its poor families from 20 per cent to 11 per cent, almost by half.

Can such a pace be maintained? After all, it is estimated that by 1975 the number of aged family heads will have increased by only 9 per cent as compared to 1962, while population will have increased by 21 per cent during the same period. But the variety and complexity of factors that press upon the poverty situation in America will in all probability leave the structure of poverty unchanged. And no matter what projections are employed—even a crude straight line—the long-term rate of decrease in the incidence of poverty will still leave 10 per cent of the population behind the rest of us. One assumes, of course, that high levels of economic activity will continue.

We ought not to feel complacent about exits from poverty and decreases in the numbers of poor stemming from prosperity. In 1964 there were still 34 million Americans below the poverty line, according to Mollie Orshansky.[24] The nation's poor may be fewer in number, but the gap between poverty and non-poverty has widened. In 1959 the median income of $6,070 for four-person families was twice the SSA Poverty Index. In 1964 the median income for such a family was $7,490, nearly two and a half times the index. But the income of the poor in 1964 totaled 59 per cent of estimated need, a mere 2 percentage points gain over 1959. Prices and living standards had moved with income, leaving the poor "outbid and outspent." The rapid expansion of the economy in 1964 proceeded about twice as fast as the rate by which deficits for the poor were being reduced.

Some will argue that the poor are simply a statistical category—people fall in and climb out in rapid succession. Stephen Thernstrom, a Harvard historian, cites the example of graduate students,[25] but at the same time he overlooks the larger and more significant situations of Appalachia and other permanent pockets of rural poverty, the fatherless family, the aged, and the urban Negro. Nor is he impressed by the fact that 40 per cent of parents receiving AFDC (Aid to Families with Dependent Children) were themselves raised in a home where public assistance was received. He does not see that this represents a condition of social entrapment for these families from which there is little escape.

Admittedly, the statistical definition of poverty is no simple matter. There are exits and there are entrances, even in an affluent society, but an increase in annual income of $50 or $100 a year over the official cut-off line does not make a family substantially less poor than it was before. Somewhere along the spectrum of income and family size, people begin to feel less oppressed, less tension in their lives, and able to acquire those little amenities that make material existence less desperate. But there are millions of persons in this country who have not yet made that passage, and there are millions who never will.

Notes

1. Charles Booth, *Life and Labour of the People in London*, 1891–1903; B. S. Rowntree, *Poverty: A Study of Town Life*, London, 1922; J. N. Morgan, M. H. David, *et al.*, *Income and Welfare in the United States*, New York, 1962.

2. *Report of the Council of Economic Advisers*, Washington, D.C., 1964.

3. Morgan, David, *et al.*, *op. cit.*, p. 190.

4. H. P. Miller, "The Dimensions of Poverty," in B. B. Seligman, ed., *Poverty as a Public Issue*, New York, 1965, pp. 36ff.

5. *Ibid.*, p. 39; O. Ornati, *Poverty amid Affluence*, New York, 1966, pp. 10ff.

6. S. M. Miller and M. Rein, "The War on Poverty: Perspectives and Prospects," in Seligman, *op. cit.*, p. 281.

7. J. K. Galbraith, *The Affluent Society*, Boston, 1958.

8. M. Harrington, *The Other America*, New York, 1962, pp. 175ff.

9. M. Orshansky, "Consumption, Work, and Poverty," in Seligman, *op. cit.*, pp. 52ff.

10. M. Orshansky, "Counting the Poor: Another Look at the Poverty Profile," *Social Security Bulletin*, January 1965, p. 4.

11. *Idem*, "Who's Who Among the Poor," *ibid.*, July 1965. Cf. also E. G. Holmes, "Spending Patterns of Low Income Families," *Adult Leadership*, May 1965.

12. From Orshansky, *Social Security Bulletin*, January 1965.

13. *New York Times*, May 3, 1965; December 12, 1965.

14. L. Keyserling, *Poverty and Deprivation in the United States*, Washington, D.C., 1962.

15. R. D. Friedman, *Poverty: Definition and Perspective*, Washington, D.C., 1965.

16. P. Townsend, quoted in Ornati, *op. cit.*, p. 2.

17. Friedman, *op. cit.*, p. 12.

18. Chamber of Commerce, *The Concept of Poverty*, Washington, D.C., 1965.

19. Morgan, David, *et al.*, *op. cit.*, p. 194.

20. R. J. Lampman, "Income Distribution and Poverty," in M. S. Gordon, ed., *Poverty in America*, San Francisco, 1965, pp. 102ff.

21. Ornati, *op. cit.*, pp. 28ff.

22. *Business Week*, July 17, 1965.

23. *New York Times*, January 28, 1966.

24. M. Orshansky, "Recounting the Poor—A Five Year Review," *Social Security Bulletin*, April 1966, pp. 20ff.

25. Stephen Thernstrom, "Poverty in Historical Perspective" in a forthcoming Harvard University Press book edited by D. P. Moynihan.

The category of poverty emerges, not in terms of low income or deprivation, but when those who suffer from want are given aid. The crux of the problem lies in the unilateral relationship of dependence. The poor must be enabled to give as well as to receive. There is an impersonal quality in the relationship between the paid social worker and his client that is suggested by the terminology "case" and "object of care." The use of peers as paraprofessionals may provide a more personal element.

The Sociology of Poverty

Lewis A. Coser

Discussions of the extent of poverty in a given society usually have been dogged by definitional problems. One man's poverty is another's wealth; minimal standards in a developed industrial society may be viewed as Utopian goals in an underdeveloped one. What may be felt to constitute unendurable deprivation in a society where the underprivileged compare their lot with that of others more favorably placed in regard to the distribution of income and wealth, may be accepted as legitimate in societies where no such comparisons are socially available or culturally sanctioned.

One may argue that a poor man is one whose economic means are not commensurate with the economic ends he seeks; yet this does not stand up under scrutiny. In societies that exhibit a strain toward anomie, a disjunction between the ends that are striven for and the means available for attaining them, boundless appetites forever create new dissatisfactions at every level reached. This seems to be typical not only of the deprived but of very large strata of the population. The economies of such societies are geared precisely to the creation of ever new needs.

Rather than taking as a point of departure the condition or felt condition of those presumed to be poor, this paper will attempt to provide a different perspective. Following Simmel's lead, poverty will be dealt with as a social category that emerges through societal definition.[1] Just as in Durkheim's view crime can best be defined as consisting in acts having "the external characteristic that they evoke from society the particular reaction called punishment,"[2] so I shall argue here that the poor are men who have been so defined by society and have evoked particular reactions from it. From this perspective, the poor have not always been with us. In Oriental societies, for example, deprivation was not socially visible and not within the focus of social awareness. The modern observer might have discerned

From "The Sociology of Poverty" by Lewis A. Coser, *Social Problems*, Fall, 1965. Reprinted by permission of the journal *Social Problems*, The Society for the Study of Social Problems, and the author.

there a great prevalence of want and misery, yet the members of the society themselves did not perceive poverty and were unaware of its prevalence. In such societies, the condition of those who were deprived did not seem to touch the sensibilities of the upper strata; and it is, after all, they who determine the conscience and consciousness of the society. The deprived, insofar as they were recognized at all, were simply put into the same category as, say, the victims of disease or natural disaster. They did not exist phenomenologically as a separate category.

Historically, the poor emerge when society elects to recognize poverty as a special status and assigns specific persons to that category. The fact that some people may privately consider themselves poor is sociologically irrelevant. What *is* sociologically relevant is poverty as a socially recognized condition, as a social status. We are concerned with poverty as a property of the social structure.

In medieval society, the poor had the function of affording the rich the opportunity for socially prescribed "good deeds." In the Catholic injunction to give alms the concern was not essentially with the physical condition of the poor but primarily with the moral condition of the rich. The giver rather than the recipient tended to be the moral center of attention. The good works of the Christian man were considered a major avenue to salvation. Giving alms hence was meant to increase the chances of the giver in the next world and not primarily to improve the chances of the poor in this. The poor were not considered in their own right but mainly as a means toward the other-worldly ends of the rich. This peculiar function of the poor was, however, of some consequence for the society for it helped to unify the Christian community.

The medieval status of the poor was very different from that assigned to the poor in Puritan England. Here they were given the social position of the "eternally damned"—confirming to the righteous the fitness of their survival. To the Puritan conscience, the poor, having no calling, were not considered a part of the society. Writes William Perkins, a leading 16th century Puritan preacher, "Rogues, beggars, vagabonds . . . commonly are of no civil society or corporation, nor of any particular Church: and are as rotten legges, and armes, that droppe from the body . . . to wander up and downe from yeare to yeare to this ende, to seek and procure bodily maintenance, is no calling, but the life of a beast." He specifies in another passage: ". . . wandering beggars and rogues, that passe from place to place, beeing under no certain Magistracie or Ministrie, nor joyning themselves to any set societie in Church, or Commonwealth, are plagues and banes of both, and are to bee taken as main ennemies of this ordinance of God."[3] The poor are here defined as not belonging to the body of society and hence not subject to the bonds of solidarity which bind all its members. The poor, like Indian untouchables, are assigned a status which marks their exclusion from the social order.

In modern societies the deprived are assigned to the core category of the poor only when they receive assistance. It might be objected that the category of the economically deprived is presently much larger than that of the assisted poor. Whereas the latter englobes around 8 million persons in contemporary America, between 40 and 50 million fall into the former category. However, the point is precisely that the current widespread discussion of the problems of poverty can be seen in large part as an effort to broaden the core category of the poor by insisting that millions not heretofore included deserve societal assistance. If I understand Michael Harrington and his co-thinkers aright, they argue in effect that a redefinition of the problem of poverty is required so that the very large number of deprived who have so far not received assistance can be included among the poor receiving societal help of one kind or another.

It is not a person's lack of economic means that makes him belong to the core category of the poor. As long as a man continues to be defined primarily in terms of his occupational status, he is not so classified. Doctors, farmers, or plumbers who have suffered financial reverses or strains are still typically called doctors, farmers, or plumbers. "The acceptance of assistance," argues Georg Simmel, "removes the man who has received it from the precondition of the previous status; it symbolized his formal declassification."[4] From that point on his private trouble becomes a public issue. In individual psychological terms the sequence of events leads from the experience of deprivation to a quest for assistance; the matter is reversed however in sociological perspective: those who receive assistance are defined as being poor. Hence, poverty cannot be understood sociologically in terms of low income or deprivation but rather in terms of the social response to such deprivations.

The modern poor are a stratum that is recruited from heterogeneous origins, and individual members of this stratum have a great number of differing attributes. They come to belong to the common category of the poor by virtue of an essentially passive trait, namely that society reacts to them in a particular manner. The poor come to be viewed and classified not in terms of criteria ordinarily used in social categorization, that is, not by virtue of what they do, but by virtue of what is done to them. To quote Simmel again: "Poverty hence presents a unique sociological constellation: a number of individuals occupy a specific organic position within the social whole through purely personal fate; but it is not personal destiny of personal conditions which determine the position but rather the fact that others —individuals, associations, or social totalities—attempt to correct this state of affairs. Hence it is not personal need which makes for poverty; rather, the sociological category of poverty emerges only when those who suffer from want are receiving assistance."[5]

Though the poor are recognized as having a special status in modern societies, it is still a status that is marked only by negative attributes, that is, by what the status-holder does *not* have. This distinguishes him from any other status-holder in that it does not carry with it the expectation of a social contribution. This lack of expectation of a social contribution by the poor is symbolized by their lack of social visibility. Those who are assigned to the status of the poor offend the moral sensibilities of other members of the society who, unwittingly, or wittingly, keep them out of their sight. What is at issue here is not only physical segregation into special areas and districts that right-minded citizens would not normally care to visit and that are typically not shown to tourists, but also a kind of moral invisibility. The Gradgrinds and Bounderbys of Victorian England held views of the poor that were not very far removed from those of their Puritan ancestors. They consequently repressed awareness of the facts of deprivation. Only the persistent agitation of a host of reformers finally led to the horrified discovery by proper Victorian gentlemen that Britain was in fact split into "two nations." This accounts for the fact that, though general well-being and standards of living clearly increased in England during the nineteenth century, perceived deprivation increased throughout the century as human misery gained at least some visibility.

Lest it be believed that we deal here only with the more remote past it may be well to remind us of a very similar trend in the recent history of the United States. John K. Galbraith remarked upon this a few years ago when he wrote: "In the United States, the survival of poverty is remarkable. We ignore it because we share with all societies at all times the capacity for not seeing what we do not wish to see. Anciently this has enabled the noble-man to enjoy his dinner while remaining oblivious to the beggars around his door. In our own day it enables us to travel in comfort throughout South Chicago and the South."[6] At the present moment, when poverty is suddenly receiving frontline attention among politicians, scholars and the mass media, it is difficult to remember that only recently it seemed hardly visible at all. Five years ago the editors of *Fortune* magazine published a volume, *America in the Sixties,*[7] in which they attempted to forecast the major social and economic trends of the next decade. They concluded that soon depri-vation would no longer be with us at all. They announced with self-con-gratulatory flourish that "only" 3,600,000 families have incomes under $2,000 and that if a family makes over $2,000 it cannot be considered de-prived at all. Two years later Michael Harrington's *The Other America,*[8] followed by a spate of other books and articles, suddenly helped to picture deprivation as the central domestic issue in the United States and led to the emergence of a new social definition of poverty. The deprived in America now were seen as constituting about 25 percent of the population all of whom deserved assistance. The number of objectively deprived is not likely to have changed appreciably between the complacent fifties and the self-critical sixties, but the extent of perceived deprivation changed drastically. As a consequence, what appeared as a peripheral problem only a few years ago suddenly assumes considerable national salience.

[I should like to point out here that it will not do to argue that the statistics indicating the extent of deprivation were available all along. In the first place it is not the availability of statistics but their use which is of social significance. Furthermore, it can be argued that a society bothers to keep accurate statistics mainly of those phenomena it deems worthy of attention. Some extreme cases from totalitarian societies come readily to mind. As Everett Hughes has reminded us in his examination of German Statistical Yearbooks, in the Nazi and pre-Nazi period, "From earlier work with German official statistics, I was practically certain that the pre-Nazi German had a religion, but not a race. The statistical German was the opposite of the statistical American, who had a race but no religion. . . . Race in the pre-Nazi Yearbooks was a characteristic of stallions."[9] But all Yearbooks under the Nazi regime contained, among others, a category "Racial Classification of People who Married in X Year." A characteristic which was hitherto officially unnoticed was suddenly made visible through statistics. Or, to give another example, "In Lebanon there has not been a census since 1932 for fear that taking one would reveal such changes in the religious composition of the population as to make the marvelously intricate political arrangements designed to balance sectarian interests unviable."[10] Finally, in the 1941 Indian census there were 25 million tribal peoples, but in 1951, after independence was attained, the number had shrunk through what has been called "genocide by definition" to 1.7 million.[11]

No such drastic surgery was, of course, performed on American statistics. Yet one cannot help but be struck by the fact that, to give one example, the number of underprivileged will vary greatly depending on where you fix the income line. Thus the aforementioned *Fortune* study defined deprivation as a family income under $2,000 and concluded that there were only 3,600,000 poor families. Robert Lampman used the $2,500 cut-off for an urban family of four and on this basis came to the conclusion that 19 percent of the American population, 32,000,000 people, were underprivileged. In the same period, the AFL-CIO, using a slightly higher definition of what constituted low income, found that 41,500,000 Americans— 24 percent of the total population—have substandard incomes. After all these studies were published, the Bureau of Labor Statistics issued a report containing newly calculated budgets for urban families of four which showed that previous calculations had underestimated minimal budgetary requirements. Harrington concludes on the basis of these new figures that the deprived number more nearly 50,000,000.[12]]

Enough has been said to indicate the extent to which objective misery and perceived deprivation may diverge. We can now return to the initial statement that, in modern societies, persons are assigned a position in the status category of the poor when they receive assistance. Receipt of such assistance is predicated upon the society's willingness to assume a measure of responsibility for the poor and upon its recognition of the fact that they are effectively a part of the community. But what are the terms upon which such assistance is granted and what are the consequences for the recipient?

Here I would like to contend that the very granting of relief, the very assignment of the person to the category of the poor, is forthcoming only at the price of a degradation of the person who is so assigned.

To receive assistance means to be stigmatized and to be removed from the ordinary run of men. It is a status degradation through which, in Harold Garfinkel's words, "the public identity of an actor is transformed into something looked on as lower in the local schemes of social types."[13] In this perspective, the societal view of a person becomes significant in so far as it alters his face. Once a person is assigned to the status of the poor his role is changed, just as the career of the mental patient is changed by the very fact that he is defined as a mental patient.[14] Let me give a few illustrative instances of what is at issue here.

Members of nearly all status groups in society can make use of a variety of legitimate mechanisms to shield their behavior from observability by others; society recognizes a right to privacy, that is, the right to conceal parts of his role behavior from public observation. But this right is denied to the poor. At least in principle, facets of his behavior which ordinarily are not public are in their case under public control and are open to scrutiny by social workers or other investigators. In order to be socially recognized as poor a person is obligated to make his private life open to public inspection.[15] The protective veil which is available to other members of society is explicitly denied to them.

Whereas other recipients of social services may upon occasion be visited at home by investigators, most of their contact with the agency is likely to be in the agency rather than in their private homes. Generally, in modern society, the exercise of authority—except within the family—is separated from the home. With regard to the poor on relief, however, this is not the case. Here their home is the place in which most contacts with the agency investigators are likely to take place. They are typically being investigated *in situ* and hence have much less of a chance to conceal their private affairs from the superordinate observers. Such an invasion of home territory, because it prevents the usual stage management for the visit of outsiders, is necessarily experienced as humiliating and degrading.

When money is allocated to members of any other status groups in society, they have the freedom to dispose of it in almost any way they see fit. Here again, the treatment of the poor differs sharply. When monies are allocated to them, they do not have free disposition over their use. They must account to the donors for their expenses and the donors decide whether the money is spent "wisely" or "foolishly." That is, the poor are treated in this respect much like children who have to account to parents for the wise use of their pocket money; the poor are infantilized through such procedures.

As the above examples make clear, in the very process of being helped and assisted, the poor are assigned to a special career that impairs their previous identity and becomes a stigma which marks their intercourse with others. Social workers, welfare investigators, welfare administrators and local volunteer workers seek out the poor in order to help them, and yet, paradoxically, they are the very agents of their degradation. Subjective intentions and institutional consequences diverge here. The help rendered may be given from the purest and most benevolent of motives, yet the very fact of being helped degrades.

Assistance can be given either by voluntary workers or by professionals. The former pattern prevailed till roughly World War I, the latter has come to predominate in our days. Such professionalization of assistance has had two divergent sets of consequences for the recipient. To be cared for by a professional who is paid for his work means that the recipient need not be grateful to him, he doesn't have to say thank you. In fact he can hate the person giving assistance and even display some of his antagonism without losing the institutionally provided aid. Professionalization removes the personal element in the relationship and marks it as an impersonal transaction thereby freeing the recipient both from personal embarrassment and from personal obligation. When the poor is, so to speak, "promoted" to a case he may be spared certain personal humiliations. Yet this is not the whole story. The very manner of bureaucratic procedure used in dealing with a person on relief is different from that employed with respect to, say, an unemployed person. Receipt of unemployment insurance is seen as an unquestioned right which has been earned. Control by the donor agency over the recipient is minimal. Here it stands in contrast to control over the person on relief where control is a precondition for relief. Hence the professional in an agency dealing with the unemployed has little power over persons he serves, but the welfare investigator or the case worker has a great deal of power over the assisted poor. This power was considerably increased, it may be remarked in passing, when the giving of assistance shifted from so-called categorical assistance to granting case workers leeway to vary assistance according to the specific needs of the client. This change of policy was instituted for humanitarian and benevolent reasons, to be sure. But it stands to reason that it has greatly increased the discretionary power of the case worker over the client.

Prescribed impersonality has still other effects on the relationship between professionalized welfare workers and the recipients of aid. As long as volunteers or other non-professionals were the main dispensers of charity, condescension was likely to mark the relationship between donors and recipients of aid, but it was also likely to be characterized by a fairly high level of spontaneity. The relationship was so defined as to make a *reciprocal* flow of affect and emotion between the two actors possible, even if it did not always, or usually, occur. But professionalization by definition prevents the flow of affect. This is not due to happenstance but to the institutionalization of a structurally asymmetrical type of relationship. Those who render assistance have a job to do; the recipient is a case. As in every type of bureaucratic procedure, the impersonal aspects of the case must of need take precedence over distracting personal considerations. In fact, case workers or investigators would be incapacitated in the exercise of their tasks were they to indulge in "over-rapport," that is, in an undue consideration of the personal needs of the client. Excessive sympathy would impair role performance. The welfare worker, moreover, is not supposed to deserve esteem for his accomplishments from the recipient of aid but rather from professional peers and superiors. The client who is defined as "poor" has little if any possibility of controlling his behavior. Hence there exist built-in insulating mechanisms which insure that professional concern with the poor does not corrupt the professional into considering the poor as anything but an object of care and a recipient of aid. In this way the status discrepancy between them is continuously reaffirmed. This is accentuated, moreover, in those cases where welfare workers are of lower middle class origin and feel that close association with clients might endanger the respectable status they have but recently achieved.

The professionals and the poor do in fact belong to two basically different worlds. In Alexander Solzhenitsyn's fine novel about Russian concentration camps, *One Day in the Life of Ivan Denisovich*,[16] occurs an episode in which the hero attempts to get some medical relief from the man in charge of the infirmary but is turned away with indifference. He thereupon reflects, "How can you expect a man who's warm to understand a man who's cold." This beautifully captures the gist of what I have been trying to say. As long as social workers and the poor belong to the opposite worlds of those who are warm and those who are cold, their relationship is necessarily an asymmetrical one. As in other aspects of case work, those in need address those who can relieve some of their wants as supplicants, and the asymmetry is not only one of feelings and attitudes, it is also an asymmetry of power. This is an extreme case of unilateral dependence. Peter Blau's formulation is helpful here: "By supplying services in demand to others, a person establishes power over them. If he regularly renders needed services they cannot readily obtain elsewhere, others become dependent on and obligated to him for these services, and unless they can furnish other benefits to him that produce interdependence by making him equally dependent on them, their unilateral dependence obligates them to comply with his requests lest he ceases to continue to meet their needs."[17]

Blau stresses here that unilateral dependence comes into being when the receiver of benefits is not in a position to reciprocate with benefits that he can in turn bestow upon the donor. This, I believe, touches upon the crux of the matter. The poor, when receiving assistance, are assigned a low and degraded status by virtue of a determination that they cannot themselves contribute to society. Their inability to contribute in turn degrades them to the condition of unilateral receivers. Built into the system of relief is not only the definition of their being non-contributors, but the expectation that they are not even potential contributors. In an instrumentally oriented society, those who cannot give but only receive and who are not expected to give at a future time are naturally assigned the lowest status. They cannot engage in activities that establish interdependence and this is why they cannot be given social recognition. Poverty, therefore, can never be eliminated unless the poor are enabled to give as well as to receive. They can be fully integrated into the social fabric only if they are offered the opportunity to give.

In order to be able to serve, they must first be able to function at optimum capacity. Devices such as a guaranteed minimum income for every citizen, assuring him freedom from pressing want, may very well be a precondition for the abolition of dependency. But it is a precondition only. It needs to be considered not as an end in itself but only as a means which permits the poor to be free from anxiety while they train themselves for the rendering of such services to the community as will make them interdependent with others.

I showed earlier how the core category of the poor arises only when they come to be defined as recipients of assistance. We now see that correlatively the poor will be with us as long as we provide assistance so that the problem of poverty can be solved only through the abolition of unilateral relationship of dependence.

This is not the place to spell out in detail concrete measures which will "solve" the problem of poverty. I know of no such global solutions at the present moment. But I wish to indicate at least the direction in which, I believe, such solutions are to be looked for. I am impressed, for example, by the number of recent experiments, from Mobilization for Youth to Alcoholics Anonymous, in which "some people who do not seem to benefit from *receiving* help often profit indirectly when they are *giving* help."[18] A number of such projects have of late used a variety of nonprofessionals recruited largely among the poor. The New York State Division for Youth and several other agencies for example employ former youthful offenders in interviewing and related tasks. Howard University's Community Apprentice Program trains delinquent youth to be recreation, child welfare, and research aides. Mobilization for Youth employs indigenous leaders as case aides, homework helpers, and the like. These jobs offer employment opportunities for the underprivileged and hence serve directly to reduce poverty by transforming dependent welfare cases into homemakers, and former delinquents into researchers.[19] This indigenous non-professional, as

Frank Riessman and Robert Reiff have written, "is a peer of the client and can more readily identify with him. He possesses no special body of knowledge which makes him an expert and can feel, therefore, that in reversed circumstances the client could do the same job just as easily. In the place of subtle patronage or *noblesse oblige* concepts, he is likely to feel that 'there but for the grace of God go I.' To the indigenous non-professional, 'helping others' is a reciprocal process. . . ."[20]

These are only a few and still very feeble beginnings, but I believe that they point in the right direction. The task is to create valued status positions for those who were formerly passive recipients of assistance. Such valuable status positions can only be those in which they are required and enabled to make a social contribution and become active partners in a joint undertaking of mutual aid. This can be done through helping others with whom but recently they shared similar problems or through working in large-scale projects similar to a domestic Peace Corps or a replica of the New Deal's Civilian Conservation Corps. Yet another case in which the poor may themselves contribute to the abolition of the status they occupy arises when they cease "acting poor," i.e., when they reject the role behavior which is required by the status. When the poor begin to react actively, when they refuse to continue to be passive recipients of aid, they undermine the very status that they occupy. This is why rent strikes, demonstrations, and other political activities by the poor should be seen as avenues of activization which tend to lead to a restructuring of their relationships in the community.

Simmel observes that though the notion of assistance necessarily implies taking from the rich and giving to the poor, it nevertheless was never aimed at an equalization of their positions in society. As distinct from socialist endeavors, it does not even have the tendency to reduce the differences between rich and poor but rather accepts and bolsters them.[21] Or, as T. H. Marshall once put it, "The common purpose of statutory and voluntary effort was to abate the nuisance of poverty without disturbing the pattern of inequality of which poverty was the most obvious unpleasant consequence."[22] This is why what I have suggested diverges sharply from most previous policies. It aims not at alleviating poverty but at abolishing it through the elimination of the despised status of the receiver of assistance. It is, to be sure, a Utopian proposal. But, as Max Weber, that supreme realist, has argued, "Certainly all political experience confirms the truth— that man would not have attained the possible unless time and again he had reached out for the impossible."[23]

Notes

1. Georg Simmel, *Soziologie,* Leipzig: Duncker und Humblot, 1908, pp. 454–493. I have relied very heavily on Simmel's hitherto untranslated essay, "Der Arme," in the above volume. In fact, much of what I say in the

first part of this paper is little more than a restatement of some of Simmel's seminal ideas.

2. Emile Durkheim, *The Rules of Sociological Method,* New York: The Free Press of Glencoe, 1950, p. 35.

3. Quoted in Christopher Hill, *Puritanism and Revolution,* New York: Schocken Books, 1964, pp. 227–228.

4. Simmel, *op. cit.,* p. 489.

5. *Ibid.,* p. 493.

6. John K. Galbraith, *The Affluent Society,* Boston: Houghton Mifflin, 1959, p. 333.

7. The Editors of *Fortune, America in the Sixties,* New York: Harper Torchbooks, 1960, p. 102. Note the following additional comment: "Only about a million domestic servants, marginal farm operators, and farm laborers and their families still look truly poor." *Ibid.,* p. 102.

8. Michael Harrington, *The Other America,* Baltimore: Penguin Books, 1963.

9. Everett C. Hughes, *Men and Their Work,* New York: The Free Press of Glencoe, 1958, p. 146 and p. 150.

10. Clifford Geertz, "The Integrative Revolution" in Geertz (ed.), *Old Societies and New States,* New York: The Free Press of Glencoe, 1963, p. 126.

11. *Ibid.*

12. Harrington, *op. cit.,* pp. 192–194.

13. Harold Garfinkel, "Conditions of Successful Degradation Ceremonies," *American Journal of Sociology,* 61, (March, 1956), p. 420.

14. Cf. Erving Goffman, *Asylums,* New York: Doubleday Anchor Books, 1961, *passim.*

15. On the notion of observability, cf. Robert K. Merton, *Social Theory and Social Structure,* New York: The Free Press, 1957, pp. 374–375, and Rose Laub Coser, "Insulation from Observability and Types of Social Conformity," *American Sociological Review,* 26, pp. 28–39.

16. Alexander Solzhenitsyn, *One Day in the Life of Ivan Denisovich,* New York: E. P. Dutton, 1963.

17. Peter Blau, *Exchange and Power in Social Life,* New York: John Wiley and Sons, 1964, p. 118.

18. Robert Reiff and Frank Riessman, *The Indigenous Nonprofessional,* New York: National Institute of Labor Education, Mental Health Program (mimeo, p. 11).

19. *Ibid.,* p. 6.

20. *Ibid.,* p. 12.

21. Simmel, *op. cit.,* p. 459.

22. T. H. Marshall, *Class, Citizenship and Social Development,* New York: Doubleday Anchor Books, 1965, p. 105.

23. Gerth and Mills (eds.), *From Max Weber,* New York: Oxford University Press, 1948, p. 128.

Shame, pride, resentment, and hope are some of the emotions evidenced in the descriptions of individual families who constitute our modern poor. Poverty has many causes, and therefore there is need for a many-faceted approach to the solution of the problem.

The Poor Who Live Among Us

Lee E. Dirks

The job-seeking cook's helper shuffled slowly along the dingy corridor of a Lower Manhattan employment center, a pitiful figure in an ill-fitting suit and soiled "white" shirt. Pausing, he straightened his flowered tie and made small talk with a stranger:

"A shame about President Kennedy," he said. "They ever catch the guy that did it?"

On Bad Off Mountain, in the mine country of West Virginia, a retired cement mason drew his tall, spare frame erect and inhaled the chill January air. Happy in the freedom of retirement, he boasted of his hunting prowess ("seven bear 'n a dozen coon so far this winter"). Then he summed up his condition in life:

"I'm gettin' along real well—and thank Old Master for every bit of it."

They Would Be Called "Poor"

So different, so distant, the spry West Virginian at home in the hills and the jobless New Yorker who had never heard of Lee Harvey Oswald share one thing in common: by almost any measurement of material wealth, most Americans would call them "poor."

For years, the nation's prosperity has obscured the poor. Now that they have been "discovered," it appears the emotions of politics will over-simplify everything about them.

President Johnson, declaring "unconditional war on poverty in America," asserts that one fifth of all American families have incomes "too small to meet their basic needs." He'll soon send Congress a special message on how he proposes "not only to relieve the symptoms of poverty but to cure it—and, above all, to prevent it."

"You Will Never Catch Up"

Senator Barry Goldwater, a candidate for the Republican Presidential nomination, scoffs that declaring war on poverty "is like greyhounds chas-

From "The Poor Who Live Among Us" by Lee E. Dirks. *The National Observer*, January 27, 1964. Reprinted by permission of *The National Observer*.

ing a mechanical hare. You never will catch up. There will always be a lowest one third or one fifth." He questions what can be done to help the poor: "Most people who have no skill have had no education for the same reason—low intelligence or low ambition."

Poverty is real. But it is also complex. There is no community of the poor, no chemistry of the poor.

Poverty knows no East or West, no North or South. It plagues West Virginia, yes, but it flourishes too in the fertile San Joaquin Valley of California and in the shadow of Phoenix's South Mountain. The District of Columbia, among all the states, has the nation's highest per capita income —and some of the nation's most oppressive slums.

Poverty has many causes. Poor education handicaps many Americans, and automation makes the skills of some obsolete. Ill health can break the will and the ability to work; it can break the bank account, too. Divorce and desertion rob families of their breadwinner. Alcohol and drugs drag some into poverty. A few of the poor—beatniks, religious ascetics—deliberately choose poverty.

Sometimes They Sink Slowly

Poverty strikes some swiftly—as when a business goes bankrupt or huge medical bills stream in. Some people sink into poverty slowly, victims of dwindling job opportunities or perhaps of the erosion of their own self-respect. Most often, they have been born into poverty and stay there until they die, even as their brothers or sisters escape.

Poverty does different things to different people. Walk into the home of a poor family. A stench may offend the nostrils; filth may offend the eyes. Or the home may look immaculate.

The "poor" range from the destitute to the outwardly comfortable. No one starves to death in America; government food programs and private welfare agencies see to that. But millions get by on starchy diets that make them paunchy but not healthy. Millions live in housing with inadequate heating and sanitation facilities that breed disease.

The Term Is Misleading

The poor don't agree on whether they're poor. Some deny that they are poor; judged by the standards of their neighbors or by their past way of living, *poor* may indeed mislead. Others consider themselves poor, but even these respond to their poverty differently, unpredictably: they see poverty as a challenge, and dream of breaking out of it; or perhaps they see poverty as a conqueror, and yield to despair.

Only the poor can know poverty; only they can understand it. The economist who tries to define poverty with statistics can't know poverty—

nor can the reporter who spends hours observing the poor, interviewing them, but retreating at night to the luxury of a filet mignon and the comfort of a clean motel room. Nor, indeed, can the social worker who injects himself—and his background and his prejudices—into the neighborhoods of the poor by the day or even by the year.

Poverty cannot be defined; it cannot be measured. Who can measure a man's needs? A man's longings?

The Social Security Administration places the cost of an "economy-plan" budget for a nonfarm family of four at $3165. No family in New York City could live adequately on this amount. But most families in small communities in Georgia, say, do.

Lacking any more precise measurement, many private and government economists call a family poor if its yearly income is below $3000; an individual, if he earns less than $1500. By this standard one fifth of the nation's people are poor.

Just six years ago, in his book *The Affluent Society,* John Kenneth Galbraith drew the "hard-core" poverty line much lower—at incomes of $1000. A fellow economist, Leon Keyserling, uses the figure $4000 for stark poverty, $6000 for families he calls "deprived." Whatever the figure, economists admit that it is arbitrary—that some below it cannot by any definition be adjudged poor, that some above it should be.

What role does welfare play among the poor, what role can it play? One eighth of all Americans live in families with incomes that qualify them for relief in their states. It's widely agreed these persons comprise the "hard-core" poor. Yet only one sixth of all families with incomes below $3000 actually receive welfare payments.

Poverty, then, has many faces, many forms, many nuances. There is no simple way to describe the poor, no simple way to solve their problems.

"Pobre?" the Puerto Rican woman exclaimed. "Ha! I'm not poor. I'm rich." "Rich" because she has food to eat. "Rich" because welfare pays her rent. "Rich" compared with her girlhood in Puerto Rico.

Rosita P., forty-seven, was frying codfish cakes at the stove of her tiny kitchen (three feet by five feet) on New York City's Lower East Side. She had come to New York twelve years before.

Rosita lives entirely on her welfare check; her husband disappeared years ago. To support herself and her two children, she receives $99 every two weeks ($2574 a year). Of this, nearly half—$46 every two weeks —goes to the landlord as rent for their ill-lighted, overheated three-room flat in the basement of a dilapidated apartment building.

With the rest, she buys food, second-hand clothing, an occasional item of furniture. An old television set and an equally aged record-player provide entertainment. Prominently displayed in the slim collection of records:

John Fitzgerald Kennedy's speeches. Kennedy newspaper photographs—and little else—adorn the walls.

Like half of New York City's 700,000 Puerto Ricans, Rosita never reached the eighth grade. Her children remain in school at fourteen and eleven, though, and when they finish, Rosita hopes to find a job. If she does, she can hope for little better than day after day of drudgery in a low-paying job.

Rosita complains little; she and her children live more comfortably than they did in Puerto Rico. But she wonders about the day when "progress" will come to her neighborhood in the form of high-rise apartments: "Some day house go down," she says. "Then?" Then, she knows, she will have to pass progress by and search for another ill-lighted, overheated flat.

Death, divorce, desertion, and illegitimacy deprive many families of a male breadwinner, and this unquestionably contributes to poverty. In 24 per cent of all families with incomes below $3000, a woman is head of the household.

One of Rosita's neighbors, a Puerto Rican woman of forty-three whose husband died and who supports four children, receives $3224 a year from welfare. Yet few would deny that she is poor: she lives frugally, and has bought no dress for herself for eleven years; her $90-a-month apartment is so poorly maintained by the landlord that a five-foot chunk of ceiling plaster not long ago fell on her and two daughters sleeping with her. At another extreme, another close neighbor of Rosita's has five children but no husband. She never had a husband; each of her five children has a different father.

For all their problems, Puerto Ricans on New York's Lower East Side display little of the sullen hopelessness of many of their fellow poor. Perhaps they remember too well how they lived when they lived in rural Puerto Rico.

Will S., a seventy-seven-year-old Negro, lives at the end of a muddy, rutty clay road a few miles south of Fort Mill, South Carolina. On one side of his backyard is the well from which Will draws water; on the other side is the family privy.

And Will does have a family. He has his wife Hattie, sixty-five, his two daughters, and his daughters' children, twelve in all. All sixteen persons live in the four-room house. One daughter's husband stays there sometimes too; sometimes he doesn't. The other daughter has no husband and never had.

Will is the breadwinner. His sole income: a monthly Social Security check of $55.30 ($663.60 a year). Occasionally his daughters earn $2 or $3 a day washing, ironing, or cleaning for white families nearby.

Will had been a tenant farmer until he "retired" two years ago. He had hoped to save a bit the last two years, but "we had two bad years in a row. I didn't come clear either year."

Now, says Will, "I mostly just lay here in the house studyin' about all them children." He "studies" most about how to feed them: "I buy fatback, pinto beans, white grits, rice, and sometimes a little meat like chicken or some eggs." The children wear cast-off clothes given them by white families in the neighborhood. But school costs worry Will: "Them lined pads they write on costs a lot, and most of 'em have to have a dime every single day to eat on. Them dimes add up fast."

Will is no isolated case. He belongs to a category of the poor who have just two skills—the skill to make things spring up from the soil, and the skill to live on little or nothing while doing so.

His forebears of two generations ago lived in slavery. He came along in an age of paternalism, when the landlords—while hardly showering their tenants with worldly goods—provided a roof, a fireplace, a garden plot, and credit at the store for life's necessities.

But this way of life, too, is disappearing, prodded by the inevitable trend toward large, mechanized farms. To live at roughly the average American standard of living, it's widely agreed, a farmer must have at least 325 acres, good credit at a nearby bank, and a sizable investment in machinery. Yet few of the nation's 350,000 full-time family farms approach these proportions.

Over 40 per cent of all Negroes who live on farms earn less than $1000 a year. White farmers do better, but not much: 50 per cent earn less than $3000. In a society that produces more than enough food, many low-income farm families—56 per cent, according to a government study—have diets deficient in at least one of the basic nutrients. Will's family, fed on fatback and rice, is not alone.

Forsaking the South

Americans are escaping this way of life. They are escaping it, in fact, in tidal proportions. Into the cities in the past four decades have streamed 27 million Americans—a migration greater than the one that brought 21 million Europeans to America's cities between 1880 and 1920.

Claude L. is one who moved north in the great migration. So is Boyd J. Both forsook the South in the early 1950's; both chose Detroit and its monotonous assembly lines. Both have been rejected by America's industrial society, transformed into internal aliens in their own land.

"You breathe—and you exist. You're not going ahead—and you ain't even standing still. You're going backwards, and you can't do one thing about it."

Boyd, age fifty, father of thirteen, and white, tries to explain how it feels to be out of work, nearly out of hope, and dependent on the community for the necessities of life.

"The only time it really bothers me is when it hurts the kids," he says. "Sometimes the other kids at school make fun of them for my bein' on welfare. The older girls have to make the same dress do for months on end and when other girls are always buyin' new things."

Boyd leaps up to cuff his shouting seven-year-old into sullen silence. He walks back through a litter of toys, newspapers, and partly devoured slices of bread and sits down.

"It's disgusting to have to live this way," exclaims his wife. "Look at my hair. Don't you think I'd like to get it fixed up?" Her hair hung down in straight, stringy strands. She wore no makeup. Below the old house dress that hung on her heavy frame, her feet were bare.

"Too Old to Get a Job"

Less than six years ago, Boyd had been making good wages operating a heavy stamping machine in an auto body plant. Today he gets $109.60 every two weeks ($2850 a year) from the city welfare department. Boyd was laid off in August 1957 during auto model changeover time. Last November his five years' seniority expired, and he was dropped from the plant recall lists.

"I got applications in every place in town," he says. "But everybody keeps tellin' me I'm too old to get a job."

On welfare since he was laid off, he puts in fifty-two hours every two weeks on jobs the city requires of welfare recipients able to work. "Funny thing about that," he says. "I tried to get a job with that department once and they told me I was too old for heavy labor. But now I do the same kind of work for the same department and they think I'm great—as long as I'm doing it on welfare."

He motions at a new console television set. "Present from one of our married daughters," he says. "The welfare wouldn't let us buy one ourselves, but there's no law against us gettin' one as a gift."

Though Boyd resents welfare's intrusions on his freedom, it provides him and his family $27.50 for rent and $61 for food stamps every two weeks. They buy about $125 worth of clothing twice a year with certificates redeemed at major Detroit department stores. City hospitals provide free medical and dental care, which has helped especially when severe attacks of asthma have struck their two-year-old and nine-year-old boys.

"When one hits, we've got to run for a taxi or find a neighbor because we don't have a car," says Boyd's wife. "The fits are bad enough that we can have a telephone in the house if we want one—they don't let most people on relief have them. Trouble is, we can't afford one."

Like most people who are poor, Boyd and his wife think the best chance their children have lies in their education. "Look at those little fellas over there," says Boyd. "When they grow up, they won't get any place at all without high school educations, and most likely college to boot."

So far, Boyd's four oldest children have quit school before graduation. But if statistics prove anything, he's right about his children's chances. Of the nation's families with breadwinners who didn't go beyond the eighth grade, 37 per cent last year had incomes of less than $3000. Only 12 per cent with breadwinners who finished high school earned less than $3000.

Only Thirty-six, but a Negro

Claude L., who came to Detroit the same time as Boyd, was laid off at the same time too. Unlike Boyd, he has his age going for him. He's thirty-six. But he has something against him too: he's a Negro.

"Why, just the other day Claude showed up at a factory to get a job at the same time this white man did," says Claude's wife. "Claude had more experience, but the white man got the job. You see that all the time."

Claude's race makes up 20 per cent of Detroit's population—and perhaps 80 per cent of its relief rolls. With generally less education, less job training, less seniority in the factories, Negroes find industry more demanding. For the nation as a whole, Negroes represent 10 per cent of the population, but 21 per cent of those with incomes below $3000.

Jobs Are Not for Them

The Reverend David W. Barry, executive director of the New York City Mission Society, knows the plight of the urban poor from years of working with them: "Jobs are increasing in the cities, but jobs are not for them. Once the way to escape from poverty was hard work, drudging work. There is still drudgery among the urban poor, but the supply of these jobs has long since fallen behind the demand.

"For today's poor there is something worse: no work at all, just the dreary security of a relief check or pension check that gives minimum food and clothing and some kind of shelter, but no promise of anything beyond, no promise that a strong back and willingness to work will let them inch up the ladder of success."

And then the final indignity: "Every magazine and television advertisement, with its beautiful women and sleek cars and new washing machines, shouts at them that they are a failure, for they do not share in your picture of what American life is like." For those who suffer it, the indignity is greater, perhaps, than was the indignity of poverty during the Depression. For during the Depression, poverty was a common fate; today it is an isolated phenomenon, largely out of sight and therefore largely out of mind in an otherwise affluent America.

She Sees a Bright Side

Some who have fled rural poverty have fled, in turn, the poverty of the cities. Consider Helen B., now a twenty-eight-year-old mother of eight, who left the West Virginia hills a decade ago to seek a better life in Indianapolis. Her second husband, a West Virginia man whom she met in Indianapolis, worked for a while as a redcap and then as a taxi driver until an accident put him out of work. At forty-five and with a third-grade education, he could find no other job. Confined to a tiny three-room apartment ("the kids had no place to play; they was gettin' on my husband's nerves"), they decided to return to West Virginia and the security of welfare.

"I can't imagine anyone ever livin' any worse'n we did when we moved in," she says. For several days in the cold of winter they had no beds to sleep on, no stove to cook on, and few blankets to keep them warm.

Even today, no one could walk into their home and question for a moment that they are poor. A stench permeates the air; coal dust smothers the floor, the tables, the walls. A single coal stove heats the house. The five-month-old baby, hacking with a cough he has had since birth, lies in a wooden box suspended on metal tubing near the stove. In a corner, the family's only source of entertainment—an ancient table-model radio—plays softly all day long.

"I've never been used to this kind of life," confesses Helen. But even she sees a bright side: "At least my husband is working for what we have— he works for the state to get his relief check. It's good. He comes home tired, like other men do. He plays with the kids; he doesn't growl at them like he used to. And now I know exactly how much I can spend for food and clothes."

West Virginia is proud of its Work and Training program, which requires able welfare recipients to work for their payments at $1 an hour. It was the first state in the union to adopt the program; for nearly a year, it operated on a verbal agreement between state and federal officials.

Automation in the Mines

Sidney W. is an able-bodied West Virginian who's out of work, but he doesn't qualify for the relief program: he's single.

The other day Sidney hollered a warning at a motorist gunning his car up a snow-covered hillside road in tiny Thurmond, West Virginia. "Can't none of us read nor write," he admitted later in the sanctity of the home he shares with his mother and sister. "I went to school 'til I was sixteen, and the only daggone thing I learned to do was how to chew tobacco."

Sidney loads coal for a living. Or he did until last summer. Automation has come to the mines of West Virginia as it has come to the rest of the country, and Sidney may never go back to the mines.

But neither will Sidney likely leave West Virginia. In his thirty years, he never has. Chimes in his mother, who supports him on her Social Security check: "We'd move away from Thurmond; there's nothing here. But where to? Page Fork? Glen Jean? Costs too much to live there."

Live in an Obsolete Culture

Across the continent, Aurilio M. shook his balding head and took another bite on the unlighted cigar he has learned to make last all day. "Poverty?" he said. "Yes, we have poverty in northern New Mexico. We live in what they call an economically depressed area."

Then he laughed. "You know," he said, "when the rest of the world was in the Depression, we didn't notice it at all."

Even today, when nearby Los Alamos County enjoys the second-highest per capita income in the nation, Aurilio's Rio Arriba County suffers from its primitive heritage. Like the nation's 650,000 Indians, Spanish-Americans in the Southeast live in an obsolete culture.

Aurilio doesn't consider himself poor—not by his standards. He's selling used cars now, pulling down $200 a month ($2400 a year). A few weeks ago he was working as a night watchman on a construction project. Before that he was a janitor for a school in a nearby mountain village. Jobs in Aurilio's area, heavily dependent on a seasonal tourist business and periodic public works projects, are low in pay, short in length. In his memory, it has never been otherwise.

Fishing Supplies the Meat

Joseph M., octogenarian farmer in Orange County, Florida, knew a better life once. Born on a Slovenian farm under the rule of Emperor Franz Josef of Austria, he came to the United States when he was seventeen and built up a profitable butcher shop in Omaha. Eventually, though, supermarkets drove him out of business; after he and his wife lost their two sons in World War II, they bought a modest ten-acre farm in Florida.

The couple still farm the land, earning about $1600 a year from their sales of chickens, eggs, and vegetables. Like many farm families, they own their own home and pay almost nothing for food because they grow it themselves. Joseph enjoys fishing; except for an occasional chicken that has served its purpose as an egg-producer, his fishing supplies their table with the only meat or fish the family ever eats.

Joseph and his wife, and millions like them, make up the one third of the nation's under-$3000-income families that are headed by a person over sixty-five. They live frugally and even manage to save a little by paring expenses: "We used to go to church in Omaha, but we can't afford it now, what with the collection plate and having to buy Sunday clothes."

For all their frugality, Joseph and his wife insist they need little more. "Window curtains, drapes, washing machines, new dresses?" she asks. "We eat good. We're decent people. What more?"

Plant Went Bankrupt

Not far away, a family that once knew affluence now knows only misery. The former president of a small manufacturing plant in Iowa, Albert A. now clerks in a grocery store to bring in an income of $1600 a year. Under his son's management, the plant in Iowa went bankrupt and Albert's savings evaporated.

Albert detests his job in the store. His wife has become an alcoholic. Both admit that they have seriously considered suicide.

No one knows the thoughts of Roosevelt H. as he shuffles silently along West Madison Street, capital of Chicago's Skid Row. He tugs down on a beaten Air Force enlisted man's cap and adjusts a tattered scarf to protect himself from the winter wind that skips along the street carrying dust and debris.

"I can't tell you the times I've spent most of the night walking," says Roosevelt. "Many times I've walked from downtown to 95th (eleven miles) and then turned around and walked back. On the real cold nights—like when it's near zero—I walk out to the county hospital and play sick. By the time they examine you, it's daylight and you can leave. I'm ashamed to tell you that, but it's the truth."

Shame, pride, resentment, hope—these are but a few of the emotions of those that Americans call "poor." As the emotions of poverty are all but infinite, so are the causes and the possible cures.

One Monday in January 1964, Walter Heller, chairman of the President's Council of Economic Advisers and chief strategist of the War on Poverty, settled onto the brown-leather couch in his Washington office and said, "We're not starry-eyed about this. It can't be accomplished overnight."

"What's more," he said, "there will always be some residue of people who truly don't have the mental and physical ability to earn an income. And there will always be some who don't have the motivation. But even that core of poverty is subject to reduction by intelligent rehabilitation."

Later that day the Council of Economic Advisers, in its annual report to the President, discussed poverty and the various "cures": "It's roots are many and its causes complex. . . . No single program can embrace all who are poor, and no single program can strike at all the sources of today's and tomorrow's poverty."

The words will be forgotten in the politics of 1964's summer. But they will be no less true.

The fact that poverty and suffering are present among both white and black people is small consolation to the black minority. Poverty is humilating and de- meaning and makes people defenseless against those who prey upon and victim- ize the less fortunate. The only way to improve a ghetto is to extinguish it, because anything else merely perpetuates the attitudes and conditions that underlie the inequalities in our society.

Fifth Avenue, Uptown

James Baldwin

There is a housing project standing now where the house in which we grew up once stood, and one of those stunted city trees is snarling where our doorway used to be. This is on the rehabilitated side of the avenue. The other side of the avenue—for progress takes time—has not been re- habilitated yet and it looks exactly as it looked in the days when we sat with our noses pressed against the windowpane, longing to be allowed to go "across the street." The grocery store which gave us credit is still there, and there can be no doubt that it is still giving credit. The people in the project certainly need it—far more, indeed, than they ever needed the project. The last time I passed by, the Jewish proprietor was still standing among his shelves, looking sadder and heavier but scarcely any older. Further down the block stands the shoe-repair store in which our shoes were repaired until reparation became impossible and in which, then, we bought all our "new" ones. The Negro proprietor is still in the window, head down, work- ing at the leather.

These two, I imagine, could tell a long tale if they would (perhaps they would be glad to if they could), having watched so many, for so long, struggling in the fishhooks, the barbed wire, of this avenue.

The avenue is elsewhere the renowned and elegant Fifth. The area I am describing, which, in today's gang parlance, would be called "the turf," is bounded by Lenox Avenue on the west, the Harlem River on the east, 135th Street on the north, and 130th Street on the south. We never lived beyond these boundaries; this is where we grew up. Walking along 145th Street—for example—familiar as it is, and similar, does not have the same impact because I do not know any of the people on the block. But when I turn east on 131st Street and Lenox Avenue, there is first a soda-pop joint, then a shoeshine "parlor," then a grocery store, then a dry cleaners, then the houses. All along the street there are people who watched me grow up, people who grew up with me, people I watched grow up along with my brothers and sisters; and, sometimes in my arms, sometimes underfoot, sometimes at my shoulder—or on it—their children, a riot, a forest of children, who include my nieces and nephews.

When we reach the end of this long block, we find ourselves on wide, filthy, hostile Fifth Avenue, facing that project which hangs over the avenue like a monument to the folly, and the cowardice, of good intentions. All along the block, for anyone who knows it, are immense human gaps, like craters. These gaps are not created merely by those who have moved away, inevitably into some other ghetto; or by those who have risen, almost always into a greater capacity for self-loathing and self-delusion; or yet by those who, by whatever means—War II, the Korean war, a policeman's gun or billy, a gang war, a brawl, madness, an overdose of heroin, or, simply, unnatural exhaustion—are dead. I am talking about those who are left, and I am talking principally about the young. What are they doing? Well, some, a minority, are fanatical churchgoers, members of the more extreme of the Holy Roller sects. Many, many more are "moslems," by affiliation or sympathy, that is to say that they are united by nothing more—and nothing less —than a hatred of the white world and all its works. They are present, for example, at every Buy Black street-corner meeting—meetings in which the speaker urges his hearers to cease trading with white men and establish a separate economy. Neither the speaker nor his hearers can possibly do this, of course, since Negroes do not own General Motors or RCA or the A&P, nor, indeed, do they own more than a wholly insufficient fraction of anything else in Harlem (those who *do* own anything are more interested in their profits than in their fellows). But these meetings nevertheless keep alive in the participators a certain pride of bitterness without which, however futile this bitterness may be, they could scarcely remain alive at all. Many have given up. They stay home and watch the TV screen, living on the earnings of their parents, cousins, brothers, or uncles, and only leave the house to go to the movies or to the nearest bar. "How're you making it?" one may ask, running into them along the block, or in the bar. "Oh, I'm TV-ing it"; with the saddest, sweetest, most shamefaced of smiles, and from a great distance. This distance one is compelled to respect; anyone who has traveled so far will not easily be dragged again into the world. There are further retreats, of course, than the TV screen or the bar. There are those who are simply sitting on their stoops, "stoned," animated for a moment only, and hideously, by the approach of someone who may lend them the money for a "fix." Or by the approach of someone from whom they can purchase it, one of the shrewd ones, on the way to prison or just coming out.

And the others, who have avoided all of these deaths, get up in the morning and go downtown to meet "the man." They work in the white man's world all day and come home in the evening to this fetid block. They struggle to instill in their children some private sense of honor or dignity which will help the child to survive. This means, of course, that they must struggle, solidly, incessantly, to keep this sense alive in themselves, in spite of the insults, the indifference, and the cruelty they are certain to encounter in their working day. They patiently browbeat the landlord into fixing the heat, the plaster, the plumbing; this demands prodigious patience; nor is patience usually enough. In trying to make their hovels habitable, they are perpetually throwing good money after bad. Such frustration, so long endured, is driving many strong, admirable men and women whose only crime is color to the very gates of paranoia.

One remembers them from another time—playing handball in the playground, going to church, wondering if they were going to be promoted at school. One remembers them going off to war—gladly, to escape this block. One remembers their return. Perhaps one remembers their wedding day. And one sees where the girl is now—vainly looking for salvation from some other embittered, trussed, and struggling boy—and sees the all-but-abandoned children in the streets.

Now I am perfectly aware that there are other slums in which white men are fighting for their lives, and mainly losing. I know that blood is also flowing through those streets and that the human damage there is incalculable. People are continually pointing out to me the wretchedness of white people in order to console me for the wretchedness of blacks. But an itemized account of the American failure does not console me and it should not console anyone else. That hundreds and thousands of white people are living, in effect, no better than the "niggers" is not a fact to be regarded with complacency. The social and moral bankruptcy suggested by this fact is of the bitterest, most terrifying kind.

The people, however, who believe that this democratic anguish has some consoling value are always pointing out that So-and-So, white, and So-and-So, black, rose from the slums into the big time. The existence—the public existence—of, say, Frank Sinatra and Sammy Davis, Jr., proves to them that America is still the land of opportunity and that inequalities vanish before the determined will. It proves nothing of the sort. The determined will is rare—at the moment, in this country, it is unspeakably rare—and the inequalities suffered by the many are in no way justified by the rise of a few. A few have always risen—in every country, every era, and in the teeth of regimes which can by no stretch of the imagination be thought of as free. Not all these people, it is worth remembering, left the world better than they found it. The determined will is rare, but it is not invariably benevolent. Furthermore, the American equation of success with the big time reveals an awful disrespect for human life and human achievement. This equation has placed our cities among the most dangerous in the world and has placed our youth among the most empty and most bewildered. The situation of our youth is not mysterious. Children have never been very good at listening to their elders, but they have never failed to imitate them.

They must, they have no other models. That is exactly what our children are doing. They are imitating our immorality, our disrespect for the pain of others.

All other slum dwellers, when the bank account permits it, can move out of the slum and vanish altogether from the eye of persecution. No Negro in this country has ever made that much money and it will be a long time before any Negro does. The Negroes in Harlem, who have no money, spend what they have on such gimcracks as they are sold. These include "wider" TV screens, more "faithful" hi-fi sets, more "powerful" cars, all of which, of course, are obsolete long before they are paid for. Anyone who has ever struggled with poverty knows how extremely expensive it is to be poor; and if one is a member of a captive population, economically speaking, one's feet have simply been placed on the treadmill forever. One is victimized, economically, in a thousand ways—rent, for example, or car insurance. Go shopping one day in Harlem—for anything—and compare Harlem prices and quality with those downtown.

The people who have managed to get off this block have only got as far as a more respectable ghetto. This respectable ghetto does not even have the advantages of the disreputable one, friends, neighbors, a familiar church, and friendly tradesmen; and it is not, moreover, in the nature of any ghetto to remain respectable long. Every Sunday, people who have left the block take the lonely ride back, dragging their increasingly discontented children with them. They spend the day talking, not always with words, about the trouble they've seen and the trouble—one must watch their eyes as they watch their children—they are only too likely to see. For children do not like ghettos. It takes them nearly no time to discover exactly why they are there.

The projects in Harlem are hated. They are hated almost as much as policemen, and this is saying a great deal. And they are hated for the same reason: both reveal, unbearably, the real attitude of the white world, no matter how many liberal speeches are made, no matter how many lofty editorials are written, no matter how many civil-rights commissions are set up.

The projects are hideous, of course, there being a law, apparently respected throughout the world, that popular housing shall be as cheerless as a prison. They are lumped all over Harlem, colorless, bleak, high, and revolting. The wide windows look out on Harlem's invincible and indescribable squalor: the Park Avenue railroad tracks, around which, about forty years ago, the present dark community began; the unrehabilitated houses, bowed down, it would seem, under the great weight of frustration and bitterness they contain; the dark, the ominous schoolhouses from which the child may emerge maimed, blinded, hooked, or enraged for life; and the churches, churches, block upon block of churches, niched in the walls like cannon in the walls of a fortress. Even if the administration of the projects were not so insanely humiliating (for example: one must report raises in salary to the management, which will then eat up the profit by raising one's rent; the management has the right to know who is staying in your apartment; the management can ask you to leave, at their discretion), the projects would still be hated because they are an insult to the meanest intelligence.

Harlem got its first private project, Riverton—which is now, naturally, a slum—about twelve years ago because at that time Negroes were not allowed to live in Stuyvesant Town. Harlem watched Riverton go up, therefore, in the most violent bitterness of spirit, and hated it long before the builders arrived. They began hating it at about the time people began moving out of their condemned houses to make room for this additional proof of how thoroughly the white world despised them. And they had scarcely moved in, naturally, before they began smashing windows, defacing walls, urinating in the elevators, and fornicating in the playgrounds. Liberals, both white and black, were appalled at the spectacle. I was appalled by the liberal innocence—or cynicism, which comes out in practice as much the same thing. Other people were delighted to be able to point to proof positive that nothing could be done to better the lot of the colored people. They were, and are, right in one respect: that nothing can be done as long as they are treated like colored people. The people in Harlem know they are living there because white people do not think they are good enough to live anywhere else. No amount of "improvement" can sweeten this fact. Whatever money is now being earmarked to improve this, or any other ghetto, might as well be burnt. A ghetto can be improved in one way only: out of existence.

Similarly the only way to police a ghetto is to be oppressive. None of Commissioner Kennedy's policemen, even with the best will in the world, have any way of understanding the lives led by the people they swagger about in two's and three's controlling. Their very presence is an insult, and it would be, even if they spent their entire day feeding gumdrops to children. They represent the force of the white world; and that world's real intentions are, simply, for that world's criminal profit and ease, to keep the black man corraled up here, in his place. The badge, the gun in the holster, and the swinging club make vivid what will happen should his rebellion become overt. Rare, indeed, is the Harlem citizen, from the most circumspect church member to the most shiftless adolescent, who does not have a long tale to tell of police incompetence, injustice, or brutality. I myself have witnessed and endured it more than once. The businessmen and racketeers also have a story. And so do the prostitutes. (And this is not, perhaps, the place to discuss Harlem's very complex attitude towards black policemen, nor the reasons, according to Harlem, that they are nearly all downtown.)

It is hard, on the other hand, to blame the policeman, blank, good-natured, thoughtless, and insuperably innocent, for being such a perfect representative of the people he serves. He, too, believes in good intentions and is astounded and offended when they are not taken for the deed. He has never, himself, done anything for which to be hated—which of us has?—and yet he is facing, daily and nightly, people who would gladly see him dead, and he knows it. There is no way for him not to know it: there are few things under heaven more unnerving than the silent, accumulating contempt and hatred of a people. He moves through Harlem, therefore, like an occupying soldier in a bitterly hostile country; which is precisely what, and where, he is, and is the reason he walks in two's and three's. And he is not the only one who knows why he is always in company: the people who are watching him know why, too. Any street meeting, sacred or secular, which he and his colleagues uneasily cover has as its explicit or implicit burden the cruelty and injustice of the white domination. And these days, of course, in terms increasingly vivid and jubilant, it speaks of the end of that domination. The white policeman, standing on a Harlem street corner, finds himself at the very center of the revolution now occurring in the world. He is not prepared for it—naturally, nobody is—and, what is possibly much more to the point, he is exposed, as few white people are, to the anguish of the black people around him. Even if he is gifted with the merest mustard grain of imagination, something must seep in. He cannot avoid observing that some of the children, in spite of their color, remind him of children he has known and loved, perhaps even of his own children. He knows that he certainly does not want *his* children living this way. He can retreat from his uneasiness in only one direction: into a callousness which very shortly becomes second nature. He becomes more callous, the population becomes more hostile, the situation grows more tense, and the police force is increased. One day, to everyone's astonishment, someone drops a match in the powder keg and everything blows up. Before the dust has settled or the blood congealed, editorials, speeches, and civil-rights commissions are loud in the land, demanding to know what happened. What happened is that Negroes want to be treated like men.

Negroes want to be treated like men: a perfectly straightforward statement, containing only seven words. People who have mastered Kant, Hegel, Shakespeare, Marx, Freud, and the Bible find this statement utterly impenetrable. The idea seems to threaten profound, barely conscious assumptions. A kind of panic paralyzes their features, as though they found themselves trapped on the edge of a steep place. I once tried to describe to a very well known American intellectual the conditions among Negroes in the South. My recital disturbed him and made him indignant; and he asked me in perfect innocence, "Why don't all the Negroes in the South move North?" I tried to explain what *has* happened, unfailingly, whenever a significant body of Negroes move North. They do not escape jim-crow: they merely encounter another, not-less-deadly variety. They do not move to

Chicago, they move to the South Side; they do not move to New York, they move to Harlem. The pressure within the ghetto causes the ghetto walls to expand, and this expansion is always violent. White people hold the line as long as they can, and in as many ways as they can, from verbal intimidation to physical violence. But inevitably the border which has divided the ghetto from the rest of the world falls into the hands of the ghetto. The white people fall back bitterly before the black horde; the landlords make a tidy profit by raising the rent, chopping up the rooms, and all but dispensing with the upkeep; and what has once been a neighborhood turns into a "turf." This is precisely what happened when the Puerto Ricans arrived in their thousands—and the bitterness thus caused is, as I write, being fought out all up and down those streets.

Northerners indulge in an extremely dangerous luxury. They seem to feel that because they fought on the right side during the Civil War, and won, that they have earned the right merely to deplore what is going on in the South, without taking any responsibility for it; and that they can ignore what is happening in Northern cities because what is happening in Little Rock or Birmingham is worse. Well, in the first place, it is not possible for anyone who has not endured both to know which is "worse." I know Negroes who prefer the South and white Southerners, because "At least there, you haven't got to play any guessing games!" The guessing games referred to have driven more than one Negro into the narcotics ward, the madhouse, or the river. I know another Negro, a man very dear to me, who says, with conviction and with truth, "The spirit of the South is the spirit of America." He was born in the North and did his military training in the South. He did not, as far as I can gather, find the South "worse"; he found it, if anything, all too familiar. In the second place, though, even if Birmingham *is* worse, no doubt Johannesburg, South Africa, beats it by several miles, and Buchenwald was one of the worst things that ever happened in the entire history of the world. The world has never lacked for horrifying examples; but I do not believe that these examples are meant to be used as justification for our own crimes. This perpetual justification empties the heart of all human feeling. The emptier our hearts become, the greater will be our crimes. Thirdly, the South is not merely an embarrassingly backward region, but a part of this country, and what happens there concerns every one of us.

As far as the color problem is concerned, there is but one great difference between the Southern white and the Northerner: the Southerner remembers, historically, and in his own psyche, a kind of Eden in which he loved black people and they loved him. Historically, the flaming sword laid across this Eden is the Civil War. Personally, it is the Southerner's sexual coming of age, when, without any warning, unbreakable taboos are set up between himself and his past. Everything, thereafter, is permitted him except the love he remembers and has never ceased to need. The resulting, indescribable torment affects every Southern mind and is the basis of the Southern hysteria.

None of this is true for the Northerner. Negroes represent nothing to him personally, except, perhaps, the dangers of carnality. He never sees Negroes. Southerners see them all the time. Northerners never think about them whereas Southerners are never really thinking of anything else. Negroes are, therefore, ignored in the North and are under surveillance in the South, and suffer hideously in both places. Neither the Southerner nor the Northerner is able to look on the Negro simply as a man. It seems to be indispensable to the national self-esteem that the Negro be considered either as a kind of ward (in which case we are told how many Negroes, comparatively, bought Cadillacs last year and how few, comparatively, were lynched), or as a victim (in which case we are promised that he will never vote in our assemblies or go to school with our kids). They are two sides of the same coin and the South will not change—*cannot* change—until the North changes. The country will not change until it re-examines itself and discovers what it really means by freedom. In the meantime, generations keep being born, bitterness is increased by incompetence, pride, and folly, and the world shrinks around us.

It is a terrible, an inexorable, law that one cannot deny the humanity of another without diminishing one's own: in the face of one's victim, one sees oneself. Walk through the streets of Harlem and see what we, this nation, have become.

There is a culture of poverty that is different from poverty *per se*. It is a way of life that develops among the poor. The underdeveloped nations present a particularly fertile field for the study of this subculture, and if economic development is to successfully combat poverty in these nations, it must go hand in hand with changes in the values and attitudes of the poor.

The Culture of Poverty

Oscar Lewis

In the nineteenth century, when the social sciences were still in their infancy, the job of recording the effects of the process of industrialization and urbanization on personal and family life was left to novelists, playwrights, journalists, and social reformers. Today, a similar process of culture change is going on among the peoples of the less-developed countries but we find no comparable outpouring of a universal literature which would help us to improve our understanding of the process and the people. And yet the need for such an understanding has never been more urgent, now that the less-developed countries have become a major force on the world scene.

In the case of the new African nations that are emerging from a tribal, nonliterate cultural tradition, the paucity of a great native literature on the lower class is not surprising. In Mexico and in other Latin American countries where there has been a middle class, from which most writers come, this class has been very small. Moreover, the hierarchical nature of Mexican society has inhibited any profound communication across class lines. An additional factor in Mexico has been the preoccupation of both writers and anthropologists with their Indian problem, to the neglect of the urban poor.

This situation presents a unique opportunity to the social sciences and particularly to anthropology to step into the gap and develop a literature of its own. Sociologists, who have pioneered in studying urban slums, are now concentrating their attention on suburbia to the relative neglect of the poor. Today, even most novelists are so busy probing the middle-class soul that they have lost touch with the problems of poverty and the realities of a changing world. As C. P. Snow has recently stated: "Sometimes I am afraid that people in rich countries . . . have so completely forgotten what it is like to be poor that we can no longer feel or talk with the less lucky. This we must learn to do."

It is the anthropologists, traditionally the spokesmen for primitive people in the remote corners of the world, who are increasingly turning

From *The Children of Sanchez* by Oscar Lewis. Copyright © 1961 by Oscar Lewis. Reprinted by permission of Random House, Inc., and Martin Secker & Warburg, Ltd.

their energies to the great peasant and urban masses of the less-developed countries. These masses are still desperately poor in spite of the social and economic progress of the world in the past century. Over a billion people in seventy-five nations of Asia, Africa, Latin America, and the Near East have an average per capita income of less than $200 a year as compared with over $2,000 a year for the United States. The anthropologist who studies the way of life in these countries has become, in effect, the student and spokesman of what I call the culture of poverty.

To those who think that the poor have no culture, the concept of a culture of poverty may seem like a contradiction in terms. It would also seem to give to poverty a certain dignity and status. This is not my intention. In anthropological usage the term culture implies, essentially, a design for living which is passed down from generation to generation. In applying this concept of culture to the understanding of poverty, I want to draw attention to the fact that poverty in modern nations is not only a state of economic deprivation, of disorganization, or of the absence of something. It is also something positive in the sense that it has a structure, a rationale, and defense mechanisms without which the poor could hardly carry on. In short, it is a way of life, remarkably stable and persistent, passed down from generation to generation along family lines. The culture of poverty has its own modalities and distinctive social and psychological consequences for its members. It is a dynamic factor which affects participation in the larger national culture and becomes a subculture of its own.

The culture of poverty, as here defined, does not include primitive peoples whose backwardness is the result of their isolation and undeveloped technology and whose society for the most part is not class stratified. Such peoples have a relatively integrated, satisfying, and self-sufficient culture. Nor is the culture of poverty synonymous with the working class, the proletariat, or the peasantry, all three of which vary a good deal in economic status throughout the world. In the United States, for example, the working class lives like an elite compared to the lower class of the less-developed countries. The culture of poverty would apply only to those people who are at the very bottom of the socio-economic scale, the poorest workers, the poorest peasants, plantation laborers, and that large heterogenous mass of small artisans and tradesmen usually referred to as the lumpen proletariat.

The culture or subculture of poverty comes into being in a variety of historical contexts. Most commonly it develops when a stratified social and economic system is breaking down or is being replaced by another, as in the case of the transition from feudalism to capitalism or during the industrial revolution. Sometimes it results from imperial conquest in which the conquered are maintained in a servile status which may continue for many generations. It can also occur in the process of detribalization such

THE CULTURE OF POVERTY

as is now going on in Africa where, for example, the tribal migrants to the cities are developing "courtyard cultures" remarkably similar to the Mexico City *vecindades*. We are prone to view such slum conditions as transitional or temporary phases of drastic culture change. But this is not necessarily the case, for the culture of poverty is often a persisting condition even in stable social systems. Certainly in Mexico it has been a more or less permanent phenomenon since the Spanish conquest of 1519, when the process of detribalization and the movement of peasants to the cities began. Only the size, location, and composition of the slums have been in flux. I suspect that similar processes have been going on in many other countries of the world.

It seems to me that the culture of poverty has some universal characteristics which transcend regional, rural-urban, and even national differences. In my earlier book, *Five Families* (Basic Books, 1959), I suggested that there were remarkable similarities in family structure, interpersonal relations, time orientations, value systems, spending patterns, and the sense of community in lower-class settlements in London, Glasgow, Paris, Harlem, and Mexico City. Although this is not the place for an extensive comparative analysis of the culture of poverty, I should like to elaborate upon some of these and other traits in order to present a provisional conceptual model of this culture based mainly upon my Mexican materials.

In Mexico, the culture of poverty includes at least the lower third of the rural and urban population. This population is characterized by a relatively higher death rate, a lower life expectancy, a higher proportion of individuals in the younger age groups, and, because of child labor and working women, a higher proportion of gainfully employed. Some of these indices are higher in the poor *colonias* or sections of Mexico City than in rural Mexico as a whole.

The culture of poverty in Mexico is a provincial and locally oriented culture. Its members are only partially integrated into national institutions and are marginal people even when they live in the heart of a great city. In Mexico City, for example, most of the poor have a very low level of education and literacy, do not belong to labor unions, are not members of a political party, do not participate in the medical care, maternity, and old-age benefits of the national welfare agency known as *Seguro Social*, and make very little use of the city's banks, hospitals, department stores, museums, art galleries and airports.

The economic traits which are most characteristic of the culture of poverty include the constant struggle for survival, unemployment and underemployment, low wages, a miscellany of unskilled occupations, child labor, the absence of savings, a chronic shortage of cash, the absence of food reserves in the home, the pattern of frequent buying of small quantities of food many times a day as the need arises, the pawning of personal goods, borrowing from local money lenders at usurious rates of interest, spontaneous informal credit devices (*tandas*) organized by neighbors, and the use of second-hand clothing and furniture.

Some of the social and psychological characteristics include living in crowded quarters, a lack of privacy, gregariousness, a high incidence of alcoholism, frequent resort to violence in the settlement of quarrels, frequent use of physical violence in the training of children, wife beating, early initiation into sex, free unions or consensual marriages, a relatively high incidence of the abandonment of mothers and children, a trend toward mother-centered families and a much greater knowledge of maternal relatives, the predominance of the nuclear family, a strong predisposition to authoritarianism, and a great emphasis upon family solidarity—an ideal only rarely achieved. Other traits include a strong present time orientation with relatively little ability to defer gratification and plan for the future, a sense of resignation and fatalism based upon the realities of their difficult life situation, a belief in male superiority which reaches its crystallization in *machismo* or the cult of masculinity, a corresponding martyr complex among women, and finally, a high tolerance for psychological pathology of all sorts.

Some of the above traits are not limited to the culture of poverty in Mexico but are also found in the middle and upper classes. However, it is the peculiar patterning of these traits which defines the culture of poverty. For example, in the middle class, *machismo* is expressed in terms of sexual exploits and the Don Juan complex whereas in the lower class it is expressed in terms of heroism and lack of physical fear. Similarly, drinking in the middle class is a social amenity whereas in the lower class getting drunk has different and multiple functions—to forget one's troubles, to prove one's ability to drink, and to build up sufficient confidence to meet difficult life situations.

Many of the traits of the subculture of poverty can be viewed as attempts at local solutions for problems not met by existing institutions and agencies because the people are not eligible for them, cannot afford them, or are suspicious of them. For example, unable to obtain credit from banks, they are thrown upon their own resources and organize informal credit devices without interest. Unable to afford doctors, who are used only in dire emergencies, and suspicious of hospitals "where one goes only to die," they rely upon herbs or other home remedies and upon local curers and midwives. Critical of priests "who are human and therefore sinners like all of us," they rarely go to confession or Mass and rely upon prayer to the images of saints in their own homes and upon pilgrimages to popular shrines.

A critical attitude toward some of the values and institutions of the dominant classes, hatred of the police, mistrust of government and those in high position, and a cynicism which extends even to the church gives the culture of poverty a counter-quality and a potential for being used in political movements aimed against the existing social order. Finally, the sub-culture of poverty also has a residual quality in the sense that its members are attempting to utilize and integrate into a workable way of life the rem-nants of beliefs and customs of diverse origins.

. . . About a million and a half people out of a total population of ap-proximately four million in Mexico City live in . . . [poverty conditions]. The persistence of poverty in the first city of the nation fifty years after the great Mexican Revolution raises serious questions about the extent to which the Revolution has achieved its social objectives. . . .

This assertion is made in the full knowledge of the impressive and far-reaching changes which have been brought about by the Mexican Revolu-tion—the transformation of a semifeudal economy, the distribution of land to the peasants, the emancipation of the Indian, the strengthening of labor's position, the spread of public education, the nationalization of oil and the railroads, and the emergence of a new middle class. Since 1940 the economy has been expanding and the country has become acutely production con-scious. Leading newspapers report daily in their headlines record-breaking achievements in agriculture and industry and proudly announce huge gold reserves in the national treasury. A boom spirit has been created which is reminiscent of the great expansion in the United States at the turn of the century. Since 1940 the population has increased by over thirteen million, to reach a high of thirty-four million in 1960. The growth of Mexico City has been phenomenal, from one and a half million in 1940 to over four million in 1960. Mexico City is now the largest city in Latin America and the third or fourth largest city on the American continent.

One of the most significant trends in Mexico since 1940 has been the increasing influence of the United States on Mexican life. Never before in the long history of U.S.-Mexican relations has there been such a varied and intense interaction between the two countries. The close co-operation during World War II, the rapid tempo of U.S. investment, which has reached almost a billion dollars as of 1960, the remarkable influx of U.S. tourists into Mexico and of Mexican visitors to the United States, the annual migra-tion of several hundred thousand Mexican agricultural workers to the United States, the exchange of students, technicians and professors, and the increasing number of Mexicans who are becoming U.S. citizens have made for a new type of relationship between the two countries.

The major television programs are sponsored by foreign controlled companies like Nestlé, General Motors, Ford, Procter & Gamble and Col-gate. Only the use of the Spanish language and Mexican artists distinguish the commercials from those in the United States. American department-store retail practices have been made popular in most of the large cities by stores like Woolworth's and Sears Roebuck and Co., and self-service super-markets now package many American brand foods for the growing middle class. English has replaced French as a second language in the schools, and the French tradition in medicine is slowly but surely being replaced by U.S. medicine.

Despite the increased production and the apparent prosperity, the uneven distribution of the growing national wealth has made the disparity between the incomes of the rich and the poor more striking than ever before. And despite some rise in the standard of living for the general population, in 1956 over 60 percent of the population were still ill fed, ill housed, and ill clothed, 40 percent were illiterate, and 46 percent of the nation's children were not going to school. A chronic inflation since 1940 has squeezed the real income of the poor, and the cost of living for workers in Mexico City has risen over five times since 1939. According to the census of 1950 (published in 1955), 89 percent of all Mexican families reporting income earned less than 600 *pesos* a month, or $69 at the 1950 rate of exchange and $48 at the 1960 rate. (There are 12.50 *pesos* to the dollar.) A study published in 1960 by a competent Mexican economist, Ifigenia M. de Navarrete, showed that between 1950 and 1957 approximately the lower third of the national population suffered a decrease in real income.

It is common knowledge that the Mexican economy cannot give jobs to all of its people. From 1942 to 1955 about a million and a half Mexicans came to the United States as *braceros* or temporary agricultural laborers, and this figure does not include "wetbacks" or other illegal immigrants. Were the United States suddenly to close its borders to the *braceros,* a major crisis would probably occur in Mexico. Mexico also has become increasingly dependent upon the U.S. tourist trade to stabilize its economy. In 1957 over 700,000 tourists from the United States spent almost six hundred million dollars in Mexico, to make tourism the single largest industry in the country. The income from the tourist trade is about equal to the total Mexican federal budget.

One aspect of the standard of living which has improved very little since 1940 is housing. With the rapidly rising population and urbanization, the crowding and slum conditions in the large cities are actually getting worse. Of the 5.2 million dwellings reported in the Mexican census of 1950, 60 percent had only one room and 25 percent two rooms; 70 percent of all houses were made of adobe, wood, poles and rods, or rubble, and only 18 percent of brick and masonry. Only 17 percent had private, piped water.

In Mexico City conditions are no better. The city is made more beautiful each year for U.S. tourists by building new fountains, planting flowers along the principal streets, building new hygienic markets, and driving the beggars and vendors off the streets. But over a third of the city's population lives in slumlike housing settlements known as *vecindades* where they suffer from a chronic water shortage and lacking elementary sanitary facilities. Usually, *vecindades* consist of one or more rows of single-story dwellings with one or two rooms, facing a common courtyard. The dwellings are constructed of cement, brick, or adobe and form a well-defined unit that has some of the characteristics of a small community. The size and types of the *vecindades* vary enormously. Some consist of only a few dwellings, others of a few hundred. Some are found in the commercial heart of the city, in run-down sixteenth- and seventeenth-century two- and three-story Spanish colonial buildings, while others, on the outskirts of the city, consist of wooden shacks or *jacales* and look like semitropical Hoovervilles.

It seems to me that . . . [a study of the life style of the poor] has important implications for our thinking and our policy in regard to the under-developed countries of the world and particularly Latin America. It highlights the social, economic, and psychological complexities which have to be faced in any effort to transform and eliminate the culture of poverty from the world. It suggests that basic changes in the attitudes and value systems of the poor must go hand in hand with improvements of the material conditions of living.

Even the best-intentioned governments of the underdeveloped countries face difficult obstacles because of what poverty has done to the poor. . . . Yet with all of their inglorious defects and weaknesses, it is the poor who emerge as the true heroes of contemporary Mexico, for they are paying the cost of the industrial progress of the nation. Indeed, the political stability of Mexico is grim testimony to the great capacity for misery and suffering of the ordinary Mexican. But even the Mexican capacity for suffering has its limits, and unless ways are found to achieve a more equitable distribution of the growing national wealth and a greater equality of sacrifice during the difficult period of industrialization, we may expect social upheavals, sooner or later.

Within our affluent society, largely ignored and unseen, at least 25 percent of the population are being maimed in body and spirit by the conditions of poverty. They are locked in by their circumstances, with little hope or opportunity for emancipation.

The Invisible Land

Michael Harrington

There is a familiar America. It is celebrated in speeches and advertised on television and in the magazines. It has the highest mass standard of living the world has ever known.

In the 1950's this America worried about itself, yet even its anxieties were products of abundance. The title of a brilliant book was widely misinterpreted, and the familiar America began to call itself "the affluent society." There was introspection about Madison Avenue and tail fins; there was discussion of the emotional suffering taking place in the suburbs. In all this, there was an implicit assumption that the basic grinding economic problems had been solved in the United States. In this theory the nation's problems were no longer a matter of basic human needs, of food, shelter, and clothing. Now they were seen as qualitative, a question of learning to live decently amid luxury.

While this discussion was carried on, there existed another America. In it dwelt somewhere between 40,000,000 and 50,000,000 citizens of this land. They were poor. They still are.

To be sure, the other America is not impoverished in the same sense as those poor nations where millions cling to hunger as a defense against starvation. This country has escaped such extremes. That does not change the fact that tens of millions of Americans are, at this very moment, maimed in body and spirit, existing at levels beneath those necessary for human decency. If these people are not starving, they are hungry, and sometimes fat with hunger, for that is what cheap foods do. They are without adequate housing and education and medical care.

The Government has documented what this means to the bodies of the poor, and the figures will be cited throughout this book. But even more basic, this poverty twists and deforms the spirit. The American poor are pessimistic and defeated, and they are victimized by mental suffering to a degree unknown in Suburbia.

This . . . is a description of the world in which these people live; it is about the other America. Here are the unskilled workers, the migrant

Reprinted by permission of The Macmillan Company from *The Other America* by Michael Harrington. © by Michael Harrington 1962.

farm workers, the aged, the minorities, and all the others who live in the economic underworld of American life. In all this, there will be statistics, and that offers the opportunity for disagreement among honest and sincere men. I would ask the reader to respond critically to every assertion, but not to allow statistical quibbling to obscure the huge, enormous, and intolerable fact of poverty in America. For, when all is said and done, the fact is unmistakable, whatever its exact dimensions, and the truly human reaction can only be outrage. As W. H. Auden wrote:

> Hunger allows no choice
> To the citizen or the police;
> We must love one another or die.

The millions who are poor in the United States tend to become increasingly invisible. Here is a great mass of people, yet it takes an effort of the intellect and will even to see them.

I discovered this personally in a curious way. After I wrote my first article on poverty in America, I had all the statistics down on paper. I had proved to my satisfaction that there were around 50,000,000 poor in this country. Yet, I realized I did not believe my own figures. The poor existed in the Government reports; they were percentages and numbers in long, close columns, but they were not part of my existence. I could prove that the other America existed, but I had never been there.

My response was not accidental. It was typical of what is happening to an entire society, and it reflects profound social changes in this nation. The other America, the America of poverty, is hidden today in a way that it never was before. Its millions are socially invisible to the rest of us. No wonder that so many misinterpreted Galbraith's title and assumed that "the affluent society" meant that everyone had a decent standard of life. The misinterpretation was true as far as the actual day-to-day lives of two-thirds of the nation were concerned. Thus, one must begin a description of the other America by understanding why we do not see it.

There are perennial reasons that make the other America an invisible land.

Poverty is often off the beaten track. It always has been. The ordinary tourist never left the main highway, and today he rides interstate turnpikes. He does not go into the valleys of Pennsylvania where the towns look like movie sets of Wales in the thirties. He does not see the company houses in rows, the rutted roads (the poor always have bad roads whether they live in the city, in towns, or on farms), and everything is black and dirty. And even if he were to pass through such a place by accident, the tourist would not meet the unemployed men in the bar or the women coming home from a runaway sweatshop.

Then, too, beauty and myths are perennial masks of poverty. The traveler comes to the Appalachians in the lovely season. He sees the hills, the streams, the foliage—but not the poor. Or perhaps he looks at a run-down mountain house and, remembering Rousseau rather than seeing with his eyes, decides that "those people" are truly fortunate to be living the way they are and that they are lucky to be exempt from the strains and tensions of the middle class. The only problem is that "those people," the quaint inhabitants of those hills, are undereducated, underprivileged, lack medical care, and are in the process of being forced from the land into a life in the cities, where they are misfits.

These are normal and obvious causes of the invisibility of the poor. They operated a generation ago; they will be functioning a generation hence. It is more important to understand that the very development of American society is creating a new kind of blindness about poverty. The poor are increasingly slipping out of the very experience and consciousness of the nation.

If the middle class never did like ugliness and poverty, it was at least aware of them. "Across the tracks" was not a very long way to go. There were forays into the slums at Christmas time; there were charitable organizations that brought contact with the poor. Occasionally, almost everyone passed through the Negro ghetto or the blocks of tenements, if only to get downtown to work or to entertainment.

Now the American city has been transformed. The poor still inhabit the miserable housing in the central area, but they are increasingly isolated from contact with, or sight of, anybody else. Middle-class women coming in from Suburbia on a rare trip may catch the merest glimpse of the other America on the way to an evening at the theater, but their children are segregated in suburban schools. The business or professional man may drive along the fringes of slums in a car or bus, but it is not an important experience to him. The failures, the unskilled, the disabled, the aged, and the minorities are right there, across the tracks, where they have always been. But hardly anyone else is.

In short, the very development of the American city has removed poverty from the living, emotional experience of millions upon millions of middle-class Americans. Living out in the suburbs, it is easy to assume that ours is, indeed, an affluent society.

This new segregation of poverty is compounded by a well-meaning ignorance. A good many concerned and sympathetic Americans are aware that there is much discussion of urban renewal. Suddenly, driving through the city, they notice that a familiar slum has been torn down and that there are towering, modern buildings where once there had been tenements or hovels. There is a warm feeling of satisfaction, of pride in the way things are working out: the poor, it is obvious, are being taken care of.

The irony in this . . . is that the truth is nearly the exact opposite to the impression. The total impact of the various housing programs in post-war America has been to squeeze more and more people into existing slums. More often than not, the modern apartment in a towering building rents at $40 a room or more. For, during the past decade and a half, there has been more subsidization of middle- and upper-income housing than there has been housing for the poor.

Clothes make the poor invisible too: America has the best-dressed poverty the world has ever known. For a variety of reasons, the benefits of mass production have been spread much more evenly in this area than in many others. It is much easier in the United States to be decently dressed than it is to be decently housed, fed, or doctored. Even people with terribly depressed incomes can look prosperous.

This is an extremely important factor in defining our emotional and existential ignorance of poverty. In Detroit the existence of social classes became much more difficult to discern the day the companies put lockers in the plants. From that moment on, one did not see men in work clothes on the way to the factory, but citizens in slacks and white shirts. This process has been magnified with the poor throughout the country. There are tens of thousands of Americans in the big cities who are wearing shoes, perhaps even a stylishly cut suit or dress, and yet are hungry. It is not a matter of planning, though it seems as if the affluent society had given out costumes to the poor so that they would not offend the rest of society with the sight of rags.

Then, many of the poor are the wrong age to be seen. A good number of them (over 8,000,000) are sixty-five years of age or better; an even larger number are under eighteen. The aged members of the other America are often sick, and they cannot move. Another group of them live out their lives in loneliness and frustration: they sit in rented rooms, or else they stay close to a house in a neighborhood that has completely changed from the old days. Indeed, one of the worst aspects of poverty among the aged is that these people are out of sight and out of mind, and alone.

The young are somewhat more visible, yet they too stay close to their neighborhoods. Sometimes they advertise their poverty through a lurid tabloid story about a gang killing. But generally they do not disturb the quiet streets of the middle class.

And finally, the poor are politically invisible. It is one of the cruelest ironies of social life in advanced countries that the dispossessed at the bottom of society are unable to speak for themselves. The people of the other America do not, by far and large, belong to unions, to fraternal organizations, or to political parties. They are without lobbies of their own; they put forward no legislative program. As a group, they are atomized. They have no face; they have no voice.

Thus, there is not even a cynical political motive for caring about the poor, as in the old days. Because the slums are no longer centers of powerful political organizations, the politicians need not really care about their inhabitants. The slums are no longer visible to the middle class, so much of the idealistic urge to fight for those who need help is gone. Only the social agencies have a really direct involvement with the other America, and they are without any great political power.

To the extent that the poor have a spokesman in American life, that role is played by the labor movement. The unions have their own particular idealism, an ideology of concern. More than that, they realize that the existence of a reservoir of cheap, unorganized labor is a menace to wages and working conditions throughout the entire economy. Thus, many union legislative proposals—to extend the coverage of minimum wage and social security, to organize migrant farm laborers—articulate the needs of the poor.

That the poor are invisible is one of the most important things about them. They are not simply neglected and forgotten as in the old rhetoric of reform; what is much worse, they are not seen.

One might take a remark from George Eliot's *Felix Holt* as a basic statement of what this book is about:

> . . . there is no private life which has not been determined by a wider public life, from the time when the primeval milkmaid had to wander with the wanderings of her clan, because the cow she milked was one of a herd which had made the pasture bare. Even in the conservatory existence where the fair Camellia is sighed for by the noble young Pineapple, neither of them needing to care about the frost or rain outside, there is a nether apparatus of hot-water pipes liable to cool down on a strike of the gardeners or a scarcity of coal.
>
> And the lives we are about to look back upon do not belong to those conservatory species; they are rooted in the common earth, having to endure all the ordinary chances of past and present weather.

Forty to 50,000,000 people are becoming increasingly invisible. That is a shocking fact. But there is a second basic irony of poverty that is equally important: if one is to make the mistake of being born poor, he should choose a time when the majority of the people are miserable too.

J. K. Galbraith develops this idea in *The Affluent Society,* and in doing so defines the "newness" of the kind of poverty in contemporary America. The old poverty, Galbraith notes, was general. It was the condition of life of an entire society, or at least of that huge majority who were without special skills or the luck of birth. When the entire economy advanced, a

good many of these people gained higher standards of living. Unlike the
poor today, the majority poor of a generation ago were an immediate (if
cynical) concern of political leaders. The old slums of the immigrants had
the votes; they provided the basis for labor organizations; their very numbers could be a powerful force in political conflict. At the same time the
new technology required higher skills, more education, and stimulated an
upward movement for millions.

Perhaps the most dramatic case of the power of the majority poor took
place in the 1930's. The Congress of Industrial Organizations literally organized millions in a matter of years. A labor movement that had been
declining and confined to a thin stratum of the highly skilled suddenly em-
braced masses of men and women in basic industry. At the same time this
acted as a pressure upon the Government, and the New Deal codified some
of the social gains in laws like the Wagner Act. The result was not a basic
transformation of the American system, but it did transform the lives of an
entire section of the population.

In the thirties one of the reasons for these advances was that misery
was general. There was no need then to write books about unemployment
and poverty. That was the decisive social experience of the entire society,
and the apple sellers even invaded Wall Street. There was political sympathy
from middle-class reformers; there were an élan and spirit that grew out of
a deep crisis.

Some of those who advanced in the thirties did so because they had
unique and individual personal talents. But for the great mass, it was a question of being at the right point in the economy at the right time in history,
and utilizing that position for common struggle. Some of those who failed
did so because they did not have the will to take advantage of new opportunities. But for the most part the poor who were left behind had been at the
wrong place in the economy at the wrong moment in history.

These were the people in the unorganizable jobs, in the South, in the
minority groups, in the fly-by-night factories that were low on capital and
high on labor. When some of them did break into the economic mainstream
—when, for instance, the CIO opened up the way for some Negroes to find
good industrial jobs—they proved to be as resourceful as anyone else. As a
group, the other Americans who stayed behind were not originally composed primarily of individual failures. Rather, they were victims of an impersonal process that selected some for progress and discriminated against
others.

Out of the thirties came the welfare state. Its creation had been stimulated by mass impoverishment and misery, yet it helped the poor least of
all. Laws like unemployment compensation, the Wagner Act, the various
farm programs, all these were designed for the middle third in the cities, for
the organized workers, and for the upper third in the country, for the big
market farmers. If a man works in an extremely low-paying job, he may not

even be covered by social security or other welfare programs. If he receives unemployment compensation, the payment is scaled down according to his low earnings.

One of the major laws that was designed to cover everyone, rich and poor, was social security. But even here the other Americans suffered discrimination. Over the years social security payments have not even provided a subsistence level of life. The middle third have been able to supplement the Federal pension through private plans negotiated by unions, through joining medical insurance schemes like Blue Cross, and so on. The poor have not been able to do so. They lead a bitter life, and then have to pay for that fact in old age.

Indeed, the paradox that the welfare state benefits those least who need help most is but a single instance of persistent irony in the other America. Even when the money finally trickles down, even when a school is built in a poor neighborhood, for instance, the poor are still deprived. Their entire environment, their life, their values, do not prepare them to take advantage of the new opportunity. The parents are anxious for the children to go to work; the pupils are pent up, waiting for the moment when their education has complied with the law.

Today's poor, in short, missed the political and social gains of the thirties. They are, as Galbraith rightly points out, the first minority poor in history, the first poor not to be seen, the first poor whom the politicians could leave alone.

The first step toward the new poverty was taken when millions of people proved immune to progress. When that happened, the failure was not individual and personal, but a social product. But once the historic accident takes place, it begins to become a personal fate.

The new poor of the other America saw the rest of society move ahead. They went on living in depressed areas, and often they tended to become depressed human beings. In some of the West Virginia towns, for instance, an entire community will become shabby and defeated. The young and the adventurous go to the city, leaving behind those who cannot move and those who lack the will to do so. The entire area becomes permeated with failure, and that is one more reason the big corporations shy away.

Indeed, one of the most important things about the new poverty is that it cannot be defined in simple, statistical terms. Throughout this book a crucial term is used: aspiration. If a group has internal vitality, a will—if it has aspiration—it may live in dilapidated housing, it may eat an inadequate diet, and it may suffer poverty, but it is not impoverished. So it was in those ethnic slums of the immigrants that played such a dramatic role in the unfolding of the American dream. The people found themselves in slums, but they were not slum dwellers.

But the new poverty is constructed so as to destroy aspiration; it is a system designed to be impervious to hope. The other America does not contain the adventurous seeking a new life and land. It is populated by the fail-ures, by those driven from the land and bewildered by the city, by old people suddenly confronted with the torments of loneliness and poverty, and by minorities facing a wall of prejudice.

In the past, when poverty was general in the unskilled and semiskilled work force, the poor were all mixed together. The bright and the dull, those who were going to escape into the great society and those who were to stay behind, all of them lived on the same street. When the middle third rose, this community was destroyed. And the entire invisible land of the other Ameri-cans became a ghetto, a modern poor farm for the rejects of society and of the economy.

It is a blow to reform and the political hopes of the poor that the middle class no longer understands that poverty exists. But, perhaps more important, the poor are losing their links with the great world. If statistics and sociology can measure a feeling as delicate as loneliness . . . , the other America is becoming increasingly populated by those who do not be-long to anybody or anything. They are no longer participants in an ethnic culture from the old country; they are less and less religious; they do not be-long to unions or clubs. They are not seen, and because of that they them-selves cannot see. Their horizon has become more and more restricted; they see one another, and that means they see little reason to hope.

Galbraith was one of the first writers to begin to describe the newness of contemporary poverty, and that is to his credit. Yet because even he underestimates the problem, it is important to put his definition into per-spective.

For Galbraith, there are two main components of the new poverty: case poverty and insular poverty. Case poverty is the plight of those who suffer from some physical or mental disability that is personal and individ-ual and excludes them from the general advance. Insular poverty exists in areas like the Appalachians or the West Virginia coal fields, where an entire section of the country becomes economically obsolete.

Physical and mental disabilities are, to be sure, an important part of poverty in America. The poor are sick in body and in spirit. But this is not an isolated fact about them, an individual "case," a stroke of bad luck. Disease, alcoholism, low IQ's, these express a whole way of life. They are, in the main, the effects of an environment, not the biographies of unlucky individuals. Because of this, the new poverty is something that cannot be dealt with by first aid. If there is to be a lasting assault on the shame of the other America, it must seek to root out of this society an entire environment, and not just the relief of individuals.

But perhaps the idea of "insular" poverty is even more dangerous. To speak of "islands" of the poor (or, in the more popular term, of "pockets of poverty") is to imply that one is confronted by a serious, but relatively minor, problem. This is hardly a description of a misery that extends to

40,000,000 or 50,000,000 people in the United States. They have remained impoverished in spite of increasing productivity and the creation of a welfare state. That fact alone should suggest the dimensions of a serious and basic situation.

And yet, even given these disagreements with Galbraith, his achievement is considerable. He was one of the first to understand that there are enough poor people in the United States to constitute a subculture of misery, but not enough of them to challenge the conscience and the imagination of the nation.

Finally, one might summarize the newness of contemporary poverty by saying: These are the people who are immune to progress. But then the facts are even more cruel. The other Americans are the victims of the very inventions and machines that have provided a higher living standard for the rest of the society. They are upside-down in the economy, and for them greater productivity often means worse jobs; agricultural advance becomes hunger.

In the optimistic theory, technology is an undisguised blessing. A general increase in productivity, the argument goes, generates a higher standard of living for the whole people. And indeed, this has been true for the middle and upper thirds of American society, the people who made such striking gains in the last two decades. It tends to overstate the automatic character of the process, to omit the role of human struggle. (The CIO was organized by men in conflict, not by economic trends.) Yet it states a certain truth— for those who are lucky enough to participate in it.

But the poor, if they were given to theory, might argue the exact opposite. They might say: Progress is misery.

As the society becomes more technological, more skilled, those who learn to work the machines, who get the expanding education, move up. Those who miss out at the very start find themselves at a new disadvantage. A generation ago in American life, the majority of the working people did not have high-school educations. But at that time industry was organized on a lower level of skill and competence. And there was a sort of continuum in the shop: the youth who left school at sixteen could begin as a laborer, and gradually pick up skill as he went along.

Today the situation is quite different. The good jobs require much more academic preparation, much more skill from the very outset. Those who lack a high-school education tend to be condemned to the economic underworld—to low-paying service industries, to backward factories, to sweeping and janitorial duties. If the fathers and mothers of the contemporary poor were penalized a generation ago for their lack of schooling, their children will suffer all the more. The very rise in productivity that created more money and better working conditions for the rest of the society can be a menace to the poor.

But then this technological revolution might have an even more disastrous consequence: it could increase the ranks of the poor as well as intensify the disabilities of poverty. At this point it is too early to make any final judgment, yet there are obvious danger signals. There are millions of Americans who live just the other side of poverty. When a recession comes, they are pushed onto the relief rolls. (Welfare payments in New York respond almost immediately to any economic decline.) If automation continues to inflict more and more penalties on the unskilled and the semi-skilled, it could have the impact of permanently increasing the population of the other America.

Even more explosive is the possibility that people who participated in the gains of the thirties and the forties will be pulled back down into poverty. Today the mass-production industries where unionization made such a difference are contracting. Jobs are being destroyed. In the process, workers who had achieved a certain level of wages, who had won working conditions in the shop, are suddenly confronted with impoverishment. This is particularly true for anyone over forty years of age and for members of minority groups. Once their job is abolished, their chances of ever getting similar work are very slim.

It is too early to say whether or not this phenomenon is temporary, or whether it represents a massive retrogression that will swell the numbers of the poor. To a large extent, the answer to this question will be determined by the political response of the United States in the sixties. If serious and massive action is not undertaken, it may be necessary for statisticians to add some old-fashioned, pre-welfare-state poverty to the misery of the other America.

Poverty in the 1960's is invisible and it is new, and both these factors make it more tenacious. It is more isolated and politically powerless than ever before. It is laced with ironies, not the least of which is that many of the poor view progress upside-down, as a menace and a threat to their lives. And if the nation does not measure up to the challenge of automation, poverty in the 1960's might be on the increase.

II

There are mighty historical and economic forces that keep the poor down; and there are human beings who help out in this grim business, many of them unwittingly. There are sociological and political reasons why poverty is not seen; and there are misconceptions and prejudices that literally blind the eyes. The latter must be understood if anyone is to make the necessary act of intellect and will so that the poor can be noticed.

Here is the most familiar version of social blindness: "The poor are that way because they are afraid of work. And anyway they all have big cars. If they were like me (or my father or my grandfather), they could pay their own way. But they prefer to live on the dole and cheat the taxpayers."

This theory, usually thought of as a virtuous and moral statement, is one of the means of making it impossible for the poor ever to pay their way. There are, one must assume, citizens of the other America who choose impoverishment out of fear of work (though, writing it down, I really do not believe it). But the real explanation of why the poor are where they are is that they made the mistake of being born to the wrong parents, in the wrong section of the country, in the wrong industry, or in the wrong racial or ethnic group. Once that mistake had been made, they could have been paragons of will and morality, but most of them would never even have had a chance to get out of the other America.

There are two important ways of saying this: The poor are caught in a vicious circle; or, The poor live in a culture of poverty.

In a sense, one might define the contemporary poor in the United States as those who, for reasons beyond their control, cannot help themselves. All the most decisive factors making for opportunity and advance are against them. They are born going downward, and most of them stay down. They are victims whose lives are endlessly blown round and round the other America.

Here is one of the most familiar forms of the vicious circle of poverty. The poor get sick more than anyone else in the society. That is because they live in slums, jammed together under unhygienic conditions; they have inadequate diets, and cannot get decent medical care. When they become sick, they are sick longer than any other group in the society. Because they are sick more often and longer than anyone else, they lose wages and work, and find it difficult to hold a steady job. And because of this, they cannot pay for good housing, for a nutritious diet, for doctors. At any given point in the circle, particularly when there is a major illness, their prospect is to move to an even lower level and to begin the cycle, round and round, toward even more suffering.

This is only one example of the vicious circle. Each group in the other America has its own particular version of the experience, and these will be detailed throughout this book. But the pattern, whatever its variations, is basic to the other America.

The individual cannot usually break out of this vicious circle. Neither can the group, for it lacks the social energy and political strength to turn its misery into a cause. Only the larger society, with its help and resources, can really make it possible for these people to help themselves. Yet those who could make the difference too often refuse to act because of their ignorant, smug moralisms. They view the effects of poverty—above all, the warping of the will and spirit that is a consequence of being poor—as choices. Understanding the vicious circle is an important step in breaking down this prejudice.

There is an even richer way of describing this same, general idea: Poverty in the United States is a culture, an institution, a way of life.

There is a famous anecdote about Ernest Hemingway and F. Scott

Fitzgerald. Fitzgerald is reported to have remarked to Hemingway, "The rich are different." And Hemingway replied, "Yes, they have money." Fitzgerald had much the better of the exchange. He understood that being rich was not a simple fact, like a large bank account, but a way of looking at reality, a series of attitudes, a special type of life. If this is true of the rich, it is ten times truer of the poor. Everything about them, from the condition of their teeth to the way in which they love, is suffused and permeated by the fact of their poverty. And this is sometimes a hard idea for Hemingway-like middle-class America to comprehend.

The family structure of the poor, for instance, is different from that of the rest of the society. There are more homes without a father, there is less marriage, more early pregnancy and, if Kinsey's statistical findings can be used, markedly different attitudes toward sex. As a result of this, to take but one consequence of the fact, hundreds of thousands, and perhaps millions, of children in the other America never know stability and "normal" affection.

Or perhaps the policeman is an even better example. For the middle class, the police protect property, give directions, and help old ladies. For the urban poor, the police are those who arrest you. In almost any slum there is a vast conspiracy against the forces of law and order. If someone approaches asking for a person, no one there will have heard of him, even if he lives next door. The outsider is "cop," bill collector, investigator (and, in the Negro ghetto, most dramatically, he is "the Man").

While writing this book, I was arrested for participation in a civil-rights demonstration. A brief experience of a night in a cell made an abstraction personal and immediate: the city jail is one of the basic institutions of the other America. Almost everyone whom I encountered in the "tank" was poor: skid-row whites, Negroes, Puetro Ricans. Their poverty was an incitement to arrest in the first place. (A policeman will be much more careful with a well-dressed, obviously educated man who might have political connections than he will with someone who is poor.) They did not have money for bail or for lawyers. And, perhaps most important, they waited their arraignment with stolidity, in a mood of passive acceptance. They expected the worst, and they probably got it.

There is, in short, a language of the poor, a psychology of the poor, a world view of the poor. To be impoverished is to be an internal alien, to grow up in a culture that is radically different from the one that dominates the society. The poor can be described statistically; they can be analyzed as a group. But they need a novelist as well as a sociologist if we are to see them. They need an American Dickens to record the smell and texture and quality of their lives. The cycles and trends, the massive forces, must be seen as affecting persons who talk and think differently. . . .

What shall we tell the American poor, once we have seen them? Shall we say to them that they are better off than the Indian poor, the Italian poor, the Russian poor? That is one answer, but it is heartless. I should put it another way. I want to tell every well-fed and optimistic American that it is intolerable that so many millions should be maimed in body and in spirit when it is not necessary that they should be. My standard of comparison is not how much worse things used to be. It is how much better they could be if only we were stirred.

For 380,000 "original" Americans, poverty is a way of life. Unemployment is staggering. Housing is substandard. Education has been neglected. Health services are minimal. The Navajos on their reservation in Arizona are a good example of poverty surrounded by opulence, and of the "invisible poor." Their circumstances demonstrate how the definition of poverty is relative to the situation.

Where the Real Poverty Is: Plight of American Indians

U.S. News & World Report

The American Indians—long out of sight and out of mind on their isolated reservations—are getting a fresh burst of attention in Washington.

Congress is being asked to vote more money for Indians' need. More help through the antipoverty program also is promised.

A committee of the Senate has jumped on the Bureau of Indian Affairs for its handling of education and other matters on reservations. Top officials of the Bureau met in Santa Fe, N.M., April 12–15, to begin an overhaul of the agency.

If Indians themselves take the promise of better days ahead with a large grain of salt, the reason is not far to seek. They have been promised better things ever since the white man began to move westward two centuries ago.

Today, abject poverty is a way of life for the average Indian. Yet the antipoverty dollars and workers that abound in big-city slums are just beginning to move to Indian reservations.

So-called *de facto* segregation existed in Indian schools long before civil-rights advocates coined the phrase. It still is the rule, not the exception. Yet, there's no busing of large numbers of white children to integrate Indian classrooms.

And medical care? On Southwestern reservations, thousands of Indians are blind, or going blind, from trachoma, an eye disease. But Government health services for Indians have been spread too thin to control the disease.

A Look at One Tribe

Typical of the plight of many tribes today is that of the Navajos. Their reservation is located in the northeastern corner of Arizona, with some land extending eastward into New Mexico and northward into Utah.

The Navajo reservation is a vast desolate land—15 million acres of desert, semi-arid plains, and mountains. Here live more than one fourth of all Indians on reservations today. Life for them contrasts sharply with that in the affluent society of the white man in such cities as Phoenix, Albuquerque and Denver, each only a few hours' drive away.

Living within the vastness of Navajo-land is a population somewhere between 106,000 and 120,000. An exact count is not possible because many families in remote areas have children without reporting them. A total of 380,000 Indians are on U.S. reservations.

When the Navajos roamed the Southwest at will, they were a proud and self-sufficient tribe. Their freedom ended with "The Long Walk" in 1865. That year, Col. Kit Carson and his troopers climaxed a ruthless, scorched-earth campaign against the Navajos by rounding up 9,000 of their men, women and children. This band was marched 300 miles to Fort Sumner, in New Mexico. The Navajos spent three years in exile.

In 1868, the U.S. Government signed a treaty with the Navajos and returned them to a reservation in their homeland. Over the years, the reservation has been expanded to its present 15 million acres.

Dineh and the Anglos

The Navajos still are a proud people. They call themselves *Dineh*, which means "the people." Americans are called "Anglos."

Navajos consider themselves superior to other Indians and other races. But tribal leaders at Window Rock, capital of the reservation, grapple with problems as monumental as those in many an underdeveloped country.

Poverty is widespread. While an income of below $3,000 a year may mean poverty in the "Great Society" of the white man, a Navajo family with that kind of money is well-to-do in the eyes of other Navajos.

Illiteracy is the rule rather than the exception. Under the 1868 treaty, the U.S. Government is supposed to give Navajo children a free education. Even so, 7 out of 10 adults are unable to read or write the English language.

Unemployment on the reservation is so high as to make so-called pockets of poverty in other parts of the U.S. look prosperous. Raymond Nakai, tribal chairman, estimates that 19,000 are jobless out of a total work force of 30,000.

Housing is substandard by any measure. Most Navajo families live in hogans—small, circular huts of log and adobe without running water or electricity. Others live in frame houses that, if anything, are less adequate than the hogans.

Infant mortality is high. It averages out at 40.3 deaths per thousand births in the first year of life. That compares to a U.S. average of 25.3.

Yet, despite high infant mortality, Navajo leaders face a population explosion. Numbers are increasing at the rate of about 3 to 4 per cent a year. The U.S. average is 1.5 per cent.

The Federal Government has been spending more than 50 million dollars a year to improve the Navajos' lot. Most of this, 36.7 million this year, is spent by the Bureau of Indian Affairs, known simply as the BIA. The rest is spent by the U.S. Public Health Service.

Kill and Cure

Says a BIA official: "People often ask: 'You've been running Indian affairs for 150 years. Why haven't you made more progress?' They forget that for the first 100 of these years we were busy killing off Indians, rounding them up, and pushing them as far out of the way as possible onto reservations in isolated areas. Only in the last generation have we made any real effort to bring the Indians into modern life."

BIA's major effort on the reservation is education. There are 48 boarding schools on the reservation. Nearly half the Navajo children must attend these because distances are too great to bus them to and from their homes. Other children go to BIA day schools and to mission schools. A few attend public schools with white children.

School attendance has improved markedly in recent years. In the 1951–52 school year, only 13,135 were in class out of a school-age population of 26,336. In the 1964–65 school year, the comparable figures were 40,256 out of 45,969. Still, that leaves nearly 6,000 children outside classrooms.

Large numbers of children arrive at school age speaking only Navajo. To help them overcome this handicap, the Bureau has preschool classes in which 6-year-olds get a year of training in the English language.

Despite all the money spent on schools, many Navajo leaders feel that the educational effort misses the mark.

A Navajo's Story

One of these is Peter McDonald, a Navajo who left the reservation to get a college education and a good job, but has returned to try to help his people.

The trouble with BIA schooling, as Mr. McDonald sees it, is that the Indian children are taught "to be like a white man, and think like a white man." The result, says Mr. McDonald: "They completely lose their self-identity as Navajos. They can't live within their own culture and they can't live in the affluent society of the white man. So you get mixed-up kids, and they give up. This is happening to many of our young people between the ages of 16 and 30."

Mr. McDonald knows from personal experience what it is like to be poor and mixed up. He dropped out of school in the sixth grade. First, he studied with his grandfather to be a medicine man—a profession still widely accepted by the Navajos. Many an educated Navajo believes that a medicine man can cure illnesses that defy modern medicine.

At the age of 15, Mr. McDonald joined the Marine Corps. After his discharge, he completed the equivalent of four years of high school in one year. Then he got a degree in electrical engineering at the University of Oklahoma. He worked for seven years for Hughes Aircraft Company. During that time, he won a master's degree at the University of California at Los Angeles.

Three years ago, Mr. McDonald left a promising career in industry and came back to the reservation to work for betterment of his people. He now heads the Navajos' antipoverty program, which gets its funds from the Office of Economic Opportunity in Washington.

Opening Rounds

The "war on poverty" is off to a small start on the Navajo reservation. Mr. McDonald thinks it offers the best opportunity Indians have had to lick their basic problems.

"Operation Head Start," funded with $500,000, now is under way at 25 locations with 700 children enrolled. Mr. McDonald says it is a big improvement over the "preschools" of the BIA because children can begin learning English sooner. He has asked for 2.5 million dollars to expand "Head Start" to at least 3,000 children at 150 locations.

Mr. McDonald is determined to get a college on Navajo land because: "No matter how much we do in economic development, so long as we don't have a college on the reservation, this place will never blossom." He hopes to get $27,000 in antipoverty funds for a study that will lead to establishment of a junior college.

Most important, tribal leaders say, is a manpower-development and training program. They have asked for 20 million dollars from the Office of Economic Opportunity to finance such a program.

Training programs of the past, in Mr. McDonald's view, "have only created a sense of frustration because, for all the talk, we're not getting people to the job or jobs to the people. Those who are trained often can't land a job because they don't have the apprenticeship, or the union qualifications."

What is needed, according to Navajo leaders, is a plan to take the unskilled Navajo all the way through testing, counseling, remedial education, on-the-job training, apprenticeship and finally into the job itself.

Richest of the Poor

For all their individual poverty, the Navajos are far better off than most other tribes. Their land is rich in minerals—coal, gas, oil, uranium, helium. Bonuses and royalties of more than $200 million have poured into the tribal treasury since 1950. Of this, about $85 million remains.

But mineral income has been declining and tribal spending has been increasing. This year the tribal budget is $26 million, against income of only a little more than $11 million.

"At the rate we're going, we'll be broke in about five years," says a member of the tribal council.

A big hope of Navajo leaders is that the tribe can attract enough industry to the reservation to provide jobs for at least some of the 19,000 now unemployed. A small beginning has been made.

At Shiprock, N.M., 300 young Navajo women now are in a work-training program in a plant of the Fairchild Semiconductor division of Fairchild Camera & Instrument Corporation.

Sixty women work at a B.V.D. Company plant in Winslow, Ariz., south of the reservation. If the Navajo women show that they are able machine operators, the B.V.D. Company may establish several plants on the reservation. According to BIA officials, the women have been turning out T shirts at a rate 30 per cent above expectations.

For the future, 30 to 40 firms have expressed interest in putting plants on the reservation. Of these, 11 have shown "strong interest" and negotiations now are in progress with six of them.

If all 11 companies should go through with plans discussed, between 5,000 and 11,000 jobs would be created.

Mining the Coal

The tribe also is beginning to cash in on its coal reserves, estimated at 758 million tons and one of the largest remaining deposits in the U.S. Until recently, this coal supply had been untapped because it was so low in quality that shipping it any distance was uneconomic.

But now, with long-distance transmission of electricity possible through new developments, steam generating plants are being built at mine sites.

Already in operation are three plants of the Arizona Public Service Company.

On April 12, negotiations were completed for two giant steam generation plants that will tap Navajo coal beds. A group of 21 private and public electric utilities known as WEST will build the plants—at Farmington, N.M., and at Mohave, Nev. The latter plant is to get coal from the reservation through a coal-slurry pipeline.

"These two plants, along with those already in operation, will make the Four Corners as big as any power center in the United States," says Washington lawyer Norman M. Littell, general counsel and claims attorney for the Navajos. Four Corners is the area where the states of Arizona, New Mexico, Colorado and Utah meet.

Thus, the outlook is not all bleak at Window Rock where Navajo leaders try to cope with the present and plan for the future.

Control of Navajo affairs rests in the tribal council, made up of 74 representatives elected from 97 chapters on the reservation. Because so many Navajos are illiterate, ballots present both names and pictures of the candidates.

Politicking is one lesson that the Navajos have learned well from the whites. Elections are to be held in November, and already the air at Window Rock is filled with charges and countercharges of corruption and inefficiency.

This preoccupation with politics hampers the Navajos, according to J. Bruce Wiley, a Denver management consultant who advises the tribe on its antipoverty program.

"The trouble is that anything one faction suggests is prima facie evidence to the opposing faction that it is no good," says Mr. Wiley. "Until real leadership emerges, we're going to have practically no progress at all."

The Council in Session

The tribal council meets four times a year at Window Rock in a round, hogan-shaped building with huge, polished wooden beams radiating outward from the center. The white plaster walls are adorned with frescos of Navajo life and history.

The men dress in their go-to-town uniform of cowboy boots, Levis, plaid shirts, short jackets and Western hats.

Older women wear long skirts of flowered cotton or pleated satin with overblouses of velvet, topped off by colorful hand-woven shawls. Younger women wear blouses cut like cowboy shirts with flared skirts or tapered slacks.

Old ways on the reservation are undergoing gradual change. While a herd of sheep still is the major status symbol and evidence of wealth among the older Navajos, younger ones seem to prefer a new status symbol—the pickup truck, preferably blue or light green.

Some of the younger generation are getting away to college. There is a scholarship fund derived from interest on 10 million dollars on deposit in the U.S. Treasury. In the 1964–65 academic year, 536 Navajos entered college. Of these, 122 dropped out. In the current year, 596 are in college.

The Relocation Program

As with other Indian tribes, there have been attempts to move Navajos off the reservation into the mainstream of U.S. life.

Under the "direct employment-assistance program" started in 1952, a total of 6,500 Navajo men and women have been relocated in such areas as San Francisco, Los Angeles, Denver, Dallas, Chicago and Cleveland. The Government pays transportation and initial living expenses and helps the Navajo find a home and a job.

A BIA official estimates that about one third have returned to the reservation. Mr. McDonald, however, puts the figure closer to 50 per cent and says:

"One reason for this failure is that people from the reservation haven't learned to live with people outside. As a result, many have tagged relocation as not the right thing to do. Now others don't want to leave because they feel the program is unsuccessful."

But basically, says Mr. McDonald, most Navajos feel that "the reservation is their home and they want to make a go of this place."

Bootstrap Businesses

One of the most hopeful omens for the future has been the success of the Navajos in self-help projects, says Graham Holmes, BIA superintendent on the reservation.

One such project is the 10-million-dollar sawmill of the Navajo Forest Products Industries north of Window Rock. This enterprise is owned by the tribe and managed by a group of Navajos and outside experts. The sawmill, largest in New Mexico, employs 450 persons. More than 90 per cent are Navajos. Annual payroll is 1.5 million dollars.

In 1965, the sawmill did a gross business of 3.5 million dollars and had a net profit of $450,000. Profits were plowed back into the business.

Other tribal enterprises include two restaurants, a gift shop and a one-third interest in a Window Rock bank.

The tribe also gets a share of the profits from several motels in Arizona and New Mexico. And the tribe has $100,000 invested in a marina on Lake Powell, the reservoir behind Glen Canyon Dam recently completed on the Colorado River.

A major enterprise is the Navajo Tribal Utility Authority, launched in 1960. It now has 212 employes, and 1,367 customers for gas, 4,029 for electricity and 980 for water and sewerage.

This fledgling utility, admittedly, has made only a tiny beginning on this vast reservation. Tribal leaders, however, are optimistic about its future. They say that, as more jobs are created, living standards will rise, and there will be more utility customers. The result will be more jobs in the utility.

Clearly, this illustrates the basic problem for the Navajos: how to start an economic cycle that will feed on itself, generating more and more jobs and better and better living conditions.

Broken Promises

Another problem, say Navajo leaders, is that the white man still tries to push the Indian around on occasion. As an immediate example, they point to a big irrigation project promised for the reservation from the Government's development of the San Juan River.

When the project was authorized by Congress, the tribe was promised enough water to irrigate 110,630 acres—enough to support more than 1,000 families. Now, say tribal leaders, the Government wants to provide only enough water for around 75,000 acres, taking the rest of the water to augment supplies for areas in New Mexico, mainly Albuquerque.

Officials of the Interior Department, which is in charge of the work, say the project is being restudied to determine the feasibility of irrigation of all the acreage first planned.

The project is now under construction, with enough water due to arrive in 1971 to irrigate 10,000 acres. Target date for finishing the project is 1980.

Is there any solution in sight for the problems of American Indians?

One man who has spent a lifetime working with the Indians says that the most important step that could be taken to solve their problem would be to make the Bureau of Indian Affairs an independent agency because: "As long as the Bureau is in the Department of the Interior, its policies will change with every Administration and every whim of politicians in Washington."

With a more stable policy toward Indians, said this man, business and industry would be more likely to bring jobs to reservations.

"A Terrific Potential"

The need for jobs on the reservations is one thing on which there is widespread agreement. Says Mr. Wiley, the management consultant working with the Navajos:

"The actual potential for development is terrific.

"If I had guts enough to break loose from my status symbols, pull out and come here, not only could I become a millionaire, but I could start any one of a half dozen industries that could employ many hundreds of Navajos."

Thus, Mr. Wiley poses the big question: Will business and industry leaders take a chance in this desolate land where the latest status symbol is a pickup truck?

Poverty *per se* need not be a totally destructive force, but modern poverty tends to degrade its victims and impel them toward criminal behavior, violence, vice, disease, and other forms of personal disorganization. The affluent portion of a society will inevitably be affected by the presence of these elements because the sights, sounds, and smells of poverty cannot be shut out. Poverty is a public nuisance and a private misfortune.

How Much Is Enough?

George Bernard Shaw

It is generally agreed that poverty is a very uncomfortable misfortune for the individual who happens to be poor. But poor people, when they are not suffering from acute hunger and severe cold, are not more unhappy than rich people: they are often much happier. You can easily find people who are ten times as rich at sixty as they were at twenty; but not one of them will tell you that they are ten times as happy. All the thoughtful ones will assure you that happiness and unhappiness are constitutional, and have nothing to do with money. Money can cure hunger: it cannot cure unhappiness. Food can satisfy the appetite, but not the soul. A famous German Socialist, Ferdinand Lassalle, said that what beat him in his efforts to stir up the poor to revolt against poverty was their wantlessness. They were not, of course, content: nobody is; but they were not discontented enough to take any serious trouble to change their condition. It may seem a fine thing to a poor woman to have a large house, plenty of servants, dozens of dresses, a lovely complexion and beautifully dressed hair. But the rich woman who has these things often spends a good deal of her time travelling in rough places to get away from them. To have to spend two or three hours a day washing and dressing and brushing and combing and changing and being messed about generally by a lady's maid is not on the face of it a happier lot than to have only five minutes to spend on such fatigues, as the soldiers call them. Servants are so troublesome that many ladies can hardly talk about anything else when they get together. A drunken man is happier than a sober one: that is why unhappy people take to drink. There are drugs that will make you ecstatically happy whilst ruining your body and soul. It is our quality that matters: take care of that, and our happiness will take care of itself. People of the right sort are never easy until they get things straight; but they are too healthy and too much taken up with their occupations to bother about happiness. Modern poverty is not the poverty

From *Intelligent Woman's Guide to Socialism and Capitalism* by George Bernard Shaw. By permission of The Society of Authors, on behalf of the Bernard Shaw Estate.

that was blest in the Sermon on the Mount: the objection to it is not that
it makes people unhappy, but that it degrades them; and the fact that they ✗
can be quite as happy in their degradation as their betters are in their exal-
tation makes it worse. When Shakespear's king said

Then happy low, lie down:
Uneasy lies the head that wears a crown,

he forgot that happiness is no excuse for lowness. The divine spark in us
flashes up against being bribed to submit to degradation by mere happiness,
which a pig or a drunkard can achieve.

Such poverty as we have today in all our great cities degrades the poor,
and infects with its degradation the whole neighborhood in which they live.
And whatever can degrade a neighborhood can degrade a country and a ✗
continent and finally the whole civilized world, which is only a large
neighborhood. Its bad effects cannot be escaped by the rich. When poverty
produces outbreaks of virulent infectious disease, as it always does sooner
or later, the rich catch the disease and see their children die of it. When it
produces crime and violence the rich go in fear of both, and are put to a
good deal of expense to protect their persons and property. When it produces bad manners and bad language the children of the rich pick them up
no matter how carefully they are secluded; and such seclusion as they get
does them more harm than good. If poor and pretty young women find, as
they do, that they can make more money by vice than by honest work, they
will poison the blood of rich young men who, when they marry, will infect
their wives and children, and cause them all sorts of bodily troubles, sometimes ending in disfigurement and blindness and death, and always doing
them more or less mischief. The old notion that people can "keep themselves to themselves" and not be touched by what is happening to their
neighbors, or even to the people who live a hundred miles off, is a most
dangerous mistake. The saying that we are members one of another is not ✗
a mere pious formula to be repeated in church without any meaning: it is
a literal truth; for though the rich end of the town can avoid living with the
poor end, it cannot avoid dying with it when the plague comes. People will
be able to keep themselves to themselves as much as they please when they
have made an end of poverty; but until then they will not be able to shut
out the sights and sounds and smells of poverty from their daily walks, nor
to feel sure from day to day that its most violent and fatal evils will not
reach them through their strongest police guards.

Besides, as long as poverty remains possible we shall never be sure
that it will not overtake ourselves. If we dig a pit for others we may fall into
it: if we leave a precipice unfenced our children may fall over it when they
are playing. We see the most innocent and respectable families falling into
the unfenced pit of poverty every day; and how do we know that it will not
be our turn next?

It is perhaps the greatest folly of which a nation can be guilty to attempt to use poverty as a sort of punishment for offences that it does not send people to prison for. It is easy to say of a lazy man "Oh, let him be poor: it serves him right for being lazy: it will teach him a lesson." In saying so we are ourselves too lazy to think a little before we lay down the law. We cannot afford to have poor people anyhow, whether they be lazy or busy, drunken or sober, virtuous or vicious, thrifty or careless, wise or foolish. If they deserve to suffer let them be made to suffer in some other way; for mere poverty will not hurt them half as much as it will hurt their innocent neighbors. It is a public nuisance as well as a private misfortune. Its toleration is a national crime.

The disorder that has been rampant in urban centers recently is partly an out-
growth of the failure of government agencies to cope with the mounting needs
for public services. Frustration, dissatisfaction, tension, hostility, and an
urge to action have developed into serious problems for the police as a result
of the unresolved grievances. There must be concerted efforts to improve the
relationship between the poor and the rest of the community.

What Can Be Done?

Barbara Ritchie

The racial disorders during the summer of 1967 reflect, in part, the failure
at all levels of government—Federal and state as well as local—to come to
grips with the problems of our cities. The ghetto symbolizes the dilemma
created by a widening gap between human needs and public resources, and
a growing cynicism regarding the commitment of community institutions
and leadership to meet these needs.

The problem has many dimensions—financial, political, and institutional. Almost all cities, and particularly the central cities of the largest
metropolitan regions, are simply unable to meet the growing need for public services and facilities with the funds that can be raised from traditional
sources of municipal revenue. Many cities are structured politically in such
a way that great numbers of citizens, particularly minority groups, have
little or no representation in the processes of government. Finally, some
cities lack either the will or the capacity to use effectively the resources that
are available to them.

Instrumentalities of Federal and state government often compound
the problems. National policy, expressed through a very large number of
grant programs and institutions, rarely exhibits a coherent and consistent
perspective when viewed at the local level. State efforts, traditionally focused on rural areas, often fail to tie in effectively with either local or
Federal programs in urban areas.

Meanwhile, the decay of the central city continues. The revenue base
of the central city has been eroded by the retreat of industry and of middle-
class families to the suburbs. Its budget and tax rate have been inflated by
rising costs and increasing numbers of dependent citizens. And its public
plant—schools, hospitals, and correctional institutions—has deteriorated
because of age and long-deferred maintenance.

From *The Riot Report:* A Shortened Version of *The Report of the National Ad-
visory Commission on Civil Disorders* by Barbara Ritchie. Copyright © 1969 by
Barbara Ritchie. All rights reserved. Reprinted by permission of The Viking Press,
Inc., and Curtis Brown, Ltd.

Yet, to most citizens the decay remains largely invisible. Only their tax bills, and the headlines they read concerning crime or "riots," suggest that something may be seriously wrong with the city.

There are, however, two groups of people that live constantly with the problem of the city: public officials and the poor, particularly poor residents of the racial ghetto. The relationship of these two groups is a key factor in the development of conditions underlying civil disorders.

Our [the Commission's] investigations of the 1967 riot cities establish that:

> Virtually every major episode of urban violence in the summer of 1967 was foreshadowed by an accumulation of the unresolved grievances of ghetto residents against local authorities (often, but not always, the police). So high was the resulting underlying tension that routine and random events, tolerated or ignored under most circumstances (such as the raid on the "blind pig" in Detroit), became the triggers of sudden violence.
>
> Not only was there a high level of dissatisfaction, but confidence in the willingness and ability of local government to respond to Negro grievances was low. Evidence presented to this Commission in hearings, field reports, and reserach analyses of the 1967 riot cities establishes that a substantial number of Negroes were disturbed and angry about local governments' failures to solve their problems.

Several developments have converged to produce this volatile situation.

First, there is a widening gulf in communications between local government and the residents of the erupting ghettos of the city. As a result, many Negro citizens develop a profound sense of isolation and alienation from the processes and programs of government. Although all residents of our larger cities experience this lack of communication, it is much more difficult for the low-income, poorly educated citizens to overcome. And because the poor are disproportionately supported by and dependent upon programs administered by agencies of local government, it is they who more often are subject to real or imagined official discourtesy, seeming disinterest, or arbitrary administrative actions.

Further, as a result of the long history of racial discrimination, the grievances of Negroes often take on personal and symbolic significance transcending the immediate consequences of a particular event. For example, inadequate sanitation services are viewed by many ghetto residents as not merely instances of poor public service but as manifestations of racial discrimination. This perception reinforces existing feelings of alienation and contributes to a heightened level of frustration and dissatisfaction, not only with the administrators of the sanitation department but with all the representatives of local government. This is particularly true with respect to the police, who are the only public agents on duty in the ghetto twenty-four hours a day, and who bear the burden of a hostility toward the less visible elements of the system.

The lack of communication and the absence of regular contacts with ghetto residents prevent city leaders from learning about problems and grievances as they develop. As a result, tensions which could have been dissipated if responded to promptly mount unnecessarily, and the potential for explosion grows inevitably. And once disorder erupts, public officials are frequently unable to fashion an effective response. They lack adequate information about the nature of the trouble and its causes, and they lack rapport with local leaders who might be able to influence the community.

Second, many city governments are poorly organized to respond effectively to the needs of ghetto residents, even when those needs are made known to appropriate public officials.

Most middle-class city dwellers have limited contacts with local government. When contacts do occur, they tend to concern relatively narrow and specific problems. Furthermore, middle-class citizens, although subject to many of the same frustrations and resentments as ghetto residents in dealing with the public bureaucracy, find it relatively easy to locate the appropriate agency for help and redress. If they fail to get satisfaction, they can ask for the assistance of elected representatives, friends in government, or a lawyer. In short, the middle-class city dweller has relatively fewer needs for public services and is reasonably well positioned to move the system to his benefit.

On the other hand, the typical ghetto resident has interrelated social and economic problems which require the services of several government and private agencies. At the same time, he may be unable to identify his problems in terms of the complicated structure of government. Moreover, he may be unaware of his rights and opportunities under public programs and unable to obtain the necessary guidance from either public or private sources.

Current trends in municipal administration have had the effect of reducing the capacity of local government to respond effectively to these problems. The pressures for administrative efficiency and cost cutting have brought about the withdrawal of many operations of city government from direct contact with neighborhood and citizen. Red tape and administrative complexity have filled the vacuum created by the centralization of local government. The introduction of a merit system and a professionalized civil service has made management of the cities more business-like, but it has also tended to depersonalize and isolate government. And the rigid patterns of segregation prevalent within the central city have widened the distance between Negro citizens and the city hall.

In most of the riot cities surveyed by the Commission we found little or no meaningful coordination among city agencies, either in responding to the needs of ghetto residents on an ongoing basis or in planning to head

off disturbances. The consequences of this lack of coordination were particularly severe for the police. Despite the fact that they were being called
upon increasingly to deal with tensions and citizen complaints that often
had little, if anything, to do with police services, the police departments of
many large cities were isolated from other city agencies. Sometimes they
were isolated even from the mayor and his staff. In these cities, the police
were compelled to deal with ghetto residents angered over dirty streets,
dilapidated housing, unfair commercial practices, or inferior schools—
grievances which they had neither the responsibility for creating nor the
authority to redress.

Third, ghetto residents increasingly believe that they are excluded
from the decision-making process which affects their lives and community.
This feeling of exclusion, intensified by the bitter legacy of racial discrimination, has engendered a deep-seated hostility toward the institutions of
government. It has severely compromised the effectiveness of programs intended to provide improved services to ghetto residents.

In part, this is the lesson of Detroit, where well-intentioned programs,
designed to respond to the needs of ghetto residents, were not worked out
and implemented sufficiently in cooperation with the people who were
supposed to benefit from the programs. A report prepared for the Senate
Subcommittee on Employment, Manpower, and Poverty, presented just
prior to the riot in Detroit, found that:

> Area residents . . . complain almost continually that their
> demands for program changes are not heeded, that they have little
> voice in what goes on. . . . As much as the area residents are
> involved, listened to, and even heeded . . . it becomes fairly clear
> that the relationship is still one of superordinate-subordinate, rather
> than one of equals. . . . The procedures by which HRD (the
> Mayor's Committee for Human Resources Development, the De-
> troit Community Action Agency) operates generally admit the
> contributions of area residents only after programs have been writ-
> ten; after policies have already operated for a time or have already
> been formulated; and to a large degree, only in formal and in-
> frequent meetings rather than in day-to-day operations. . . . The
> meaningfulness of resident involvement is reduced by its after-the-
> fact nature and by the relatively limited resources residents have
> at their disposal.

Mayor Alfonso J. Cervantes of St. Louis was even more explicit. In
testimony before this Commission he stated:

> We have found that ghetto neighborhoods cannot be oper-
> ated on from outside alone. The people within them should have
> a voice, and our experience has shown that it is often a voice that
> speaks with good sense, since the practical aspect of the needs of
> the ghetto people are so much clearer to the people there than they
> are to anyone else.

The political system, traditionally an important vehicle for the effective participation of minorities in decisions affecting the distribution of public resources, has not worked for the Negro as it has for other groups. The reasons are fairly obvious.

We have found that the number of Negro officials in elected and appointed positions in the riot cities is minimal in proportion to the Negro population. The alienation of the Negro from the political process has been exacerbated by his racial and economic isolation.

Specifically, the needs of ghetto residents for social welfare and other public services have swelled dramatically at a time when increased affluence has diminished the need of the rest of the urban population for such services. By reducing disproportionately the economic disability of other portions of the population, particularly other ethnic urban minorities, this affluence has left the urban Negro few potential local allies with whom to make common cause for shared objectives. The development of political alliances, essential to effective participation of minority groups in the political process, has been further impaired by the polarization of the races, which on both sides has transformed economic considerations into racial issues.

Finally, these developments have coincided with the demise of the historic urban political machines and the growth of the city-manager concept of government (according to which the city manager is not publicly elected but appointed by the city council). While this tendency has produced major benefits in terms of honest and efficient administration, it has eliminated an important political link between city government and low-income residents.

These conditions have produced a vast and threatening disparity in perceptions of the intensity and validity of Negro dissatisfaction. Viewed from the perspective of the ghetto resident, city government appears distant and unconcerned, the possibility of effective change remote. As a result, tension rises perceptibly; the explosion comes as the climax to a progression of tension-generating incidents. To the city administration, unaware of this growing tension or unable to respond effectively to it, the outbreak of disorder comes as a shock.

No democratic society can long endure the existence within its major urban centers of a substantial number of citizens who feel deeply aggrieved as a group, yet lack confidence that the government will rectify perceived injustice, and confidence in their own ability to bring about needed change.

We are aware that reforms in existing instruments of local government, and reforms in their relationship to the ghetto population, will mean little unless joined with a sincere and comprehensive response to the severe social and economic needs of ghetto residents.

We believe that there are measures which can and should be taken now. They can be put to work without great cost and without delay. They can be built upon in the future. They will effectively reduce the level of grievance and tension as well as improve the responsiveness of local government to the needs of ghetto residents.

It is vital, however, that the first-phase programs not be regarded or perceived as short-term antiriot efforts, as merely today's stop-gap remedies for cooling already inflamed situations. These programs will have little chance of succeeding unless they are part of a long-range commitment to action designed to eliminate the fundamental sources of grievance and tension.

The Commission recommends that six first-phase actions be taken by large cities facing problems of unrest, dissatisfaction, and decay in their central cities.

Develop neighborhood action task forces. The task forces should be made up of representatives of both government and community. The goal would be to achieve more effective communication between government and ghetto residents and to provide an opportunity for effective citizen participation in decision making. The Commission believes that the task-force approach could bring the energies and resources of both city government and the private sector to bear on the real needs and priorities of low-income residents, and that it could do much to generate a new sense of community.

Establish effective grievance-response mechanisms. A grievance agency, separate from operating municipal agencies, should have general jurisdiction in grievances against all public agencies and authorities, and have the authority to investigate and make public its findings and recommendations. The grievance procedure should be easy for ghetto residents to use. It should guarantee that grievants be given full opportunity to take part in all proceedings and be represented by counsel.

Expand legal services for the poor. Among the most intense grievances underlying the riots of 1967 were those which derived from conflicts between ghetto residents and private parties, especially white landlords and merchants. Resourceful and imaginative use of available legal processes could contribute significantly to the alleviation of such tensions. But ghetto residents also have need for advocacy in a variety of other contexts. The local bar bears major responsibility for devising ways of bringing increased and more effective legal aid to the poor, such aid to be financed by increased private and public funding.

Provide assistance for mayors and city councils. The capacity of the Federal government to affect local problems depends to a great extent on the capacity of city government to respond competently to Federal government program initiatives. Therefore representatives of Federal programs, mayors, and city councils need to create new mechanisms to aid in decision making, program planning, and coordination. Both state and Federal governments should offer financial assistance for developing these new, critically needed mechanisms for cooperative effort.

Sponsor meetings of legislative bodies and ghetto residents. The city legislative body should hold a series of meetings on ghetto problems— with ghetto residents participating fully—for the purpose of identifying ghetto grievances that can best be addressed by legislative action, and establishing a foundation for needed legislation.

Expand employment of ghetto residents. Local government should make a concerted effort to provide substantial employment opportunities for ghetto residents through deliberate employment, training, and upgrading of Negroes. Municipal authorities should review civil-service policies and job standards and take prompt action to remove arbitrary barriers to employment. Employment qualification tests and police records should be given careful re-evaluation. Local government action in this vital area could stimulate private employers to take similar action.

Finally, there remains the issue of leadership. Now, as never before, the American city has need for the personal qualities of strong democratic leadership. Given the difficulties and delays involved in administrative reorganization or institutional change, the best hope for the city in the short run lies in this powerful instrument. In most cities, the mayor will have the prime responsibility.

It is in large part his role now to create a sense of commitment and concern for the problems of the ghetto community and to set the tone for the entire relationship between the institutions of city government and all the citizenry.

Part of the task is to interpret the problems of the ghetto community to the citizenry at large and to generate channels of communication between Negro and white leadership outside of government. Only if all the institutions of the community—those outside the government as well as those inside the structure—are implicated in the problems of the ghetto can the alienation and distrust of disadvantaged citizens be overcome.

This is now the decisive role of the urban mayor. As leader and mediator, he must involve all groups—employers, news media, unions, financial institutions, and others—which only together can bridge the chasm now separating the racial ghetto from the community. His goal, in effect, must be to develop a new working concept of democracy within the city.

In this effort, state government has a vital role to play. It must provide a fuller measure of financial and other resources to urban areas. The crisis confronting city government today cannot be met without regional cooperation. This cooperation can take many forms—metropolitan government, regional planning, and joint endeavors. But it must be the principal goal, and perhaps the overriding concern, of leadership at the state level to fashion a lasting and mutually productive relationship between city and suburban areas.

We have cited deep hostility between police and ghetto communities as a primary cause of the disorders surveyed by the Commission. In Newark, Detroit, Watts, and Harlem—in practically every city that has experienced racial disruption since the summer of 1964—abrasive relationships between police and Negroes and other minority groups have been a major source of grievance, tension, and ultimately, disorder.

In a fundamental sense, however, it is wrong to define the problem solely as hostility to police. In many ways, the policeman only symbolizes much deeper problems.

The policeman in the ghetto is a symbol not only of law but of the entire system of law enforcement and criminal justice.

As such, he becomes the tangible target for grievances against shortcomings throughout that system: against assembly-line justice in teeming lower courts; against wide disparities in sentences; against antiquated correctional facilities; against the basic inequities imposed by the system on the poor—to whom, for example, the option of bail means only jail.

The policeman in the ghetto is a symbol of increasingly bitter social debate over law enforcement.

One side, disturbed and perplexed by sharp rises in crime and urban violence, exerts extreme pressure on police for tougher law enforcement. Another group, inflamed against police as agents of repression, tends toward defiance of what it regards as order maintained at the expense of justice.

The policeman in the ghetto is the most visible symbol, finally, of a society from which many ghetto Negroes are increasingly alienated.

At the same time, police responsibilities in the ghetto are even greater than elsewhere in the community, since the other institutions of social control have so little authority there. This is true of the schools, because so many are segregated, old, and inferior; of religion, which has become irrelevant to those who have lost faith as they lost hope; of career aspirations, which for many young Negroes are totally lacking; and of the family, because its bonds are so often snapped. It is the policeman who must deal with the consequences of this institutional vacuum, and who is then resented for his presence and for the measures this effort demands.

Alone, the policeman in the ghetto cannot solve these problems. His role is already one of the most difficult in our society. He must deal daily with a range of problems and people that test his patience, ingenuity, character, and courage in ways in which few of us are ever tested. Without positive leadership, goals, operational guidance, and public support, the individual policeman can only feel victimized. Nor are these problems the responsibility only of police adminstrators; they are deep enough to tax the courage, intelligence, and leadership of mayors, city officials, and community leaders. As Dr. Kenneth B. Clark told the Commission:

> This society knows . . . that if human beings are confined
> in ghetto compounds of our cities, and are subjected to criminally
> inferior education and pervasive economic and job discrimination,
> committed to houses unfit for human habitation, subjected to un-

speakable conditions of municipal services, such as sanitation, that such human beings are not likely to be responsive to appeals to be lawful, to be respectful, to be concerned with property of others.

To a people imbued with a deep sense of injustice the police have come to symbolize a repressive force barring any hope of escape from the ills that beset them. And while society must aid police in taking every possible step to allay ghetto grievances, it is the police who must bear a major responsibility for making needed changes.

In the first instance, they have the prime responsibility for safeguarding the minimum goal of any civilized society: security of life and property. To do so, they are given society's maximum power: discretion in the use of force.

Second, it is axiomatic that effective law enforcement requires the support of the community. Such support will not be present when a substantial segment of the community feels threatened by the police and regards the police as an occupying force.

At the same time, public officials also have a clear duty to help the police make any necessary changes to minimize as far as possible the risk of further disorders.

To meet the needs arising from five basic problem areas, the Commission recommends that city government and police authorities:

Review police operations in the ghetto to ensure the proper conduct of police officers and eliminate abrasive practices.

Provide more adequate police protection to ghetto residents so as to eliminate their high sense of insecurity and their belief in the existence of a dual standard of law enforcement.

Establish fair and effective mechanisms for the redress of grievances against the police and other municipal employees.

Develop and adopt policy guidelines to assist officers in making critical decisions in areas where police conduct can create tension.

Attempt to insure widespread community support for law enforcement by:

(1) Developing and putting into practice innovative police-community relations programs.

(2) Recruiting more Negroes into the regular police force, and reviewing promotion policies to insure fair promotion for Negro officers.

(3) Establishing a community service officer program to attract ghetto youths between the ages of seventeen and twenty-one to police work. These junior officers would perform duties in ghetto neighborhoods but would not have full police authority. The Federal government should provide support equal to 90 per cent of the costs of employing community service officers on the basis of one for every ten regular officers.

Bibliography

Bazelon, David T. *Power in America*. New York: New American Library, 1967.

Committee on Education and Labor. *Poverty in the U.S.* Washington, D.C.: Government Printing Office, 1964.

Ferman, Louis A., ed. *Poverty in America*. Ann Arbor: University of Michigan Press, 1965.

Gordon, Margaret S., ed. *Poverty in America*. San Francisco: Chandler Publishing Co., 1965.

Harrington, Michael. *The Other America*. New York: Macmillan, 1962.

Larmer, Jeremy, and Howe, Irving. *Poverty: Views From the Left*. New York: William Morrow and Co., 1969.

Levitan, Sar A. *The Great Society's Poor Law: A New Approach to Poverty*. Baltimore: Johns Hopkins Press, 1969.

Miller, Herman P. *Rich Man, Poor Man*. New York: Thomas Y. Crowell, 1964.

Ornati, Oscar. *Poverty Amid Affluence*. New York: Twentieth Century Fund, 1966.

Proceedings of the First Annual Conference on Social Issues: Poverty: Four Approaches/Four Solutions. Eugene: University of Oregon Books, 1966.

Seligman, Ben B. *Aspects of Poverty*. New York: Thomas Y. Crowell, 1968.

Photo by Gerhard Gscheidle, Photo Find, S.F.

Famine

In 1798, Thomas Malthus in *An Essay on the Principle of Population* prophesied that population would one day outstrip food supply, and many authorities are telling us that his prophecy is now materializing in certain areas of the world. Malthus pointed out that food supply increases slowly as compared with the geometric multiplication of population, which snowballs with great momentum once it gets started. There is a simple story that illustrates this point. An employer told an employee that he would pay him $10,000 for a month's work or he would pay him one cent for the first day and double his pay every day thereafter for thirty days. The employee chose the $10,000 and thereby lost over five million dollars.

In 1940 the average annual increase in world population was one percent, and by 1961 it reached two percent. At the rate of increase of two percent, the world's population of three billion will reach 23 billion in 100 years, and at the rate of three percent it would reach 60 billion.

Population increases when the birth rate (total number of live births per 1,000 population per year) exceeds the death rate (total number of deaths per 1,000 population per year). It also may grow when immigration to an area is greater than emigration from the area.

Part of the food shortage problem today is due to increasing population in areas that are unable to increase the production of food at a rate sufficient to feed all of the people. Scientific treatment and control of disease have been introduced in the less developed countries, and the death rates have been significantly lowered. No equally effective steps have been taken to encourage lower birth rates or increased food production.

The countries referred to by such terms as underdeveloped, developing, and Third World are mainly in tropical and subtropical zones and have a pattern of low per capita income, poor educational opportunities, high child mortality rates, little industrialization and use of modern technology, antiquated agricultural methods, and meager transportation systems.

There is serious threat of widespread famine in these areas within the next five or ten years. The hunger that exists there at this time, however, is not the kind associated with literal, acute starvation. It is an insidious, incipient, suboptimal nutritional state that kills just as surely, but slowly, and is seldom recognized as death due to malnutrition. Malnutrition is prevalent and persistent in these areas and causes much of the high mortality, either directly or by lowering resistance to infections.

The most common nutritional deficiencies, lack of protein and Vitamin A, are manifested in the mortality rate for children one to five years of age. The rate is from twenty to fifty times higher in underdeveloped countries than in the United States and Western Europe. Children in the poorer countries are weaned early, and the food substitutes for milk are very poor. The lack of Vitamin A causes children to have trouble with their eyes, often resulting in blindness. Anemia, beriberi, pellagra, and other diseases associated with deficient diet are frequent. Poor nutrition also contributes significantly to such conditions as poor growth, poor psychological development, and mental retardation.

Malnutrition is costly in terms of both the wasted children who die before they are old enough to become useful citizens and those who are so impaired that they are forever inadequate. It takes its toll on adults, also, by making them lethargic, low in initiative and drive, and subject to ill health and disease.

It is estimated that two-thirds of the world population live in countries in which the average diet is considerably below the minimum nutritional level required for normal health and activity. There is no question that the overall world food supply is failing to keep pace with population growth, but, in accord with the prediction of Malthus, it is not limiting the world's explosive population increase. For perhaps millions of years the food supply was effective in limiting the growth of human population. It is only in the last few hundred years that means of obtaining food have improved to the point where food supply is not operating to impede population growth.

The development of agriculture made possible the production of surplus food supplies that in turn released the labor force necessary for the beginnings of an industrial society and urban centers in a few European and Asian countries. These areas have been able to provide for a slowly increasing population, but most of Asia and Africa is still relatively untouched by modern technology. On the other hand, the most rapidly expanding populations in the world are found in these countries.

From 1958 to 1964, world food production was about equal to the population increase, but in 1964 the population grew twice as fast as food resources. In the developed countries, the rate of agricultural production has increased, whereas in the underdeveloped areas it has decreased. At the same time, rate of population growth in underdeveloped countries has increased.

A comparison of the undeveloped countries with those that are in better circumstances shows the underdeveloped countries have less acreage per person, a higher population growth rate than the advanced countries ever had, almost no opportunity for emigration, and no significant usable uncultivated areas. The continuing imbalance between population and food supply will inevitably produce famine manifested as chronic undernourishment and the resultant poor health, disease, and premature death, which will vary in degree of intensity according to the region and social class.

Food supply depends to a great extent upon agriculture, which, it seems reasonable to think, is a matter of human effort and land. But there is much more involved if production is to reach more than subsistence level in most regions. Such things as fertilization, pest control, and methods of planting and cultivation of the soil are all very complex matters and require extensive scientific knowledge to determine the proper combinations for each type of soil and climate.

Tools are an important factor, also. Without efficient machinery, production suffers. The development of agricultural production depends on industry for mechanical tools, motorized equipment, chemicals for fertilizers and pesticides, and for the research that precedes the manufacture of such items. On the other hand, the availability of labor for industry is dependent on efficient agricultural production. Because of this interrelationship, agriculture and industry must progress concurrently.

Sporadic, piecemeal aid is as ineffective as attempts to promote agriculture without regard for industry. Furnishing seed to a given area for a couple of years, supplying fertilizer to another area, and sending machinery somewhere else is wasteful and useless. A thorough program, even in one small area at a time, is needed if there are to be lasting effects.

Advances in the agricultural productivity of underdeveloped countries will necessarily entail great social change, and the difficulties to be encountered in overcoming irrational beliefs, traditional habits and customs, and superstitions are great. Peasant societies do not readily abandon the security they know in exchange for a way of life that breaks up their familiar structure.

Such are the obstacles that must be surmounted in underdeveloped countries, but not all hunger is in Asia and Africa. Hunger and malnutrition affect millions of people in the United States as well. In 1968 a citizens' committee published findings of research they had conducted that shocked the public. They found that many babies in the United States die during their first year because of malnutrition and that many who do live suffer irreversible brain damage because of lack of protein in their diets. It is estimated that 30 to 70 percent of the children from poverty backgrounds have nutritional anemia due to protein and iron deficiency. Their growth and learning are retarded, and they are more susceptible to disease. Many old people live on liquids and starches, slowly starving. Children from affluent homes may be malnourished because of neglect of their diets and bad eating habits.

Undernourishment and malnutrition are subjects that have been largely ignored by the medical profession and other professions and agencies whose functions are related to the health of our people. Very little research has been done, and there is no authoritative source of information as to the extent of the problem in the United States. The Public Health Service, the Department of Agriculture, and the Department of Health, Education, and Welfare all concede that a problem exists, but not one of them can contribute any specific data, nor have they exhibited any degree of concern about becoming involved with the situation. Private charitable organizations such as CARE have been active in feeding programs for people in other countries, but there is not the same interest in the domestic scene.

It is commonly believed that the poor in this country are adequately fed through government aid in the form of surplus food programs, food stamps, free school lunches, and other such devices. More careful examination shows much of this assistance to be illusory. The facts indicate that slow starvation is going on within our own country, particularly among cotton field workers in Mississippi, coal miners in eastern Kentucky, migrant workers in California, and Indians of Arizona, New Mexico, and Oklahoma.

According to federal government statistics, there are approximately 8.75 million families or nearly 30 million persons in poverty. Only 5.4 million persons, or 18 percent of the poor, are benefiting from food programs, and the fact is that the diets of those receiving this aid are not much improved by the additional food. A national survey made in 1965 showed that two-thirds of America's poor are not receiving minimum nutrition.

Over 300 of the poorest counties in the United States have refused to have a food assistance program of any kind, hoping to starve out the elements they consider undesirable. Some counties discontinue the programs during seasons when labor is needed, so that the poor will be forced to work for subsistence wages.

The surplus commodity distribution program is one of the food assistance plans. It has been severely criticized by those who are familiar with its operation. It is under the jurisdiction of the Department of Agriculture and has a dual purpose—to keep farm crop prices high and to provide food for those in need. The food for distribution has been largely limited to the items in surplus at any given time, such as cornmeal, flour, nonfat dry milk, peanut butter, and rice, although there is legislation in effect which would permit the department to purchase other foods for this purpose. The amount of food provided is in most cases grossly inadequate, and many families run out days before the end of the month.

Some counties locate the distribution depots at remote, inaccessible places, so that those without transportation cannot reach them. Also, bulky goods are too heavy to carry because they are packaged in quantities equal to one month's supply. In fact, relatively few of our hungry people are benefiting from this program because barriers have been made insurmountable.

The Food Stamp Program was intended to supplement the commodity program. The two objectives of the plan are to multiply purchasing power and to provide for individual choice in the selection of food. Stamps are purchased for a fraction of their dollar value when traded at a retail food market. The lower the income of a family, the less the stamps cost. In all cases one or two large cash payments are required each month in order to obtain the stamps, because nothing less than the designated minimum amount can be purchased. This cash outlay is impossible for a large percentage of poor families because they do not receive enough cash to make the purchase. The whole problem results primarily from the use of "average" figures in each income class in determining the cost and amount of stamps, and, obviously, many are below the "average."

Most families use all of their stamps before the next issue, and they are forced to "charge" their purchases. The retail merchant extends credit on the condition that the buyer will pay him from the new allotment of stamps. Thus the customer creates an ongoing debt from which there is no escape. Many merchants raise their prices on the days that the food stamps are distributed. Food stamp offices are too often inconveniently located, and they also tend to keep irregular office hours.

Approximately 20 million children per year are being fed under the National School Lunch Program with lunches that are either free or at reduced prices. This program is one of the easiest and least expensive to administer, but it is failing to reach more than one-third of the children who need it. In 1967, of the 6 million children from poverty families, only 2 million were receiving free lunches. Many schools in low-income areas have no cafeteria, and when they do have the facilities, they cannot afford the program because the state must put up $3 for every $1 of federal support.

A school lunch is certainly better than no lunch, but children may be seriously damaged from malnutrition before they reach school age. Also, a child who has had no breakfast may be in great discomfort by lunch time. The program has much potential, however. For example, with the use of fortified foods, a child could be given in the one meal the minimum nutritional requirements for the day and thus be insured against serious deficiencies.

Obviously, new and unprecedented solutions must be found to meet the crisis of overpopulation and underproduction of food. In our own country, laws made for an earlier and different period of time must be made flexible or new, or more appropriate ones must be substituted. At the international level, the problem is graver. Social inequality has caused trouble in the United States to the extent that it has forced us to take steps toward eliminating some of the factors that have perpetuated that phenomenon. The inequalities between the developed and the underdeveloped nations are the basis of a similar problem that poses a threat to the whole world. Sooner or later the underdeveloped countries will be persuaded to unite in a common front. They may then seek elsewhere for the help and leadership that the Western world has failed to provide.

The problems of food and population can be solved only by the joint efforts of the rich and the poor countries on a scale never before attempted. There is no way of knowing exactly what programs will work best in trying to alleviate the stress, but once the goal is clear and the intent is sincere, a way will be found to reach the crux of the problem. Some general principles are emerging from research and from the contacts made on a more or less experimental basis. These principles indicate the general direction our endeavors should take. It is to be noted that basic to most of the proposed solutions is a change in values by the donors or the beneficiaries of assistance, or both. The recipients must accept some responsibility for their condition and be willing to compromise some of their older values for the opportunity to survive and to participate in the world on a more meaningful and broader scale. The donors will have to widen their horizons to include in their world some of the nations that have not held high priorities heretofore.

Some of the recommendations that have been made by those who have given much thought to this problem are worth considering:

1. There must be greater international cooperation so that enough food can be distributed in the poor countries to greatly reduce the malnutrition among the population at once. Mere acts of charity are not the answer. The World Health Organization (WHO) and the World Food Program should be supported by the general population in every country. To meet nutritional needs, food supplies in the developing countries will have to be doubled by 1985. The United States, Canada, Australia, and a

few other countries will be able to meet much of this increase by expanding their cultivated areas and raising the yields per acre. However, food aid, other than disaster relief, should be considered as only an interim program to be used while more permanent and long-range solutions are materializing.

2. Increased production leading to self-sufficiency should be the overall aim of programs of assistance, and the long-range objective should be replacing aid with trade. It is neither necessary nor desirable that each country produce all of the food it needs, but rather that countries be able to produce enough goods that can be traded for food items they may lack. Differing ideologies, motivations, and interests will produce many hindrances to progress in this direction, but steady, consistent effort may be able to accomplish enough to avert disaster. The problems cannot be solved in a year or ten years. Short-term, quick payout programs will not suffice. Subsistence agriculture must be replaced with market-oriented agriculture. This change calls for urbanization, industrialization, and the development of the whole economic structure of a nation.

3. Solution of the problem will require heavy capital investment for purchases of equipment and material for industrial plants that will manufacture fertilizers, pesticides, farm machinery and tools. A fund should be created, through regular contributions from the better developed countries, to be drawn upon for the advancement of the productive capacity of the poor countries. Such aid agencies as the World Bank, the International Development Association, and the United States Agency for International Development (AID) have begun to collaborate in the support of agricultural development.

4. The developing countries do not have enough technically trained people to do the work needed or even enough to train and educate others. Large-scale plans must be adopted for training, motivating, organizing, and supervising the native labor force in each area. Teachers, technicians, engineers, agronomists, and many other workers would be required to educate the peasants of these countries to use the fertilizers, insecticides, machinery, and tools necessary in modern agriculture. This task is one of the most difficult of all, because it not only includes the teaching of skills and techniques, but also the inculcation of new values and new goals. The education of largely illiterate populations concerning the benefits to be derived from a new way of life and new habits calls for great patience and perseverance.

5. To encourage the industrialization of backward countries, world markets must be planned to cover at least basic commodities. Universal free trade works to the disadvantage of the developing countries because of the fluctuating nature of the uncontrolled market. The developed countries should rely upon expanded consumption rather than restricted production for price stabilization. Some kind of international organization is needed for

carrying on continuing research to provide a basis for price fixing, for information on the markets, and as a basis for regulating production and trade.

6. The same difficulties arise when attempts are made to promote among the wealthier nations the development of world resources for the greater benefit of all peoples, such as those encountered in trying to educate backward peoples to values that are new to them. In both cases people are unwilling and resist change, particularly when it involves sacrificing something today for the promise of a reward in a future that they do not comprehend.

The above proposals are directed at hunger in the underdeveloped nations. The problem of hunger and malnutrition in the United States is relatively easy to deal with because the resources, the necessary personnel, and the transportation and communication facilities are all present and could be focused upon the condition almost immediately. But there is one very important prerequisite; there must be a firm, sincere commitment by the people of this country to the idea that an adequate diet should be available to every child. A commitment is different from pious platitudes in favor of helping the poor, appropriations of money to study conditions, and other kinds of lip service. It implies genuine feeling and conscientious resolution toward the objective. It calls for a modification of our value system whereby every individual would feel a sense of personal responsibility for seeing that all of our children will eat well instead of believing he is fulfilling his obligations by paying taxes that he cannot escape in any event. If we, as a people, were determined to eradicate involuntary malnutrition and hunger in this country, the goal could become a reality in a short time.

There must be long-range planning to insure the future, but there is need for emergency action immediately, for example:

1. Set up emergency food programs in the 300 counties where hunger is evident, in the camps of the migrant farm workers, and on certain Indian reservations where such help would be appropriate.

2. Make full use of all funds and programs allowed under present legislation, and urge Congress to enact laws that will provide additional powers and appropriations needed.

3. Make the public aware of the extent of the problem, and solicit support for all programs designed to bring relief.

The longer-range programs should include at the very least:

1. Federal food programs unhampered by state and county governments and made available to those who need food regardless of where they live.

2. Simple methods of distributing food stamps, whereby those in need can declare their circumstances by mail or in person in a manner similar

to the filing of income tax returns, with the same kind of reliance on honesty.

3. School lunches made available to every child in every school in all grades through the twelfth, to be paid for by everyone with stamps or tickets so that no stigma would be attached to those who receive the food free or at reduced rates.

4. Research and training regarding the diagnosis and treatment of malnutrition through schools of medicine and nursing.

The extent and seriousness of the shortage of food in the world as it is related to population and environment is set forth in the first article that follows, "The Population-Food Collision Is Inevitable" by William and Paul Paddock. The authors of this article, an agronomist and a plant pathologist, have had wide experience in tropical countries in Central America, Asia, and Africa. They are convinced that famine is inevitable in the near future and that it will not be a temporary state but a condition of prolonged duration. They explain the reasons behind their thinking and also point out the fallacies in some of the solutions that have inspired much confidence.

The Citizens' Crusade Against Poverty, under the chairmanship of Walter Reuther, initiated an investigation into the following:

1. The scope of starvation and hunger in selected poverty areas throughout the United States.

2. The extent of nutritional knowledge at medical schools and within the United States Public Health Service.

3. The extent and quality of programs now existing to meet the needs of hungry people.

4. What might be recommended both for immediate relief and for long-range plans to deal with the problem.

The article "Hunger, U.S.A." is from the report that issued from the above inquiry and describes the disgraceful conditions that it uncovered.

The author of "Population, Food, and Environment: Is the Battle Lost?" is an authority on the problem of the population explosion. Paul R. Ehrlich relates the increased numbers of people to food supply and environmental deterioration and proposes four steps by which we might be able to bring about a reversal of the present population growth trend in the United States. He offers these as preferable alternatives to compulsory birth regulation. Ehrlich points to the folly of our charitable gestures in sending aid to poor countries and emphasizes the need to face the total situation from a rational standpoint, prepared for radical action and abandonment of outworn sentiments and superstitions.

The last four articles deal with ways of currently handling the problem. In "Birth Control Now" the foreign staff of *U.S. News & World Report* surveys the status of birth control practices in many countries of the world. Their findings show that the dangers of uncontrolled population growth are well known and that most countries have accepted the idea of birth control.

Marjory Bracher deals with the touchy subject of "The Right to Have Children" and makes some reasonable suggestions.

Two government assistance programs, school lunches and food stamps, are outlined in "School Lunch to Food Stamps." The role that the United States can play in alleviating the world food shortage is delineated in the final article, "The United States and World Hunger."

The world's margin of food supplies will be exhausted in ten years. Death rates continue to fall, and birth control measures cannot be made effective soon enough on a large scale to prevent serious overpopulation in many areas of the world. A billion people will be added to the world's population in the next fifteen years and four-fifths of this number will come into being in the regions least able to provide food.

The Population-Food Collision Is Inevitable

William Paddock and Paul Paddock

Not too far in the future from now a strange phenomenon came to a head in parts of the United States. The experts had foreseen the threat of catastrophe that would come about. The press had long quoted experts but usually on the inside pages. Debates had occurred in Congress but not in the strident voices of urgency. People had been worrying but always the worrying was tempered with "something will happen" to forestall the troubles. In this day and age of extraordinary scientific breakthroughs all assumed something was bound to be discovered in time. And so it was especially terrifying when the hospitals of Tacoma and Memphis suddenly filled with the dying and the maimed. Emergency wards were set up in the schools and teams of doctors rushed in from neighboring cities and the federal government mobilized a dozen bureaucracies to cope with the disaster and troops patrolled the streets to control looting. The surrounding countryside was not fully aware of the extent of the trouble until the refugees came flowing out from the cities seeking safety—at first the well-to-do and finally even the poorest people walking on foot and bent under their bundles of whatever they could carry. Yet the countryside did not provide safety because soon here also the danger overwhelmed the population. By the end of the year the trouble was compounded when suddenly Seattle and St. Louis also fell before the scourge and a new focus of disaster appeared first in Buffalo and then Albany. Now the government cordoned off the refugees because even their appearance in an untroubled area would set off a panic. Few in the still safe regions would extend help to the fleeing. The economy of the nation slowed and weakened as every man centered his attention on his own safety, on the safety of his own family.

The foregoing is a rather loose description of what happened in the

From *Famine, 1975! America's Decision: Who Will Survive?* by William and Paul Paddock. Reprinted by permission of Little, Brown and Co. Copyright © 1967 by William and Paul Paddock. Also by permission of Weidenfeld and Nicholson, Ltd., London.

old days whenever yellow fever plagues broke out in, for instance, New Orleans. Maybe this is what will be happening some day in the future when air pollution makes certain cities unlivable and the scientific breakthroughs to control it do not, after all, come about and the various levels of government are not, after all, able to stop the causes of pollution.

For 1975, however, this would be a close description of what will be happening in parts of the undeveloped world because of famine and its accompanying civil unrest. Change the name of the cities from Tacoma and Albany to Madras and Recife.

Worse, the catastrophe of these forthcoming famines and unrest will have one characteristic different from previous plagues and disasters. Until now such troubles were overcome and finished within, usually, a year or two. Famines, for instance, would cease with the next year's harvest or, at most, at the end of the rather short cycle of bad drought years.

The famines which are now approaching will not, in contrast, be caused by weather variations and therefore will not be ended in a year or so by the return of normal rainfall. They will last for years, perhaps several decades, and they are, for a surety, inevitable. Ten years from now parts of the undeveloped world will be suffering from famine. In fifteen years the famines will be catastrophic and revolutions and social turmoil and economic upheavals will sweep areas of Asia, Africa, and Latin America.

This is not a book on the population explosion. Neither is it a book on development of the undeveloped countries, nor is it a book on food production. It deals, instead, with the *consequences* of the world's inability to cope with these problems before the famines strike. It deals with the policies that must be formulated in Washington (as the true center of today's leadership and power) in order to alleviate the famines and to shorten their length.

A locomotive is roaring full throttle down the track. Just around the bend an impenetrable mudslide has oozed across the track. There it lies, inert, static, deadly. Nothing can stop the locomotive in time. Collision is inevitable. Catastrophe is foredoomed. Miles back up the track the locomotive could have been warned and stopped. Years ago the mud-soaked hill could have been shored up to forestall the landslide. Now it is too late.

The locomotive roaring straight at us is the population explosion. The unmovable landslide across the tracks is the stagnant production of food in the undeveloped nations, the nations where the population increases are greatest.

The collision is inevitable. The famines are inevitable.

It is a difficult task to convince the government official, the learned scientist, the journalist or the bewildered man in the street that a collision between exploding population and static agriculture is imminent. Always they refer to some aspect of our complex world economy or of our scientific span of knowledge that is going to deflect the famines from happening with full force. Always, it seems, the scientist who is indeed an expert in his own branch of knowledge nevertheless naïvely takes for granted that the solution lies ready for use in another branch of science.

This was, as a pertinent example, the case with me personally. In December 1965 I welcomed the invitation to attend a conference at Cornell University on the agricultural potentials of the tropics. The conference was broadly based in the sense that experts from many scientific disciplines took part. As an agronomist I know the limitations of increasing food production rapidly, especially the long time-lag between discovery of an improved technique and its final utilization out in the fields; also I have long been acquainted with the troubles of the tropical world and realize that these troubles are due primarily to limitations imposed by soil and climate or, to say it another way, our lack of know-how in coping with tropical conditions.

In my opening paper at this conference I stressed that the potentials of tropical agriculture, based on today's knowledge, are limited, but I expressed the hope that the experts from other sciences would have helpful ideas that could bring progress to the tropics quickly.

That evening I had dinner with one of the country's leading demographers, J. Mayone Stycos. "This is going to be a most significant conference," he said, "because we are going to need a solution to the food problem *fast.*"

"Don't expect any food solution to come out of this conference," I said, "for the direct reason that there is none in sight. Whatever new ideas are presented here will not change the agricultural outlook in the next ten or twenty years. What I want to learn here is the methods which the demographers like you have on tap. How can you curtail population growth so that we agriculturalists will have time to solve the food problem?"

"*Us!*" Stycos nearly shouted across the table. "We have *nothing* that will work in the next ten years. We have been counting on the agronomists to give the population men enough time."

Stycos then leafed through some clippings he took from his pocket. "Look here. The Secretary of Agriculture, Freeman, has just made a speech at the FAO Conference in Rome. He said: 'Some newly developing countries are already increasing their agricultural production at rates higher than those ever achieved by the highly developed nations—including my own.' "[1]

I replied, "No matter what is said in public and for whatever reason, the true situation is that food production in the undeveloped world *is* nearly static. I *know* the food possibilities in these countries. I *know* that future food increases, based on today's techniques, are limited and can only change slowly."

Hereupon I took out of my briefcase my own handful of clippings. "What about all these statements from the demographers? This one claims that in most of the world man's fertility will decline in the next five or ten years[2] and this one says we have one or two generations ahead of us before the number of people becomes hopeless."[3]

Stycos's answer was simply, "It isn't so. This I *know*. Fertility may decline a little, but mortality will decline even more. The net result in the next ten years will be an increase in the number of people greater than anything the world has ever dreamed of."

I asked, "What if the governments, especially the U.S., gave all the money needed, eliminated all the bureaucratic bottlenecks, did away with all the religious taboos, everyone gave fullest support? Could this stop the overpopulation in time to avoid the famines?"

Stycos leaned back, thought for a while and said slowly, "As a demographer I would relish such support. Yes, by 1975 you might lower the birth rate by a few points. In a region like Central America you might reduce the birth rate from fifty to forty-five or even forty per thousand in ten years. That would be a major, a truly major achievement."

I said this was not enough.

Stycos added, "Of course, it would accumulate and go down faster after that."

My own answer was that this still would not be fast enough. The world's margin of food supplies will already have been passed in ten years.

Regarding valid experts basing their hopes in provinces other than their own, it is pertinent that Roger Revelle, director of the Harvard Center for Population Studies, when he testified on this subject before the Committee on Agriculture of the House of Representatives, spoke primarily of hopes not in his own field, that is, population control, but of his hopes for increasing food production, a field in which he is not trained.[4]

Today twelve thousand people died of hunger in the world. Tomorrow another twelve thousand will die.[5]

These deaths, however, are nothing more than the warning whistle of the locomotive rushing down the tracks toward the immovable landslide of static food production in the hungry nations. There is neither a new agricultural method nor is there a birth control technique on the horizon which can avert the inevitable famines.

Don't call this pessimism. It is merely sad realism.

"We are in the presence, perhaps, of a turning-point in human affairs so immense that we do not perceive it: 1966 may be the year in which sufficiency in food disappears from the world and famine becomes a recurrent and habitual condition. No doubt those not immediately affected will 'learn to live with it,' as with the housing shortage or overcrowded schools. No doubt—for a decade at least—actual starvation will be rare and localized, and disaster on the grand scale will be forestalled by modern means of transport and by emergency actions. . . . But, once the overall trend is the wrong way, it will get progressively harder to reverse."[6]

So much has been written about the population explosion. The columns of statistics, the plethora of data. By now, even the most serious worriers are dulled with the flow of percentages and the trends and the graphs.

The natural reaction is to turn wearily away to other matters. Yet, as with a tumor, the stinging effect of the population explosion will not die down. It continues to eat the vitals. Always the hour of crisis moves closer. Each new set of statistics, of facts, merely illustrates that previous estimates of the increases in population have been too low.

In 1947 I was stationed in Kabul. We at the American Embassy were caught in an argument between our friends the British and our friends the Afghans. This particular incident concerned the size of the population of Afghanistan. No census had ever been taken. Whose guesswork were we to believe?

A drought had developed and the Afghan government had appealed to the Embassy for flour. Washington immediately agreed, and the British also immediately promised to facilitate shipment through the port of Karachi and to forward the flour by rail to Quetta and Peshawar, the only practical routes into landlocked, remote Afghanistan.

Everyone was in accord as to the percentage of Afghan population that was affected by this drought and in need of relief. But how many people were there? The Afghans claimed the country's population totaled 10 million. The British said, "Nonsense." Their long-accepted estimate was 7 million. The Afghan officials said their figure was based on the number of people vaccinated in a cholera scare the previous year, when even the nomads were vaccinated. The British still claimed 7 million.

The difference of over 25 per cent was important, not only for the amount of flour to be shipped from the United States but, equally important, for the amount of dock and railroad space the British were to arrange for transshipment. This was the year of the division of the Raj into independent Pakistan and independent India. Communal riots were erupting all over the subcontinent and the harried British were noble even to give time and effort to facilitate these shipments into Afghanistan.

Anyway, the flour, especially packaged in sealed cans to survive the hot Red Sea passage, did arrive from Karachi, through the Khyber Pass, across the Jalalabad Desert, over the Lattaband Pass and down to Kabul. It was distributed to the bakeries around the country. The crisis ebbed and passed—not, for the record, due to the American flour which turned out to be of a type the Afghans did not know how to use for bread, although eventually it was all consumed.

But the distribution through the bakers definitely proved that Afghanistan's population was much more than 7 million and, in fact, over 10 million (today it is over 15 million).

When you read any population figure from an undeveloped country, add to it! And also from anywhere else. For instance: "Recent population projections [for the U.S.] for the end of the century have ranged all the way from 263 million to 388 million, but most experts are reluctant to be pinned down to long-term figures, pointing out that the most reliable study in the early '40's projected a population of 165 million for the year 2000—a figure exceeded more than a decade ago."[7] As recently as 1964, United States officials were talking about a world population of 6 billion people in the year 2000. Today they say it will be 7 billion!

The easiest statistic to grasp is the one that tells in how many years the population of a country will double. It illustrates, for one thing, how quickly the country must double the amount of food it produces in order to maintain the current level of nutrition, however low that may be (in addition, of course, to doubling the number of houses, schools, sanitation facilities, etc.).

What if the population of the Netherlands were to double in twenty years? Aside from where to put the new people in that already pressed-together country, could its currently thriving economy and its equitable social structure possibly absorb all the strains such a population influx would cause? One result would surely be a drastic lowering of Holland's present living standard. Yet in the field of urban organization Holland has, I guess, about the most efficient, most intelligent government to be found anywhere, and its regulations to govern city and rural planning have long been refined to a degree undreamed of in the United States or elsewhere.

If the experienced Hollanders could barely cope with a population doubling within a generation, the outlook is indeed gloomy for the weak governments and uneducated communities of Honduras, Ceylon, the Ivory Coast, and also the miscellaneous corners like the Fiji Islands, Martinique, and—you name it!

A momentous date with the world's birth control experts was 1957, the year the first widespread testing of the new intrauterine coil for women was completed (this is a small, inexpensive plastic loop or coil, simple and quick for a doctor to insert, requiring little attention once in place, and is 85 per cent effective in preventing conception).

Taking 1957 as our benchmark, the accompanying table gives the year when the populations of the following prolific countries will have *doubled*.[8]

The first adequate population forecasts were based on an effort at a worldwide census in 1950. When in 1960 the second worldwide census was taken, most of the earlier predictions had to be discarded because the new data showed a faster growth rate than had previously been thought possible.

Venezuela had believed on the basis of the 1950 census that its population would double in 26 years; now the 1960 census showed a doubling in 18. Korea 25 years instead of 50. India 33 years instead of 54. Peru 27 years instead of 37.[9]

India during this decade between the two censuses had increased its

Predicted Population Doubling Dates	
Costa Rica	1973
Burundi	1974
Syria	1974
Mauritania	1975
Libya	1976
Taiwan	1977
Dominican Republic	1977
Ivory Coast	1977
Mali	1977
Venezuela	1978
Vietnam	1978
Honduras	1979
Malaysia	1979
Mexico	1979
Mongolia	1979
Panama	1979
Philippines	1979
Brazil	1980

population 20.5 per cent—in contrast to 13.3 per cent in the preceding decade.[10]

Nigeria's 1963 census pulled a startling surprise for that country's planners. The census counted 56 million people—19 million more than the highest estimate had anticipated.[11]

In 1958 the United Nations estimated that in 1970 the population of "the less developed world" would be 2,950,000,000; in 1965 this figure was revised upward to 3,070,000,000.[12]

An important lesson must be hammered home from these figures. Inaccurate as population statistics in the hungry nations may be, the evidence shows them to be on the low, on the conservative, side. Looking at them realistically, they indicate only one trend: the locomotive of population explosion is gaining momentum faster each day.

There are several dynamics making this inevitable.

Population Dynamic Number One: The Death Rate

Recently, I visited in Washington the library of the Population Reference Bureau and asked for some information on death rates in the developing countries. This Bureau is the mother lode of all population information and it has been the spearhead, thanks to its president, Robert Cook, in awakening the American public to the dangers of uncontrolled human fertility.

"You want to know about death rates! Great!" they said. "We've been trying for years to get people interested in death rates, to get people to understand that the 'explosion' is due primarily to falling death rates and not to changing birth rates."

With everyone's preoccupation over birth control, we all seem to ignore the fact that the death rate is still dynamic, *still* going down. The end result is the same as an increase in birth rates.

Until this century the history of the world had been pockmarked by a steady series of afflictions from plague, cholera, diphtheria, smallpox and other pestilences. However, it now has been half a century since the world has had a major pandemic with a significant toll of deaths (when 25 million died of influenza in 1919).[13] Few people can grasp the dramatic speed with which death rates have fallen, especially in the undeveloped countries. It all came about overnight.

By 1948 it was clear that a new interest in health work existed in many countries where no such interest had existed before the war. . . . Mass inoculations required little coercion. The efficiency of DDT and antibiotics in control of infections was known because of our war experience. And the significance of BCG for tuberculosis was also known. But no one realized their full potentialities in 1948.

It was clear, by 1948, that the death rates in the non-industrial countries could be made to decline—but no one knew how rapidly. No one knew how well the controls effected by such agents as DDT would be accepted. No one fully realized that mass public health controls could produce such rapid and widespread results. Japan, which is not a "non-industrial" country, had a crude death rate of 8.9 in 1951—half of that which existed in 1946. Ceylon, perhaps a better example, had a death rate of only 10.14 in 1954—half of its 1946 rate. These changes were hardly predictable in 1948.[14]

The effectiveness of modern-day medicine—the rapidity with which it can be disseminated and the eagerness with which people accept it—has resulted in the drastic changes in the death rates shown in the table.
. . . The drop in death rates has been so spectacular that many believe they cannot go lower. On the contrary, . . . trends show not only

Falling Death Rates in the Hungry World[15]
(per thousand)

	1935	1950	1965	1980*
World	25	19	16	12.7
Asia	33	23	20	13
Africa	33	27	23	18
Latin America	22	19	12	8.2

* Projected.

room for a further fall of the death rate but a clear forecast that it *will* fall.

Look at the low death rates already achieved in the following four undeveloped countries:[16]

Taiwan	5.7 per thousand
Ceylon	8.7
Hong Kong	4.9
Singapore	5.7

These low death rates are due in part to the populations having today a higher percentage of young people. . . . But another major factor is better medical care; and what these countries have achieved, the other undeveloped areas will strive also to achieve. The table of current death rates below shows how much room for a further dynamic fall is possible.

1965 Death Rates[17] (per thousand)	
El Salvador	10.8
Guatemala	17.3
Mexico	10.4
Chile	12.0
Ivory Coast	35.0
Senegal	23–29
Upper Volta	27–31
Iran	23–27
India	21–23
Indonesia	19–23
South Korea	11–13

If by 1975 the "death rate in Guatemala fell somewhere near the 1950 United States level [9.6][18]—a not unlikely development—this alone would increase the number of women reaching the beginning of the child-bearing period by 36 per cent and the number at the end of the child-bearing period by 85 per cent. . . . This drop in the death rate in the child-bearing period has and will have in the next few years a gigantic effect on the birth rate."[19]

The mortality rates remain dynamic. They will continue their downward rush in the years ahead—until checked by famine.

A friend of mine, a charming lady in her fifties who had never traveled in the undeveloped world, happened to do an important favor for a member of the family of a ruling potentate of one of the semi-backward nations (whom I would like to name but it probably would not be of benefit to him). She was invited to visit the royal family and gladly accepted. Her plane arrived at evening and the ride to the palace through the capital city, pleasantly exotic in the half-light, was a delight despite the clouds of dust swirling everywhere. At dinner with the highly cultured ruler and his wife and children she was told the rainy season was long overdue, and the next morning the first rains did burst forth. Afterwards, she took a walk outside the palace gate and along the rutted main street and saw people eagerly scooping up the water out of the puddles along with the horse manure and anything else that had happened to accumulate during the dry season. They used the water for cooking, for drinking, for, in a word, normal living. Sickened, my friend asked the ruler why he allowed this, why he did not provide sanitation facilities and clean water at least in his capital city. After all, this was not a destitute country; compared to many it was recognized as prosperous. The ruler replied, "I know it is not pleasant to see people drinking from the ruts in the road, and we do have enough money at least to change things here in the city. But the problem is not that simple. Rather, I have not been sure in my own mind how to handle this problem. So I have visited other countries, especially India, to see what happens when a city gets pure drinking water. My decision was that when India learns how to feed all of the people who have been kept alive because of the good water, then I shall order a modern water system here." My friend was not convinced this was right but she was intelligent enough to accept it as a thought-out policy.

My own opinion is that this ruler is an exceedingly wise man. Although he could never announce such a policy publicly, he has, in various ways, held back spending tax moneys on public health. Some hospitals and clinics have been built and staffed by aid-giving countries and the aura of progress in medical services is believed in by the local people. Yet there has been no all-out effort by the government along these lines; this must be a major factor why the population increase rate is not out of hand and why the nation, compared to its neighbors, is relatively prosperous.

Population Dynamic Number Two: The Younger Generation

The people are already here who will cause the famines. Birth control techniques are for the future; they cannot affect the present millions of hungry stomachs.

Today, nearly half of the people in the undeveloped world are under the age of fifteen years. Dr. B. R. Sen, director-general of the Food and Agriculture Organization of the United Nations (FAO), says: "Even if birth control measures were adopted on a wide scale, population would still increase substantially because of the large number of children who will be forming their own families ten, twenty and thirty years from now."[20]

In Latin America, for instance, the increasing percentage of children in the population means that by 1975 there will be 60 per cent *more* marriages formed than in 1960.[21] The potential for further population increase is truly enormous.

By 1975 Latin America (and most of the undeveloped world as well) will find itself in the position of a friend of mine who is now a professor at one of the leading universities. John returned from World War II in 1946, was married and settled down to a serious graduate study program. In the subsidized days of the G.I. Bill and the confidence of a returning marine, he had four children in quick succession. After a stint in the business world he accepted an excellent teaching position. His salary moved up to $10,000 in 1955 and to $15,000 by 1960. He made a down payment on his house and was marked as a comer in his profession. By 1965 he was making $20,000—a fine record for someone only fifteen years out of graduate school, a good record for anyone!

In 1965 his first child entered college. It cost John $2,500 a year. In 1966 his second child entered college. Now it was costing him $5,000 a year for education, a real financial burden for this hard-working, energetic professor. By 1967 when his third child is in college it will cost him $7,500 a year. Now his savings will be gone and he will take out another mortgage on his house. And when his last child enters college, his 1968 education bill will come to $10,000 a year! A $20,000 salary does not go far under such circumstances.

The hungry world is in a position similar to John's. The only difference, really, is that when John has his fourth child educated, he can begin to recoup his savings. The hungry world's problem is just beginning and the time of recoupment will not be in this century.

By farming farther and farther up the hillsides (until all the extra land is used up), by borrowing more and more funds from the international agencies (until credit is exhausted), by receiving from the well-fed countries more and more of their surplus food (but now the surplus is about gone), the hungry world has been able to keep its children alive. But the children are getting bigger, they eat more, they need more calories to stay alive and now there are more and more of them and, worse, even the children themselves are having children. The family grows ever larger and so do the problems of the parent country.

Therefore, between now and 1975 we shall see much of the hungry world exhaust its capacity to cope with the population that is *already* here, that is already eating, that is demanding more at the dawn of each day. This is the built-in inevitability of the dynamic of today's generation.

Population Dynamic Number Three: The Birth Rate

Until the 1950's the maximum birth rate physiologically possible in a population was believed to be forty-five births per thousand.

For the classical European population it was quite simple to calculate: out of every thousand people there were 500 women; of these 410 were either too young or too old for child-bearing or were, for some reason, nonfertile; another 45 had just had a child and there was not time to conceive and deliver another in the current year.

In 1945, then, the 45 per thousand figure was fixed in academic circles as the formula for the maximum possible birth rate.

By the 1950's, though, this was refuted in the undeveloped nations. Today, a dozen countries have birth rates above the 45 figure. The numbers 48, 49, 50 appear in the statistics. No one really knows how the women manage these figures. But they do. Costa Rica's birth rate, for example, in 1940 was 44.9; in 1950 it was 49.2; in 1960 it was 50.0; today it is 50.2.[22]

Part of the blame can be placed on the higher percentage of young people found in these populations today (thus, a larger reproductive age group). Another part of the blame probably comes from our having each year a more accurate set of birth statistics. But yet another part can be placed on improved health. Healthy people are simply more fertile. Good health decreases the number of stillbirths, miscarriages, and spontaneous abortions. Good health increases the frequency of intercourse.[23]

Although improved living conditions, such as those sometimes brought on by industrialization, are often given as a reason for a decreased birth rate, actually the evidence seems to be the opposite. As industrialization breaks down traditional social patterns, there is first of all, apparently, an increase in the birth rate. A couple of decades later the birth rate may fall off, but not at first. For example, changes in the social pattern can bring about greater marital stability to non-legal unions; or, as in India, the breakdown of taboos on the remarriage of widows could raise the number of births in the population.[24]

Although the reasons behind the dynamism of the increases in birth rate are still vague and uncertain, the statistics of their reality are clear.

Population Dynamic Number Four: Man's Reproductive System

Man has been evolving and reproducing for a million years. Those who expect science to be able to find quickly a birth control method which can successfully circumvent this million years of such single-mindedness both overestimate modern science and underestimate the efficiency of the reproductive system which evolution has provided man.

Most of us have been confident that science soon will find some effective way to control births because we cannot bring ourselves to believe the appalling population figures projected for the coming generation. We have fallen back on the hope that "something" will be devised quickly to limit the statistics.

Let me now do away with such false hopes for the coming decade.

The False Hope of Limited Families

Most important, we forget that people love children. This is a key characteristic that man and his wife have acquired through the million years of evolution. The simple love for children itself guarantees this book's predictions.

Surveys in undeveloped countries indicate that nearly always the average woman does not become concerned with family planning until she has four or five children. In Chile, for instance, interviews have shown that the people there consider the ideal number of children per family is four. Forty-two per cent of the families in that country have not achieved this ideal.[25] In rural India the preferred number averages above four.[26]

Thus, we can assume that with the "perfect" birth control method available to all, 42 per cent of the Chilean parents would still not want to use it—and similar data shows that neither would the average Indian farm wife unless she already had four children. Their reasons for this ideal figure for a family have nothing to do with the cost of bringing up the children, with the teachings of the Catholic Church (in Chile), privacy of parents in the homes, etc. People *love* children.

Also, it is discouraging to note that certain societies demand surplus children.

> In many countries, grown-up children who will support their aged parents are the chief form of social security. If a man and his wife do not have at least one adult male child, they have little to look forward to when they can no longer work to support themselves. Under conditions of high child mortality, the average married couple needs to produce many children to be sufficiently certain that at least one boy will survive to become a man. Only in this way can they ensure their own future security. Whenever infant and child mortality can be brought down to a low enough level, the probability in an individual family that a male child will survive becomes very much greater, and the pressure for large numbers of children correspondingly lessens. This is one of the principal reasons the profession of public health needs to be deeply involved in the problems of family planning and population control.[27]

The False Hope of the IUD

The intrauterine device (IUD) for women is the big hope today among population experts working in the undeveloped countries. It is already widely accepted, factories are under construction in many countries to mass-produce it cheaply. This is the only thing on the horizon which looks as if it might make a fast enough impact on birth rates in the foreseeable future in the hungry nations. But . . .

They cannot insert the IUD's fast enough!

Dr. Alan F. Guttmacher, president of Planned Parenthood–World Population, recently told a Senate committee how impressed he was with the speed with which the IUD can be inserted. He told of seeing a Chinese woman doctor with a team of well-trained nurses make insertions in seventy-five patients in three hours.[28] That averages out as one patient every two minutes and twenty-four seconds. Dr. Jack Lippes, the inventor of the most widely used type of IUD, states that a physician can insert one IUD every six minutes.[29]

Neither of these two figures is fast enough.

Each year in India an additional 850,000 women enter childbearing age.[30] Dr. Lippe says: "The greatest shortage in India is time. The birth control revolution must be instituted in less than ten years. If in ten years India adds another 200 million people to its population, neither India nor her friends will be able to feed these new numbers."[31] He adds that a program of 25 million coil insertions by 1969 could lead to a real drop in the Indian birth rate.

Such a target figure would be a true achievement, but current trends and the current slow tempo of India's governmental organizations would seem to make it unrealistic. Progress of this program, however, can be checked upon before 1969. Dr. Lippes expects 3 million insertions to be made in 1966 and 6 million in 1967.[32] It will be indicative of India's ability to handle such a program if these figures are achieved, figures which are huge elsewhere but modest in view of India's crisis.

In addition to the unproven ability of the Indian government to operate such a crash program, there is also the problem of the lack of medical personnel available for this work. Since it is believed that the insertion of the IUD is sufficiently delicate to require a physician, a key to the success of any such program depends on the number of doctors available, and this I discuss later.

An extra complication in India which has not received much publicity is that women are reluctant to let male doctors insert the coils. Yet India has only about eight thousand women doctors.[33] As in most other countries, a large proportion of these doctors do not want to move from the cities to the villages, the place where the most serious part of the problem lies.[34]

India is perhaps an unfair example. Everything seems so much harder in India!

At the other extreme is Taiwan, also an untypical example.

[Taiwan] has an ideal setting for a family planning program: fundamental to the success of any attempt to slow population growth are the social and economic conditions and attitudes which

determine individual family size. Taiwan is going through a transition from a traditional to a modern society. The island is becoming industrialized to a great extent. Literacy and education are
widespread, and the transportation and communication systems are
good.[35]

Taiwan is considered such an ideal example that as many as a hundred foreign visitors a month sometimes come to study its family planning
program.[36] Yet Taiwan expects to insert less than 150,000 IUD's in 1967.
Thus, what will be the end result of this "ideal" situation? ". . . even with
an intensive family planning program to accelerate the present decline in
the birth rate, the population [of Taiwan] will still double before the turn
of the century."[37]

And do not forget the coil is not recommended for use until after a
woman has already given birth to a child, thus lessening the percentage
able to take advantage of it. And of those who do, 30 per cent lose or remove the IUD within the first year.[38]

Unfortunately, many governments and many aid officials put sole
faith in the IUD; they fail to devise overall programs making use of all
methods open for population control. In fact, those few governments of the
undeveloped areas which have launched tentative birth control programs
"seem to have fallen into the 'technological fallacy' which has long marked
Western thinking in this area. They have adopted, in other words, a kind of
blind faith in gadgetry of contraception."[39]

I offer as an aside the suggestion that retired doctors and nurses from
the United States and elsewhere might well be engaged as technicians (by
the Peace Corps perhaps) to insert IUD's as part of the population control
programs in these countries. Knowledge of the local language would not be
necessary. Such a group of medical persons ("The Coil Corps") working
full time solely with IUD's could indeed have an impact on a nation or on a
single province. The usefulness of the IUD as a birth control program is in
direct proportion to the doctors available.

The False Hope of the Pill

The Pill, it is accepted in most scientific circles, will stop the reproductive
process of the Cuzco Indian, the farm maid of Upper Volta and the Bali-
nesian novitiate as effectively as of the Baltimore housewife. However, if
any one of these cannot afford to buy a new supply at the end of the week
or is illiterate and does not read the directions correctly or just fails, for
whatever reason, to take the pills regularly, then all bets are off.

No birth control method needs a stronger motivation than does the
present type of the Pill inasmuch as it requires daily attention, hours away
from knowing whether or not it is going to be needed. Such motivation is

just as scarce in the hungry world as in Baltimore. Thus, it is not entirely a matter of affluence or literacy. Remember also that when a woman goes off the Pill, or forgets to take it regularly, her fertility is heightened!

Yet let us assume that somehow or other the government of an undeveloped country is able to persuade most women to take the Pill. Imagine what would happen if a rumor suddenly spread through the countryside that, after a year's use, the Pill caused cancer or two-headed births. Such a rumor would be difficult if not impossible to correct in an illiterate population. That such a rumor would get started must be accepted as a probability. Consider, for instance, the similar rumors in our country that have circulated, especially when the product of one drug firm (not of the other firms) was questioned by the Department of Health, Education and Welfare.

Actually, the medical profession itself is not united in its opinion about the Pill. The *Medical Letter,* a non-profit drug-advisory service for physicians, said in its February 1966 issue that women for whom the Pill had been prescribed "should be informed of the present status of knowledge about the possible risks involved." In the light of recent reports about clotting, eye damage and related disorders in some users, the publication said, "it is necessary to repeat the advice . . . that women who can satisfactorily use topical contraceptive measures should not use oral [the Pill] contraceptives."[40]

A few years from now there is little doubt the current intensive research in this field will develop new types of pills or injections that will be startlingly effective, such as the current reports of studies on a "morning after" pill, a "monthly" pill, injections valid for a year for both men and women, etc. Unfortunately, today's Pill, successful though it is with individuals, is an unfirm foundation on which to build a nation-wide campaign. Instead, it should be only one part of a program that utilizes actively all varieties of population control.

The False Hope of Sterilization

In India, "of all the methods tried so far [to control population growth], only sterilization has yielded significant results."[41] In 1957 Madras State started a policy of voluntary subsidized male sterilizations (a free operation plus a bonus of $7.50, and a three- to six-day holiday with pay for government employees). Gradually, other states started similar programs. Also the government in Delhi, after prolonged procrastination, has now come out in favor of this and has established a goal of 5,000,000 male sterilizations by the end of 1970.[42] "Had India embarked on this policy 15 years ago with fervor, the country by now could have cut its birth rate in half."[43]

The strength of a sterilization program is that it has a cumulative effect as the men overcome their initial psychological rejection of it and learn not to be fearful of the operation. It takes, unfortunately, a determined government, full medical services and a prolonged education and propaganda campaign in order to achieve significant results. In this, India is typical. Even with the glaring catastrophe of overpopulation constantly before them, the officials at Delhi have only now turned their attention to this campaign which some of the provincial states had initiated several years earlier.

Now it is too late. India does not have enough doctors for a massive sterilization program. Nor are the Indian men yet ready to accept it.

Only Taiwan, Korea and Pakistan of all the other undeveloped nations have instituted sterilization programs.[44] This can be an important tool in the future, but not in time to stop the famines.

The False Hope of Japan

At every turn today in the demographic field the phenomenal success story of the Japanese in achieving a dramatic lowering of the birth rate is emphasized. Between 1951 and 1961 that country cut its birth rate in half and will, in fact, by the end of this generation not quite maintain its present population. Those who refuse to believe the end results of the world's population explosion always say, "If Japan can do it, so can other countries when the need arises." In fact, even Ronald Freedman, president of the Population Association of America, recently predicted that India and Pakistan are able to go through a fertility decline similar to that in Japan.[45]

There is not a chance of this, unfortunately, within the time period we are speaking of here.

What did Japan have in its favor which today's hungry nations do not have?

JAPAN IS A TIGHT LITTLE ISLAND

The Japanese are packed, compressed, into an area the size of Montana with 685 persons per square mile (4 for Montana). Herein lies a basic observation that it does not seem possible for a government to push successfully for a birth control program until the people themselves demand it. This they do not do until everyone is practically standing on top of one another.

The year 1947 was the Moment of Truth for Japan. Upon losing World War II it lost its dreams of expansion. Suddenly, the people realized that their future had to be found *within* their own boundaries. With a birth rate of over 34 per thousand this realization brought a universal groundswell to do "something." It was not simply a movement of sociologists and intellectuals.

No similar feeling of "standing room only" exists in any hungry, undeveloped nation today of which I know. This is usually because most of these nations have a lot of empty (useless) land that gives the illusion that there is plenty of space available for the oncoming populations. This is borne out by one often used, misleading type of statistic, that of population per square mile in a country. Thus, Brazil has only 24 people per square mile, Indonesia 180, Ethiopia 44. Even India (377) has a population density of about half that of Japan.

In the densely populated highlands of Guatemala where I once lived for several years, there is the firm belief that when things get too crowded people can always move to the empty department of the Petén, an area which actually few Guatemalans have ever seen. Only the trained agronomist realizes that, until new agricultural techniques are found, this type of jungle area cannot support more than the few thousand persons now there —which is why, of course, it is empty.

This dangerous illusion of "vast" empty spaces in these countries was typically expressed by the influential N. Viera Altamirano, editor of *El Diario de Hoy* in the capital of continental Latin America's most populated country, El Salvador (330 people per square mile).[46] He wrote that Latin America as a whole needs "two billion more inhabitants" and that the resources of Central America are sufficient for a population ten times her present size.[47] To this I give no comment!

THE JAPANESE WERE NOT ADVERSE TO ABORTIONS

The Japanese people in 1947 did not wait for science to come up with a new gadget, such as the later-developed IUD, to limit man's reproductive capacity. The government legalized abortion in 1948. The results were startling:[48]

> 1950   320,000 abortions
> 1955   1,200,000 abortions

More than any other single factor, the opportunity to have an abortion performed under safe and easily available conditions and, above all, legally, is the cause of Japan's success in population control. Such a method is completely taboo in much of the hungry world.

THE JAPANESE POPULATION IS LITERATE

Most of the hungry world is illiterate—and it is going to stay illiterate throughout this generation, and probably much longer.

Japan has had a compulsory education program since 1872. Illiteracy is so rare that the census no longer bothers to tabulate it. The last year for which figures were given was 1948 when the illiteracy rate was 1.1 per cent. In contrast Africa's is 84 per cent, Latin America's 40 per cent.[49]

Most demographers affirm that literacy is an important prerequisite for an effective birth control program (although I wonder, as a non-demographer, if this condition cannot be bypassed by other forms of government propaganda).

JAPAN HAS A RELATIVELY LOW PROPORTION OF FARMERS

Farmers everywhere always have more children than city folk. Children are an asset in the rural area where their labor can be used; but they are a liability in the city where they contribute little but consume a major part of the family income. As long ago as 1930 only one out of every three Japanese farmed.[50] Today, in contrast, two out of every three farm in Asia, Africa and Latin America.

JAPAN HAS A LARGE MEDICAL PROFESSION

Physicians say that trained doctors, not just technicians or nurses, are necessary to the effective application of birth control techniques to a population. If such reasoning is sound (and I am not sure that a corps of technicians could not be trained adequately enough for specific jobs such as insertion of the IUD's), then the undeveloped countries can never expect to catch up in the next ten years with the large number of doctors in Japan. Note the great gap between Japan and these other nations in inhabitants per physician:[51]

Physicians in Japan and the Hungry World	
	Inhabitants per Physician
Japan	900
Mexico	1,800
Costa Rica	2,200
Brazil	2,500
Panama	2,500
Syria	5,200
Libya	5,800
India	5,800
Malaysia	6,500
Pakistan	11,000
Gambia	16,000
Mauritania	26,000
Nigeria	27,000
Vietnam	29,000
Afghanistan	32,000
Mali	39,000
Indonesia	41,000
Burundi	66,000
Upper Volta	76,000
Ethiopia	96,000

THE JAPANESE LOWERED THE SIZE OF THEIR "IDEAL" FAMILY

At a dinner recently I had the good fortune to be seated next to a most delightful young Japanese wife who, however, seemed to lapse regularly into moments of preoccupation. The dinner was for her husband, who had just completed his graduate work, and the two were returning the following week to Japan. Making conversation, I said, "Watching you this evening, I would say that you have mixed feelings about returning to Japan."

She laughed and then, suddenly becoming quite serious, said, "Yes, but not for any reason you might think. We have been here almost five years and I'm homesick and can hardly wait to get home. But when I came here I had only one child. Now I have four. How am I going to face my friends at home?"

I looked at her so blankly that she continued, "You are not understanding me, are you? What I mean is that I could have returned happily with two children or maybe even three. But with four children no one will be able to understand—a family this size is really against public opinion."

And it is. For years the Japanese government, prodded on by an aggressive press which found that the subject sold newspapers, has made population control a major preoccupation of the people. Now in all levels of this generation's society it is accepted as unpatriotic not to practice family limitation.

How different in the backward nations!

In 1965 Senator Robert F. Kennedy, who at this writing has nine children, exuberantly shouted to a crowd in the highlands of Peru, "I challenge any of you to produce more children than I have."[52]

They cheered him in Catholic Latin America. In Japan he might well have drawn an official rebuke.

THE GOVERNMENT OF JAPAN HAS FIRMLY SUPPORTED POPULATION CONTROL

Before one develops any hope that a population control method will be effective in a given country, he should recognize the importance for total and aggressive backing from the government there. It is true that government attitudes are changing in this respect in some places, but not fast enough to give an impact in the next ten years.

Relevant also is the widespread belief among certain political leaders that the power of a country is determined by the size of its population. Some observers have noted that the most active opposition to birth control in Latin America is not the Catholic Church but the left-wingers who claim that birth control programs will castrate their nation's hope for power.

What leader of a hungry nation does not now use the population growth in his country to argue on behalf of the need for new markets, for more foreign aid, to justify educational and medical programs and expensive industrialization—and more P.L. 480 food shipments? Losing a war as Japan did, and thus being forced to turn inward to its own resources, is a dilemma the leaders of these other nations have not experienced.

Of course, it is today politically advantageous for the new governments of the new nations to blame their backwardness on the economic and metro-pole-centered policies of their former rulers. Now that they have thrown off colonialism (usually by nothing more than an intensive propaganda form of agitation), the leaders feel obliged to shout that paradise has arrived. To say that national problems now stem mostly from too many people having too few resources is to deny to colonialism its proper damnation.

Such was clearly the case when in December 1965 I attended the organizational meeting of the Committee on the World Food Crisis. The press that week had carried daily stories of imminent famine in India. President Johnson had just announced a stepped-up food shipment program to that subcontinent. Studies were under way to expand the Indian port facilities to receive these rush shipments. There was an atmosphere of pending calamity in the room of this committee, engendered by the dismal statistics presented by earlier non-Indian speakers.

Then, in contrast, K. S. Sundara Rajan, Economic Minister of the Indian Embassy and Executive Director for India of the World Bank, rose to speak. The grave food situation in India, he said, was due to having "the worst drought in the last 100 years" (something, obviously, for which the Indians themselves could not be blamed). Then he added, "The average Indian in 1965 is better fed than he was 20 or 30 years ago." (In other words, better fed than under British colonialism.) Although Rajan acknowledged that the food from the United States (which was then shipping 20 per cent of its entire wheat production to India, mostly as P.L. 480 Food) was helpful "in keeping prices stable and removing under-nutrition, . . . much the greatest part of the increased food supplies came from our own production. . . . With great efforts we stepped up the production of our food grains . . . in 1950 and 1951." [53] (That is, after the British were gone; these dates, in any case, are rather meaningless in the present crisis, fifteen years later.)

With such statements still coming fom high Indian officials, how can one expect population control to be taken seriously in Delhi and by the Indian public?

JAPAN IS NOT UNDER THE INFLUENCE OF THE CATHOLIC CHURCH

The press now often points to changes that may be developing within the Catholic Church with respect to many of its formerly rigid beliefs and traditions. Even concerning the Catholic Church's prohibition against artificial birth control it is pointed out that a large proportion of Catholics do not obey. For instance, 80 per cent of all United States Catholic couples married ten years or longer use some form of artificial birth control.[54] Studies also show that in no society in the world are there any significant differences in the attitude toward family planning between the Catholics and their neighbors, whether in Puerto Rico where the Catholics are in the majority or in Jamaica where they are in the minority or in Lebanon where they are evenly balanced.[55]

But the official Catholic position is quite different. Rev. Dexter L. Hanley of the Jesuits testified before the Senate Committee on Government Operations in August 1965, saying: "I affirm what is already well-known —that according to the theological, moral and authoritative pronouncements of the Catholic Church, the only morally acceptable form of voluntary family regulation is through continence, either total or periodic."[56]

Is there a reader of this book who believes such a practice of continence will have any effect on world population growth?

Thus, the problem is not the Catholic laity but the restraining hand of their church in the halls of government.

The former director of the United Nations World Health Organization (WHO), Brock Chisholm, has written:

> No person can get anywhere in any agency of the United Nations or in any of its committees or commissions, who tries to talk frankly about population problems and their solution. The Population Commission . . . makes terrifying reports every year but it does not make any constructive recommendations because it is not allowed to. Every committee . . . is under the influence of the Roman Catholic Church—and no delegate from the United States, from Canada, from France, from Britain or any of many other countries is in a position where he can ever begin to defy that taboo.
>
> I've seen it done. Once when an innocent proposal had been made by the chief delegate from Norway to the effect that the World Health Organization should set up a medical committee to study the medical aspects of population problems, representatives of six governments, chiefs of delegations, immediately got up and said that if this question were even discussed their governments might have to withdraw from the World Health Organization.[57]

Chisholm made this statement in 1959. In 1966 the ban against involvement in population control within the United Nations was still in force: "The World Health Organization refused today to assume international leadership in developing family planning as an answer to the population explosion. . . . The birth-control issue once threatened to disrupt the 18-year-old agency because the predominantly Roman Catholic member states opposed its even being raised. It was not until last year that the Assembly approved for the first time some action in the field . . . [but] it was carefully stipulated that this was not to 'involve operational activities.' "[58] Opposition to WHO action in this field was led by France, supported by Argentina, Austria, Belgium, Brazil and Mexico.

"The 30-nation executive board of the United Nations Children's Fund, at its annual meeting early this month in Addis Ababa, voted to defer action on the recommendations of the UNICEF director general that UNICEF consider government requests for assistance in family-planning programs. The recommendations specifically excluded the furnishing of birth-control devices or advice. A varied bloc of nations, led by the Soviet Union and predominantly Roman Catholic countries in Latin America, opposed the director general's report."[59]

"Nowhere [in Mexico] is the rate of population growth less than 3 per cent and in some northern states it is 4 per cent or more. Nowhere are any practical steps to limit this growth discernible. When the question was broached, officials of all types took shelter behind a stock answer: 'We are a Catholic country.' "[60] The citizens of Mexico will for a surety live up to current predictions of an 80,000,000 population in 1987 as compared to 40,000,000 today.[61]

As of this writing press reports from Rome indicate that the current study by the Catholic Church of the problem of birth control may alter its position and sanction certain contraceptives, especially, it is rumored, the use of the Pill. Even if this change is allowed, it will take many years for the lower clergy throughout the world to cease at least passive opposition and to support the programs. Or so it has been with some of the other changes initiated at Rome.

In any case, it seems highly doubtful that the Catholic Church, in spite of its other modernizing changes, will cease active opposition to overall population control in the hungry nations, opposition to the IUD, opposition to legalized abortion, opposition to sterilization. In such areas as Latin America this church's dictum is the major, usually invincible, barrier. Other non-Catholic areas are affected by the same barrier as it prevents or hinders action in the American AID programs, in the Peace Corps, and, of course, in all agencies of the United Nations.

But not in Japan.

Japan is indeed an important case study with respect to population control. It is indeed the pioneer that shows how the birth rate of any nation can be cut in half within a decade.

The tragedy is that no government in any one of the hungry, soon-to-be-starving nations is physically capable or psychologically prepared to duplicate the factors that were responsible for Japan's success.

As the perfect illustration of this whole problem I reprint in full a press dispatch I noticed on an inside page of the morning newspaper:

With four out of 10 of her people under 15 years of age, Turkey is preparing to undertake a program of family planning.

Reducing Turkey's annual population increase of 2.5 per cent—one of the highest in the world—has become an economic necessity. Turkey's population will more than double in 30 years unless the rate is reduced. The rate in the United States is 1.6 per cent.

The vast population growth has slowed economic progress. Heavily burdened with more than $2 billion in foreign debts and a foreign trade deficit above $146 million, Turkey has 1.25 million more mouths to feed than it had two years ago.

Despite more new schools, the illiteracy rate is on the increase. Unemployment is rife and there is an acute housing shortage.

Dr. Nusret Fisek, director general of the Ministry of Health, says a successful program of family planning is "absolutely imperative." The program calls for free provision, through the social health system, of intrauterine loops, devices about the size of a 50-cent piece that have an excellent record of preventing conception. The Government will also supply pills that control ovulation for a token charge of 33 to 55 cents a month.[62]

Here, in a nutshell, is reflected the dilemma of the undeveloped world. Only now is Turkey "preparing to undertake a program of family planning." Not fifteen years ago. Not ten years ago. Only now. In the last two years Turkey's population increased by 1,250,000. The population will double in thirty years. The nation is overwhelmed by foreign debt payments and an unfavorable trade balance; how will it finance purchases of food from abroad except through charity from other nations?

The world must make room for a billion people to be added to the world's population over the next 15 years. This fact in itself is significant. But even more significant, fully four-fifths of this total will be added in the food-short, less developed regions—regions where the fertility of the people is already outstripping the fertility of the soil.[63]

The United Nations loves to promote mouth-watering terms like the Geophysical Decade, the Year of the Quiet Sun, the International Cooperation Year, etc. What the United Nations should do—and the very thought of it would cringe the stoutest heart at the Delegates' Bar—is to promote a Childless Year.[64]

Malthus, the economist, summarized it as graphically as is possible: population will increase in geometrical progression—1, 2, 4, 8, 16, 32—but food will increase in arithmetical progression—1, 2, 3, 4, 5, 6. . . .

Notes

1. Orville L. Freeman, Secretary of Agriculture, address at the United Nations Biennial Conference of the Food and Agriculture Organization, Rome. Nov. 23, 1965.

2. Ronald Freedman, president, Population Association of America, *New York Times,* Apr. 24, 1965.

3. Roger Revelle, director, Harvard Center for Population Studies, "The University Population Center," *Harvard Public Health Alumni Bull.* (Jan. 1965), p. 15.

4. *World War on Hunger,* Hearings before the House Committee on Agriculture, 89th Cong., 2d Sess., on H.R. 12152, H.R. 12704, and H.R. 12785, Feb. 14, 1966, p. 23.

5. Rep. Harold D. Cooley, as quoted by Felix Belair, Jr., *New York Times,* Feb. 23, 1966.

6. Editorial, *New Statesman,* Jan. 21, 1966, p. 69.

7. *Time,* May 6, 1966.

8. Population Reference Bureau, Washington, D.C., *World Population Data Sheet,* Dec. 1965.

9. United Nations, Department of Economic and Social Affairs, *Provisional Report on World Population Prospects as Assessed in 1963* (1964), p. 120.

10. *Ibid.*

11. Population Reference Bureau, press release, Dec. 7, 1964.

12. United Nations, Department of Economic and Social Affairs, *World Population Prospects up to the Year 2000* (1965).

13. MacFarlane Burnet, *Natural History of Infections and Diseases,* 3d ed. (Cambridge: Harvard Univ. Press, 1962), p. 308.

14. Warren S. Thompson, *The Population Ahead,* ed. Roy G. Francis (Minneapolis: Univ. of Minnesota Press, 1958), p. 126.

15. *Population Bulletin of the United Nations,* No. 6 (1962), p. 17; and Population Reference Bureau, *World Population Data Sheet,* Dec. 1965.

16. Population Reference Bureau, *World Population Data Sheet,* Dec. 1965.

17. *Ibid.*

18. U.S. Department of Health, Education and Welfare, *Vital Statistics Indicators* (Feb. 1966).

19. Jean Mayer, "Food and Population: The Wrong Problem?," *Daedalus* (Summer, 1964), p. 834.

20. *Washington Post,* June 4, 1963.

21. Irene B. Taeuber, "Population Growth in Latin America: Paradox of Development," *Population Bull.,* Vol. 18 (Oct. 1962), p. 128.

22. United Nations, Department of Economic and Social Affairs, *Provisional Report on World Population Prospects as Assessed in 1963* (1964), p. 120.

23. Ansley J. Cole and Edgar M. Hoover, *Population Growth and Economic Development in Low-Income Countries* (Princeton: Princeton Univ. Press, 1958).

24. J. Mayone Stycos, "Problems of Fertility Control in Under-Developed

Areas: Marriage and Family Living," in *Population, Evolution, Birth Control*, ed. Garrett Hardin (San Francisco: W. H. Freeman, 1965), p. 321.

25. Lee Rainwater, *Family Design, Marital Sexuality, Family Size and Contraception* (Chicago: Aldine, 1965), p. 120.

26. *Ibid.*

27. Roger Revelle in *World War on Hunger*, Hearings before the House Committee on Agriculture, 89th Cong., 2d Sess., on H.R. 12152, H.R. 12704, and H.R. 12785, Feb. 14, 1966, p. 41.

28. Alan F. Guttmacher, statement before the Senate Subcommittee on Foreign Aid Expenditures of the Committee on Government Operations, 89th Cong., 1st Sess., on S. 1676, Aug. 10, 1965.

29. *Washington Post*, Aug. 8, 1965.

30. Calculated on the basis of a 2.4% annual increase in a population of 482 million, taken from *World Population Data Sheet* (see n. 8 above).

31. Population Crisis Committee, Washington, D.C., "Birth Control Expert Reports on Family Planning in India," news release, June 21, 1966.

32. *Ibid.*

33. Kasturi Rangan, *New York Times*, Jan. 24, 1966.

34. *Ibid.*

35. Robert W. Gillespie, *Family Planning on Taiwan* (New York: Population Council, Apr. 1965), p. 7.

36. Population Council, *Studies in Family Planning No. 6* (Mar. 1965).

37. Gillespie, p. 7.

38. Byung Moo Lee and John Isbister, "The Impact of Birth Control Programs on Fertility," in *Family Planning and Population Programs*, ed. Bernard Berelson *et al.* (Chicago: Univ. of Chicago Press, 1965), p. 740.

39. Leo F. Schnore, "Social Problems in the Underdeveloped Areas: An Ecological View," *Social Problems*, Vol. VIII (Winter, 1961), p. 187.

40. *Washington Post*, Feb. 20, 1966.

41. S. Chandrasekhar, "A Billion Indians by 2000 A.D.?," *New York Times Magazine*, Apr. 4, 1965.

42. Population Council, *Studies in Family Planning No. 9* (Jan. 1966).

43. *Ibid.*

44. *Ibid.*

45. *New York Times*, Apr. 24, 1965.

46. All population density figures are from Agency for International Development, Statistics and Reports Division, *Selected Economic Data for the Less Developed Countries* (June 1965).

47. *El Diario de Hoy*, San Salvador, Jan. 25, 1962, as quoted by J. Mayone Stycos, "Opinions of Latin American Intellectuals on Population Problems and Birth Control," *Annals of the American Academy of Political and Social Science*, Vol. 360 (July 1965), p. 19.

48. Irene B. Taeuber, *The Population of Japan* (Princeton: Princeton Univ. Press, 1958).

49. For the source of these percentages, see n. 46.

50. Taeuber, p. 90.

51. United Nations, *Statistical Year Book* (1964).

52. Drew Pearson, *Washington Post,* Nov. 30, 1965.

53. K. S. Sundara Rajan, address before the Committee on the World Food Crisis, Washington, D.C., Dec. 9, 1965.

54. Robert C. Cook, president, Population Reference Bureau, Washington, D.C., in conversation with the author, Aug. 30, 1966.

55. J. Mayone Stycos, "Obstacles to Programs of Population Control—Facts and Fancies," *Marriage and Family Living* (Feb. 1965), p. 6.

56. Dexter L. Hanley, statement before the Senate Subcommittee on Foreign Aid Expenditures of the Committee on Government Operations, 89th Cong., 1st Sess., on S. 1676, Aug. 24, 1965.

57. Brock Chisholm, "Dangerous Complacency Toward Biological Warfare," *The Humanist* (Jan.–Feb. 1960), p. 15.

58. *New York Times,* May 19, 1966.

59. *International Development Review,* Vol. 3, No. 6 (June 15, 1966).

60. Henry Gininger, *New York Times,* June 8, 1966.

61. Population Reference Bureau, *World Population Data Sheet,* Dec. 1965.

62. *New York Times,* Jan. 2, 1966.

63. Lester R. Brown, address before the Pacific Northwest Farm Forum, Spokane, Wash., Feb. 8, 1966.

64. Robert Cassen, *New Statesman,* Jan. 21, 1966, p. 96.

There is a high incidence of malnutrition among the poor in the United States. Young children who have less than adequate diets suffer from illnesses that have serious and lasting effects. Malnutrition is a problem also among the aged, the migratory farm workers and the Indians. The ultimate cost of these conditions is so great that steps must be taken to relieve the problem of hunger in the U.S.A.

Hunger, U.S.A.

Citizens' Board of Inquiry

We have found concrete evidence of chronic hunger and malnutrition in every part of the United States where we have held hearings or conducted field trips.

These conditions are *not* confined to Mississippi.

Moreover, on the basis of studies, statements of professionals and lay observers, and newspaper accounts, collected from sources throughout the country, we are convinced that chronic hunger and malnutrition are not confined to those places we visited personally but are national in scope and distribution.

In the course of our research we made an extensive attempt to collect all available medical and nutritional studies evaluating the nutritional status of the poor and found that, without exception, those studies reveal a prevalence of chronic hunger and malnutrition hitherto unimagined.

This prevalence is shocking. A thousand people who must go without food for days each month would be shocking in a wealthy nation. We believe that, in America, the number reaches well into the millions. And we believe that the situation is worsening.

Our first impressions of these severe conditions came not from professionals, not from medical journals, but from the people whose lives are virtually consumed in seeking the food they lack the money to buy.

Wherever we went, we heard the voices of the poor, speaking not in medical terms, not with precise analysis of foods consumed in grams or ounces—but telling us of constant, chronic, unremitting hunger.

After a point, the voices merge into a characterization of a pervasive condition. In Alabama, we were told of a survey just completed of over 1800 Negro heads of households representing families totaling over 10,000 persons. The story that survey told follows the litany:

From *Hunger, U.S.A.*, Report by the Citizens' Board of Inquiry Into Hunger and Malnutrition in the United States. Reprinted by permission of The New Community Press. Copyright 1968.

*babies whose mothers are unable to nurse them receiving no milk
at all but fed instead with water drawn directly from wells and
creeks.*

*children showing the listlessness characteristic of malnutrition, who
let flies climb around their eyes and mouths, who show little interest in playing with each other, who just sit idly when not working,
who sleep a great deal in school.*

*adults suffering from cycles of dizziness and "fallinout," who find
upon visiting the doctor that they need to discontinue starchy and
fatty food—pork products, especially fatback and cornbread, biscuits, beans and grits—their basic diet.*

women who have become bloated from poor diet.

And the story did not vary when we turned north to Boston—where
Dr. Wheeler[1] stated:

"Inevitably, I compared what I saw there with my experiences
in Mississippi and Appalachia and I left Boston with the strongly
held opinion that the problems there are only different in degree
from what we have seen elsewhere.

"I think we saw enough to conclude tentatively that in the
northeastern United States also there is a great group of disadvantaged people living just at or below a minimum level of subsistence
and that their children are malnourished, hungry, ill-clothed, and
are being deprived of the opportunity of ever becoming healthy,
well adjusted, and productive citizens."

This is, in brief, the story of hunger in the United States that this report will explore. Having heard this testimony and much more, we turned
to the medical profession and medical and nutritional journals to learn just
how seriously hunger in the United States affected the health of the poor.
The unequivocal and uncontradicted thrust of testimony by doctors and
the studies we received reemphasized the problems of hunger and malnutrition in objective medical terms.

We were struck by the high incidence of anemia, growth retardation,
protein deficiencies and other signs of malnutrition among the poverty
population.

Repeatedly, we found high proportions of poor infants and children—
Negro, Mexican-American and white, urban and rural—suffering from
anemia. And we have learned that, among the young, anemia can have
serious and lasting medical and even emotional effects.

A young resident physician at Boston City Hospital reported to us the
signs of malnutrition which he and his fellow doctors see regularly among
poor children. He commented that it was a generally accepted fact among
the doctors in the hospital that hemoglobin levels in children from poor
districts were significantly lower than in children coming to suburban hospitals from higher economic groups. He also mentioned that in his experi-

ence the major cause of death in the first year of life is pneumonia, no longer an important killer except in the weak, malnourished and chronically ill.

In Columbia, South Carolina, Dr. Donald Gatch[2] testified:

"I don't find [it] at all uncommon in my patients, in my preschool Negro children who come in, to have a hemoglobin from 6 to 8 gms./100 ml." (Anemia is characterized by low hemoglobin levels. A level of 11 gms./100 ml. is considered below normal. A level of 6 to 8, as here, is considered extremely low.) "I don't put them in the hospital, I just give them some iron and they usually leave. . . ."

In Hazard, Kentucky, Dr. David Steinman,[3] testified and subsequently provided supplemental information describing serious anemia problems among infants in eastern Kentucky:

"Among the infants (infants tested ranged from six weeks to the day of their second birthday) we found in Martin County, out of a total of 220 tested, a rate of 23.6% who had anemia." (Anemia defined as hematocrit below 32%. Hematocrit is another widely used method for identifying anemia.)

Dr. Steinman's testimony was echoed more recently in testimony offered by Dr. Doane Fisher, Pediatrician, Harlan County, Kentucky.[4]

"Anemia remains a very great problem in our infants; and very many of the infants have severe anemia by the time they reach age one. . . . I think another very significant point is when we compare our children who are from the poorer families—these children on the whole spend half again to twice as long for each hospital admission . . . by this I mean . . . if two children have pneumonia and one is poor we expect it will take twice as long to get this child well and out of the hospital because he has the handicaps of anemia, parasites, and poor nutrition standing behind him."

In San Antonio, Texas, the Board heard testimony from doctors at Green Charity Hospital that severe cases of anemia were commonplace, that children one year old frequently weighed less than their birth weights and three-, four- and five-year-olds weighed around 20 pounds.

In Washington, D.C., Dr. Margaret Gutelius,[5] interviewed by a member of the Board, summarized a study conducted in Washington in 1967 of 460 Negro children from low income families. Fifteen percent of the children were supported by public assistance. Iron deficiency anemia was found in 28.9 percent of the total number and reached a peak of 65.0 percent in children from 12 to 17 months of age.

During our Birmingham, Alabama, hearing, we questioned Dr. H. F. Drake, a physician from Huntsville:

Dr. Carter: "You mentioned signs of nutritional deficiencies that you see in your practice. Could you just forget for a few moments that there's a lay audience here and be specific about which signs you see. . . ."

Dr. Drake: "Well, perhaps I can list a few. I see a tremendous number of iron deficiency anemias—hypochromic, microcytic anemias."

From Chicago Dr. Morten Andelman[6] reported to us concerning studies he is currently conducting among children in that city:

"In 1964 we were able to demonstrate that 76% of our infants become anemic before they are two years of age. The exact significance of this has not as yet been definitely established. In our observations we were able to demonstrate that the incidence of upper respiratory infections were almost twice as great in those infants who become anemic than in those whose anemia was prevented by early administration of iron in the formulas."

Dr. Nathan J. Smith[7] estimates that in Seattle, Washington, between 50 and 75 percent of all poverty infants between six and 36 months of age suffer from nutritional deficiency anemia compared to five percent of infants seen in private practice.

In Cincinnati, Boston, Chicago, St. Louis, Columbus, Ohio, and Augusta, Georgia, reports collected by the Board of hospital admissions of children (poor and non-poor) six to 36 months old revealed an average of 20 percent suffering from nutritional anemia. Presumably in the poverty population, the percentage would be higher. This is in fact borne out by studies of Headstart and other preschool children.

These studies have been summarized by L. J. Filer, Pediatrician at the University of Iowa, School of Medicine.[8]

In Chicago (1967), 31.6 percent of the children examined were suffering from anemia (hemoglobin levels below 11 gms./ 100 ml.).

In New York City (1963), 41.3 percent of one-year-olds from low income families had hemoglobin levels below 10 gms./ 100 ml. Among children below three years, 27.3 percent had abnormally low hemoglobin levels.

In Pittsburgh, 16.4 percent of all children studied between 6 and 36 months and 19.0 percent of non-white children had hemoglobin levels below that considered normal.

In Baltimore (1965) the mean hemoglobin concentration of children from low income backgrounds was found to be lower than that of rural Pakistani infants.

In addition the Board learned that:

In Mississippi, 62.1 percent of 847 Headstart children in four Mississippi counties have hemoglobin levels well below that considered normal.[9]

In Alabama,[10] "80% of the (709) children tested had hemoglobin values of 9.4 grams or less. An expected normal would be
11.0 to 13.0 grams."

The board found both in hearings and studies that pregnant women
in poverty suffered from nutritional deficiencies and were constantly anemic.

In San Antonio the Board was informed that at a large charity hospital a minimum of one blood transfusion was given prophylactically to
many pregnant mothers during child birth as part of their regular prenatal
care.

Vera Burke, Director of Social Services for the Texas County Metropolitan Health District which operated Green Charity Hospital in San Antonio, and Dr. Charles Hilton, a prominent pediatrician, reported that
among the nutritional problems they see daily are severely anemic pregnant
women. Mrs. Burke also stated that 25 percent of babies had birth weights
less than five pounds—and that malnutrition could well have been an important factor in causing this.

The Board learned that a study of unwed mothers 18 years and under,
being conducted at Yale Medical School, revealed that approximately 23
percent were suffering from anemia.

Among the specific examples of diets which fail to provide essential
nutrients, Dr. Gilbert Ortiz observed in San Antonio a woman in her eighth
month of pregnancy who had one meal a day consisting of tortillas. And
Harry Huge, in a field visit to Lee County, Florida, was told by public
health officials that most expectant mothers have a low protein intake.

During pregnancy nutritional demands rise dramatically. Nutritional
supplements used routinely by the middle class are virtually unknown to
the poor.

Dr. David Steinman told the Board at the Hazard, Kentucky, hearing
about a study documenting poor diets among pregnant women:[11]

". . . [T]heir findings can be summarized as these: 72% of the
prenatal patients have had some protein from meat, fish or poultry
and 95% had some protein from another animal source.

"However, quantitatively the amounts nowhere approached
the recommended daily dietary allowance of 78 grams a day. This
78 grams a day is that recommended for women in the second half
of pregnancy.

"When teen-age prenatal patients were considered, the rates
were much worse.

"They determined Vitamin A and Vitamin C levels and they
were grossly inadequate. An adequate source of Vitamin A appeared in only 18% of the patients' histories, and Vitamin C in
only 31%."

A U.S. Government survey of Blackfoot Indians, published in December 1964,[12] found the caloric intake of pregnant women was 51 percent of the National Research Council recommended dietary allowance (RDA).

The caloric intake of lactating women was 33 percent of RDA. Also, lactating women consumed an average of 33 percent of the recommended allowance for protein and 31 percent of the allowance for iron. Because two-thirds of RDA is widely accepted as the standard for minimum nutrition, these women were receiving about one-half the protein and iron necessary for a minimally adequate diet.

A 1954 study of 67 Negro pregnant women in Louisiana, published in the *Journal of the American Dietetic Association*,[13] found 38 percent ate laundry starch and 25 percent ate clay. Eighty percent of the diets of pregnant clay eaters and 100 percent of the diets of the non-pregnant clay eaters were noted "fair" to "poor."

A similar study of 86 Alabama women in 1959[14] found 48 percent were clay eaters, 26 percent were cornstarch eaters, and seven percent ate other unusual substances. All the women were from low income families. (All but seven of the clay and starch eating women were pregnant.) Similar phenomena have been reported in Washington, D.C., and Los Angeles.

The most recent and definitive study of clay and starch eating (or geophagia) prepared by Dr. James A. Halsted[15] states:

(1) All studies of pregnant women in the poorest socio-economic groups show a high incidence of either clay or starch eating, from 40 to 50 percent in Negroes and lower numbers in white women.

(2) A mild iron deficiency anemia often appears to accompany the eating of laundry starch by pregnant women, especially those of poor economic status in the southern part of the United States. The mechanism for this anemia is not understood nor has it been adequately studied.

(3) Nevertheless, it has long been recognized by physicians'practicing in poverty areas and in developing nations that geophagia leads to anemia.

(4) In 1906 it was established that in India "clay is eaten by people already anemic, and the more they eat it the more anemic they become."

(5) Indeed, the ability of clay to markedly reduce iron absorption has recently been substantiated.

(6) When combined with food it may rob the body of essential metals such as iron and zinc, producing deficiencies of these minerals.

Finally, a 1960 study of 571 pregnant Negro women in Nashville, Tennessee,[16] showed them consistently falling below RDA for thiamine, riboflavin and ascorbic acid. (They scored above the RDA on Vitamin A due to large consumption of greens.) The poorest were consistently below the average of all pregnant women studied and there was a direct correlation between dietary deficiencies and low socio-economic status.

The board found evidence of retarded growth (abnormally low heights and weights) attributable to malnutrition in both urban and rural poverty areas.

Dr. David Steinman provided the Board with studies showing that six-year-olds from Appalachia were one to two inches shorter than national (Boston-Iowa) norms. This observation was confirmed in conversations with the Assistant Medical Director of Job Corps, Dr. Macht, who informed members of the staff that doctors at the Job Corps centers reported that the youngsters from Appalachia aged 16–21 who entered the centers tended to be generally below normal in height. The crippling effect that growth retardation can have on lives of the poor is discussed below. (We have learned that if poor nutrition goes unchecked in early childhood and growth is consequently retarded, the effects may include irreversible brain damage.

Dr. Doane Fisher's recent testimony in eastern Kentucky substantiated these findings:

> "Our hospital admits 30–50 children per month . . . mostly very low income; . . . our nutritional problems are borderline but they are real . . . example: we surveyed 109 preschoolers for our rural day care centers . . . criteria . . . family income less than $1,000; 30 percent fell below the third percentile for height; now by definition only three percent should have . . . fallen below. This means that a third of our children were significantly statistically below the size they should be which is pretty good evidence that something was wrong nutritionally earlier in life. Seventeen and one-half percent fell below the third percentile in weight— the reason for this difference is . . . they had been under day care food service and one can regain weight easier than height. . . . We have a sharp comparison between the infants who come to our clinic and those who visit us privately up near the United States Steel Co. in Lynch. There is a dramatic contrast between the two groups; a quarter of the infants from low income families are dramatically below norms in weight; the converse is true for the other group—a quarter of them are overweight."

The Board during its field trip to Boston received a report of a comprehensive biochemical dietary study of low income children conducted by the faculty of the Harvard School of Public Health.[17] The study established that in the Roxbury District (one of Boston's poorest) teenagers—both white and Negro—ranked in the lowest percentiles for height and weight.

A 1967 Baltimore study[18] characterized median height for 842 low income preschool children so far below the national (Boston-Iowa) standard as to be closer to norms for underdeveloped countries.

When asked about the dimensions of the food problem in the San Antonio area, Vera Burke reported to the Board that she has seen infants one year old weighing as little as seven pounds and others who actually weigh less than they did at birth.

Dr. Charles Bernard Hilton testified at the same hearing:

"I have seen children at Robert B. Green, just as any doctor who has worked there has seen children, three, four, five years old, all weighing 20 pounds. I was told today that there was a one-year-old baby weighing eight pounds, who [when properly fed] gained three pounds in one month. In my well-baby clinics, I know of at least 10 children who came to us at the age of two to four months and all of them weighed the same as their birth weights."

Dr. Milton Senn, Sterling Professor of Pediatrics at Yale, told a similar story about his visit to Mississippi:[19]

"Children in Mississippi appeared uniformly thin. I did not weigh them but I would judge that more than 50 percent are less than the third percentile in weight."

We have identified severe protein deficiency resulting in the most severe protein diseases—Kwashiorkor and Marasmus. Protein deficiency in early childhood may cause permanent brain damage.

Dr. James Carter personally identified cases of two severe protein deficiency diseases—Kwashiorkor and Marasmus—generally thought to exist only in underdeveloped countries. On a field trip to Hualapi and Navajo Indian Reservations in Arizona, Dr. Carter heard reports that three or four cases of Kwashiorkor per year have been recorded at the United States Health Service Hospital in Tuba City, Arizona. We were informed that such cases were increasing in frequency.

The illustrative case histories of protein deficiency diseases included:[20]

A one-and-one-half-year-old Navajo girl, brought to the hospital because of swelling, irritability and loss of appetite of one week's duration. Parents considered her well until the onset of swelling. She had received "no milk for a long time" and had rarely been given meat. Diet consisted primarily of tea, soda water and beans.

An 11-month-old Navajo girl, brought to the clinic because of swelling. Said to have been well until four months before when swelling of the hands, feet and labia was noted. Since that time had refused to eat well and had lost weight. There had been intermittent vomiting. Swelling recurred one day prior to admission and according to mother made the child appear less starved.

A two-year-old Navajo girl, admitted because of sudden swelling. One month before a mild diarrhea began. Ceased two days prior to admission at which point the swelling occurred. Child had been increasingly listless. For the month during which there was diarrhea the child was fed nothing except "soup" and soda water and occasionally whole milk.

Rose Jones and Harold E. Schendel in their study "Nutritional Status of Selected Negro Infants in Greenville County, South Carolina,"[21] report:

    29 percent (10) of the subjects had serum albumin concentrations associated with marginal protein nutrition;

    61 percent had total protein concentrations below that considered normal (6.0 gm. per 100 ml.).

Dr. Nathan Smith of Seattle also told us:

"We have been made aware of a high incidence in all age groups of low serum protein values which would appear to be related to inadequate dietary intakes of protein. Our experience with older children in the pediatric clinic has clearly demonstrated to us irregular, inadequate nutritional practices in the urbanized low-income family."

A study by Graciela Delgado and Public Health officials in 1961[22] reports the occurrence of Kwashiorkor and Marasmus among the infants of Negro migrant agricultural workers in Palm Beach County, Florida.

There is on record in the *American Journal of Diseases of Children*[23] a documented case of Kwashiorkor in a Puerto Rican child living in the Bronx. No other treatment except whole cow's milk feedings resulted in complete recovery of the child.

The board found evidence of a high incidence of parasitic diseases associated with malnutrition on its visits to South Carolina, Florida, Mississippi, Alabama, and Indian reservations.

The "Report of a World Health Organization Expert Committee," 1967,[24] states that:

"Studies have not been carried out to determine whether malnutrition affects the susceptibility of the human host to infection with hookworm or is related to the number of adult worms in the gut. On the other hand, there is clear evidence that the development of hookworm disease after infection takes place is influenced by the state of the host's iron reserves, and probably also by depletion of the exchangeable albumin pool.

"Some observations indicate that in infected subjects prolonged or periodic starvation may cause increased migration of the worms from the gut to aberrant sites. This may explain the greater frequency of complications requiring surgery and other complications in some regions."

In January 1968, a study of 80 preschool children from two communities in Beaufort County, South Carolina, was conducted.[25] The results of this study are essentially the same as those of an earlier study described to the Board by Dr. Gatch:

"An extremely high rate of parasitic infection was the only out-standing problem. Of the 55 fecal specimens, 30 (54.5%) showed a high incidence of ascaris (round worms) and trichuris (whip worm) infection. Though this rate is not as high as that for the same age group in the prior study, it is still a serious problem. The children tested were primarily infected with round worms. . . .

"The seriousness of worm infection is not always realized. . . . The eggs are taken into the body through the mouth. They go into the intestines where they hatch and the larvae (baby worms) enter the circulatory system as if they were food. Eventually the larvae reach the lungs where they mature. While these worms are developing in the lungs there is a danger of pneumonia. As the de-veloping worms grow they cause irritation and are usually coughed up and are then swallowed to return to the intestines. There they grow and thrive on the food which would otherwise be used by the body. Intestinal parasitic infestations, therefore, can be associated with nutritional deficiencies, loss of weight, listlessness, and even bowel obstruction. If left to thrive in a person's body, worms can cause death."

At the Birmingham, Alabama, hearing, Dr. H. F. Drake of Huntsville, Madison County, responded to the question: "Are parasites a big problem for these people?"

Dr. Drake: "Much larger than is generally recognized. Very defi-nitely so . . . there was a time in my practice when I disregarded it and said, 'oh, there are no worms here,' until a four-year-old vomited a double-handful on my examining table one day. Since that time, I have checked for them. But there are parasites here, very definitely. . . . I don't see in my area much hookworm dis-ease. I see primarily ascaris infestation, pinworms, and from time to time amoebic dysentery."

On a field trip to Florida migrant camps, Harry Huge interviewed officials of Lee County Health Department who informed him that 435 persons were treated in Lee County in 1966 for parasitic diseases; 39,424 were treated for parasitic diseases in the entire state of Florida; that cases of hookworms and other parasitic diseases were seen quite often.

In December, 1967, the Board conducted a field trip in Mississippi. Dr. James F. Schwartz, Emory University School of Medicine, submitted a report of that trip to the Board stating that:

"MAP (Mississippi Action for Progress) is now paying the State Health Department Laboratories $3.00 for each stool examination for parasites. Of 2,500 stool examinations, between 30 and 40 percent revealed parasites. The State Health Department has agreed to supply the medicine, Piperazine, to treat worms, but in several counties at the County Health Department level the medicine was not supplied to the children with worms. Apparently the State Health Department did not send out information and directives."

Studies that have dealt with the nutritional status of the aged indicate that there may be serious nutritional problems among this population group.

The survey conducted by USDA[26] in Rochester, New York, in 1965, of 283 households composed of individuals 65 years of age or older, revealed that 50 percent of the diets being consumed failed to provide adequate levels of one or more protective nutrients, especially calcium and Vitamin C.

Interviews in New York City with nutritionists provide the following composite picture of the nutritional problems of the aged:

"The major health problems of the aging include: diabetes, arteriosclerosis, heart disease, and hypertension. Diet may be related. But both the health and nutritional status of the aging must be viewed as the sum total of long years of living on the marginal limits of nutritional adequacy."

The elderly were characterized by one nutritionist as living on a "tea and toast" diet and by a doctor as subsisting primarily on "mushy foods and soups."

One of those interviewed, Mrs. Marcella Katz, has personally taken nutritional histories of the aging and noted that the protein intake of the aging is very low. They often do not drink milk. Their meat usually consists of chicken backs and wings.

Some of the nutritional problems of the aging are directly attributable to lack of money. One nutritionist observed that "Older persons living on fixed or limited income find that the one area which can be cut is food." It was reported that some chew gum in lieu of eating because they cannot afford food. The aging are unwilling to use their scant savings for everyday needs such as food.

One elderly person interviewed reported that he had $20 a month left after fixed expenses such as rent. When asked how it was possible to manage on such a sum, he responded, "You'd be surprised how much clean garbage there is."

But the nutritional problems of the aged are more complex than money. Loneliness, lack of mobility, lack of eating or cooking facilities, and shopping problems all add a special dimension.

The aging are victims of a cycle. Poor nutrition leads to low energy levels, which in turn lead to no moving or traveling around. Lack of carfare, in and of itself, presents nutritional problems:

"About two years ago a member of a Senior Center in New York City was asked why he could not come to the Center more than once a week, since he was particularly active and enthusiastic and had assumed a leadership role in the affairs of the Center. He replied that 'I have to go without my dinner one day a week to pay carfare for coming to the Center. I can only manage this one day a week.' "

Restaurants, by and large, try to avoid a clientele of older people who take a long time eating and spend little money.

Eating alone tends to become something to get done and over with. And many older people live in single rooms without cooking facilities. (This tends to be understated in surveys which consider a hot plate or a kitchen in the building to be a "cooking facility" for the residents.)

Food shopping poses additional special problems. In a large city such as New York the elderly tend to live in poor neighborhoods and shop in neighborhood stores where prices may be higher or the quality not as high. Many of the elderly live alone, and food often is not packaged for individuals but for families. The size of the food package may make it too large to carry about easily, may require more storage space than the elderly typically have and may contain so large a quantity that much of the contents of what is bought must be discarded due to spoilage.

Roughly one-third of the poor are aged. And they would appear to have a unique set of nutritional problems and nutritional needs. Because they are relatively immobile, have to live on limited and fixed incomes, are lonely, are afraid of the neighborhoods they live in, and because they live and eat alone, obtaining, selecting, preparing and eating food becomes a chore of overwhelming proportions and with none of the compensating social values that meals and eating traditionally have in the family or communal context.

The incidence of malnutrition is likely to be high among migratory farm workers and Indians—but once again data is sparse.

Among Negro migrant agricultural workers in Palm Beach County, Florida, it was found:

> *34 percent* ate no citrus fruits and *82 percent* ate less than one-half the minimum requirements.

> *97 percent* of the families fell below half the recommended allowances for milk and milk products.

> *84 percent* of the persons examined had dental caries and *35 percent* had lost permanent teeth.

> *63 percent* of the families ate no green or yellow vegetables and the rest ate less than half the minimal allowances suggested by USDA.

> Cases of scurvy, rickets, nutritional edema, and Marasmus were observed.

Board members have attested to seeing similar conditions on their trips to migrant camps in Florida. Moreover, Gerald Frawley, Executive Director of the Variety Children's Hospital in Miami, sent to the board a summary of examinations performed in his outpatient department last month on the migrant children from Immokalee.

"The findings in the report are most startling. It is rather incredible that out of 23 children, we found 38 clinical diseases—a most extraordinary morbidity rate for such a group."

Eleven cases of iron deficiency anemia were diagnosed among the 23 children examined. Similar conditions have been reported among migrant workers in Gary, Indiana, and San Antonio, Texas.

Mrs. Barbara McDonald, a Public Health Nutritionist who has worked with the Navajos for many years, has written.[27]

"Nutritional diseases constitute the most serious and widespread health threat throughout the Navajo Indian health area. Malnutrition is endemic and is not accurately reflected by the present method of collecting and analyzing data. Malnutrition provides an ever-present contributing and complicating factor to other health problems and illnesses. Under-reporting of nutritional diseases is frequent."

From Seattle Dr. Nathan J. Smith reports on conditions among the Quinault Indians:

nutritional anemia among children is almost universal; and there is widespread incidence of rickets and low serum proteins.

Analysis of the findings of the Public Health Service nutrition survey of the Blackfoot Indian Reservation in Montana found:

significant segments of the population with borderline intakes of calories, protein, calcium, iron, and Vitamins A and C;

high incidence of dental caries due to deficient fluorine intake;

almost 22 percent of the population fell into the underweight classification of less than 90 percent of standard weight when compared to a normal North American population.

And the picture did not change when we moved from migrant camps to urban areas.

Throughout this chapter, we have documented serious problems in our largest cities, in Boston, Baltimore, Cleveland, and in New York. Our field trip and staff investigations in New York City presented us with a composite picture that summarizes the plight of the urban poor: From Dr. Harold Wise, Internist, associated with Montefiore Hospital and a neighborhood health center in the Bronx:

"We see hunger over a weekend, the period immediately before the next welfare check is due, and a lot of malnutrition mostly manifested in iron deficiency anemia, and susceptibility to infection. Doctors and nurses here at the health center sometimes shell out of their own pockets to tide a family over a weekend. Malnutrition is more prevalent in the children, but it is seen also in the adults."

From Dr. Laurence Feinberg, Pediatrician, Montefiore Hospital:

"We now see about three cases a month of malnutrition at Montefiore and Morrisania Hospitals combined. I see about four or five cases of rickets a year in the Bronx. The most common reason for 'failure to thrive' (a category of diagnoses for children) is insufficient caloric intake, resulting in a cycle of diarrhea and further insufficient caloric intake.

"You do see some starvation in urban areas for the following reasons:

"1. For many, food is too costly;

"2. Mental illness in parents from various economic groups;

"3. Insufficient attention to children's nutrition;

"4. Gastro-intestinal diseases become a vicious cycle, often caused by some degree of malnutrition and causing further malnutrition;

"5. Cultural patterns—e.g., people coming from a tropical Spanish-speaking environment to a temperate, English-speaking environment. Superstitions and folk habits influence choice of diet."

From Eugene Barron, pediatric-psychiatric social worker, Downstate College of Medicine, Kings County Hospital, Brooklyn:

"A classic case is that of a mother with three children on welfare. The youngest child, seven months old, was brought by the mother to Kings County and diagnosed as a 'failure to thrive' case (a general category of sub-normal growth with undetermined cause). A second child was then treated for second-degree burns, but the mother did not follow through on medical care and reinfection occurred. The third child (three years old) had rickets. The mother didn't know, thought the child was just 'bowlegged.' "

From a private physician in Brooklyn:

"A large number of people in the area I serve have nutritional problems. Protein deficiencies resulting from lack of meat and eggs are particularly common. Diets consist primarily of carbohydrates. Weakness and lassitude are common results or manifestations of these poor diets. I would guess that a delay in growth may also be a result. Diets are not balanced and are not adequate. Over half the population in the area of Brooklyn where my practice is located are Puerto Rican. Puerto Rican food habits include: rice and beans, sweet potatoes and fruits typical of the tropics. . . ."

From a public nurse, New York City Department of Public Health:

"A month ago, an eight-year-old girl came to me with a stomach ache. Questioning revealed that she had had no breakfast and only oatmeal for supper the night before. I took her to the kitchen and negotiated a bottle of milk and a slice of bread."

And finally from a second grade teacher in New York City:

"I did a survey of my 25 kids in November, 1967: Two had fruit for breakfast, the others only black coffee or a slice of dry bread. I took them to a grocery store, bought breakfast foods (with my own money) and we had a cooking lesson—and breakfast in the classroom. I give my kids milk each morning. They count on it. One kindergarten teacher told me that she has some children each year who have ravenous appetites for the small snack and repeatedly fight other children for theirs and for extras. In her afternoon session, some children arrive hungry (after the 'lunch' hour). The snack is lighter in the afternoon, as the session is shorter."

We are not the only ones, or even the first ones who have "discovered" hunger and malnutrition in America: others—Senate committees, the Director of the Poverty Program, investigators from the Department of Agriculture, newspaper reporters—have described similar findings.

The report that first opened our eyes to hunger in America told of intolerable conditions in Mississippi.[28]

From New Orleans the Board received a report from Revius Ortique, past President of the National Bar Association, that a reporter from a local TV station had recently uncovered the fact that 1,000 persons living in tar paper shacks surrounding the city dump relied upon the food they scavenged there for survival. This situation came to light when the city decided to institute a charge for dumping garbage at the city dump. The resultant decrease in use of the dump caused severe hardship and an outcry from the families who depended upon the steady flow of garbage in order to survive.

In Des Moines, Iowa, Mark Arnold, a reporter for the *National Observer,* found cases of hunger, sickness and deprivation that seem inconceivable, especially in a state in the heart of the nation's bread basket and in the state on which national standards of satisfactory nutrition and physical development are based. His stories tell of people digging in the dump for food, sick people unable to afford the diet required to control their illness and infants dying for lack of milk.

He reported these interviews:[29]

Mrs. Fay L., a thin, 68-year-old widow, who lives alone on $45 a month: "I know I should be eating more meat to get the protein with my heart trouble and all, and most of the time I get a little hamburger almost everyday. Doctor says I should be drinking fruit juices too, but I figure I can get some Vitamin C from lemonade, it's a lot cheaper. . . . When you keep busy you don't mind being hungry so much. I don't hardly notice when mealtime goes by if I'm playing the piano or reading my Bible."

Mrs. Florence M., 26 with two small children, whose husband is unable to find work: "We mooch same's other folks, I guess. One thing we always got is milk 'cuz my ma keeps a goat. We don't always eat the same things all the time either. One day I'll fix macaroni for lunch, the next day spaghetti, or potatoes so we get a little variety too. . . . I had a steak once, about three months ago. A boy friend of my husband's was servin' it and invited us over. Imagine that, me going 26 years without tastin' steak. I took one little bitty bite and said, 'Boy it sure was worth waitin' for.' "

Early in April, two officials from the Department of Agriculture, Howard Davis and William Seabron, traveled to Mississippi to view at first hand the reported conditions of hunger. Their findings were summarized in a report to Secretary Freeman:

"There are clear evidences of malnutrition and unmet hunger.

"A typical hardship case is that of Mr. and Mrs. Leroy Brown, 514 North Beauchamp, Greenville, Mississippi. They have eight children. Mr. Brown is a cement finisher helper and has intermittent employment. He had gone to work the morning prior to our arrival only to find that a subcontractor had slapped a lien on the job and it had closed down. He was unemployed. We asked him about participating in the Food Stamp program and he indicated that he could never save enough money to do this. His children had no shoes and few clothes. He has rent of $20 a month, water $3, and he uses butane gas which costs him $1 a week. He claims he has no winter work and gets behind in all his bills during this period. The children go to school usually with no breakfast and get no lunch at school. They get only one meal a day and this usually is something like beans and white potatoes. Every once in a while they have chicken wings or necks.

"Mrs. Annie White, 300 Ethel Street, Cleveland, Mississippi, has six children. She signed up for the Food Stamp program but was unable to participate because of no income. We asked what she had had for breakfast and she said rice and biscuits. We asked where she got the food and she said it was left over from March commodities. She had tried to get on welfare but without success. We saw a young baby in her house whose stomach and navel was extended, possibly from malnutrition or hunger.

"There are families existing on no discernible income. . . ."

Sargent Shriver referred to the results of an NIMH study[30] where social workers listened to the poor and heard:

"There was no food in the house and I didn't want them to go to school hungry and then come home hungry too. I felt that if I kept them at home with me, at least when they cried and asked for a piece of bread, I would be with them and put my arms around them."

Mr. Shriver testified in July, 1967:

"When I was in Alaska, I saw problems which are in Alaska as challenging or as tragic as perhaps those in Mississippi. For example I found out that out of 35,000, 36,000, 37,000 poor people—and I mean desperately poor people—in Alaska, something like 142 are getting food assistance in toto."

The Georgia Director of Family and Children Services has stated:

"The other day I saw a place you wouldn't believe exists in the U.S. It looked like a slum on a hillside of some Latin American country. Hundreds of shacks . . . little kids running around with their bellies sticking out . . . women and children—no men. It was pathetic."

As our study was drawing to a close, an appeal for food donations to help residents of the nation's capital survive the winter appeared in the Washington, D.C., newspapers:

"Friendship House has put out an emergency appeal for canned goods to help its needy families survive one of Washington's toughest winters.

"Ruth Melby, Director of Consumer Education at Friendship, called the need 'desperate.' One SE senior citizen, speaking of rising food costs, said, 'It used to be that we went hungry the last few days of the month; now it's the last 15 days of the month.' "

And what we have found is more than substantiated by every available food consumption study: The poor simply do not eat what they need to eat—their diets are inadequate.

Dietary intake studies of food actually consumed establish that substantial proportions of the poor in fact subsist on grossly inadequate diets.

Medically confirmed diagnoses of malnutrition provide the firmest evidence that serious malnutrition exists but characteristically tell us little about the magnitude and severity of the problem. Conversely, the evidence drawn from studies reporting grossly inadequate diets is less conclusive than medical evidence in establishing malnutrition but is most significant in indicating that we are dealing with a widespread phenomenon. These normally are not accompanied by medical corroboration of malnutrition and sometimes are methodologically questionable.

Consumption studies corroborate the initial observation based on medical studies: There is a high incidence of malnutrition among the poor.

In Boston's Roxbury section, the Harvard School of Public Health in 1967 studied a group of predominantly Negro nine- to 13-year-olds and found:

64 percent had less than two glasses of milk a day;

30 percent had unsatisfactory meal ratings for two or more of the four days of the study;

A majority had less than one serving of citrus fruit a day; the average number of servings was 0.4 per day;

The ratings were as bad or worse than the poorest groups surveyed 15 to 20 years earlier;

99.8 percent had unsatisfactory ratings in consumption of

green and yellow vegetables; the average number of daily servings—0.2.

A New York City study of elementary school children concluded:[31]
73.2 percent had poor diets; 20.2 percent of the diets were
adequate, only 6.6 percent were excellent.

Children whose families were not on welfare had twice the
frequency of "excellent" ratings as those from welfare families.
Sources of proteins [milk, meat and eggs] were served less than
once a day for almost half the families.

A 1967 study of teenagers from low income families in Berkeley,
California,[32] showed that the nutrient intakes were less than two-thirds of
RDA in the following proportion:

	% of girls	% of boys
Iron	50%	10%
Calcium	50	20
Vitamin A	25	30
Vitamin C	25	33
Calories	15	20

A 1963 Cleveland study of public assistance families reported that:

More than 60 percent of the families had "poor or very poor"
food intake; more than one-fourth rated very poor.

Only one in 12 families and one in 15 children were getting
what nutritionists consider a good diet.

20 percent of the children—most under 12—had less than
one glass of milk a day.

A 1964 county-wide follow-up study of the families on public
assistance found 80 percent had substandard diets while the other
20 percent were marginal.

A survey reported of families in rural Pennsylvania receiving federal
food assistance in the form of surplus commodities,[33]

two-thirds had intakes below normal (RDA) for calcium
and Vitamins A and C.

Calories and riboflavin were low in more than half.

Protein, thiamine and iron were deficient in 40 percent.

A dietary intake study in Mississippi Delta Counties in 1967 conducted by the Department of Agriculture concluded:[34]

"The average food consumption and nutrient content of the diets
of the families eligible for the food stamp program in Washington
County and for the food donation program in Sunflower County
are considered poor" (defined as meeting less than ⅔ of the

RDA). "The quality of the diets of participants and non-participants was about equal."

The Child Development Group of Mississippi conducted two studies in 1967 to determine the kinds of diets Headstart children were getting. The first study of families, most of whom received all or part of their food from surplus commodities, found:[35]

50 percent of the families had some meat three or less meals a week; 18 percent had meat only once a week;

18 percent had meat only once a week or not at all.

The testimony of the poor told us there was hunger. Doctors, nutritionists, school teachers, government officials and many others told us there was hunger and malnutrition. Professional journals, newspaper articles, and various other reports confirmed what we heard. There are hunger and malnutrition in America. They are widespread and are becoming worse.

But why, it may still be asked, should this be a matter either for national concern or for priority treatment, given the large number of competing demands on this nation? What happens to infants who are malnourished? If malnutrition at every age is dangerous, is chronic hunger by itself a cause for concern? A number of doctors and psychologists have provided us with the answers to these and other related questions. The answers need no embellishment. The facts, we feel, speak for themselves.

The Effects of Hunger and Malnutrition

In the latest *Rockefeller Foundation Quarterly*, George Harrar writes:[36]

"We have long known that severe food shortages and famines can have immediate injurious effects on human beings. We have all seen pictures of children with bloated bellies and emaciated bodies. Their physical constitutions are so weakened by hunger that they are highly vulnerable to all manners of other illnesses. It is also common knowledge that certain dietary deficiencies can later cause severe skeletal damage such as occurs in rickets. Contemporary research, however, has indicated that malnutrition may also have long range and more insidious effects on children and may even damage internal organs such as the liver.

". . . There is accumulating evidence to show that an inadequate and unbalanced diet, occurring at a highly crucial and prolonged period in the development of an infant or young child, may affect its mental capacities to a degree where its ability to learn is seriously impaired. The visible effects of malnutrition may be corrected and may disappear, and the child may seem to be restored to full health and vigor. But the effects on mental development may not be readily apparent and often may be perceived only when the child manifests difficulty in competing with normal children."

The damage caused by malnutrition begins even before birth and can affect future generations.

Dr. Frederick Solomon summarized this relationship:

"It is well known that low income women have greatly increased chances of producing premature infants and/or having 'complicated' pregnancies and deliveries. It is also known that such offspring will then have greatly increased risk of brain damage or (in the case of prematures) slow development and special needs. As far as I can tell from the medical literature, the causes of prematurity and other complications of pregnancy . . . include: (1) small bone size in the expectant mother (probably due to poor nutrition and illness in her childhood); (2) poor nutrition and infectious disease during the pregnancy. . . ."

An article in a recent issue of the *Journal of Pediatrics*[37] reported that women whose small stature is attributable to malnutrition are prone to give birth prematurely and the substantially higher incidence of birth defects among premature babies indicates that the effects of malnutrition thus may extend beyond a single generation.

There is increasing evidence that lack of protein in the diet of youngsters can cause severe and irreversible brain damage.

Dr. Joseph Brenner briefly summarized the evidence in testimony to the Senate Subcommittee on Employment, Manpower and Poverty:

". . . Increasing evidence has come from different countries, especially from Mexico and South Africa, to suggest that infants, who both before and after birth, were deprived of the kinds of food which are necessary for normal bodily growth, suffer not only visible damage to their bodies but also damage to the central nervous system, to the brain.

Now one of the tragedies of this finding, if, indeed, it proves to be substantiated, is that while the damage to the bodily tissues from early malnutrition can be repaired in the main by subsequent better nutrition and medical care, no matter how well you feed children who are sadly deprived of food during the prenatal and immediate postnatal period, if they have suffered brain damage the likelihood is that this cannot be remedied."

Dr. Willard Johnson, in an article[38] discussing whether school lunches are too late to avert the permanent effects of malnutrition, notes:

"The nutritionists are saying these days that calories alone are not enough for the proper development of young children. Neither is it sufficient to add minerals and vitamins to the diet. The most critical factor seems to be protein.

Aaron Altschul of the Research Service of the U.S. Department of Agriculture [said]:

'This [protein deficiency] is especially serious for pre-school children. Their brains reach 90 percent of full weight before age four. If they don't get enough protein in that critical period, the brain just never does develop properly.'

The implications of this finding are tremendous. Not that giving adequate protein to children in their early years would be a panacea, but without it all other efforts may be doomed to failure or to mere partial success.

It is a common observation that the children of the 30 million poverty-stricken people in the United States may get enough food through welfare programs. But do they get enough proteins? Mostly they eat starchy foods—potatoes, grits, cornpone, breads, beans, and so forth. If the family has meat, cheese, nuts or fish, it goes mostly to adults. So children suffer brain damage that is never overcome, irrespective of the amounts of protein consumed later.

These children, being deprived of normal brain development, do not do well in school. They do not have the intelligence, the initiative, or the motivation that stems from normal brain capacity. The many other deficiencies caused by poverty, the emotional and social damages of broken homes, and the lack of normal living conditions all reinforce the outcome of this early nutritional imbalance, so that these children become adults who perpetuate the same conditions for their children."

Dr. Nevin S. Scrimshaw, head of the Department of Nutrition and Food Science at MIT, has presented a thorough analysis of this nutritional blight. Discussing the field studies of Dr. Joaquin Cravioto, the pioneer of research into brain damage and malnutrition, Dr. Scrimshaw explained:[39]

"Retardation in physical growth and development was found to depend upon family dietary practices and on the occurrence of infectious disease. It was not related to differences in housing facilities, personal hygiene, proportion of total income spent on food, or other indicators of social and economic status. Under these circumstances, the investigators found test performance of preschool and school children to be positively correlated with body weight and height."

If protein deprivation does, indeed, cause irreversible brain damage, then the evidence accumulated by the Board is all the more disturbing. We found specific instances of children suffering from two severe protein deficiency diseases named Kwashiorkor and Marasmus. But more pervasive are the findings of anemia which characterize high percentages of infants and children from poverty populations. Contrary to the assumption of laymen who think anemia involves solely an iron deficiency, a finding of anemia may indicate either an iron deficiency or a *protein deficiency,* or both. Thus, our widespread findings of anemia may in turn be indicative of widespread protein deficiency among infants and young children at a critical stage in the development of their central nervous system.

Malnutrition causes lowering of resistance to infection and consequently is a prime cause of infant mortality after weaning and a significant contributory cause of parasitic infection, worms, viruses, and bacterial diseases.

A report of a World Health Organization Expert Committee states:[40]
"Experimental work confirms the clinical impression that severe protein deficiency and generalized malnutrition increase the susceptibility of the host to many infectious diseases."

The relationship between malnutrition and infant mortality is discussed below.

Dr. Frederick Solomon made the following observation:
"A poorly nourished child is a child who will be more likely to become clinically ill rather than throwing off an infection. A child whose intake of protein, calories and vitamins has been deficient will not only have less resistance to catching a disease, but his clinical course will be more severe and prolonged once he has become ill. Furthermore, there is a vicious circle between borderline malnutrition and communicable disease, so that the presence of one illness exhausts the body's resources so that the child is even less resistant to catching the next infectious disease to which he is exposed."

Other direct effects of malnutrition include listlessness and apathy, shortened life expectancy, disabilities resulting from inadequate growth and diseases such as blindness, rickets, scurvy, and pellagra that result from deficiencies of a particular nutrient.

Yet, those consequences which result from classical instances of malnutrition represent only the tip of the iceberg. Each extreme case is indicative of a far greater number of borderline cases. Each case identified and documented is indicative of many undocumented and unreported.

But we wish to emphasize that hunger and a general condition of insufficient nourishment take a toll far greater and at least as significant as any of the classical forms of malnutrition which result from the deficiency of a particular nutrient.

We wish to distinguish the conditions we have seen of widespread, chronic and unremitting hunger from the extreme famine state with which some of us have had first hand familiarity abroad. We found instances of malnutrition and undernutrition as severe as those we have seen abroad. But far more typical of the Board's experience was the condition of chronic hunger, and continuous undernutrition which tends to be dismissed as minor or unimportant by the American people and even by segments of the medical profession. Beyond those cases of malnutrition clinically diagnosed are the far vaster number of Americans who never get enough to eat, who never get adequate nutrition, who waste away or suffer the corpulence and gross overweight of a diet comprised almost entirely of starches.

The cost of this chronic hunger and undernutrition takes many forms: educational, psychological and social.

Hunger for food overrides hunger for knowledge.

A child comes to school with no breakfast—except perhaps a cup of coffee. He has no lunch and no money for a school lunch. He may carry some candy to nibble on to appease his appetite. Teachers and principals have repeatedly told the Board the obstacle which hunger places in their way—in the form of listlessness, fights over food, inattentiveness, acute hunger pangs, withdrawal, a sense of failure.

The ultimate costs are to be found in patterns of social unrest, distrust, alienation, withdrawal, and frustration.

Dr. Robert Coles provides this description of what it means to a child to be hungry more or less regularly. The children, he notes:

"become tired, petulant, suspicious and finally apathetic.

One will talk with them and play with them and observe their behavior and ask them to draw or paint pictures. From all that one can learn the aches and sores of the body become for a child of four or five more than a concrete physical fact of life, bring in the child's mind a reflection of his worth, and judgment upon him and his family of the outside world by which he not only feels but judges himself.

They ask themselves and others what they have done to be kept from the food they want or what they have done to deserve the pain they seem to feel.

In my experience with families in the Delta, their kind of life can produce a chronic state of mind, a form of withdrawn, sullen behavior. I have seen some of the families I know in the South go North and carry with them that state of mind and I am now working with them in Boston. They have more food, more welfare money, and in the public hospitals of the northern city certain medical services.

But as one tape records their expressed feelings and attitudes month after month, one sees how persistently sickness and hunger in children live on into adults who doubt any offer, mistrust any goodness or favorable turn of events as temporary and ultimately unreliable.

I fear that we have among us now in this country hundreds of thousands of people who have literally grown up to be and learned to be tired, fearful, anxious, and suspicious and in some basic and tragic sense simply unbelieving.

All one has to do is ask some of these children in Appalachia who have gone north to Chicago and Detroit to draw pictures and see the way they will sometimes put food in the pictures or draw pictures of trees which they then explain are ailing with branches in some way falling. All one has to do is ask them what they want, to confirm the desires for food and for some kind of medical care for the illnesses that plague them."

The hunger we have seen contributes directly to the schisms which threaten our society today.

In a land of affluence and agricultural plenty, it cannot help but aggravate a sense of injustice, of grievance, of frustration and revolt.

This takes many forms. They range from school absenteeism and food stealing in schools to the massive problems of urban unrest and violence where chronic hunger, combined with other grievances, lowers the frustration level, intensifies one's sense of distrust and outrage at the society as a whole and increases tensions to the breaking point.

The problem is not one peculiar to (or confinable to) Mississippi, though there are some who would seem to want to draw comfort and complacency from that myth. As Dr. Robert Coles pointed out:

"When a sick, chronically malnourished child leaves a plantation or mountain hollow for Chicago or Detroit, rural poverty becomes urban poverty. Internal migration in this country has recently been enormous. Had the same dislocated people come from outside, we should no doubt have all kinds of emergency plans to help them and also help the area in which they settled."

Joshua Lederberg summed up the overall costs of hunger and malnutrition:[41]

"The geopolitical impact of this facet of nutritional science comes from the vicious cycle of malnutrition, mental retardation, indolence and unemployability—a vicious cycle that afflicts depressed peoples throughout the world, be they have-not nations or have-not ghettos."

Order of Magnitude and Probable Pattern of Distribution

We recognize that no definitive estimate can now be made regarding the number of people suffering from hunger and malnutrition in the United States.

On July 12, 1967, Dr. William Stewart, Surgeon General of the United States, stated:

"We do not know the extent of malnutrition anywhere in the United States."

Senator Clark asked:

"Are you able to say whether in your estimate, there is a lot of it, or, on the other hand, not much?"

Dr. Stewart: "Among the population . . . there is a fair amount of it. I cannot say what the extent is because we just don't know.

. . . We have been trying to get ourselves to do this kind of work in the United States. We can do it all over the world but not in the United States."

It is hoped that under the new Partnership for Health legislation, such data will soon be available. It is significant that Drs. Arnold Schaefer and Ogden Johnson, the experts responsible for conducting such studies for the Public Health Service abroad, have been designated to take charge of this assignment. The legislation calls for an initial report within a few months— by summer, 1968.

Nonetheless, it is possible to assert with a high degree of probability that we face a problem which, conservatively estimated, affects 10 million Americans and in all likelihood a substantially higher number.

We base this conclusion upon the following reasoning: the incidence of malnutrition correlates directly with income levels; the percentage of the poor affected by hunger and malnutrition ranges conservatively between one-third and one-half. The federal government estimates that there are approximately 29 million Americans considered to be below the poverty line.

Correlation: all available evidence indicates that the incidence of malnutrition correlates directly with income levels.

A. This correlation emerges from our hearings and field trips, from professional observations, personal interviews, and newspaper accounts summarized above.

B. This correlation is corroborated by the many medical and dietary intake studies summarized above.

C. This correlation is directly substantiated by both the 1955 and 1965 nationwide Household Consumption Studies conducted by the Department of Agriculture.

The 1955 study states:

"Among city families, dietary adequacy, as measured by the percentage of household diets meeting allowances in all of eight nutrients, was closely related to income. At each successively higher income level a greater percentage of diets met allowances, a relationship that existed among both northern and southern families. There was a tendency for those of the higher income levels whose diets did not meet the recommended dietary allowances to fail in a single nutrient only. At the lower income levels a somewhat larger percentage of households failed in four or more nutrients."

The correlation between income and dietary adequacy is reaffirmed in the recently released dietary analysis of the 1965 nationwide consumption study conducted by the Department of Agriculture.

The report states:

"At each successively higher level of income, a greater percentage of households had diets that met [recommended dietary] allowances."

Moreover, the nutritional status of Americans has actually deteriorated since 1955 and 1965:

"About 20 percent of the diets in 1965 were poor, . . . and about 15 percent in 1955."

D. This correlation (between low income and malnutrition) is further substantiated by the impact of low income upon postneonatal mortality—a nutritionally related phenomenon. Postneonatal mortality rates state the incidence of infant mortality *from one month to one year.*

After the period of weaning, nutrition becomes a chief factor in a child's life. Poor nutrition lowers a child's resistance and increases his susceptibility to disease. Since malnutrition may manifest itself as weakened resistance to disease, the autopsy may conclude that the infant died of pneumonia or flu or some other disease, but the evidence reviewed indicates that malnutrition may make the difference between life and death when infection does occur.

Dr. Joseph Brenner testifying before the Senate Subcommittee on Employment, Manpower and Poverty on July 11, 1967, called attention to the toll being taken of the infant poor during their first year:

"During the first few months of his life an infant has a slowly diminishing immunity to disease that has been acquired from the mother before birth. By the time of his weaning he must start replacing his immune substances by those that his body produces. For that he needs adequate body tissues and adequate nutrition to build them. This is vital between the time of weaning when a few months old and about two years of age."

The correlation between malnutrition and poverty is reflected in postneonatal mortality rates. During the first month of life—the neonatal stage —poverty infants die at only a slightly higher rate than infants from higher income groups.

From the second to the 12th month, a startling disparity occurs between different income groups. The rate of death for the infant from an affluent family drops to approximately one-third the neonatal (first month) rate. The death rate for the poor infant may drop—but nowhere as radically; and in the poorest counties, the postneonatal rate will actually rise appreciably above the neonatal rate. As a result, the odds that the poor infant will die during the second to 12th month is approximately three times that of the non-poor infant. In the poorest counties, the disparity shoots up to five to 10 times the national average of postneonatal mortality.

Although nutrition is not the exclusive factor causing death, it is the primary factor *added* as a cause of death during the postneonatal stage. This marked divergence between rich and poor reflects the importance of nutrition which, after weaning, can only be supplied by prepared foods.

Thus, for instance, in Wolfe County, Kentucky, the second poorest county in the United States, a county with a 100 percent white population, the neonatal rate for infants is 16.3 per 1,000 births—actually below the

national average for white infants, 17.3 per 1000. However, the postneonatal rate in Wolfe County is 13.2 per 1,000—higher than twice the
national average for white infants, 5.9 per 1000.

The pattern is unbroken from state to state:

   (a) In virtually every state the highest postneonatal mortality
   rates occur in counties with higher percentages of poor families than
   counties with the lowest postneonatal mortality rates. . . .

   (b) In virtually every state, the postneonatal rate in the poorest county dramatically exceeds the postneonatal rate for the
   wealthiest county. . . .

*Magnitude: available evidence indicates that the percentage of poor affected
by hunger and malnutrition range between one-third and one-half of the
poor.*

A. These percentages characterize the degree of malnutrition-related
conditions found in the studies summarized above.

B. Field trips, observations and interviews confirm the impression that
hunger and malnutrition prevail where one finds heavy concentrations of
poverty.

C. The nationwide Household Consumption Studies conducted both
in 1955 and 1965 reveal that more than a majority of the poor have inadequate diets.

Thus the 1965 study observes:

   "Almost two-thirds, 63 percent, of the households with incomes
   under $3,000 had diets that did not meet the allowances for one or
   more nutrients.

   "Over one-third, 36 percent, of the households with incomes
   under $3,000 had 'poor' diets. At this income level poor diets oc-
   curred most frequently among urban households in the North Central and rural households in the South."

This analysis does not reveal the actual severity of the problem because it lacks a breakdown for families under $3,000 per year. In rural
areas, failure to provide such a breakdown averages the poorest of the poor,
with incomes of less than $1,000, with families of $3,000 (which in some
rural areas constitutes a livable income). For instance, the 1955 study reveals that 71% of farm families in the South with incomes under $1,000
had inadequate diets. The 1955 consumption study revealed that percentages of those with inadequate diets rose markedly as income fell from
$3,000 to $2,000 to $1,000 and less:

   38% of city families with incomes between $1,000 and $2,000 were
   deficient in dietary intake of four or more of the eight nutrient clas-
   sifications as compared with 30 percent of city families with income
   between $2,000 and $3,000.

All of these percentages are subject to challenge because they are based
upon RDA which some nutritionists consider to be inflated minimum daily

requirements. Nonetheless, these percentages provide at least a gross indication of the order of magnitude of the problem with which we are confronted.

D. Each fatality which comprises the postneonatal mortality rate— just as with every diagnosed case of rickets, Kwashiorkor or Marasmus— may indicate a substantially larger and unrecorded number of infants suffering from malnutrition ranging from near fatal to borderline.

Notes

1. Dr. Raymond Wheeler, a member of the Board of Inquiry, observed described conditions during a medical field trip to Boston in January, 1968.

2. Practicing physician, Beaufort County, South Carolina.

3. Resident Physician, University of Kentucky School of Medicine.

4. Dr. Fisher's testimony was given to the Senate Subcommittee on Employment, Manpower and Poverty during its February trip to eastern Kentucky.

5. Director, Child Health Center, Children's Hospital, Washington, D.C., Associate Professor of Pediatrics, George Washington University School of Medicine.

6. Resident Physician, Chicago, Illinois. Dr. Andelman over the past few years has directed various studies to the nutritional well-being of preschool children.

7. Pediatrician in Chief, King County Hospital, Seattle, Washington.

8. Filer, L. J., "The United States Today—Is It Free of Public Health Nutrition Problems—Anemia"; Presented to American Public Health Association, Miami Beach, Florida, October 24, 1967.

9. Britton, A. B.; "High Incidence of Anemia Among C.D.G.M. Children"; Memo to the Director and the Chairman of CDGM, dated July 6, 1967.

10. Testimony of Dr. Allen C. Mermann, Department of Pediatrics, Yale University Medical School, and private practice Guilford, Conn., Hearings Before the Subcommittee on Employment, Manpower and Poverty of the Committee on Labor and Public Welfare, United States Senate, 90th Congress, Hunger and Malnutrition in America, July 11, 1967, pp. 53–56.

11. Garland, B., "A Preliminary Evaluation of the Nutritional Status of 416 Pregnant Women in Eastern Kentucky," Jan. 1967 (unpublished).

12. Blackfoot Indian Reservation, Nutrition Survey August–September, 1961; U.S. Public Health Service, Dec. 1964.

13. Edwards, C. H., McSwain, H., Haire, S.; "Odd Dietary Practices of Women"; Journal of American Dietetic Association, Vol. 30, October 1954, p. 976.

14. Edwards, C. H., McDonald, S., Mitchell, J. R., Jones, L., Mason, L., Kemp, A. M., Laing, D., and Trigg, L.; "Clay and Cornstarch Eating Women," Journal of American Dietetic Association, August, 1959, p. 810.

15. See Halsted, James A. and Prasad, Ananda, "Syndrome of Iron Deficiency Anemia, Hepatosplenometaly, Hypogonadism, Dwarfism, and Geophagia." Transactions of American Clinical Climatological Assoc., Vol. 72, 1960, pp. 130–149. Halsted's most recent work, quoted here, is to be published soon.

16. Studies discussed in report of National Vitamin Foundation, Inc., "How Well Nourished Are Americans," in 1963.

17. Myers, M. L., O'Brien, S. C., Mabel, J. S., Stare, F. J.; "A Nutritional Study of School Children in a Depressed Urban District—II Biochemical Findings." Harvard University, 1967.

18. Stine, O. C., Saratsiotis, J. B., Furno, O. F.; "Appraising the Health of Culturally Deprived Children"; *The American Journal of Clinical Nutrition,* Vol. 20, No. 10, October, 1967.

19. Senate Subcommittee Hearings, pp. 5–8.

20. Wolf, C. B., Kwashiorkor on the Navajo Indian Reservation, U.S. Public Health Service.

21. Jones, R. E. and Schendel, H. E., "Nutritional Status of Selected Negro Infants in Greenville County, South Carolina"; *The American Journal of Clinical Nutrition,* Vol. 18, No. 6, June, 1966.

22. Delgado, G. Brumback, C. L., and Deaver, M. B.; "Eating Patterns Among Migrant Families," U.S. Dept. of HEW, Public Health Reports, Vol. 76, No. 4. April, 1961.

23. *American Journal of Diseases of Children,* 1966, Vol. 112, pp. 76–78.

24. Report of World Health Organization Expert Committee: "Nutrition and Infection" World Health Organization, Technical Report Series No. 314, 1965, p. 11, et. seq.

25. Jeffery, G. M. "Study of Intestinal Helminth Infections in a Coastal South Carolina Area." Public Health Reports, Vol. 78, No. 1, January, 1963.

26. LeBovit. "A Study of Low Income Householders of Rochester, North Carolina; Average Age over 70 Years." Dietary Adequacy and Nutritional Status in U.S. *Dairy Council Digest,* Vol. 38, No. 6, Nov.–Dec. 1967.

27. "Nutrition of the Navaho," U.S. Public Health Service, Division of Indian Health, Window Rock, Arizona, June, 1965, page 30.

28. Poverty, Hunger and Federal Food Programs. Background information prepared for Subcommittee on Employment, Manpower and Poverty of the Committee on Labor and Public Welfare, United States Senate, July 1, 1967 (hereafter Senate Subcommittee Background Information on Hunger), pp. 59, 60, 61.

29. Arnold, Mark. "You Won't Find Many Are Dying from Hunger but Malnutrition Problem Is Very Large Even in Bountiful Iowa": *The National Observer,* August 7, 1967.

30. NIMH study, quoted by Sargent Shriver, from Study on Welfare, Outreach, 1965.

31. Christakis, G., Miridjanian, An., Nath, L., Khurana, H. S., Cowell, C., Archer, M., Frank, O., Ziffer, H., Baker, H., James, G.; "A Nutritional Epidemiologic Investigation of 642 New York City Children," 1967 (unpublished).

32. Diets of high school students in Berkeley, California; Hampton, M. C., Huenemans, R. L., Shapero, L. R., Mitchel, B. W.; *Journal of American Dietetic Association,* 50:385, 1967.

33. Survey conducted by General Accounting Office. Methodology and results reported to us by Public Health Service.

34. Adelson, Sadye F., "The Dietary Situation Among Low-Income Households in Two Mississippi Delta Counties."

35. "Survey of Family Meal Patterns," Child Development Group of Mississippi, Nutrition Services Division, May 17, 1967, and July 11, 1967 (two surveys).

36. *Rockefeller Foundation Quarterly Report*, 1967.

37. See Drillien, Cecil M., *The Growth and Development of the Prematurely Born Infant*, Livingston, Edinburgh and London, 1964, pp. 7–8, 73–95.

38. Johnson, W., "Protein and Poverty, or School Lunches are Too Late," *Child Welfare*, June, 1967.

39. Scrimshaw, Nevin S., "Infant Malnutrition and Adult Learning," *Saturday Review*, March 16, 1967, page 64.

40. Report of World Health Organization Expert Committee: "Nutrition and Infection," World Health Organization, Technical Report Series No. 314, 1965, p. 11, et. seq.

41. Lederberg, J., "Evidence Links Poor Diet to Forever-Stunted Minds," *The Washington Post*, January, 1968.

It is simple logic that given a limited space, such as the earth, and a growing population, sooner or later the growth must and will stop. Immediate and drastic steps must be taken to overcome the barriers to population control, and meaningful inducements must be offered to individuals and nations to encourage birth control. Every possible aid must be applied to increase food supply.

Population, Food, and Environment: Is the Battle Lost?

Paul R. Ehrlich

The facts of human population growth are simple. The people of the earth make up a closed population, one to which there is no immigration and from which there is no emigration. It can be readily shown that the earth's human population will remain essentially closed—that no substantial movement of people to other planets is likely and that no substantial movement to other solar systems is possible. Now, a closed population will grow if the birth rate exceeds the death rate, and will shrink in size if the death rate is greater than the birth rate. Over the past half-century or so a massive increase in man's understanding and utilization of death control has resulted in a rapid rise in the rate of growth of the human population (a rate which is equal to the birth rate minus the death rate). So, we have a closed, growing population. And, intriguing as the prospect may be to certain irresponsible politicians, economists, and religious leaders, we will not achieve an infinite population size. Sooner or later the growth of the human population must stop.

On the "later" side it has been possible to compute when physical limitations, notably the problem of dissipating the heat produced by human metabolic processes, will put an end to growth in the solar system. We are forever barred from exporting a significant part of our population to the stars, so the theoretical maximum for the solar system coincides closely with the extreme possible numerical peak for *Homo sapiens*. This peak would be reached, at the current growth rate, in far under 1500 years. Indeed, if we are confined in large part to the planet Earth (and there is every reason to believe we will be), the end will be reached in less than 1000 years. For those interested in such long-range thinking there is one more cheery datum —the rate of increase of the population is itself accelerating!

On the "sooner" side we must face considerably less certainty. A fantastic world effort over the next decade at changing the attitude of people

From "Population, Food, and Environment: Is the Battle Lost?" by Paul R. Ehrlich. Reprinted by permission of Paul R. Ehrlich and the Editors of *The Texas Quarterly*.

towards family size and developing, promoting, and distributing birth control technology might conceivably arrest population growth at two to three times its present level—if nothing untoward intervenes. On the other hand, it is quite within our power to reduce the population size to zero tomorrow, should we opt for thermonuclear war. But, later or sooner, one thing is certain. The human population *will* stop growing. This halt must come through either a decrease in the birth rate, or an increase in the death rate, or a combination of the two. A corollary of this is that anyone or any organization opposing reduction in the birth rate is automatically an agent for eventually increasing the death rate.

Since we need have only an academic interest in theoretical limits on the size of the human population, I am going to address my remarks to the very real crisis we face this instant. In particular I want to examine the relationship of our current population growth to food resources and the quality of our environment. Finally, I want to examine what, if anything, can be done to give our descendants a world to live in.

At the moment it is shockingly apparent that in the battle to feed humanity our side has been routed. In 1966 the population of the world increased by some seventy million people, and there was no compensatory increase in food production. Indeed, in areas such as Africa and Latin America there has actually been a decrease in food production over the past two years. According to the United Nations Food and Agriculture Organization advances in food production made in developing nations between 1955 and 1965 have been wiped out by agriculture disasters in 1965 and 1966. All this means that last year, on the average, each person on earth had 2 per cent less to eat. The reduction is, of course, not uniformly distributed. Starvation already is a fact in many countries. Only ten countries, including the United States, grew more food than they consumed—all other populous countries, including Russia, China, and India, imported more than they exported. Last year the United States shipped one quarter of its wheat crop, nine million tons, to India. In spite of this aid, serious famines still threaten the Indian population. And, what is worse, our aid has retarded the development of grain production in that country. Our wheat reserves are now so low that they can no longer serve as antistarvation insurance for the Indian subcontinent. Every month there are some one and a half million more Indians. Should India's present population growth continue for another ten years it would take the *entire* grain production of the United States to relieve the Indian food shortage.

Agricultural experts state that a tripling of the food supply of the world will be necessary in the next thirty years or so, if the six or seven billion people who may be alive in the year 2000 are to be adequately fed. Theoretically such an increase might be possible, but it is becoming increasingly clear that it is totally impossible in practice. A few months ago I would have told you that *if* we had ideal conditions of research, development, and international cooperation we might triple our food production by then—if we started immediately. I would then have examined the possibility of meeting such assumptions. You would have been treated to the history of the unsuccessful attempts of the International Whaling Commission to control the hunting of whales, as a sample of the kind of international cooperation we can anticipate. I would have explained why the idea that our food supply can be dramatically increased by harvesting the sea is a gigantic hoax. Then I would have told you about some of the unhappy physical and social barriers in the way of attempting to produce much more food on the land.

All of this, however, now seems to me to be beside the point. There is not going to be any massive tooling up to meet the food crisis. There is not going to be any sudden increase in international cooperation. Even if there were a miraculous change in human attitudes and behavior in this area, *it is already too late to prevent a drastic rise in the death rate through starvation.* In a massively documented book, *Famine 1975!,* William and Paul Paddock recently stated:

> A locomotive is roaring full throttle down the track. Just around the bend an impenetrable mudslide has oozed across the track. There it lies, inert, static, deadly. Nothing can stop the locomotive in time. Collision is inevitable. Catastrophe is foredoomed. Miles back up the track the locomotive could have been warned and stopped. Years ago the mud-soaked hill could have been shored up to forestall the landslide. Now it is too late.
>
> The locomotive roaring straight at us is the population explosion. The unmovable landslide across the tracks is the stagnant production of food in the undeveloped nations, the nations where the population increases are greatest. The collision is inevitable. The famines are inevitable.

The Paddocks predict that the time of famines will be upon us full-scale in 1975. The U.S. Department of Agriculture estimates that America can continue to feed the developing countries until 1984. Which estimate is more correct will depend in part on the validity of the assumptions on which they are based, and in part on such things as the weather. My guess is that the Paddocks are more likely correct, but in the long run it makes no difference. A great many people are going to starve to death, and soon. There is nothing that can be done to prevent it.

Much of the Paddocks' book deals with the problem of how the United States should behave in the time of crisis. We are the only country which will be in a position to *give* food to starving countries, and the amount of food which we will be able to donate will fall far short of world-wide needs. We will be forced to choose who will live and who will die. The Paddocks suggest that we place each country in one of three categories based on the method used to classify wounded entering a military hospital:

1. Those who will die regardless of treatment.
2. Those who will survive regardless of treatment and regardless of the agony they may suffer.
3. Those who can be saved if given prompt treatment.

India, where population growth is colossal, agriculture hopelessly antiquated, and the government incompetent, will be one of those we must allow to slip down the drain. This year C. Subramaniam, former Minister for Food and Agriculture of India, speaking at Stanford University blamed the United States for not giving his country enough food to get her through the last couple of years. He blamed drought for India's problems, and predicted a massive increase in Indian agriculture which would "save the day" by yielding nineteen million more tons of grain a year. This from an ex-official of a government which itself *officially* predicted in 1959 that a serious gap would appear in 1965–66 between demand and available food in India. This man is trying to tell us that in the next eight years India is going to find a way to produce enough food to support some 120 million more people than they cannot feed today—a challenge which would tax a highly efficient agricultural system. Millions of Indians will die because of governmental attitudes exemplified by Subramaniam. They will die because some religious organizations have blocked attempts over the years to get governmental and United Nations action under way to control human birth rates. They will die because scientists have managed to persuade many influential people that a technological rabbit can always be pulled out of the hat to save mankind at the last moment. They will die because many people, like myself, who recognized the essential role of overpopulation in the increasing woes of *Homo sapiens* could not bring themselves to leave the comforts of their daily routine to do something about it. Their blood will be distributed over many hands.

But then, what good can a partitioning of guilt do? Perhaps some people will recognize their culpability and mend their ways—too late. What's done is done, to coin a phrase. We must look to the survivors, if there are to be any. We must assume that the "time of famines" will not lead to thermonuclear Armageddon, and that man will get another chance, no matter how ill-deserved. What I'd like to consider now is what we can do today that would improve the probability of man's making the most of a second chance, should he be lucky enough to get one.

Of course, the most important thing that we must do is to educate people and change many of their attitudes. We must, for example, alert people to the possible environmental consequences of attempting continually to increase food production. They must be made aware of subtle biological properties of our environment which, if ignored, may lead to very unsubtle future calamities. For instance, one of the basic facts of population biology is that the simpler an ecological system (or ecosystem) is, the more unstable it is. A complex forest, consisting of a great variety of plants and animals, will persist year in and year out with no interference from man. The system contains many elements, and changes in different ones often cancel one another out. Suppose one kind of predator eating small rodents, say foxes, suffers a population decline. Its role in the forest may be assumed by another predator, perhaps owls. Such compensation may not be possible in a simpler system. Similarly, no plant-eating animal feeds on all kinds of plants, and the chance of a population explosion of a herbivore completely defoliating a mixed woodland is virtually nil.

Man, however, is a simplifier of complex ecosystems, and a creator of simple ecosystems. For instance, he persists in creating systems which consist almost entirely of uniform stands of a single grass—wheatfields and cornfields are familiar examples. Any farmer can testify to the instability of these ecosystems. Without human protection such an ecosystem rapidly disappears.

Plans for increasing food production invariably involve large-scale efforts at environmental modification. Land must be cleared, water must be provided, fertilizers must enrich soils, and pesticides must be used against organisms which compete with us by eating our crops. It seems unlikely that, if we should choose to push ahead with increasing world food production on a monumental scale, this push will be accompanied by an upsurge in the level of ecological sophistication of those responsible for directing the effort. We can expect more bad land management, such as caused the American dust bowl and, indeed, is ruining soils in many parts of the world today. Farming practices are often followed which lead to the loss of topsoil or the rapid conversion of soil into unmanageable compacted material. Soil is often "mined" by grazing or single-crop farming. Minerals taken up by plants are not returned to the soil when crops or cattle are marketed. Careless irrigation also ruins soils, by permitting the building up of salts. Another factor, often unappreciated, is poisoning of the soil. If we attempt to greatly increase the agricultural yield of the earth it seems certain that the use of synthetic pesticides, already massive, will be increased. And, synthetic pesticides are one of man's most potent tools for simplifying ecosystems. They not only reduce the diversity of life above ground, but long-term applications almost certainly reduce the diversity in the soil. Remember that soil is not just crushed rock. It contains a rich flora and fauna which are essential for its fertility.

Do we want to embark on a program which would involve a great increase in the usage of synthetic pesticides? In spite of massive publicity the intimate relationship between pesticides and environmental deterioration is not widely recognized. Unfortunately, the entire issue has been clouded by the efforts of health nuts on one side and paid industrial propagandists on the other. One group urges a return to nature which, even if it were desirable, is now clearly impossible. The other would have us believe that food did not exist until synthetic organic pesticides provided it for us, and that these chemicals are the only way in which our health can be maintained. Both sides tend to concentrate on consideration of direct toxic effects on man, rather than looking at the entire ecological picture. I think this is a serious mistake.

Of all the synthetic organic pesticides, we probably know the most about DDT, the oldest and most widely used chlorinated hydrocarbon insecticide. Virtually all populations of animals the world over are contaminated with it. Concentrations in the fat bodies of Americans average 11 parts per million, and Israelis have been found to have as much as 19.2 parts per million. More significant in some ways has been the discovery of DDT residues in such unlikely places as the fat bodies of Eskimos, antarctic penguins, and antarctic seals. Pesticide pollution is truly a world-wide problem.

DDT breaks down only very slowly, and will last for decades in soils. A recent study of a Long Isand marsh which has been sprayed for twenty years for mosquito control revealed up to thirty-two pounds per acre of DDT in the upper layer of mud. Unhappily, the way DDT circulates in the ecosystem leads to a concentration in carnivores. The danger to life and reproductive capacity of meat-eating birds may be approaching the critical now, and the outlook for man if current trends continue does not seem healthy. The day may soon be upon us when the obese people of the world must give up diets, since metabolizing their fat deposits will lead to DDT poisoning. But, on the bright side, it is clear that fewer and fewer people in the future will be obese. We must remember that DDT has been in use for only about a quarter of a century. It is difficult to predict the results of another fifty years of application of DDT and similar compounds, especially if those years are to be filled with frantic attempts to feed more and more people. Of course, DDT is just one of many synthetic substances with which we are dosing our environment. In addition to their direct toxic threat to man, these compounds all have the effect of simplifying ecosystems and thus aggravating the instability created by man's agricultural and other activities.

Pest organisms ordinarily have large populations—that, indeed, is why they are pests. The large size of their populations makes them much more likely to have the kind of reserve genetic variability which leads most easily to the development of resistant strains. Therefore, extermination of a pest by use of synthetic pesticides is unlikely—and, in fact, is almost unknown. The usual picture is one in which the pesticide decimates the natural enemies of the pest, while the pest develops resistant strains. These problems of pesticides are just one example of a trend which has accompanied the expansion of the human population. The more we have manipulated our environment, the more we have been required to manipulate it. The more we have done with synthetic pesticides, the less we have been able to do without them. The more we have deforested the more flood control dams we have had to build. The more farmland we have subdivided the more pressure we have created to increase the yield on the land remaining under culti-vation and to farm marginal land. This trend has been enhanced by an un-happy historical factor. The earth has come largely under the control of a culture which traditionally sees man's proper role as dominating nature, rather than living in harmony with it. It is a culture which equates "growth" and "progress" and considers both as self-evidently desirable. It is a culture which all too often considers "undeveloped" land to be "wasted" land. Un-questionably people's attitudes toward their physical environment need changing if we are to make the grade—attitudes which unfortunately are among the most basic in Western culture. And, unfortunately, the state of our physical environment is just part of the problem.

Perhaps more important than recent changes in our physical environ-ment are those in our psychic environment. Unhappily, we cannot be sure of the significance of these latter changes—although riots, the hippie move-ment, and increased drug usage are hardly cheery signs. We can't even be sure of how much of an individual's reaction to these environmental changes will be hereditarily conditioned, and how much it will be a function of his culture. Let me quote part of what three biologists recently have written on the subject:

"Unique as we may think we are, we are nevertheless as likely to be genetically programmed to a natural habitat of clean air and a varied green landscape as any other mammal. To be relaxed and feel healthy usually means simply allowing our bodies to react in the way for which 100 millions of years of evolution has equipped us. Physically and genetically we appear best adapted to a tropical savanna, but as a cultural animal we utilize learned adaptations to cities and towns. For thousands of years we have tried in our houses to imitate not only the climate, but the setting of our evolutionary past: warm, humid air, green plants and even animal com-panions. Today, if we can afford it, we may even build a greenhouse or swimming pool next to our living room, buy a place in the country, or at least take our children vacationing on the seashore. The specific physio-logical reactions to natural beauty and diversity, to the shapes and colors of nature (especially to green), to the motions and sounds of other animals, such as birds, we as yet do not comprehend. But, it is evident that nature in our daily life should be thought of as a part of the biological need. It cannot be neglected in the discussions of resource policy for man." (H. H. Iltis, P. Andrews, and O. L. Loucks. "Criteria for an Optimum Human Environment." Manuscript, 1967.)

Man clearly has gone a long way toward adapting to urban environ-ments and despoiled landscapes. We badly need to understand the effects of this adjustment, especially in terms of group behavior, and to be able to predict the effects of further changes in man's perceptual environment. It is important to note that our perceptual systems have evolved primarily to react to stimuli representing a sudden change in our environment—a lion's charge, a flaring fire, a child's cry. Long-term changes often are not noticed. We tend not to perceive a friend's aging, or the slowing of our reflexes. If the transition from the Los Angeles of 1927 to that of 1967 had occurred overnight Angelenos surely would have rebelled. But a gradual forty-year transition has permitted southern Californians actually to convince themselves that the Los Angeles basin of 1967 is a suitable habitat for *Homo sapiens.*

It is clear that man's present physical and psychic environment is far from optimum, and that permitting today's trends to continue is likely to lead to further rapid deterioration. We also know that we will have a dramatic increase in the death rate in the near future, an increase we can do nothing about. What then should be our course of action?

I think our first move must be to convince all those whom we can that the planet Earth must be viewed as a space ship of limited carrying capacity. It must be made crystal clear that population growth must stop, and we must arrive at a consensus as to what the ideal size of the human crew of the Earth should be. When we have determined the size of the crew, then we can attempt to design an environment in which that crew will be maintained in some sort of optimum state. The socio-political problems raised by such an approach are, of course, colossal. People within cultures have different ideas on how close they want to live to their neighbors, and cross-cultural differences in feelings about crowding are obvious. The only way I can think of for achieving a consensus is for people to start voicing opinions. So here goes.

I think that 150 million people would be an optimum number to live comfortably in the United States. Such a number is clearly enough to maintain our highly technological society. It is also a small enough number that, when properly distributed and accommodated, it should be possible for individuals to find as much solitude and breathing space as they desire. With a population stabilized at such a level we could concentrate on improving the quality of human life at home and abroad. And, what a pleasure it would be to work toward an attainable goal instead of fighting the miserable rear guard action to which runaway population condemns us.

After all, what do we gain from packing more and more people into the United States? Those encouraging population growth in the hope of keeping our economy expanding must realize the consequences of such advocacy. Some men would doubtless accumulate considerable wealth, and would be able to retreat from riot-torn cities to the increasingly smoggy countryside in order to live. If thermonuclear war does not solve their children's problems permanently, what kind of a world will those children inherit? Will their heritage include social disorder and unemployment on an unprecedented scale? Will they have to wear smog masks as a matter of routine? Will they enjoy mock steaks made from processed grass or seaweed? Will they have to be satisfied with camping under plastic trees planted in concrete? Will they accept regimentation and governmental control at a level previously unheard of? Will they fight willingly in small wars and prepare diligently for the big one? Above all, will they be able to retain their sanity in a world gone mad?

Let's suppose that we decide to limit the population of the United States and of the world. How can such limitation be accomplished? Some biologists feel that compulsory family regulation will be necessary to retard population growth. It is a dismal prospect—except when viewed as an alternative to Armageddon. I would like to suggest four less drastic steps which might do the job in the United States. I suggest them in the full knowledge that they are socially unpalatable and politically unrealistic.

The first step would be to establish a Federal Population Commission with a large budget for propaganda which supports reproductive responsibility. This Commission would be charged with making clear the connection between rising population and lowering quality of life. It would also be charged with the evaluation of environmental tinkering by other government agencies—with protecting us from projects such as the FAA's supersonic transports or from the results of the Army Engineers' well-known "beaver complex" (which some predict will only be satiated when evey gutter in the country has a dam thrown across it). Commission members should be distinguished citizens, as free as possible from political or bureaucratic meddling.

The second step would be to change our tax laws so they discourage rather than encourage reproduction. Those who impose the burden of children on society should, whenever they are able, be made to pay for the privilege. Our income tax system should eliminate all deductions for children, and replace them with a graduated scale of increases. Luxury taxes should be placed on diapers, baby bottles, and baby foods. It must be clear to our population that it is socially irresponsible to have large families. Creation of such a climate of opinion has played a large role in Japan's successful dealing with her population problem.

Third, we should pass federal laws which make instruction in birth control methods mandatory in all public schools. Federal legislation should also forbid state laws which limit the right of any woman to have an abortion which is approved by her physician.

Fourth, we should change the pattern of federal support of biomedical research so that the majority of it goes into the broad areas of population regulation, environmental sciences, behavioral sciences, and related areas rather than into short-sighted programs on death control. It is absurd to be preoccupied with the medical quality of life until and unless the problem of the quantity of life is solved. In this context we must do away with nonsense about how important it is for "smart" people to have large families in order to keep *Homo sapiens* from being selected for stupidity. It is far from established that the less intelligent portion of our population is outreproducing the more intelligent. Even if a reproductive disparity did exist, the worst consequence over a period of a few generations only would be a slight lowering of average intelligence—a slight and *reversible* lowering. And, the consequences of such a lowering, if any, would be a small price to pay for the survival of mankind. Besides, who is going to determine how to measure intelligence and who will decide which people can be permitted to breed? There surely won't be voluntary abstention on the part of the less intelligent —I've never even met anyone who thought he was in the stupid half of the population! *Quantity is the first problem.* If we can lick that one perhaps we will buy the time for scientists in fields such as biochemical genetics to solve some of the problems of quality. If we don't solve the quantity problem, the quality problem will no longer bother us.

All of these steps might produce the desired result of a reversal of today's population growth trend. If they should fail, however, we would then be faced with some form of compulsory birth regulation. We might, for instance, institute a system which would make *positive* action necessary before reproduction is possible. This might be the addition of a temporary sterilant to staple food, or to the water supply. An antidote would have to be taken to permit reproduction. Even with the antidote freely available, the result of such a program would be a drastic reduction in birth rates. If this reduction were not sufficient, the government could dole out the antidote in the proper quantities. If we wished to stabilize the American population at its present level, each married couple could be permitted enough antidote to produce two offspring. Then each couple who wished could be given a chance in a lottery for enough antidote for a third child— the odds carefully computed to produce the desired constancy of population size. At the moment the chances of winning would have to be adjusted to about two out of five, assuming that all couples wanted to play the game.

An attempt to institute such a system is interesting to contemplate, especially when one considers the attitude of the general public towards fluoridation. I would not like to be the first elected official seriously to suggest that a sterility agent be added to our reservoirs! Perhaps it might seem that we can start such a program by treating the wheat we ship to India, or fish meal we ship to South America. Or can we? As you doubtless realize, the solution does not lie in that direction. For one thing, saying that the population explosion is a problem of underdeveloped countries is like telling a fellow passenger "your end of the boat is sinking." For another, it is naive to think that Indians or Brazilians are any more anxious to be fed fertility-destroying chemicals with their daily bread than are Americans. Other people already are suspicious of our motives. Consider what their attitude would be towards an attempt to sterilize them en masse.

If we can solve the population problem at home then we will be in a position to make an all-out effort to halt the growth of the world's population. Perhaps we can shorten the time of famines and lay the groundwork for avoiding a second round of population-food crises. Our program should be tough-minded. We should remember that seemingly charitable gestures such as our grain exports to India have actually harmed rather than helped Indians in the long run. I think that we should:

1. Announce that we will no longer ship food to countries where dispassionate analysis indicates that the food-population unbalance is hopeless.

2. Announce that we will no longer give aid to any country with an increasing population until that country convinces us that it is doing everything within its power to limit its population.

3. Make available to all interested countries massive aid in the technology of birth control.

4. Make available to all interested countries massive aid for increasing yield on land already under cultivation. The most important export in this area should be trained technicians, not fertilizer. We need to establish centers in the country where technicians can be trained not only in agronomy, but also in ecology and sociology. Many of the barriers to increased yields are sociological, and all increase should be made in a manner which minimizes environmental deterioration.

5. Accept the fact that if we can use our power to further military goals then it can also be used for the good of mankind as well. Extreme political and economic pressure should be brought on any country impeding a solution to the world's most pressing problem. A good way to start would be to urge the Vatican to bring its policies into line with the desires of the majority of American Catholics. Much of the world would be horrified at our stand, but as a nation we're clearly willing to go against world opinion on other issues—why not on the most important issue?

Well, perhaps if we get on the ball and set a good example the United States can lead the way in focusing the world's attention on the cause of its major sickness rather than upon the symptoms. Perhaps we can shift our efforts from the long-term pain-depressing activities to the excising of the cancer. The operation will require many brutal and callous decisions. The pain will be intense, but the disease is so far advanced that only with radical surgery does the patient have any chance of survival.

The rate of growth in the population of the underdeveloped countries is more dreadful in terms of possibilities than the threat of nuclear war, and these nations will continue to grow much more rapidly than the developed areas of the world. In many nations, developed and underdeveloped, the use of measures to control family size—abortion, sterilization, or contraceptive devices—is on the upswing, but in some countries where the population problem is severe no progress in family planning has occurred.

Birth Control Now: A Survey

U.S. News & World Report

In a world full of dangers, one danger is coming to be feared more than any other.

That danger is overpopulation. . . .

The world today contains about 3.5 billion people. That is double the population of 50 years ago and three times that of a century ago.

By the year 2000, according to projections made by the United Nations, the world's population will be about 6 billion.

That means that in the next 31 years the world will acquire 2.5 billion additional people—an increase of more people than existed on this earth only 20 years ago.

How to feed these added billions of people is only part of the problem that such a startling population explosion presents.

Increasing upheaval. What officials and experts are beginning to realize is this: The more people there are and the more crowded their living conditions become, the greater grows the likelihood of violence and upheaval.

Riots, revolutions and wars are foreseen as almost inevitable products of the overpopulation that lies ahead.

This is noted: Most of the huge population growth will occur in those parts of the world that already are overcrowded, that are poorest and least able to feed and support more people.

These also are the areas where unrest is greatest today, and where pressures of expanding population already are contributing to revolution or aggression.

At present, 2.5 billion people—or 70 per cent of the world's population—live in underdeveloped regions of Asia, Africa and Latin America.

Reprinted from "World's No. 1 Worry—Too Many People," *U.S. News & World Report,* March 17, 1970. Copyright 1970 U.S. News & World Report, Inc.

By the year 2000, there will be about 4.7 billion people—or 77 per cent of the world's population—in such regions. China, which is already bursting at the seams with nearly 740 million people, will have more than 1 billion. India, hungry and riotous with 540 million today, will have a billion people by the turn of the century.

Asia will contain, all told, 3.46 billion inhabitants, which is almost as many as the world contains today.

Africa, even less developed than Asia, will have a total population of 768 million by 2000—more than double its present population.

Latin America, struggling now to support 280 million, will have about 638 million.

Developed areas. By contrast, the more developed areas of the world —Europe and North America—will grow much more slowly in population than the already crowded and underdeveloped areas.

Europe, now supporting some 450 million people fairly comfortably, will have about 527 million by the year 2000. The United States, where some 200 million people live in relative affluence today, will have about 318 million by that time. Soviet Russia, growing at about the same percentage rate, will see its population increase from about 240 million now to 353 million.

The noncontributors. Along with rapid population growth in underdeveloped countries will come another significant change: a growing proportion of young people. Thus a larger share of the population will be dependent and nonproductive—demanding food and other necessities of life but contributing little to producing those necessities. The result will be to limit the ability of backward economies to meet the needs of their expanding populations.

Lauchlin Currie, once an official of the U.S. Government and now an adviser to the Government of Colombia, recently said this:

"I regard the rate of growth in the population of the underdeveloped countries as the single most important obstacle to development and, hence, the single most important problem of the world, even outranking the threat of nuclear warfare in terms of ultimate dread possibilities."

Concern over an ever-expanding population is turning worldwide attention to diverse aspects of a growing debate—the argument over "artificial" birth control and family planning.

For example: Just how widespread is the practice of limiting births, whether legal or illegal? Do laws for or against contraception mean much, actually? What is the attitude of people in other countries toward self-regulated family planning, regardless of religious or governmental directives?

For answers, members of the staff of "U.S. News & World Report" in world capitals checked into the situation. Their findings:

London

Big social changes—including the legalization of abortion—recently have been introduced in Britain.

The Abortion Act, which went into effect in 1968, makes it possible for a woman to have a free abortion in a National Health Service hospital. The only requirement is that two physicans must first agree that such treatment is necessary to the woman's physical or mental well-being.

In essence, medical circles agree, this makes it possible for almost any woman to have an abortion, since it is nearly always possible to find two doctors who would agree on such a course.

In the past, abortions were theoretically illegal, but were permitted in many cases. Latest estimates are that from 15,000 to 50,000 abortions a year are being performed in Britain.

Another big change is the increasing presence of Family Planning Association centers. These give free advice—and free supplies such as the birth-control pill—to applicants. Today there are 780 such clinics throughout the country, paid for by voluntary subscriptions but often supplied with free offices by local governments.

About 500,000 women and men received advice from these centers last year. Tens of thousands of others sought advice from doctors.

It is estimated that more than three fourths of British married couples practice some form of birth control. Reliance on the pill, now used by about 1 million British women, is increasing rapidly. Only half of that number had used the pill in 1966.

Interest also has been expressed in Britain about an "abortion pill," which is under development. Medical circles say such a pill is expected to be ready for distribution in a few years.

Paris

Since 1920, France has had a law making it a criminal offense to give out birth-control information, and putting contraception and abortion on the same criminal footing. This law was revised last year to permit the sale of contraceptives.

The French Movement for Family Planning, founded in 1956, is credited with the recent growth of popularity of the birth-control pill. It is estimated that 500,000 women in France now use this form of contraception and that 1 million will be using it by 1970.

A recent book by a group of young doctors says that the most important step toward birth control is education. They say: "Everyone has heard of the pill, but only one woman in 1,000 knows exactly what contraception is about."

There is no real sex education in French schools, and contraception remains largely a taboo subject.

After the pill, the next most favored method of contraception in France is the intrauterine loop. Women who prefer the loop do so because it can become a permanent method once it has been inserted by a doctor. However, the loop has to be checked every six months, and cannot be used by all women.

A recent test of loop insertions revealed 8.4 per cent expulsions, 0.2 per cent infections, 4.1 per cent heavy bleeding, and 2.22 per cent pregnancies. Other tests indicated that pregnancies during use of the pill were only 0.15 per cent.

Abortion is forbidden in France. However, official figures show that there are about 250,000 induced abortions annually. Unofficial sources put this figure at a total of 1 million.

The Conseil National de l'ordre des Medicins, France's highest medical authority, last year rejected proposals from a commission on population problems to liberalize the law against abortions. The law is even less likely to be changed since the latest Papal Encyclical on birth control.

Bonn

Contraceptives of all kinds are easily available in West Germany. The pill has been in use since 1962 and is gaining in popularity. About 1.4 million women—13 per cent—in the age group from 16 to 45 take the pill.

Abortions are illegal, except when decreed by doctors to save the life of a mother or for other ethical reasons. Nevertheless, the abortion rate in West Germany is described as alarmingly high. For every 1 million live births, unofficial estimates indicate that there are 200,000 to 1.5 million abortions annually.

Sprays, the loop and other devices are no longer in favor, since they are considered too bothersome and not 100 per cent effective.

Recent polls show that the majority of all young West German couples desire at least two children, but prefer to space them according to their professional and family plans. Even young Catholic couples say: "We prefer to have the pill and not play Roman roulette."

Rome

In Italy—right on the Vatican's doorstep—any kind of "artificial" birth control is illegal, but the practice flourishes just the same.

In a nation where nearly 100 per cent of the people are at least nominal Roman Catholics, abortion is widespread and use of the pill is becoming more and more popular. There is no evidence to show that the papal encyclical on birth control has caused any diminution of these practices. In fact, it is noted by an official of the Italian equivalent of the Family Planning Association that the encyclical produced such a flood of publicity in the Italian press—where the actual advertising of contraceptive devices is also illegal—that it might have even acted as a spur to their use.

Despite the ban on contraceptive devices, the pill is easy to get in Italy. This is because it can legally be prescribed as a remedy for any woman suffering from any gynecological disorder. There are at least eight different brands of the pill on sale in Italian drugstores.

Doctors appear in general to have no compunction about prescribing the pill, even when they know it will be put to contraceptive use. Drugstores are similarly permissive. It is not uncommon for pharmacists to sell the pill across the counter without a prescription.

Use of the birth-control pill still tends to be confined mainly to the more educated, middle-class Italians. The loop is relatively unknown here.

Abortion, though outlawed, has been practiced for centuries among rich and poor alike. One source estimates that at least 1 million abortions are carried out in Italy each year. An illegal abortion is said to cost about $128 at current rates, and clinics where such operations are performed are easy to find.

Thus, despite the church ban on birth-control devices—and the ostensible illegality of them—Catholic Italy has a birth rate not much higher than Britain's.

Stockholm

Birth-control methods, including legal abortion and sterilization, have long been used in Sweden and elsewhere in Scandinavia.

Experience in Sweden shows clearly that sex education in schools and easy access to contraceptives at low cost do not guarantee effective birth control. Social misfits, mentally retarded people and many youngsters fail to use contraceptives—often under the influence of liquor.

Widespread use of the pill in recent years has been charged with an alarming increase in venereal diseases. Reported cases of gonorrhea after the vacation period in 1968 were running up to 50 per cent higher than a year ago. Syphilis, too, is spreading again.

At the same time, the pill has failed to reduce the number of illegitimate births and abortions. In Sweden, the total of illegitimate births rose from 11,500 in 1960 to 18,000 in 1966.

Under a liberal abortion law, applications for legal abortions climbed from a temporary low of 4,085 in 1960 to 7,380 in 1967. As many as 95 per cent of all applications were granted last year, as against 62 per cent in 1960. Legal abortions are free under Government welfare programs.

Contrary to popular belief, Sweden does not permit abortions for foreigners except in emergency cases. Many American women who have tried to get legal abortions here have been rejected.

Despite the liberal attitude prevailing in Scandinavia, the number of illegal abortions is surprisingly high—up to 20,000 a year in Sweden.

A Swedish law of 1941 also permits sterilization for eugenic, social or moral reasons. Over the past 15 years, about 25,000 persons have been sterilized—90 per cent on medical grounds.

Bucharest

Communist governments in Eastern Europe encourage people to have more children by paying subsidies to mothers of big families, and by providing nurseries and kindergartens where working mothers may leave their children. In Russia, for example, more than 3.5 million mothers of four or more children are drawing monthly state subsidies.

Many different kinds of contraceptives are available. So is instruction in their use by gynecologists and midwives. However, contraceptives often are of poor quality and are not produced in sufficient quantity.

Accordingly, there is widespread incentive to resort to abortion. Recognizing this, and hoping to keep down the number of abortions performed on the sly under dangerous medical conditions, most Communist governments have adopted easy abortion policies. The one exception is Rumania, where—in 1966—abortions were outlawed except for rare cases.

Except in Poland and East Germany, a fee is charged for voluntary abortions, while abortion on medical grounds is free in all countries.

The Soviet Union recently decided to begin mass manufacture of intrauterine devices, after its Health Ministry ruled against the pill as a contraceptive for health reasons.

Cairo

Despite having one of the world's most serious population problems, Egypt's Government has not given birth control high priority.

And, without Government action, little can be done in this field, since the masses of people with the largest families—the peasants—do not have the knowledge or means to act on their own.

At present, both the pill and intrauterine devices are slowly being introduced. About 300,000 women are taking the pill, but this is still less than 4 per cent of the "target group"—fertile women with at least two children—that the program is trying to reach. Experts say it is unlikely that this number will ever increase very much, because of shortages in the supply of pill ingredients, and because so little is being done to promote the desirability of birth control. Use of the loop also is on a very modest scale.

Unlike the situation in Catholic countries, there is no major religious obstacle to overcome in mainly Moslem Egypt. But there are superstition and suspicion to cope with. Many Egyptians—including "intellectuals"—believe that Western emphasis on the desirability of birth control is just a plot to keep underdeveloped countries such as Egypt from becoming big countries.

Ottawa

Growing use of the pill and other birth-control measures, in spite of strong laws against the sale of contraceptives and against the dissemination of birth-control information, is believed to be a major cause of Canada's declining birth rate in recent years.

The laws are generally disregarded, except in areas where the Catholic Church is strong, such as in rural parts of Quebec Province. No one has been prosecuted in Canada for the illegal sale of contraceptives since 1961.

The birth-control laws, as well as Canada's law prohibiting abortion, are being changed. New provisions of the Food and Drugs Act will permit sale and dissemination of birth-control medicines, instruments and information.

A new law on abortion will permit establishment of a "therapeutic-abortion committee" in each hospital. The committee would be empowered to approve abortions in any case where continued pregnancy "would or would be likely to endanger life or health."

Mexico City

Birth-control work in Mexico consists of training and research programs and clinics throughout a country where the population is growing at a rate of 3.5 per cent a year. Control methods are the pill, intrauterine devices, injections and the rhythm method—for those who prefer it, and their number is small.

It is estimated that 1 million women are using the pill. Results are described as highly satisfactory, with only minor side effects which decrease with use.

The programs are sponsored by private organizations. The Mexican Government, anxious to avoid conflicts with the Roman Catholic Church, is not involved.

Use of the intrauterine loop is growing, although one doctor describes it as "good for some women and not for others."

Clinics in Mexico now are working with three types of contraceptive injections—effective for one month, two months or three months. The results are reported good, especially with women who are incapable of remembering to take pills regularly.

The rate of abortion in Mexico is estimated at one for each live birth.

Rio De Janeiro

Latin-American women are showing increasing determination to limit the size of their families by whatever means are available.

Abortion is the most common form of birth control, especially in the big cities, but the pill is catching up, particularly in the middle and upper income groups. Intrauterine loops are the most controversial, and the rhythm system is the most discredited.

The Brazilian Family Welfare Society estimates that 4,000 abortions a day—about 1.5 million annually—are performed in Brazil. This works out to one abortion for three live births.

The ratio is reversed in neighboring Uruguay, where there are three abortions for each live birth. Other South American countries fall in between.

Brazil has a constitutional ban on the distribution of contraceptives or birth-control information through the mails or in public. But doctors say that family-planning clinics are allowed to operate without interference, in the hope that they will reduce the abortion rate.

The loop is widely used in Chile, where one doctor devised a low-cost loop made of nylon fishing line. The pill is described as the overwhelming favorite among Argentine women, most of whom use some form of birth control.

The Family Welfare Society in Rio de Janeiro estimates that 1.5 million Brazilian women—almost 10 per cent of the 18 million women of childbearing age—use the pill and many other contraceptives.

Tokyo

In Asia, most countries are trying to contain populations which are increasing 3 per cent or more a year. But finding effective ways is proving difficult.

Two or three years ago, the intrauterine device was hailed as revolutionary—the cheapest, easiest way to cut the number of births to reasonable levels. Asia, with at least 2 million insertions, has become the largest market in the world for the loops.

Today, enthusiasm for the loops has waned. Results have been less than satisfactory. Some programs have been supplemented with the more expensive, more controversial pill.

Experts ask, what are the alternatives? Older contraceptive methods are unreliable. Injections and experiments with "immunization" are inadequately tested. The conclusion now being reached by leaders in family planning:

Induced abortion may be the only effective means of reducing population, particularly in areas of the world where education standards are low and poverty is widespread.

In three Asian countries, abortion is already considered the most dependable check on spiraling populations.

Japan pioneered, legalizing the operation in 1948. Abortion by qualified doctors gets major credit for reducing the birth rate to a modest 1 per cent gain per year—one of the lowest in the world.

In two neighboring countries, abortion is illegal but widely practiced. An estimated one out of every three pregnancies in South Korea is now terminated by abortion. The cost is $3 to $8. In Taiwan, abortion—costing about $6—is at least as important as the loop in curbing population growth.

Family-planning programs have been under way in Taiwan since 1964, with the aim of reducing the population growth rate from 3 to 2 per cent a year. Results of a program to insert 600,000 loops by 1970 have been mixed. Many women complain about them for one reason or another, and the retention rate is only 60 per cent after 18 months.

The Republic of Korea has had comparable experience with a program begun in 1962. Over 1 million loops have been inserted, but at least 2 out of every 10 are removed for various reasons.

Both countries are supplementing their IUD programs with pills, a more complicated and costly procedure.

Bangkok

In South Asia, the world's most critical area of population growth, only three countries—India, Pakistan and Singapore—have national programs aimed at controlling births. Malaysia is beginning one.

The Philippine Republic has no program, and is further inhibited because about 85 per cent of its population is Catholic and leans toward the "conservative" wing of the Church.

Thailand, a relatively underpopulated country by Asian standards, but one which is beginning to feel the pinch of population versus agricultural productivity, has no program yet. Indonesia, a nation of more than 110 million people and a high-density population in some areas, has no program worth mentioning.

Pakistan and India—both growing rapidly—have had major birth-control programs for years. But neither has made much of a dent in its birth rate.

Pakistan aims to have 5 million couples of childbearing age practicing birth control regularly by 1970. Right now, it looks as if the goal will be met. Some 2.4 million couples have begun some form of birth control: the loop, the pill or conventional contraceptives. In addition, 180,000 men and women have been sterilized.

India's program is 15 years old, but the population is nevertheless growing at a rate of about 2.5 per cent a year—and threatens to climb to 3 per cent, which could mean disaster.

At first, the loop was seen as the answer to India's control needs, but results have been disappointing. Now, sterilization is being stressed, and a "finder's fee" of $1.33 is being offered to anyone who brings a person to a clinic for the simple operation.

It is not uncommon for the public to overreact when faced with a critical issue. The threat of the population problem could conceivably arouse people to the point where they would pass laws extremely restrictive in nature regarding the right to have children. The consequences of restricting the right to have children would be most unfavorable, but such restrictions are likely unless we recognize both that this right, like any other, must be exercised responsibly, and that the right to have children includes as well the right not to have children.

The Right to Have Children

Marjory L. Bracher

One of the striking effects of the population growth of the last one hundred years is that it has reversed the moral obligation of centuries from the duty to have children to a duty not to have them. Even where such a reversal is not yet acknowledged it is on its way, swept in on the tide of high growth rates. How long the new obligation will prevail depends on the degree of population pressure generated in the future. As long, however, as this reversal of duty obtains, it will be necessary to protect *the right to have children*.

Under the necessity to lower the birth rate, the question naturally arises: *Who* will do the lowering? Who will have fewer children? Where people see plainly that numbers are threatening their own personal values, a large proportion of couples may be motivated to have fewer children. But where there is sharp conflict between quality-of-life and the family-size ideal, or where population pressure exists but is not identified, there will not be a spontaneous and widespread movement on the part of couples to have smaller families. Then the question of who shall have the privilege of childbearing and who shall be denied it becomes critical. And the right to have children can be in danger.

The right to have children belongs at the head of the basic list of human rights, for it is essential to the continuation of human life. There is no basic human right that has not at times been threatened or denied. Unless it is universal, belonging to all, it is safe to no one. We delude ourselves if we think this right would somehow be immune to threat.

As a right it cannot be fully protected unless it also includes the right of the couple to determine for themselves how many children they will have. No limit on offspring could be enforced without compulsory infanticide. Neither could a minimum number be required without an intolerable

"The Right to Have Children" from *S.R.O. Overpopulation and You* by Marjory L. Bracher. Reprinted by permission of Fortress Press.

invasion of privacy to establish lack of fecundity in those couples unable to reproduce.

Further, unless a couple is to be excused from child-bearing only on established proof of infecundity, they must be granted the right not to have children by their own free choice. Both the right *not* to have, and the right to determine the number, must be regarded as inherent to the right to have children.

One obstacle to a free exercise of the right is the ancient emphasis on the obligation to have children. Actually the moral *duty* to have children and the moral *right* to have them exist side by side. Both work to the same end, the perpetuation of life. The intent of both is to responsibility. Each one contains certain dangers. And each can be a corrective to the other.

In former centuries conditions were such as to create a strong emphasis on the duty to have offspring. There was the constant presence of too-early death, and there were obligations to family, tribe, or nation, for subsistence, defensive, and religious needs. While reproduction was considered an obligation on all, in practice exceptions were made. The privilege of devoting oneself to a celibate life in the service of religion has been recognized in many cultures.

In the Christian world, at least as early as the time of Augustine, procreation was considered obligatory on all married couples, and has continued so up to the present day. The danger in this strict interpretation of the duty to reproduce is that it impinges on the right of a free exercise of the procreative function. The right to no children was repudiated not by inference only but explicitly.

Under the changed conditions of the twentieth century with its rapid population growth, insistence on a universal duty to have children no longer works toward the effect that was intended. Instead of serving to maintain life and its quality, it would tend to over-population and in the long run would work against life.

Under today's conditions, insistence on the obligation to have children places the couple in a moral dilemma. On the one hand they are told it is their moral duty as responsible persons to have children; on the other hand they are under moral necessity, again as responsible persons, not to have (that is, to restrict). One way out of the dilemma is for the spokesman for one side to say how many children would satisfy the "duty," while a spokesman for the other would determine the proper quota from that side, leaving the couple to hope that the figures might prove identical. Such a solution is of course impossible, even if a figure could be agreed upon: the man and woman would no longer be free, but stripped of their essential human character—the right and the necessity to make their own choices. Duty would have completely destroyed responsibility and thus would have denied its own claim.

At present we are still trying to solve this moral dilemma. When the nineteenth-century trend to smaller families became evident, the wide-spread reaction was to put even stronger emphasis on the duty to have children (and to denounce as evil any attempts to restrict family size). Efforts were made to define the size that would still be regarded as "responsible" and to formulate exceptions to childbearing that would be morally allowable. But the duty is still reiterated, as the following recent statements from spokesmen within the churches show. "The couple must consider their responsibility before God to have children. The minister must remind them of their responsibility for bearing children."[1] "Couples . . . need to be vigilant lest they are putting their own comfort ahead of their duty."[2] "Until a family has had all the children that can be psychologically and economically managed, the decision would (have) to be to have children."[3] ". . . willful and permanent refusal to have children on principle . . . is not in accord with the proper will of God."[4] While the intent of all these is to remind people of their responsibility, to the extent that they do not recognize the right to decide the number of children, or to have none, they deny a couple their right to act in full responsibility.

How far we have gone toward solving the dilemma is indicated in the many statements from church bodies now recognizing the right of parents to decide the number of children, and the right to decide the means by which they will achieve the family size they think proper. More and more the imperative implicit in rapid population growth is being recognized.

What happens when there is strong emphasis on rights rather than on duty? First, there is the risk always inherent in human freedom that the rights of others will be disregarded. Under conditions of population pressure, the right of the couple to determine the number of children, exercised without regard of other couples, would tend to deprive those couples of the children that rightfully would be their share.

Under today's rapid increase the second risk is that strong insistence on one's rights might only add to numbers and enlarge the problems. The greater the population pressure, the greater is the possibility that irresponsible exercise of the right to children would be a danger to the whole community. And the more it became a threat, or people feared that it might, the greater the danger that the right would be denied or curtailed.

In a time of heavy or long-continuing population pressure, there will be a tendency to deny both the duty and the right to have children. Under these conditions the right will be more in need of protection than will the duty.

The right to have children has an importance, beyond that of perpetuating the race, that we are only beginning to sense. It is expressed in Erikson's concept of *generativity*. He points out that the fashion of emphasizing the dependence of children on adults "often blinds us to the dependence of the older generation on the younger one. *Mature man needs to be needed, and maturity needs guidance as well as encouragement from what has been produced and must be taken care of"*[5] (italics mine). Perhaps only the barren have been aware of this need; the others have been too busy with their children to see it. But we have only to imagine a world without children to sense how quickly the immediate purpose would go out of life.

To "have" children is generally regarded as a blessing, while rearing and educating them tends to be spoken of in terms of responsibility and burden. How much is the "guiding" of children a need to the adult, and therefore also a blessing? The concept of generativity as a fundamental characteristic of men and women deserves exploration. It may be expected to further point up the importance of preserving our right to have children.

It is likely that fears about depopulation have always tended to be exaggerated. Certainly with the hindsight of history we can see that maximum breeding has never been required to perpetuate the race. Nor is it necessary that every person replace himself. As we have seen, even the considerable normal incidence of sterility and of low fecundity have not been a threat to the perpetuation of life, however much they have been a cause of personal heartache. The genes of sterility and low fecundity breed themselves out; the proportion of sterility in a population does not tend to increase.

The duty to perpetuate life falls upon the group, upon the population as a whole, rather than being obligatory on each and all individuals. (In a certain sense, of course, the individual shares the obligation falling on the group.) In contrast to the duty, the right to have children belongs not only to the group. It must be the right of every couple. Further, it must be the right of the individual, to exercise within marriage; otherwise it could be taken from him by forcible sterilization.

Only a generation who had not known Hitler could deny the possibility of the seemingly inviolable being violated. Under extreme population pressure a time could come when the right to have children would need legal protection. But its best and ultimately its only protection lies in our granting to each other the right to have children or not, and to determine the number for ourselves. It is a present as well as a future need.

Another aspect of the matter deserves attention. It is not without significance that positive statements about the duty of a couple to have children often go on to point out the *selfishness* of not having children, or at least to warn against the danger of such a sin. No one seems concerned over the motives for having children. The assumption is always that the having can only be good, while not having is suspect (unless there is plain evidence of a certain few allowable reasons). There is no hesitation to name the specific selfishnesses: desire for comfort, wealth, luxury, ease, higher standard of living, fear of responsibility, discomforts of pregnancy, loss of beauty. No one so much as mentions the self-serving or ego-centered motives for having children, yet they are many and widely prevalent. And their ill effects, when there are such, fall upon the children.

Underneath admonitions on the duty to have children there lie not only ancient, fear-prompted, pro-natalist attitudes, but the very human tendency to envy the person who is free of the burden we bear (even when it is a "burden" we don't really want to give up), and to resent the person who does not share a responsibility that we have taken on. (There is also the more generous impulse to insist that others should have the joys we have—such as marriage!) If we yield to these temptations even when there is no threat of depopulation, we shall have to be on guard when population pressure brings its own occasions for envy and resentment, with consequent temptation to invade the rights of others.

The couple with a genuine love for children and with ample means to support four or more, who decide out of a sense of responsibility to the national welfare to have only three, will find it hard to feel kindly toward the neighbors who have six or eight. The parents who long for a third child "because if something happened to one then we'd be a one-child family, and that just isn't good" will resent the families who have "more than their share, the way things are these days." The school district that is religiously divided will have increased tension when the system sags under the weight of an obviously higher birth rate in one religious community. The many children in families living on Aid to Dependent Children can give rise to a hot political issue, all the hotter when others are denying themselves children they actually want. The question of what is a fair share in family size could become a real one. It is now for many persons. It would increase in urgency as population pressures build up.

It is easy to say: What right has the Palestinian Arab to breed at the astronomical rate of 54 per 1,000? But unless the refugee is secure in his right to have children, and to his own choice in the number, none of us is secure in the right. The right to have children must belong to the refugee, to the poor, to every race, to those of any political belief or religion, and to all classes.

The right must also cover the right of the sterile to seek a cure for their sterility, no matter how populous the country may already be.

One thorny question remains. Does not the good of the group transcend the rights of the individual? Does not society have the right to curtail the freedom of the individual for the sake of all? Under extreme population pressure would not the state have the right to regulate reproduction?

In seeking an answer, the private nature of the sex act must be considered as well as the fact that it comprises two functions. It is the most difficult of all human acts to subject to outside control. In the ultimate sense there are only two ways in which the state could abrogate the right to reproduce: by forced sterilization and by a police-administered infanticide. Even an absolute state control of marriage would not necessarily prevent births without the reinforcement of these two measures. No government could stay long in power if it advocated such measures, to be applied extensively. The danger is that, under population pressure, attempts might be made to curtail or deny the reproductive right of certain classes or persons.

Group control over reproduction can never be control in the absolute sense. The group can develop norms, reinforced by moral and religious teaching and by the application of sanctions, which may be of considerable effect. But in the end, reproduction is determined by couples. The fact that it cannot be regulated by the state lays upon each couple a heavier responsibility for self-regulation.

Perhaps we shall always needs some reminder of our duty to perpetuate life, just as we are always in need of the law to remind us of our responsibility and to set limits against our weaknesses. But under the stress of growing population it is clear that we shall need to guard every couple's right to have children. The best way is by voluntarily limiting one's own fertility as a contribution to the welfare of all.

Notes

1. James M. Robinson, "Birth Control—Right or Wrong?" *Crises in Morality,* ed. by C. W. Scudder (Nashville: Broadman Press, 1964). This is a book by ministers in the Southern Baptist church.

A Bureau of the Census release of March 1957 gave data relating fertility to religion (the only time the Bureau has asked for fertility information by religious denomination). Baptists, including non-white, tended to have even more children than Catholics (who have a higher fertility pattern than Protestants). According to the *Population Bulletin* (September, 1964), a major conclusion of *The Third Child,* a volume reporting the findings of a study conducted by the Office of Population Research at Princeton University, states that religion "is strongest of all major *social* characteristics in its influence on fertility." But I think it would be difficult to know whether Southern Baptist fertility (and attitudes on birth control) are a reflection of the fact that this denomination is largely farm and southern in membership, or whether farm and southern populations tend to be more strongly influenced by teachings of their religion.

2. The Lambeth Conference, 1958.

3. James A. Pike, "The Vocation of Parenthood," *Birth Rate and Birth Right,* ed. by Marian Maury (New York: Macfadden Books, 1963), p. 191.

4. Helmut Thielicke, *The Ethics of Sex* (New York: Harper and Row Publishers, 1964), p. 206.

Thielicke's position is strongly and consistently pro-natal, though he does recognize that certain circumstances, health and other, would require that there be no children. He tries to solve the dilemma by invoking Kant's "moral necessity," so that prevention of birth becomes "involuntary." That he may not be altogether satisfied with this solution is indicated when he says "husband and wife would have to live in God's forgiveness." Moral necessity demands what moral duty prohibits! Thielicke does concede the fact of a "population explosion," but for an answer to the problems it may pose he looks to the "sociological and economics." His rejection of birth control on any but a limited scale and for individual couples in exceptional circumstances of their own, leads him to place his faith in manipulation of what I have called the *situation* factor rather than any "manipulation" of the population.

5. Erik H. Erikson, *Childhood and Society,* 2nd ed. (W. W. Norton & Company, Inc., 1961), pp. 266 ff.

The basic food assistance programs designed to combat hunger and malnutrition in the United States are the school-lunch, commodity-donation, and food-stamp programs. Experience has demonstrated inadequacies in these programs, but measures are being taken to eliminate such inadequacies as they come to light. In addition, efforts are now being made to educate people regarding nutrition, since it has been recognized that food programs are not enough—proper eating habits must be instilled as well.

School Lunch to Food Stamps: America Cares for Its Hungry

Samuel C. Vannerman

Hunger hurts. It hurts physically, mentally, and emotionally. It is a harsh and ugly word that has no place in the American scheme of things.

Nutrition is a quiet word—a grey word—it carries no image of anger or harshness. It is a positive word, and it has an important role in the American scheme of things.

Americans are gradually becoming aware that hunger and, more particularly, poor nutrition still do exist within our borders.

In the last 30 years, the United States has steadily expanded and improved its program to improve nutrition among children and low-income families.

One example is the national school lunch program, enacted in 1946. Congress, in the National School Lunch Act, declares its policy to safeguard the health and well-being of children and encourage consumption of nutritious foods.

The Act authorizes giving cash and foods to schools that offer a nutritionally balanced lunch to children, without profit. Such lunches include a half-pint of milk, a protein-rich food, a vegetable and/or fruit, and enriched bread with butter or margarine.

The National School Lunch Act also requires that a child who cannot pay the full price of the lunch shall get it free or at a reduced price. The lunch program is further intended for all children, regardless of their ability to pay.

The special milk program—a dual-purpose program—was enacted in 1954. By providing Federal cash assistance to help reduce the cost of milk served to children, nutrition would receive a boost while at the same

From "School Lunch to Food Stamps: America Cares for Its Hungry" by Samuel C. Vannerman. Reprinted from *Food for Us All,* The Yearbook of Agriculture, 1969. Washington, D.C., U.S. Government Printing Office.

time strengthening the market for sales of fluid whole milk. This program was, in many respects, a stopgap until a complete lunch, including milk, could be made available to all children.

The oldest of our food assistance programs is the commodity donation program for low-income families. It was started some 30 years ago, when an amendment to law authorized encouraging consumption of agricultural commodities through donating them to low-income persons, among other means.

Originally, the foods offered to State and local governments for donation to needy families were limited to foods acquired by the Federal Government under price support and surplus removal programs.

For many years, the foods offered depended, primarily, on supply factors and bore little direct relationship to the nutritional needs of the family. In late 1960, for example, the donated foods included lard, flour, cornmeal, nonfat dry milk, and rice. The assumption had always been that donated foods would provide some help and free some of the family's food purchasing power to buy other foods needed.

Over the postwar years there had been little awareness of how many people—or how many families—were trying to live, trying to survive on the donated foods and little else.

Early in 1961, steps were taken to build on what had been done, and try some new approaches to improving nutrition. The first step was to increase the quantity and variety of the donated foods offered—with special emphasis upon assuring the continuing availability of protein items.

The second step was to introduce the food stamp program on a pilot basis. The food stamp program uses a different technique from that of the donation program. Food stamps are used to increase a family's existing food purchasing power. Families are required to purchase food coupons in amounts that reflect their normal level of food expenditure based on family size and income. This on-going food purchasing power is then supplemented by additional food coupons provided free of charge. On the average, families pay about $6 for every $10 worth of coupons they receive. Families shop for food in the food stores of their choice that are authorized to redeem the food coupons. Virtually every food store in every community which has the program is authorized to accept food coupons. Families may buy any food they wish with the exception of a few imported products.

Here again, we have a dual-purpose program. Families have an opportunity to improve their nutrition while broadening the demand for farm products—particularly for perishable items such as meat, poultry, dairy products, and fruits and vegetables.

The food stamp program was tested on a gradually expanded basis before enactment of substantive legislation in 1964. This legislation contemplated a continuing gradual expansion of the program so it could be made available to every county and city that wanted it. Under one provision of the Food Stamp Act, a local jurisdiction may have the commodity program or the food stamp program but not both, since essentially they are directed toward the same end—improved family nutrition.

During these years, every effort was made to encourage State and local governments to join one program or the other. Funding of the food stamp program has never been sufficient to cover all of the counties that have wanted the program, but these counties have been urged to initiate a donation program as an interim step. Rates that many families had to pay for their stamps were reduced, effective in February 1969.

In mid-1967, a review of program coverage, geographically, revealed that many of the thousand lowest-income counties in the country did not have a food assistance program for the low-income families. Many of these, with a limited tax base, felt they could not afford the donation program under which the costs of storage, distribution, and certification are borne by local governments with, in most instances, very limited help from the State. The U.S. Department of Agriculture moved to offer these local governments assistance in meeting local costs for the donation program. Similar assistance for a food stamp program is barred by language in the Food Stamp Act that limits financial assistance for administration to a portion of certification expenses.

Many counties accepted the offer of financial assistance. Many managed to find funds, locally, to join the program. But some counties simply said they did not want a food assistance program under any circumstances. In these instances, USDA moved to meet the larger responsibility to all our low-income families by using its own personnel to operate a commodity donation program in these counties. At the same time, USDA said it would stand aside any moment that the local government would agree to operate the donation program with or without financial assistance.

Meanwhile the nutritive value and the variety of the foods offered under the donation program were stepped up. In early 1969, 22 foods were offered which, if they are all accepted by State and local governments and used by eligible families, will provide from 80 to 150 percent of the minimum daily requirements for all nutrients as recommended by the Food and Nutrition Board of the National Research Council. Since these foods amounted to some 35 pounds per person, each month, and most areas provide only a monthly distribution, some very practical limitations are encountered in terms of a large family's ability to get the food home and store it.

Also, in mid-1967, modifications were made in the food stamp program to make it more fully responsive to the needs of participating families. The purchase requirement for the lowest-income families was dropped to 50 cents a month per person, with a maximum of $3 for a family of six or more.The first month's purchase requirement for all families was reduced by half to give them time to adjust their budgets to the purchase requirement. Adjustments were made in the determination of farm income so that farm laborers and others would not be priced out of the program.

In February 1969, the price of stamps was further reduced, but the reduction was limited by the appropriation available. Some further modifications are now under consideration.

As indicated above, modifications have been made whenever food stamp program experience has demonstrated a need for change. Still further changes are under consideration to assure that the program is as effective as possible in assisting low-income families toward the goal of an adequate diet.

To further emphasize the national commitment to improved nutrition, the President has issued a call to convene a White House conference on nutrition in the fall of 1969.

It has become increasingly clear that total community involvement is necessary if malnutrition is to be eliminated. The 1969 White House conference will summon the thinking and the ideas and the recommendations of the widest possible range of concerned people from both the private and the public sector toward this end.

An additional supplementary food program is underway in both food stamp and commodity donation areas to provide the low-income pregnant women and new mothers and their young children with special foods to meet their special needs.

The goal over the next several years is to have a family food assistance program operating in every county and independent city in the country— there are still more than 400 that do not participate.

Child nutrition.   Hand-in-hand with the evolution in family food assistance programs has been a similar development to improve child nutrition. Program growth under the school lunch program since its start in 1947 had been steady, but the progress made was deceiving.

Behind the pleasant growth figures of 6 to 7 percent annually lay the unpleasant truth that millions—literally millions—of children had been bypassed. The students in small rural schools and the students in the urban elementary schools had become the forgotten children. The free and reduced price requirement in the National School Lunch Act was impossible to meet in the absence of greater funding. Many schools, knowing that their youngsters couldn't pay enough to make a viable lunch program, had declined to sign up. Others did come into the program but were only able to offer a fraction of the free and reduced price meals that were necessary.

The first major forward step of this decade was taken in 1962 when the school lunch formula for apportionment of Federal funds to the States was revised to reward those States making the greatest effort to increase participation. The previous formula had tended to reward the stand-patters and discourage increased participation—the more meals you served, the less you received per lunch. The second major step in that amendment was one authorizing a higher rate of reimbursement, per meal, in those schools drawing attendance from low-income areas. This provision was much needed and was enacted rather easily but was not funded until the 1964–65 school year and, then, only to a very limited extent.

It was apparent that many schools could not participate in the lunch program because they were unable to finance the cost of even simple, basic food service equipment. At the same time, increasing numbers of educators were finding that all too many children came to school without breakfast or with a totally inadequate one. They fell asleep at their desks—they became listless and inattentive or bored and restless. In the Child Nutrition Act of 1966, the Nation moved to meet this need. Legislation authorized a pilot school breakfast program. It authorized assistance in financing school food service equipment in low-income area schools. And it authorized help to the States in strengthening their technical assistance capabilities so as to get food service programs into a substantial number of schools that either had no programs, or where an on-going program was eking out a quite precarious existence.

In 1968, still another forward step was taken with legislation that authorizes food service assistance to day-care centers, summer day camps, neighborhood houses, settlement houses, summer recreational projects— almost any situation where children are gathered together in organized groups and can be reached with a food service. This bill also extended the school breakfast program which during its pilot stage had proved its value many times over.

Meanwhile, during these past several years, the Congress has provided a level of funding for the regular lunch program that will assure a steady rate of reimbursement per meal and allow for expansion of the regular program. For fiscal 1969, the Congress provided $45 million over and above the money appropriated for what might be considered the regular child food service activities. The major share of these funds—$43 million— was allocated to provide free and reduced price meals to around 2 million additional needy children who could not have been reached with the money available under the regular child food service appropriations.

We have, then, a situation where the regular school lunch program can continue to grow and expand while additional and new resources are being applied to get to the neediest children. And, as child food service grows, so does this big market for the Nation's farmers—nearly $1 billion is spent locally for foods needed in the lunch and breakfast programs.

Our national goal is a food service program available to every school child, priced at a level so that every child may participate. New approaches are being tested to minimize the cost of equipment, for example, through the use of centralized kitchens serving a number of satellite schools.

There is one more major drive under way that affects both the family food assistance programs and the child nutrition programs—an all-out effort to get across the nutrition message. This drive seeks to explain why good nutrition is important and to make good nutrition part of everyone's life. The actual existence and participation in the food programs is not enough—people need to know why they should eat certain foods. And this applies to all of our families, however poor or however affluent.

In almost every discussion of the population-food problem the continuing role of the United States as provider is emphasized. Our efforts in the past have failed to make the countries which received help self-sufficient, and they must become so because we cannot indefinitely bear their burdens. Through the application of our market system and the use of American capital, the development of the poor countries could be hastened, but the countries themselves must be motivated to help themselves. They must be willing to modify some of their deep-seated customs and traditions in order to attract investors.

The United States and World Hunger

Duncan Norton-Taylor

The prospect of a world whose population is doubling every thirty years or so has inspired a number of nightmares. Professor J. H. Fremlin, a prestigious physicist of Birmingham University in England, has described one he had in an article in the magazine *New Scientist*. Looking ahead eight hundred years, and speculating about how all the people would be fed, he saw how "waste products could in principle be changed back into food compounds with the absorption of little more energy. Cadavers could be homogenized," and additional photosynthesis for the production of extra crops could be arranged for by the orbiting of immense mirrors that would continuously reflect the sun around the earth. But the mirrors would have created an insoluble problem of overheating, and the world, having produced a population of 12 quadrillion, would then have reached, in Fremlin's phrase of finality, a "dead end."

But there are visions, almost as unpleasant as Fremlin's, that have the more disquieting effect of being real and immediate: of the human population stabilizing itself in the manner of the animal world—through mortal conflicts between species, through degeneracy and reduction in the birth rate due to stresses of overcrowding (what one experimenter with rats calls "pathological togetherness"), and through death from hunger.

Disease may simply stalk quietly through populations debilitated by malnutrition. Such visions come into closer focus in Mrs. Indira Gandhi's India, now not only threatened again by famine, but haunted by the realization that the production of its croplands continues to fall steadily behind the requirements of its multiplying population.

The same predicament in varying degrees of seriousness has overtaken about two-thirds of the people of the world. The leaps in population

From "What the United States Can Do About World Hunger" by Duncan Norton-Taylor, *Fortune,* June 1966. Reprinted by permission of *Fortune.*

are most rapid in those regions least able to support them—the so-called underdeveloped nations, sometimes politely called the "less developed," or "developing," nations. The French have a noncommittal phrase for them— the *tiers monde,* which limits the grouping to those underdeveloped countries not in the Communist bloc, thus reducing to some extent the magnitude of our concern. But in this struggling area, which we cannot cast out, are most of Africa and Latin America, and an Asia that still includes, most burdensomely, India with its 500 million. This is the Third World, crying out, not always humbly, for help.

No problem presses on this generation of men more remorselessly. Few decisions or actions (outside of a nuclear decision) will be more critical in the next few years than those taken to resolve this dilemma of populations and human sustenance. All of modern humanism's skills and technologies are available to get the world out of its predicament at least in this century. The test is one of men's will to act.

The burden rests heavily upon the U.S., which for two decades has been sharing its abundance with hungry nations and now is called upon to rush emergency aid to India. But this country cannot continue on this course indefinitely, and shouldn't if it could, for such handouts merely put off crises, and even compound them. If there is any discernible solution it must be to raise the Third World to a state where it can feed itself. The point is being made over and over again today by Congressmen and the President, to each other and to the needy nations. But how is it to be brought about?

They have no simple answer—there is none. But certainly one answer must lie in what the U.S. has accomplished for itself and how it has done it. This nation has been able to grow food to a fantastic extent beyond the needs of its people. Granted its natural endowment of land, the U.S. has nevertheless multiplied the capacity of that land through the exploitation of technology and capital investment. These are the American products that both the government and American business should export in quantity to the agricultural economies of the Third World.

Capital can build irrigation canals in India, supply pumps and tube wells to tap the fresh water under the saline marshes of the Indus River basin in West Pakistan. Capital can supply tools and machinery, pesticides, fertilizers, provide training in modern methods. Most important of all, U.S. capital can create an atmosphere that is conducive to self-help. In the countless analyses of the subject, one fact stands out: that is the lack of incentive in the poverty-stricken, potentially rich, farmlands of the Third World. The factors inhibiting food production are traditionalism, lethargy, and hopelessness, not, at the moment, any lack of arable land. Capital generates incentive by producing goods and creating demand, and it widens the distribution of the fruits of labor. This is the market system so familiar to Americans.

The difficulties of transplanting the process are undeniable. Socialistic prejudices, hostility, and suspicion confront U.S. capital. American businessmen are reluctant to move into such an inclement and ostensibly unrewarding environment. But in the urgency of the situation, solutions to these difficulties must be found, and some, indeed, have been found and are being pressed by enterprising businessmen and administrators. It is inconceivable that there should be no answer at all to the dilemma.

A Hypothesis: 48 Million Left to Starve

Let us look at the dimensions of what is sometimes sportingly called the race between people and food. . . . The world population has doubled since 1900. Nothing is altogether inevitable, but enough female children have already been born to produce enough babies to raise the population to 7.4 billion by the year 2000. The populations of the Third World, which now number about 1.5 billion, are growing at rates of around 2.5 percent a year. The enormity of this growth becomes clear when one realizes that, at the 2.5 percent a year rate, Latin America will go from 212 million in 1960 to 569 million in the year 2000.

The sudden acceleration of population growths all over the world began in the Forties, when the availability of DDT and the antibiotics transformed a problem that was only slowly evolving into the dimensions it has now attained. Death rates began dropping abruptly. Right after World War II they were as high as thirty per thousand in many of the Third World countries, and since then they have declined to around twenty. Meanwhile the birth rates in the Third World have continued to exceed forty per thousand.

Birth rates may be the more opaque side of the dilemma. While farming isn't much fun, as one corporation economist remarked, reproducing is. There is also a poignant aspect to the situation: peasants in poverty-stricken regions look to their children as a kind of social security for themselves in an uncertain old age; and the higher the infant mortality rate, the more babies they are apt to produce. But this also suggests an encouraging angle: an improvement in economic conditions tends to lower the birth rates. In highly developed Western European countries, birth rates are down to about seventeen per thousand. It would be tragic, however, to wait on such a development, for the situation also works the other way around: increasing hordes of hungry people retard economic progress.

And the hordes have been getting hungrier. Before the war, according to the American Society of Agronomy, the countries of the Third World were, all together, net exporters of some 11 million metric tons a year of corn, wheat, rice, and other grains to the world's industrial nations. From 1948 to 1952 the flow reversed: the Third World countries imported an average of four million tons a year. As population growth gained momentum (and as many people migrated to urban centers), the net flow of imports increased: to 13 million tons a year between 1957 and 1959, to 25 million tons in 1964. It was not a matter of increasing trade but a matter of want. Even the 25 million tons were not enough to make up the growing food deficits.

The size of these deficits is difficult to measure with any exactitude, because opinions differ (as they differ in almost every aspect of the subject of food) as to what precisely constitutes an adequate diet. A Department of Agriculture study ("Changes in Agriculture in 26 Developing Nations") fixed on some 2,500 calories per day as adequate, which is about the average consumption in Mexico, and posed an interesting hypothesis to illustrate how short of this level was India's average food consumption in 1963. If India had distributed its supply of food as far as it would go even at only a 2,300-calorie level, 48 million out of that country's 480 million in that year would still have been left totally without food.

The study found an average per capita intake of calories below "desirable" levels in eleven of the twenty-six countries it examined: Colombia, Tanganyika (now part of Tanzania), Sudan, Tunisia, Egypt, Iran, Jordan, India, Pakistan, the Philippines, Thailand. And because of the uneven distribution of food in the other fifteen countries, many people there were suffering from malnutrition and undernutrition. Diets barely adequate in calories can be hazardously low in nutriments, such as proteins, necessary for good health.

At a seminar of experts in Estes Park, Colorado, last summer, the prediction was made that in 1980 the deficit in the underdeveloped countries would be somewhere between 47 million and 240 million metric tons of food, depending on whether populations were to be fed subsistence diets or adequate ones. These figures included mainland China; by removing China one reduces the overall figures somewhat (by around 25 percent) but this statistical exercise doesn't relieve the plight of the rest.

How Capital Can "Substitute for Land"

There is hope in one statement in the Agriculture Department report: most of the countries of the Third World have the potential of feeding their own people *and could have surpluses* within ten to twenty years. That hope rests on pointing economic development toward attaining self-sufficiency in food. One economist, Professor Theodore W. Schultz of the University of Chicago, takes encouragement from the way capital has transformed some of the old and congested farmlands of Europe, an experience more pertinent, perhaps, than that of the U.S., with its huge acreages. In his book, *Transforming Traditional Agriculture,* Schultz observes that Western Europe "with a population density much greater than Asia's and with a poor endowment of farm land generally, has been increasing its agricultural production at a rate that would have been thought impossible only a couple of decades ago. Italy, Austria, and Greece, for example, with less arable land per capita than India and with farm land inferior to India's, have increased agricultural production at a rate of 3.0, 3.3, and 5.7 percent per year respectively, compared to 2.1 for India."

"New land obviously is not the explanation," says Schultz. "It is the same old endowment of mostly poor land. If anything, the total area devoted to arable farming has been declining somewhat." In Israel, heavily populated by European stock, "between 1952 and 1959, production more than doubled although farm employment rose only a fourth." Israel's growth, too, was stimulated by capital investment. As in Europe, it created the factors of production "that substitute for land": modern implements, machinery, new seed strains, chemicals to fight pests and plant diseases, chemicals to enrich the earth.

India's story is a sorry contrast to this kind of progress. But at the same time India is a good case study of what capital might do to lift a poor country out of its ruck. As recently as 1952–53, India's annual output of chemical fertilizer nutrients totaled only 60,000 metric tons. Now it produces nearly 400,000 tons a year and uses more than 700,000 tons of fertilizer. It is estimated that India could increase production by 50 percent in the next five years if it improved its methods of farming and used three times this amount of fertilizer. India cannot afford to import such amounts, being lamentably short of foreign exchange. But with its own fertilizer plants, it would be freed from the need to import fertilizer and eventually the need to import food. Scarce foreign exchange could go instead into modernizing production and processing facilities. (One lack is up-to-date storage. Uncounted tons of grain are destroyed by rot and rats.) In time, India might even be able to export food and thus earn exchange for industrial development.

The injection of outside capital into the agricultural economy would also tend to draw out native capital from India's financial institutions and, what is especially important, from the farmers themselves. The Agriculture Department declares that most of the twenty-six developing nations it studied "probably have a larger capacity for savings and new capital formation than their per capita incomes and past rates of capital accumulation indicate." An Indian farmer, with an investment of no more than $68 in livestock and $11 in implements and machinery, may arrive at the end of the season with a small cash surplus. But instead of using it to buy more efficient implements or fertilizers, or even to acquire more land and thus increase his next season's profit, he puts his money in jewelry, or splurges it on ceremonies of birth, marriage, or death. The hope is that deep-seated customs will change under the impact of modern capitalism.

The Critical Failure of PL 480

For a number of years, of course, the U.S. has been pouring capital into the Third World—and on a large scale. Billions of dollars worth of government aid has gone out from these shores in both currency and commodities. The unhappy part is that U.S. foreign-aid policy, for one reason or another, has so far failed in one vital respect: it has not made the indigent countries able to feed themselves.

In the last eleven years the U.S. has shipped, mostly to Third World countries, food that has cost it some $25 billion. Some of this food was shipped in emergencies and the recipient countries were not billed for it at all. Most of the tonnage was paid for in local currencies, which can enjoy only a vague kind of status in the Budget Bureau's accounts. This was the food that went out under the legislative aegis of Public Law 480.

PL 480 was originally put together in the Eisenhower Administration with the idea of disposing of some of the country's large Commodity Credit Corporation surplus; helping stave off famine abroad; encouraging the export of U.S. agricultural products, and world trade; and promoting U.S. foreign policy. The program (once called "Food for Peace" and now probably to be renamed, at President Johnson's suggestion, "Food for Freedom") has been put to many splendid uses. It saved an uncountable number of lives; it did level off U.S. surpluses—wheat, for example, is now down to what is deemed a prudent reserve. And the act did foster world trade in agricultural commodities in several instances and to the profit of American business. In 1954, Taiwan was unable to purchase anything from the U.S.; in 1965, no longer in need of aid, it bought $36 million of U.S. farm products. Japan, which has received $376 million worth of PL 480 aid since 1954, is now a spectacular world trader and the U.S.'s biggest customer for food grains. These success stories were right in line with what a lot of people kept thinking PL 480 was supposed to do in the end: put a billion and a half people in the Third World on their feet. But it never did.

The failure grew partly out of some early notions about priorities. The experts urged the Third World countries to get cracking first on industrial development, on the theory that they needed to create foreign exchange and this was the way to do it. In India, American food shipments along with some substantial improvement in India's own farm economy (which was soon to level off) gave rise to a complacency about the onrushing population and rising demands. Instead of helping India to learn how to feed itself, PL 480 had a disincentive effect on agricultural development. The Indians strove proudly to industrialize. "Nothing was dearer to their hearts than steel mills," says an Agriculture Department economist. Professors and Indians were not the only ones making the mistake. "In the mid-Fifties," the economist recalls, "American bankers and U.S. foreign-aid people examined the underdeveloped countries. They were interested in seeing them develop industry, not agriculture."

Despite the worsening food situation, the idea of giving priority to industrial development has persisted. PL 480 provides that the local currency a country pays for the purchase of American food can be borrowed back for various investments that the U.S. approves of, or given back to the countries in grants. The three countries that have received the most PL 480 aid are India, Pakistan, and the United Arab Republic, and not surprisingly, they are the biggest recipients of such loans and grants. India has put very little of such money into agriculture, Pakistan a bit more. Most of these funds went into industrial development and public works. Egypt, so far, has put almost nothing at all into agriculture, but has put $22 million into industry, $403 million into an account merely labeled "general and miscellaneous."

Let 'em Eat Sugar

U.S. policy under PL 480 was muddled by conflicts in goals and responsibilities. Legislative direction and effective control of the program lay with the House and Senate agricultural committees, whose members, coming chiefly from the South and the Midwest, had to keep in mind their farming constituencies. The Department of Agriculture has obediently carried out Congress' demands for protective restrictions. Herbert Waters, assistant administrator for material resources in the Agency for International Development, recalls how the earnest efforts of his office to promote self-help were undone by such restrictions. Shipments of U.S. wheat encouraged South Koreans to get away from their almost exclusively rice diets, as a result of which they had a rice surplus. They wanted to sell some of it to Japan. But Agriculture made it clear that so long as the South Koreans were getting PL 480 wheat they couldn't export their rice. Eventually they were permitted to do so, but only if they bought a ton of U.S. wheat for every ton of rice they exported. Such protectionism was also applied to the export of Pakistani rice to India. And since Turkey was getting PL 480 soybean oil, that country was tied down in its export of olive oil.

One promising innovation in the program was the provision for so-called "Cooley loans," named after Chairman Harold Cooley of the House Agriculture Committee. The local currency proceeds from the sale of U.S. commodities may be borrowed by U.S. firms that might want to do business in the Third World or by local people who are going to buy U.S. goods. But this borrowing is further circumscribed. A rider disallows such borrowing when the enterprises might be competitive with a domestic American enterprise. Who would have thought that a mushroom venture would come under such a ukase? But a request for such a loan in South Korea has been shelved because AID recollected how help given to mushroom growers in Taiwan had once stirred up Congressman Paul Dague's constituents in Pennsylvania's mushroom country. Dague is ranking minority member of the House Agriculture Committee.

Now, with PL 480 about to expire and the time come to devise a new program, this attitude is changing, according to Chairman Cooley. "Some members still think we shouldn't encourage people to compete with us. But the feeling is not as widespread as it was. The new concept is to help the countries help themselves."

But one exchange during the House hearings on a new bill indicated that some Congressmen may be hard to budge. Vice Chairman W. R. Poage, of Texas, expressed his exasperation over the fact that India was producing about five million bales of cotton. "That land that is producing cotton could produce food," he told Secretary of Agriculture Freeman, who was testifying before the House committee. "I see some folks are laughing about this," Poage noted, "but to me it is a deadly serious problem." Why shouldn't the U.S., he demanded, tell the Indians to put some of that cotton acreage into something they can eat? "We can say that to them. And let us say to them that we will give you cotton to take the place of what you do not grow." And, for that matter, Poage wanted to know, why should the U.S. be buying sugar from India? "They ought either to eat it themselves," he said, "or they ought to be growing something on that sugar land they need themselves."

"It is not a simple problem, as I know you thoroughly realize," replied Freeman. "If you rejected desperately needed exchange that India might get by selling sugar, which she would use to buy fertilizer, and that fertilizer in turn makes it possible for them to double their wheat and rice output—why you then would come to the conclusion that we either say, 'We concur in your producing sugar or cotton,' or we say, 'We will make the fertilizer available.' "

After this mild demurrer, the Secretary retreated, breathing at one point, "If anybody in Washington needs any advice it is me. Thank you for any you have given me."

So it remains to be seen just how Cooley's "new concept" will work out.

Message From a Dutch Uncle

President Johnson, for his part, seems determined that the Third World should now understand that the U.S. is inclined to help only those who help themselves. With an air of having reached the end of his string, he stipulated in messages to Congress early this year that the financing of the bulk of American food shipments must eventually (within the next five years) be in dollars instead of local currency. Under the current program there have been some hard-currency transactions on credit terms as long as twenty years at 2½ percent. Less than 10 percent of such loans so far have been paid back.

But the most significant passages in the President's message were aimed at the Third World itself. From now on, he said, the recipients of U.S. aid must "make basic improvements in their own agriculture . . . bring the great majority of their people—now living in rural areas—into the market economy . . . make the farmer a better customer of urban industry and thus accelerate the pace of economic development."

The President, while sounding like a Dutch uncle, was not threatening to let the Third World starve: "Even with their maximum efforts abroad, our food aid will be needed for many years to come." Nevertheless, he gave the Third World something brand new to think about, not the least of which was its attitude toward U.S. aid, public *and* private. "Only these people and their leaders," he said, "can . . . create the climate which will attract foreign investment."

"Threats and Rumors of Expropriation"

The climate has been rough. A committee of businessmen, educators, and government and labor leaders, headed by Arthur K. Watson, chairman of I.B.M. World Trade Corp., studied the problem of "Private Enterprise in Foreign Aid." And in its report last summer it pointed out that while U.S. businessmen are used to taking risks, not many of them are accustomed to accepting "political instability, threats and rumors of expropriation, systems of pervasive discretionary regulation, prospects of rapid inflation and devaluation, and other novel features of overseas investment." And in the face of all this, the eagerness of U.S. capital to go into the underdeveloped countries is petering out.

Watson's committee found that a total of $13.3 billion of U.S. private investments had been put into underdeveloped countries up to 1964. But the *rate* at which these investments are increasing has been insignificant, compared to the needs and possibilities. And most of the increase has been in the more advanced countries, especially of Latin America; roughly 20 percent of the increased capital was from profits generated in these countries and plowed back. Petroleum and mining, not surprisingly, accounted for well over one-half the $13.3 billion; manufacturing for $2.5 billion, and "other" business activities for $3.3 billion. Very few companies have been willing to risk scratching for profits on the farms: some manufacturers of chemical fertilizers (including a few oil companies) and a few food-processing and farm-equipment firms.

The committee for its part made certain proposals aimed at the President himself. It recommended that the U.S. Government should accept the idea of international arbitration of investment disputes; it should support an investment code under international sponsorship; there should be an increase in government guarantees against overseas losses due to inconvertibility, military hazards, etc. And the income-tax laws should be amended to encourage overseas investments. The committee also recommended that AID select a number of key countries for intensive study and that an explicit program be developed for the improvement of the investment climate in those selected countries.

"We Give the Farmer a Reason to Grow"

A few companies have taken their narrow chances in the agricultural economies of the Third World. It is interesting to see how they are making out, for it does indicate what capital can do with encouragement. These ventures cannot be said to be very large, but the companies are doing moderately well or they wouldn't be planning to expand, as some of them are, cautiously.

Corn Products, for example, is introducing Latin Americans to such novelties as milk fortifiers, baby foods, custard powder, and packaged soups. Its wholly owned subsidiary in Argentina, Refinerías de Maíz, buys all its supplies locally, thus providing a cash market for the farmer. Management of the operation is in local hands.

Corn Products has also found a way to enrich edible corn starch with soybean oil, which it is marketing under the label "Maizena," and in order to increase its margin of profit on this new food the company is showing Brazilian farmers how to grow soybeans, which now have to be imported from the U.S. "We're part of the economy," said Alexander McFarlane, Corn Products' chairman. "In a modest way we give the farmer a reason to grow." What concessions does Corn Products want in a foreign investment? "No harassment. Equal opportunities with the national companies—no special favors. If we're treated equitably, we'll take our chances."

H. J. Heinz is in Venezuela with a subsidiary, Alimentos Heinz, which processes vegetables and fruits grown on small farms. Heinz introduced new strains that give better quality and yields. Junius F. Allen, in charge of Heinz's international operations, relates that the company built a factory in the farming town of San Joaquin (pop. 6,000). "We went in as the first steady industrial employer. The reactions of people to steady income were marked. They began to wear better clothes. At first they'd just peer into our cafeteria or just buy a Coke. But after a time they began to eat the hot lunch. They began to buy bicycles to get to the plant. It was the first step up, the first kind of mobility. We improved their standards in hygiene by providing clean washrooms. People respond to example. Perhaps an even greater impact was made on the agriculture of the community, for Heinz supplied a market for their produce which had not existed before. Heinz provided assistance which allowed the farmers to increase their yield and hence their incomes. The average yield of tomatoes of these farmers, for example, doubled in four years."

Sermons in Half a Dozen Dialects

In Brazil, Mexico, and Peru agricultural services are provided by Anderson, Clayton for local farmers who grow cotton seed, peanuts, and soybeans for a line of cooking and salad oils, shortening, and margarine that the company processes and markets. It finances seed, fertilizers, and insecticides, and gives advice on planting and harvesting. The plants provide plenty of local employment—6,000 jobs in Brazil, 4,500 in Mexico, 800 in Peru—and Anderson, Clayton feels, like Heinz, that it is generating incentives by providing the means for a higher standard of living.

Not the least of the handicaps these companies have to overcome is that of communication in regions where the illiteracy rate may run as high as 50 percent. Esso Chemical, which has worldwide fertilizer operations through affiliates, has developed a system of chain teaching; they train their salesmen to train local people, who in turn train larger groups to go out into the fields and preach capitalism and modern farming—sermons that may have to be rendered in one of half a dozen different dialects. International Minerals & Chemical is carrying the message of fertilizer into every corner it can reach. The gist of its sermon: NPK (nitrogen, phosphate, and potash) is a substitute for land; i.e., it can multiply the yield of one acre as many as 500 times. The average consumption of fertilizer nutrients in the Third World countries is around five pounds per acre. Some Dutch farmers use as much as 400 pounds per acre.

Some U.S. firms have already set up fertilizer plants abroad on a limited scale. I.M.C., with Standard Oil of California, is building a $70-million plant in Visag in India with a capacity of 350,000 tons, which should be in operation in 1967. I.M.C. and Standard have accepted a minority position in the Visag enterprise; Indian interests own 53 percent. This is not the kind of situation that appeals to very many U.S. corporations; they are reluctant to grant even a minority position to Indian interests, which may not appreciate the vigorous ways American business does things. But Armour is in a deal with India's big industrial firm of Birla Gwalior Ltd. to operate a $50-million ammonia-urea complex in Goa. The two companies hold 51 percent of the equity; Indian private money has taken up the rest.

A Plan for 20 Million Peasants

These companies have been fairly bold, within the limits of their accountability to their stockholders. They have been resourceful and sometimes imaginative. But some people who have studied the problem believe that it calls for an even more creative approach.

One such person is Simon Williams, a consultant once hired by I.M.C. to do a survey of world hunger. He has a scheme he would like to test with a pilot project in Mexico, where he would set up a corporation in partnership with 1,000 small farmers under "paternal" American management. The farmers would share ownership of the corporation through stock purchased on credit and paid for out of the surplus crops Williams is sure they could produce under skillful direction. He saw such a corporation financed by some $5 million of equity capital within ten years and working capital of $2 million to $3 million. Williams admits that the decision on the part of Americans to invest must "be motivated primarily by the desire to increase food supplies and to stimulate rural economic development."

Nevertheless, he sees American investors making a "substantial profit every year, as well as recovering their investment in twenty years." In those twenty years the farmers would have acquired ownership of the corporation. Williams has confidence in their intelligence and thriftiness. "We have to find new forms of organization," he says, "that will be acceptable to both capital and the political powers. We need new institutions, new attitudes so that investment can become meaningful. The opportunity was never better than now to experiment with new forms."

But the idea looked much too experimental to one banker who studied the scheme. He thought it was a fine notion but pretty idealistic and he was not sure Williams had figured out a feasible debt-equity ratio. "No banker would touch it with a ten-foot pole," he said. I.M.C., for its part, decided it had "too many other things on its plate."

The fact is, Charles Dennison, an I.M.C. vice president, has an interesting scheme of his own for India. (I.M.C. wants it to be known that the plan is Dennison's, not the company's.) An earnest and ebullient man, Dennison proposes to set up a consortium that would include a fertilizer company, seed, insecticide, and pesticide companies, a farm-implement maker, a fisheries enterprise, and a food processor, all under one top manager. The project would be capitalized at something around $100 million. Indian private investors would be invited to subscribe for shares; most of the debt structure would be government money, in rupees, including PL 480 rupees, which could be used to purchase made-in-India components for the consortium's facilities.

The consortium would train the farmers in a selected geographical area, and would sell them the products of its various technologies. "The Indian farmer is illiterate but shrewd," says Dennison. "Education is the heart of the thing." The consortium would go into operation with 1,000 to 2,000 distributors, who should be able, he figures, to reach upwards of two million peasants.

Crucial to the whole scheme would be a generous farm-credit program, and either a free market or a government policy on farm prices that would give farmers an incentive to produce.

Dennison sees other consortiums, profiting from example, beginning similar operations in neighboring regions. The participants might well include not only U.S. and Indian partners but European companies (e.g., Montecatini, I.C.I., Dutch State Mines). This should allay Indian suspicions that their country was being invaded by an American "neo-colonialism."

With ten such projects going, India could look forward to its farmers' producing the bulk of the 185 million tons or so of grain the country will need for an adequate level of consumption in 1980. India would then be able gradually to reduce its grain imports while increasing imports of other foods, thus becoming a market, instead of an object of continuing charity, for the U.S.

Dennison has taken his scheme to Secretary Freeman, who thinks it is admirable in concept but questions whether enough attention has been given to "its nuts and bolts." Another government official feels the Indian Government would think twice before letting foreign interests cut such a wide swath into their economy. Dennison himself has told Indian officials: "Here is a scheme. Tear it down or alter it any way you want. But please recognize that it is an attempt to deal with this problem on a scale big enough and fast enough to solve it." His basic motive, he says, is to help the Indians while generating profits for everyone. No one exposed to Dennison's missionary zeal can doubt him.

The Unthinkable Alternative

There has been a modest marshaling of a variety of public and philanthropic forces on the farms of the world's underdeveloped regions. Besides AID, the United Nations' Food and Agricultural Organization and private foundations, notably the Ford and Rockefeller foundations, are supporting agricultural laboratories and training centers, helping to develop new seed strains and introducing new technologies in farm management. The foundations have sent money and personnel into the Philippines, India, Pakistan, the Middle East, Africa, and Latin America, and have contributed funds to American land-grant universities to enable them to send both advisers and equipment into the foreign field. A typical outlay of Ford Foundation funds was the $300,000 it put up to experiment in crossbreeding West Pakistan's wheat with high-yielding Mexican dwarf strains.

FAO has some 2,000 employees in its Rome headquarters analyzing data and mapping areas from African deserts to Amazon rain forests that might be turned into croplands. And some 2,600 FAO people are in the field in many roles, teaching the techniques of irrigation, helping farmers in their struggles against blight and disease.

But it is the U.S. that can do the most in the struggle because of the power of its capital, if it can be put to work, to fire up the human energy that resides in these populations. It cannot be emphasized enough that this country is unable to fill the food gap, or even supply the fertilizer needs of the Third World indefinitely from its own resources.

Any formula for transplanting capital and the capitalist revolution—Williams', or Dennison's, or anyone else's—will be slow to bear fruit among old and backward cultures. There is little prospect of a short-term profit for American investors, and no one, with the exception of Williams perhaps, is ready to vouch that there will be a sizable long-term profit either.

But American businessmen, singly and in consortiums, and with the support of their government, must face the fact that the world will be unsafe unless economic, as well as political stability, is brought to the countries of the Third World. Food riots that overwhelm all order can turn threats of expropriation or destruction of American properties into reality, so that investment of billions of dollars in oil, mining, and manufacturing may in the end depend very much on a determined movement of American capital into the agricultural economies of those nations. These are practical considerations. They do nothing to lessen the humanitarian concerns involved in this astounding race between people and food.

Bibliography

Borgstrom, Georg. *Hungry Planet*. New York: Macmillan, 1965.

Bracher, Marjory L. *S.R.O. Overpopulation and You*. Philadelphia: Fortress Press, 1966.

Citizens' Board of Inquiry Into Hunger and Malnutrition in the United States. *Hunger, U.S.A.* Boston: Beacon Press, 1968.

Desrosier, Norman W. *Attack on Starvation*. Westport, Connecticut: Avi Publishing Co., 1961.

Dumont, Rene, and Rosier, Vernard. *The Hungry Future*. New York: Frederick A. Praeger, 1969.

Osborn, Fairfield. *Our Crowded Planet*. New York: Doubleday and Co., 1962.

Photo by Nick Pavloff, Photo Find, S.F.

Violence

Respect for persons and for law is characteristic of the American tradition, but a propensity toward violence is a recognized strain in the same tradition. Our national independence was gained through revolution, and the 100 years thereafter saw wars, slave insurrections, Indian fighting, urban riots, murders, duels, and beatings. Abraham Lincoln in 1838 called attention to the increasing disregard for law, the growing disposition to substitute the wild and furious passions for the sober judgment of courts and the savage mobs for the executive ministers of justice.

American ambiguity toward violence was demonstrated when Emerson and Thoreau applauded John Brown at Osawatomie, and it permeates all elements of our society to this day. Martin Luther King, Jr., spoke of the schizophrenic personality of America, so tragically divided against herself. Shooting and killing countrymen is forty-eight times more frequent in America than in England or Japan, both comparably industrialized societies. Now that violence is occurring with seemingly renewed intensity, there is much bewilderment and an anxious seeking for causes.

Many different explanations for the resurgence of violence are offered, including racism, capitalism, industrialization, our origin as a frontier society, and lack of federal gun legislation. Increasingly, it becomes evident that the real answers are not to be found in simplistic formulas, but are much more profound and elusive. To understand the violence, and tolerance of violence, in

America requires a penetration beyond the superficial symptoms. An example of such analysis is found in the report of the National Advisory Commission on Civil Disorders (1968)[1] and is an expression of the conditions that they considered to be catalysts of riots:

1. Frustrated hope, generated by the civil rights struggle.
2. A climate heavy with approval and encouragement of violence.
3. The frustration of feeling powerless to move the system.
4. A new mood—particularly in the young—of self-esteem and enhanced racial pride.
5. The view of police as a symbol of white power, white racism and white repression.

In 1968 the President of the United States established a commission under the chairmanship of Milton Eisenhower to study the causes and prevention of violence and to make recommendations with respect to the prevention of disrespect for law and order; disrespect for public officials; violent disruptions of public order; and lawlessness, including assassination, murder and assault. The conclusions of this commission are sufficiently illuminating to provide some direction for our efforts toward the control of the destructive force of violence and the understanding of its potential for constructive change.

Violence is a generic term that correctly refers to many forms of behavior. Violence may be carried on by groups or institutions or by individuals. It is most often taken to mean behavior that is intended to inflict physical injury to people or damage to property.

Overt physical assault by one person upon another, such as the crime of murder, is the most obvious type of violence. Group or institutionalized violence of this type would be war. Riots are another form of the same type. Violence is often confused with power, strength, and authority.

Power implies control. It is the ability to influence the actions of others. It is not something that an individual may have independently. He must have the support of others, because without a group there is no source of power. The group, overtly or covertly, determines the *situs* of power.

Strength, on the other hand, is an attribute of a person or thing and is inherent in the individual.

Authority is power vested in persons or in offices. When authority is acknowledged, people obey commands without coercion or persuasion. Authority is relatively easy to retain so long as the group respects the person or the position of authority.

Instruments or implements that multiply human strength may be used in exercising violence. Thus, in a conflict between power and violence, violence may destroy power and achieve instant obedience, but it is not synonymous with power. In fact, as power wanes, violence frequently is substituted, and there is a resort to terror to maintain dominance. Thus power and violence are somewhat contradictory. If power is present, there is no need for violence. Violence appears when power is in jeopardy, but it does not create power in the true sense.

The impact of the ongoing war in Southeast Asia has brought forth wide support for nonviolence. Many who subscribe to the petitions and participate in the activities of the groups seeking to promote the cause of nonviolence no doubt do not understand the concept. It is not simply a way of proving one's point and gaining one's objective without engaging in ugly behavior. Nonviolent action is a way of insisting on one's just rights without violating the rights of anyone else. It is naïve to believe that the world can go on without any violence. The most to be hoped for, perhaps, is the avoidance of excess, the reduction of the use of violence to a minimum.

Some hold that violence is natural or instinctive and that study therefore should be directed only toward means of protection against this tendency of man. This approach adds little to the understanding or the control of such behavior. A more promising subject for research is the relationship between man's biological inheritance and his social experiences, because from the moment of conception the forces of inheritance and environment interact, and the result is the unique personality that characterizes each individual. While there is indisputable evidence of man's capacity to be aggressive and violent, how the social and cultural experiences of the individual operate in the shaping and conditioning of this ability is not as well established.

The emphasis of the psychological explanation of violent behavior is upon the internal balance between instigating and inhibiting factors. The probability of violent behavior occurring is dependent upon the excess of instigating factors. External conditions, such as poverty, unemployment, and social rejection, may become instigating forces if they have sufficient meaning for the individual to stimulate him to commit violent acts.

Violence is common to all societies because all normal human beings have the capacity to commit violence and to experience rage, but the rates of violent behavior differ greatly from one society to another. No satisfactory explanation for these variations has been demonstrated thus far. The crucial question is why some people are more inclined to violence than others. The characteristics most frequently present in the criminally violent persons in our society indicate the relevance of certain sociological and cultural conditions.

The findings of recent research indicate that those who have a "stake" in their society or an investment that would be jeopardized or endangered by illegal behavior are more likely to restrain their impulses toward violent activity. A "stake" may consist of material comforts, a career, a reputation, prestige, membership in a group, love and security, or any number of different things that would be more valuable to a person than the gratification that would be gained by indulging in criminal violence.

In line with this idea, the Task Force on Individual Acts of Violence[2] proposed certain steps toward social reconstruction that would help to eliminate basic causes of crime and violence:

1. The reduction of economic deprivation and degradation through programs concerned with jobs, income supplementation and homes.

2. The reduction of political alienation through programs designed to provide for greater community participation by citizens and through creation of new channels of communication between government and the poor, the underprivileged, and the unorganized.

3. The reduction of pathologies in child development through educational programs and family services.

4. The elimination of educational inadequacies through programs that provide equal, quality education, enabling every child to secure the emotional and cognitive requirements for effective adult participation.

5. The creation of new roles for youth, so that young people can lend their energies, visions, and skills to the decision-making processes of this country and learn through such participation that peaceful change can be effective within the framework of democratic institutions.

6. The reduction or elimination of prejudice and discrimination that contributes so pervasively to the alienation felt by underprivileged groups.

7. An improved response to violence among intimates.

8. The reduction of violence by official representatives of the law.

9. A more effective and sensitive program against narcotic and drug use.

10. An improved response to the role of alcohol in violence.

11. A more comprehensive program of suicide prevention.

12. A more coordinated and exhaustive research effort.

Violence may serve as a creative and constructive force; it does have this potential. For one thing, it can be effective in reaching a given end. It may be that in some cases violence is the only way of gaining a hearing or of overcoming a deadly force. The use of violence has brought about needed change, on a short-term basis, by dramatizing conditions and bringing them to public attention.

The danger inherent in the use of violence is always that the means may overwhelm the end even when it is one justifiably sought. No doubt "violence pays" under some circumstances, but it is arbitrary; it pays equally for "good" goals and "evil" goals; and once violence becomes the customary *modus operandi* it can be used for all kinds of purposes. True, violence can evoke change, but the most probable change is toward a condition of more violence.

Thus, the resort to violence, whether on an individual, group, or institutional level, is to be avoided if possible, and much can be done in this respect. The knowledge that severe frustration is conducive to violent reactions should be enough to encourage receptive attitudes that would relax the tensions present when grievances are aired. Being aware that the threat of loss or diminution of power increases the temptation to substitute violence should aid in guarding against the worst of such consequences. Primarily, a firm, unequivocal commitment to the reduction of physical violence and a sincere willingness to make the necessary sacrifices are prerequisites to the changes that would help relieve the urge to violence.

The articles included in this section are intended to provide an explanation of the presence of violence in our society, the ramifications thereof, and some suggestions for the avoidance of it as a destructive force.

The first article, "The Functions of Social Conflict," explains both the function of conflict in society and how certain forms can be dysfunctional. The author bases his analysis of conflict on the theories of Georg Simmel and the findings gained from empirical research.

The second and third selections are from Task Force Reports to the National Commission on the Causes and Prevention of Violence, and they present the historical and the contemporary picture of violence in America.

Dr. W. Walter Menninger, noted psychiatrist, describes and explains the varying responses to violence in the fourth article and admonishes against responding to violence with hate.

The mass media are always prominent in any discussion of violence in this country. "Television and Violence" presents the views of a British author on the subject.

"When Does a Riot Become a Revolution?" and "Rioting, Insurrection, and Civil Disobedience" are both concerned with rioting as related to revolution, in the past and the present. The article by Hans Toch adds some further insights on the possibilities of preventing destructive violent behavior.

The final item presents the recommendations made by the National Commission on the Causes and Prevention of Violence.

Notes

1. *Report of the National Advisory Commission on Civil Disorders* (New York: Bantam Books, 1968), pp. 16–21.

2. *Crimes of Violence,* A Staff Report Submitted to the National Commission on the Causes and Prevention of Violence (Washington, D.C.: U.S. Government Printing Office, 1969), pp. 731–754.

Conflict or the potential for conflict is present in every society. It may unify or destroy group structure. Adverse consequences are more likely where the social structure is rigid and has no provision for the expression of hostile feelings or grievances. Disruption of the social system in such cases is due more to the rigidity of the structure than to the conflict.

The Functions of Social Conflict

Lewis A. Coser

. . . Conflict within a group . . . may help to establish unity or to re-establish unity and cohesion where it has been threatened by hostile and antagonistic feelings among the members. Yet, . . . not *every* type of conflict is likely to benefit group structure, nor . . . [can] conflict . . . subserve such functions for *all* groups. Whether social conflict is beneficial to internal adaptation or not depends on the type of issues over which it is fought as well as on the type of social structure within which it occurs. However, types of conflict and types of social structure are not independent variables.

Internal social conflicts which concern goals, values or interests that do not contradict the basic assumptions upon which the relationship is founded tend to be positively functional for the social structure. Such conflicts tend to make possible the readjustment of norms and power relations within groups in accordance with the felt needs of its individual members or subgroups.

Internal conflicts in which the contending parties no longer share the basic values upon which the legitimacy of the social system rests threaten to disrupt the structure.

One safeguard against conflict disrupting the consensual basis of the relationship, however, is contained in the social structure itself: it is provided by the institutionalization and tolerance of conflict. Whether internal conflict promises to be a means of equilibration of social relations or readjustment of rival claims, or whether it threatens to "tear apart," depends to a large extent on the social structure within which it occurs.

In every type of social structure there are occasions for conflict, since individuals and subgroups are likely to make from time to time rival claims to scarce resources, prestige or power positions. But social structures differ in the way in which they allow expression to antagonistic claims. Some show more tolerance of conflict than others.

Closely knit groups in which there exists a high frequency of interaction and high personality involvement of the members have a tendency to suppress conflict. While they provide frequent occasions for hostility (since both sentiments of love and hatred are intensified through frequency of interaction), the acting out of such feelings is sensed as a danger to such intimate relationships, and hence there is a tendency to suppress rather than to allow expression of hostile feelings. In close-knit groups, feelings of hostility tend, therefore, to accumulate and hence to intensify. If conflict breaks out in a group that has consistently tried to prevent expression of hostile feelings, it will be particularly intense for two reasons: First, because the conflict does not merely aim at resolving the immediate issue which led to its outbreak; all accumulated grievances which were denied expression previously are apt to emerge at this occasion. Second, because the total personality involvement of the group members makes for mobilization of all sentiments in the conduct of the struggle.

Hence, the closer the group, the more intense the conflict. Where members participate with their total personality and conflicts are suppressed, the conflict, if it breaks out nevertheless, is likely to threaten the very root of the relationship.

In groups comprising individuals who participate only segmentally, conflict is less likely to be disruptive. Such groups are likely to experience a multiplicity of conflicts. This in itself tends to constitute a check against the breakdown of consensus: the energies of group members are mobilized in many directions and hence will not concentrate on *one* conflict cutting through the group. Moreover, where occasions for hostility are not permitted to accumulate and conflict is allowed to occur wherever a resolution of tension seems to be indicated, such a conflict is likely to remain focused primarily on the condition which led to its outbreak and not to revive blocked hostility; in this way, the conflict is limited to "the facts of the case." One may venture to say that multiplicity of conflicts stands in inverse relation to their intensity.

So far we have been dealing with internal social conflict only. At this point we must turn to a consideration of external conflict, for the structure of the group is itself affected by conflicts with other groups in which it engages or which it prepares for. Groups which are engaged in continued struggle tend to lay claim on the total personality involvement of their members so that internal conflict would tend to mobilize all energies and affects of the members. Hence such groups are unlikely to tolerate more than limited departures from the group unity. In such groups there is a tendency to suppress conflict; where it occurs, it leads the group to break up through splits or through forced withdrawal of dissenters.

Groups which are not involved in continued struggle with the outside are less prone to make claims on total personality involvement of the membership and are more likely to exhibit flexibility of structure. The multiple internal conflicts which they tolerate may in turn have an equilibrating and stabilizing impact on the structure.

In flexible social structures, multiple conflicts crisscross each other and thereby prevent basic cleavages along one axis. The multiple group affiliations of individuals make them participate in various group conflicts so that their total personalities are not involved in any single one of them. Thus segmental participation in a multiplicity of conflicts constitutes a balancing mechanism within the structure.

In loosely structured groups and open societies, conflict, which aims at a resolution of tension between antagonists, is likely to have stabilizing and integrative functions for the relationship. By permitting immediate and direct expression of rival claims, such social systems are able to readjust their structures by eliminating the sources of dissatisfaction. The multiple conflicts which they experience may serve to eliminate the causes for dissociation and to re-establish unity. These systems avail themselves, through the toleration and institutionalization of conflict, of an important stabilizing mechanism.

In addition, conflict within a group frequently helps to revitalize existent norms; or it contributes to the emergence of new norms. In this sense, social conflict is a mechanism for adjustment of norms adequate to new conditions. A flexible society benefits from conflict because such behavior, by helping to create and modify norms, assures its continuance under changed conditions. Such mechanism for readjustment of norms is hardly available to rigid systems: by suppressing conflict, the latter smother a useful warning signal, thereby maximizing the danger of catastrophic breakdown.

Internal conflict can also serve as a means for ascertaining the relative strength of antagonistic interests within the structure, and in this way constitute a mechanism for the maintenance or continual readjustment of the balance of power. Since the outbreak of the conflict indicates a rejection of a previous accommodation between parties, once the respective power of the contenders has been ascertained through conflict, a new equilibrium can be established and the relationship can proceed on this new basis. Consequently, a social structure in which there is room for conflict disposes of an important means for avoiding or redressing conditions of disequilibrium by modifying the terms of power relations.

Conflicts with some produce associations or coalitions with others. Conflicts through such associations or coalitions, by providing a bond between the members, help to reduce social isolation or to unite individuals and groups otherwise unrelated or antagonistic to each other. A social structure in which there can exist a multiplicity of conflicts contains a mechanism for bringing together otherwise isolated, apathetic or mutually hostile parties and for taking them into the field of public social activities. Moreover, such a structure fosters a multiplicity of associations and coalitions whose diverse purposes crisscross each other, . . . thereby preventing alliances along one major line of cleavage.

Once groups and associations have been formed through conflict with other groups, such conflict may further serve to maintain boundary lines between them and the surrounding social environment. In this way, social conflict helps to structure the larger social environment by assigning position to the various subgroups within the system and by helping to define the power relations between them.

Not all social systems in which individuals participate segmentally allow the free expression of antagonistic claims. Social systems tolerate or institutionalize conflict to different degrees. There is no society in which any and every antagonistic claim is allowed immediate expression. Societies dispose of mechanisms to channel discontent and hostility while keeping intact the relationship within which antagonism arises. Such mechanisms frequently operate through "safety-valve" institutions which provide substitute objects upon which to displace hostile sentiments as well as means of abreaction of aggressive tendencies.

Safety-valve institutions may serve to maintain both the social structure and the individual's security system, but they are incompletely functional for both of them. They prevent modification of relationships to meet changing conditions and hence the satisfaction they afford the individual can be only partially or momentarily adjustive. The hypothesis has been suggested that the need for safety-valve institutions increases with the rigidity of the social structure, i.e., with the degree to which it disallows direct expression of antagonistic claims.

Safety-valve institutions lead to a displacement of goal in the actor: he need no longer aim at reaching a solution of the unsatisfactory situation, but merely at releasing the tension which arose from it. Where safety-valve institutions provide substitute objects for the displacement of hostility, the conflict itself is channeled away from the original unsatisfactory relationship into one in which the actor's goal is no longer the attainment of specific results, but the release of tension.

This affords us a criterion for distinguishing between realistic and nonrealistic conflict.

Social conflicts that arise from frustrations of specific demands within a relationship and from estimates of gains of the participants, and that are directed at the presumed frustrating object, can be called realistic conflicts. Insofar as they are means toward specific results, they can be replaced by alternative modes of interaction with the contending party if such alternatives seem to be more adequate for realizing the end in view.

Nonrealistic conflicts, on the other hand, are not occasioned by the rival ends of the antagonists, but by the need for tension release of one or both of them. In this case the conflict is not oriented toward the attainment of specific results. Insofar as unrealistic conflict is an end in itself, insofar as it affords only tension release, the chosen antagonist can be substituted for by any other "suitable" target.

In realistic conflict, there exist functional alternatives with regard to the means of carrying out the conflict, as well as with regard to accomplishing desired results short of conflict; in nonrealistic conflict, on the other hand, there exist only functional alternatives in the choice of antagonists.

Our hypothesis, that the need for safety-valve institutions increases with the rigidity of the social system, may be extended to suggest that unrealistic conflict may be expected to occur as a consequence of rigidity present in the social structure.

Our discussion of the distinction between types of conflict, and between types of social structures, leads us to conclude that conflict tends to be dysfunctional for a social structure in which there is no or insufficient toleration and institutionalization of conflict. The intensity of a conflict which threatens to "tear apart," which attacks the consensual basis of a social system, is related to the rigidity of the structure. What threatens the equilibrium of such a structure is not conflict as such, but the rigidity itself which permits hostilities to accumulate and to be channeled along one major line of cleavage once they break out in conflict.

Violence in American history has appeared in many forms, from family feuding and lynching to Indian wars and assassinations. There is negative and positive violence, and each plays a different role in our value structure. Our society must acknowledge our ambiguous attitudes toward violence and examine other means of resolving our conflicts without resort to violence.

Historical Patterns of Violence in America

Richard Maxwell Brown

American violence, historically, seems to fall into two major divisions. The first is negative violence: violence that seems to be in no direct way connected with any socially or historically constructive development. Varieties of negative violence are criminal violence, feuds, lynching, the violence of prejudice (racial, ethnic, and religious violence), urban riots, freelance multiple murder, and assassination.

Negative violence by no means exhausts the range of American violence. There has been a vast amount connected with some of the most important events of American history—events that are considered constructive, positive, and, indeed, among the noblest chapters in our national history. Thus the Revolutionary War—both in its origins and its progress— was shot through with domestic violence. The Civil War, by which the slave eventually gained his freedom and the union of the nation was assured, engendered vast waves of violence. The very land we occupy was gained over the centuries in a continuing war with the Indians. Vigilante violence was used to establish order and stability on the frontier. Agrarian uprisings occurred again and again to ease the plight of the farmer and yeoman. Labor violence was part and parcel of the industrial workers' struggle to gain recognition and a decent life. Police violence has always been invoked to protect society against the criminal and disorderly. Again and again violence has been used as a means to ends that have been widely accepted and applauded. Positive violence is a broad term that relates violence to the popular and constructive movements just mentioned.

From "Historical Patterns of Violence in America" by Richard Maxwell Brown. Reprinted from *Violence in America*, A Staff Report to the National Commission on the Causes and Prevention of Violence, prepared by Hugh Davis Graham and T. Robert Gurr. Washington, D.C., U.S. Government Printing Office, 1969.

Negative Violence

CRIMINAL VIOLENCE

The salient facts, chronologically arranged, are: (1) Organized interstate gangs of criminals are an old story, going well back into the 18th century. (2) Before the Civil War, the most prevalent type of criminal activity—especially in frontier areas—was horse theft and the counterfeiting of the myriad number of private banknotes then in circulation. (3) After the Civil War a new era of crime began with the popularization of train robbery by the Reno brothers of Indiana and bank robbery by the James-Younger gang of Missouri. (4) The modern era of big-city organized crime with its police and political connections began to emerge in the early 20th century.

America has long been ambiguous about the criminal. Official condemnation of the outlaw has been matched by social adulation. The ambiguity is not restricted to America, for the British historian, E. J. Hobsbawm, has shown the existence in European history of the "socal bandit."[1] By social bandit, Hobsbawm means largely what we have come to denote by the Robin Hood symbol, i.e., the outlaw whom society views as its hero rather than its enemy, an outlook which reflects widespread social alienation.

There have indeed been American social bandits. Jesse and Frank James gained a strong popular following in mid-America after the Civil War. To the many Southern sympathizers in Missouri the James brothers, who were former Confederate guerrillas, could do no wrong, and to many Grange-minded farmers the Jameses' repeated robberies of banks and railroads were no more than these unpopular economic institutions deserved.[2] Other social bandits have been Billy the Kid (idolized by the poor Mexican herdsmen and villagers of the Southwest),[3] Pretty Boy Floyd (onetime Public Enemy No. 1 of the 1930's who retained the admiration of the sharecroppers of eastern Oklahoma from which stock he sprang),[4] and John Dillinger, the premier bank robber of the depression era. Modeling himself on an earlier social bandit, Jesse James, John Dillinger by freehanded generosity cultivated the Robin Hood image while robbing a series of Midwestern banks.[5] The rural-smalltown era of American crime came largely to an end with the demise of John Dillinger, Pretty Boy Floyd, Clyde Barrow and Bonnie Parker, and the other "public enemies" of the 1930's. With them the American tradition of the social bandit died.

While the tradition of the rural American social bandit was waxing and waning, urban crime was increasing in importance. The first urban criminal gangs arose in New York and other cities in the pre-Civil War decades, but these gangs were limited in significance and restricted to ethnic "slum" neighborhoods such as Five Points and the Bowery in New York City.[6] Murder, mayhem, and gang vendettas were a feature of the proliferation of these gangs. Meanwhile, in the early decades of the 20th century the present pattern of centralized, city-wide criminal operations under the control of a single "syndicate" or "organization" began to take shape in New York under Arnold Rothstein.[7] Converging with this trend was, apparently, the Mafia tradition of criminal organization which Sicilian immigrants seem to have brought into East Coast port cities in the decades around 1900.[8] During the 1920's and 1930's the two trends merged into the predominant pattern of centralized operations under Mafia control which the Kefauver crime investigation highlighted in 1951.[9] Systematic killing to settle internal feuds and the use of investment capital (gained from illicit activities), threats, and extortion to infiltrate the world of legitimate business have been characteristic of contemporary urban organized crime.[10]

FEUD VIOLENCE

One classic phase of negative American violence has been the family feud. This phenomenon has been generally associated with the "hillbilly" of the southern Appalachians, and, of the two great geographic locales of the family feud, one has surely been the Southern mountains. Less generally recognized has been the prevalence of the family feud in Texas and the Southwest at the same time that murderous feuds were splotching the Southern highlands with blood.

The family blood feud is virtually nonexistent in this country before the Civil War. The feud appears on the scene quite dramatically in the decades following the war. The era between the Civil War and World War I is the great era of the Southern mountain feud in Kentucky, West Virginia, and Virginia. This is the period that produced the Hatfield-McCoy feud (1873–88) of the Kentucky-West Virginia border,[11] the Martin-Tolliver (1884–87) and Hargis-Cockrell (1902–03) feuds of eastern Kentucky,[12] and the Allen family outburst at Hillsville in the Virginia Blue Ridge in 1912.[13]

The evidence is convincing that Southern mountain feuding was triggered by the animosities generated by the Civil War. The mountains were divided country where Confederate and Union sympathizers fought in rival armies and slew each other in marauding guerrilla bands. After the war old hatreds did not die out but, fueled anew by political partisanship and moonshine whisky in a region bedeviled by isolation, poverty, and minimal education, flamed up as never before. The formal law barely operated; its power was manipulated for selfish purposes by close knit political and family factions. Because regular law and order was such a frail reed, families and individuals came increasingly to depend upon their own strong arms. Each feuding family for the sake of self-defense developed its own clan leader: a man who best combined in the highest quotients the qualities of physical strength, bravery, wealth, and family leadership. Such men were "Devil Anse" Hatfield and Judge James Hargis. In the absence of an effective system of law and order, these men functioned as family "enforcers" around whom the feuding families rallied for protection.[14]

The great feuds of Texas and the Southwest were strikingly similar to those of the southern Appalachians, were about as well known in their own day, and had similar origins. As in the Appalachians, the main era of Texas feuds was between the Civil War and World War I. The Texas feuds took place principally in the central portion of the State which, like the Southern mountains, was a region of conflicting Civil War loyalties and mordant Reconstruction hatreds. The war-spawned turbulence of Central Texas was heightened by a combination of other factors: extremely rapid development of the cattle industry with its byproducts of frantic competition, rustling, and various disorders; the fact that the western margins of the Central Texas region were seared repeatedly by one of the cruelest of all American Indian wars, that of the Comanches and Kiowas with the white settlers; and, finally, by the ethnic hostility between antislavery, pro-Union German settlers and native Southern inhabitants. The result was a series of fatal feuds that were every bit as terrible as their Appalachian counterparts.[15] Not even the Hatfield-McCoy feud exceeded for length, casualties, and bitterness the great Sutton-Taylor feud (1869–99) of DeWitt and Gonzales Counties, Texas.[16] Among the major feuds of Central Texas were the Horrell-Higgins feud of Lampasas County (1876–77), the Jaybird-Woodpecker feud of Fort Bend County (1888–90), and the Stafford-Townsend-Reese-Hope feuds of Colorado County (1890–1906).[17]

In New Mexico Territory the family and factional feud was built into the political system.[18] New Mexico before World War I was probably the only American State where assassination became a routine political tactic.[19] The most deadly of all American feuds was fought in neighboring Arizona from 1886 to 1892. This was the "Pleasant Valley War" between the Graham and Tewksbury families, a conflict that was exacerbated by the Grahams being cattle men and the Tewksburys being sheep men. The bitter feud was fought, like the title phrase of Zane Grey's novel of the vendetta, "to the last man." Only with the lone survivor of the two families did it come to an end.[20]

LYNCH-MOB VIOLENCE

Lynch law has been defined as "the practice or custom by which persons are punished for real or alleged crimes without due process of law."[21] The first organized movement of lynch law in America occurred in the South Carolina back country, 1767–69.[22] It appeared again in the Virginia Piedmont during the latter years of the Revolutionary War near the present city of Lynchburg. The Virginia movement was initiated by Colonel Charles Lynch (from whom lynch law gained its name) and was employed against Tory miscreants.[23] Well into the 19th century lynch law meant merely the infliction of corporal punishment—usually 39 or more lashes well laid on with hickory withes, whips, or any readily available frontier instrument. By the middle of the 19th century, lynch law had, however, come to be synonymous, mainly, with hanging or killing by illegal group action. Organized movements of lynch law are treated below under the heading of "Vigilante Violence." By the term "lynch-mob" is meant an unorganized, spontaneous, ephemeral mob which comes together briefly to do its fatal work and then breaks up. The more regular vigilante (or "regulator") movements engaged in a systematic usurpation of the functions of law and order.

Lynch-mob violence (in contrast to vigilante violence) was often resorted to in trans-Appalachian frontier areas before the Civil War, but it became even more common after the Civil War. In the postwar period (down to World War I) lynch-mob violence was employed frequently in all sections of the country and against whites as well as blacks, but in this period it became preeminently the fate of Southern Negroes. From 1882 to 1903 the staggering total of 1,985 Negroes were killed by Southern lynch mobs.[24] Supposedly the lynch-mob hanging (or, too often, the ghastly penalty of burning alive) was saved for the Negro murderer or rapist, but the statistics show that Negroes were frequently lynched for lesser crimes or in cases where there was no offense at all or the mere suspicion of one.[25] Lynch-mob violence became an integral part of the post-Reconstruction system of white supremacy.[26]

Although predominant in the South, lynch-mob violence was far from being restricted to that section. In the West the ephemeral "necktie party" was often foregathered for the summary disposal of thief, rapist, rustler, murderer, or all-around desperado. Frenzied mobs similarly worked their will in the North and East where (as in the West) villainous white men were the usual victims.[27]

THE VIOLENCE OF RACIAL, ETHNIC, AND RELIGIOUS PREJUDICE

Lynch-mob activity by no means exhausts the violence involving whites and blacks. Racial conflict between Caucasians and Negroes is one of the most persistent factors in American violence, extending far back into the 18th century. The first slave uprising occurred in New York City in 1712 and was put down with great ruthlessness. In 1739 there was the Stono Rebellion in South Carolina, and in 1741 New York City was again wracked with fears (apparently justified) of a slave conspiracy. The result was that New York white men went on an hysterical rampage in which scores of Negroes were burned, hanged, or expelled.[28] There were a host of plots or uprisings in the 19th century: among the largest were the abortive Gabriel Prosser (Richmond, 1800)[29] and Denmark Vesey (Charleston, 1822)[30] plots. Southside Virginia was in 1831 the scene of the greatest of all American slave rebellions: that of Nat Turner in Southampton County,[31] the subject of William Styron's recent controversial novel, *The Confessions of Nat Turner*.[32] Although there was much restiveness and runaway activity on the part of American slaves, rebellion was not a major response to the slave system. Even Nat Turner's rebellion was quickly suppressed and was of little consequence compared to the great maroon enclaves and republics which rebelling and runaway slaves established in South America and the Caribbean. The American slave more typically resisted the system by passive resistance, by running away, and by making countless small, unorganized attacks on individual families, masters, or overseers.[33]

With the end of slavery and its conjoined slave patrols and black codes, the white men of the South developed a special organization for dealing with the Negro: the Ku Klux Klan. The latter has been one of the most consistent features in the last hundred years of American violence. There have been three Ku Klux Klans: the first Ku Klux Klan of Reconstruction times, the second Ku Klux Klan of the 1920's, and the third, current Ku Klux Klan of the 1950's and 1960's. The first Ku Klux Klan was employed to intimidate the Radical Republicans of the Reconstruction Era and, by violence and threats, to force the freedman to accept the renewed rule of Southern whites.[34] The second Ku Klux Klan differed significantly from both its predecessor and successor. Although the second Ku Klux Klan was founded in Atlanta in 1915, its greatest growth and strength actually took place beyond the borders of the old Confederacy. During the early 1920's it became a truly national organization. For a time it enjoyed great strength in the Southwest, West, North, and East. The strongest State Klan was in Indiana, and such wholly un-Southern States as Oregon and Colorado felt its vigor. The second Ku Klux Klan surely belongs to the violent history of America, but, unlike either the first or the third Klans, the Negro was only a secondary target for it. Although denunciation of Catholics and Jews ranked 1–2 in the rhetoric of the second Klan, recent students of the movement have shown that Klan violence—whippings, torture, and murder—were directed less against Catholics, Jews, and Negroes than against ne'er-do-wells and the allegedly immoral of the very same background as the Klansmen: white, Anglo-Saxon, Protestant. The Klan thus attacked Americans of similar background and extraction who refused to conform to the Bible Belt morality that was the deepest passion of the Klan movement of the 1920's.[35] The Ku Klux Klan resurgence of the last 10 years has been largely restricted to the South; it is only too well known for acts of violence against the civil rights movement and desegregation.

Paralleling the Ku Klux Klan have been a host of other movements of racial, ethnic, and religious malice. Before the Civil War the northeastern United States was lacerated by convent burnings and anti-Catholic riots.[36] This "Protestent Crusade" eventually bred the political Know Nothing movement. Anti-Chinese agitation that often burst into violence became a familiar feature of California and the West as the 19th century wore on.[37] In 1891, 11 Italian immigrants were the victims of a murderous mob in New Orleans.[38] The fear and loathing of Catholics (especially Irish and Italians) that often took a violent form was organized in the nonviolent but bigoted American Protective Association (APA) of 1887.[39] Labor clashes of the late 19th century and early 20th century were often in reality ethnic clashes with native old-stock Americans ranged on one side as owners, foremen, and skilled workers against growing numbers of unskilled immigrants—chiefly Jews, Slavs, Italians, and others from Southern and Eastern Europe.[40]

URBAN RIOTS

A number of examples have already exposed urban riots as one of the most tenacious strands in the long history of American violence. The situation seems at its worst today with the country widely believed to be on the verge of some sort of urban apocalypse, but the fact is that our cities have been in a state of more or less continuous turmoil since the colonial period.[41] As early as the latter part of the 17th century the nuclei of the organized North End and South End "mobs" that dominated Boston in the 18th century had already formed. Maritime riots occurred in Boston during the middle 18th century and were general in the colonies in the 1760's.[42] Leading colonial cities of the Revolutionary Era—Charleston, New York, Boston, and Newport, Rhode Island—were all flayed by the Liberty Boy troubles which embodied an alliance of unskilled maritime workers, skilled artisans, and middle-class business and professional men in riotous dissent against toughening British colonial policy as exemplified by the Stamp Act and Townshend Acts.[43]

Economic and political conditions brought more urban turmoil in the post-Revolutionary period of the 1780's and 1790's, and by the mid-19th century, with industrial and urban expansion occurring by leaps and bounds, the cities of America found themselves in the grips of a new era of violence. The pattern of the urban immigrant slum as a matrix of povery, vice, crime, and violence was set by Five Points in lower Manhattan before the Civil War.[44] Ulcerating slums along the lines of Five Points and severe ethnic and religious strife stemming from the confrontation between burgeoning immigrant groups and the native American element made the 1830's, 1840's, and 1850's a period of sustained urban rioting, particularly in the great cities of the Northeast. It may have been the era of the greatest urban violence that America has ever experienced. During this period at least 35 major riots occurred in the four cities of Baltimore, Philadelphia, New York, and Boston. Baltimore had 12,[45] Philadelphia had 11,[46] New York had 8,[47] and Boston had 4.[48] (The violence also extended into the growing cities of the Midwest and the lower Mississippi Valley; Cincinnati had four major riots during this period.)[49] Among the most important types of riots were labor riots,[50] election riots,[51] antiabolitionist riots,[52] anti-Negro riots,[53] anti-Catholic riots,[54] and riots of various sorts involving the turbulent volunteer firemen's units.[55] Except for Civil War draft riots, the urban violence subsided in the 1860's and 1870's until the year of 1877 produced a tremendous nationwide railroad strike that began along the Baltimore Ohio Railroad and spread to the Far West. Pathological rioting blistered Baltimore and great stretches of Pittsburgh were left in smoking ruins.[56] (The similarity of what befell Baltimore and Pittsburgh in 1877 and Los Angeles, Chicago, Newark, Detroit, Washington, and other cities in 1965–68 is striking.) Many other cities suffered less seriously.

The forces of law and order responded strongly to the 19th-century urban violence. The modern urban police system was created in reaction to the riots of the 1830's, 1840's and 1850's, and the present National Guard system was developed in response to the uprisings of 1877.[57] To deal with urban tumult vigilantism was also used frequently in the 19th century. The greatest of all American vigilante movements occurred in the newly settled (by Americans) but thoroughly urban and up-to-date San Francisco of 1856; other 19th-century urban vigilante movements occurred in Los Angeles, New Orleans, San Antonio, St. Louis, Cincinnati, Rochester, and Natchez.[58]

The modern era of the urban race riot was inaugurated around the turn of our present century. From 1900 to 1949 there were 33 major interracial disturbances in the United States. During this half century the peak period of violence was from 1915 to 1919 when 22 of the 33 disturbances occurred. (The 1915–19 period of racial disorder was thus comparable to the period from 1964 to the present.) Major riots occurred in Atlanta (1906), Springfield, Ill. (1908), East St. Louis (1917), Chicago, (1919), Harlem (1935 and 1943), and Detroit (1943). With the exception of the Harlem riots, whites emerged as the main aggressors in these riots and the bulk of the casualties befell Negroes.[59] Not until the summer of 1964 with the Harlem and Rochester riots and Los Angeles' Watts riot of 1965 did the pattern decisively reverse itself to the present mode of Negro initiative.[60] Since 1964 black rioting has concentrated on property destruction rather than the taking of white lives; this is a new pattern, although it was fore-shadowed in the Harlem riots of 1935 and 1943, and as early as 1947, Ralph Ellison brilliantly caught the mood of the property-destruction riot in his novel, *Invisible Man*.[61]

FREELANCE MULTIPLE MURDER

By this term I refer to the murder of many persons by one or two individuals unconnected with any larger organization. (Thus the Chicago St. Valentine's Day massacre of 1929 and the Kansas City Union Station "massacre" of 1933 are both ruled out of consideration here as being the result of large-scale, organized, underworld criminal activity.) It was the summer of 1966 that made Americans wonder whether the freelance multiple murder was becoming the characteristic American crime, for in the space of a few weeks two shocking multiple murders occurred. First, in Chicago, Richard F. Speck murdered, one-by-one, eight student nurses.[62] Then, less than a month later, Charles Whitman ascended to the top of the tower of the University of Texas library in Austin and left tower and campus strewn with 13 dead or dying and 31 wounded as a result of his unerring marksmanship.[63] The utter horror of these two killing rampages attracted worldwide attention, but not a year goes by without the disclosure of one or more multiple murderers. Speck, the hapless product of a blighted personal background, saw himself as "Born to Raise Hell." Whitman came from an upright and respectable middle-class background that was allegedly, on closer examination, a veritable witch's cauldron of tensions and hatreds.

Neither Speck nor Whitman was normal in the usual sense of the word, and the freelance multiple murderer is often a fit subject for the abnormal psychologist. (Recently it has been suggested that male killers such as Speck arise from a genetic deficiency involving a chromosomal variation.[64]) But some observers have wondered whether the anxieties and neuroses of contemporary life in America have not led to a rise in the abnormal behavior exemplified by multiple (or "mass") murder. Crime statistics are not sufficiently available to answer the question, but there have been many examples of freelance multiple murderers in American history. The annals of crime in the United States abound with them. Among the earliest were the brutal Harpe brothers, Micajah (Big Harpe) and Wiley (Little Harpe), who in 1798–99 accounted for anywhere from about 20 to 38 victims in the frontier States of Kentucky and Tennessee. Dashing babies' brains against tree trunks in sudden frenzies was a practice they may have learned from Indians. Finally, in August 1798, a party of Kentucky settlers ended the career of Micajah. Wiley escaped but was captured, tried, and hanged in Mississippi in 1804. So feared and hated were the Harpes that following death the head of each was cut off and displayed as a trophy of triumphant pioneer justice.[65]

Numerous freelance multiple murderers crop up in the 19th century. Among them was the evil Bender family of southeastern Kansas. The Benders from 1871 to 1873 did away with at least 12 unwary travelers who had the bad judgment to choose the Bender roadside house for a meal or lodging. Eventually the Benders were detected but seem to have escaped into anonymity one jump ahead of a posse.[66] Another mass murderer was H. H. Holmes (the *alias* of Hermann Webster Mudgett) of Englewood, Ill. (near Chicago), who confessed to killing 27 people from about 1890 to 1894, many of whom he lured to their death in his bizarre castlelike house while they were attending the Chicago World's Fair in the summer of 1893.[67] While example after example can be named, such questions as the actual number of multiple murders and their relationship to social conditions still await the serious study of the historian.[68]

POLITICAL ASSASSINATION

Quantitatively, assassination does not bulk large in the history of American violence, but at the highest level of our political system—the Presidency—it has a heavy impact. In a 100-year span (1865 to 1965) four Presidents (Lincoln, Garfield, McKinley, and Kennedy) fell to assassins's bullets, and others were the intended objects of assassination. One of the victims, Lincoln, was the target of an assassination of conspiracy. The other three victims—Garfield, McKinley, and Kennedy—were the prey of freelance assassins in varying states of mental instability. Charles Guiteau, the slayer of Garfield, was a disappointed officeseeker, but mental derangement seems to have been at the bottom of his action.[69] Both Leon Czolgosz, the killer of McKinley, and Lee Harvey Oswald, Kennedy's assassin, appear to have had strong ideological commitments. Czolgosz was an anarchist, and Oswald was a self-styled Marxist. Both, however, were independent operatives. Czolgosz was rejected by the organized anarchist movement of his day; nor was Oswald a member of the Communist organization in America or of any of the American Marxist splinter groups. Czolgosz seems to have been in the incipient stages of insanity.[70] Evidence amassed by the Warren Commission strongly suggests that Oswald was psychotic, but the Commission itself cautiously refrained from reaching that conclusion.[71]

Although the mortality rate of American Presidents in the last century has been a high one at the hands of assassins, some comfort can be taken in the fact that assassination has not become a part of the American political system as has happened elsewhere in the world, the Middle East, for example. None of the major political parties has resorted—even indirectly—to assassination. Notable, also, is the immunity which other high political officials—the Vice President, the Supreme Court Justices, Cabinet officers, and leading Senators[72] and Congressmen—have enjoyed from assassination.

Despite some prominent cases, assassinations at the State and local level have, on the whole, been few and far between with the exception of New Mexico Territory (discussed below). During the often chaotic Reconstruction period in the South there was once *cause célèbre:* John W. Stephens, a native white Southerner and a rising Radical Republican politician of Caswell County, N.C., was in 1870 the victim of an assassination plot by a local faction of his Klan-oriented Conservative political opponents. Stephens' killers certainly wanted him out of the way because of his political effectiveness, but the killing itself seems to have been more the result of the terrorist impulse of the Ku Klux Klan movement than any attempt to raise assassination to the level of a systematic political weapon.[73] Apparently similar to the assassination of Stephens was the killing, by "parties unknown," of John M. Clayton, Republican congressional candidate in Arkansas. Although defeated in the fall 1888 election, Clayton was contesting the result when he was killed in January 1889, while visiting Plummerville, Ark.[74]

One of the most famous political assassinations in American history took place at the State level, the fatal wounding of nationally prominent Senator Huey P. Long of Louisiana on September 8, 1935. Long's assassin seems (like the Presidential assassins) not to have been part of a political plot but to have been motivated by personal emotion and grievance, with political resentment of the "Kingfish" being distinctly secondary.[75] An earlier famous (but now forgotten) assassination of a leading State figure did stem from a context of a political conflict. This was the fatal wounding of the Governor-elect of Kentucky, William Goebel, at Frankfort on January 30, 1900.[76] Goebel was the charismatic leader of the Democratic Party in Kentucky who had been waging a hot battle against the Republicans and the railroad interests of his State. Goebel's assassination occurred during an infusion into Frankfort of thousands of anti-Goebel Republicans from the hotblooded mountain region of eastern Kentucky. Fatal feuds had often been linked with local political rivalries in the Kentucky mountains in previous decades (see the section above on "Feud Violence"), and it is not surprising that Goebel's assassins seem to have sprung from that background.[77]

Apparently the only place in America where assassination became an integral part of the political system was New Mexico Territory from the end of the Civil War down to about 1900. Many assassinations occurred, among the most prominent being that of Col. Albert J. Fountain, a leading Republican of southern New Mexico, in 1896.[78] Other leading New Mexican politicians narrowly missed being killed, and many New Mexicans were convinced that the two chieftains of the Republican and Democratic Parties, respectively, had been involved in assassination plots. Thomas B. Catron, the autocratic Republican boss, was thought by many to have been a party to one of the notable assassinations of the era; Catron himself seems to have been the target of an unsuccessful assassination attempt.[79] The recent biographer of Colonel Fountain has brought forth strong evidence to support his charge that Albert Bacon Fall, the incisive Democratic leader,[80] was guilty of leading complicity in the plot against Fountain.[81] The most important point is that virtually all political factions in New Mexico accepted and used assassination as a way of eliminating troublesome opponents.[82]

The frightening phenomenon of assassination in territorial New Mexico still awaits searching study by the historian. In the absence of such a study it is hard to say just why assassination became such a prominent political feature in New Mexico alone. The territory was indeed a violent one at the time; it was scarred by a savage Indian war (with the Apaches), numerous vigilante movements and lynch mobs, a host of criminal outlaws (Billy the Kid, Clay Allison, and others), and mordant local conflicts such as the Lincoln County war and the Maxwell Land Grant troubles. Such a high level of violence might well have had the effect of skewing the political system in the direction of assassination as a tactic, although this did not happen in neighboring Texas, which at the time was every bit as violent as New Mexico. Nor does the large Latin element of the population seem to have imputed a fatal measure of volatility to the political climate of New Mexico Territory, for native Anglo-American politicians such as Catron (from Missouri) and Fall (from Kentucky) were leaders in a political system that was characterized, often, by assassination.

A third explanation of political assassination in New Mexico is suggested by social scientists who have recently posited a "contagion phenomenon" in regard to "highly publicized and dramatic acts of deviant behavior" such as prison riots, bomb scares, slum uprisings, mass murder, and psychopathic sexual acts.[83] Beginning with the first assassination in New Mexico (that of the Territorial chief justice, John P. Slough, in 1867), it is possible that something like a "contagion phenomenon" set in to perpetuate assassination until it became a part of the political system itself. After 1900 the level of general turbulence in New Mexico life subsided. It may have been no coincidence that the politics of assassination faded, too. Students of the "contagion phenomenon" have seen it as a short-run phenomenon characterized by an accelerating pace followed by an abrupt end which might, in long-run terms, be analogous to New Mexico's experience.

The tragic history of assassination in New Mexico Territory may be an ill portent for our own era. It is conceivable that the wave of assassinations in recent years which cut down John F. Kennedy, Robert F. Kennedy, Martin Luther King, Jr., Medgar Evers, and Malcolm X is a contemporary example of the "contagion phenomenon." The danger is not to be found in the "contagion phenomenon" alone but in the grim possibility that, as happened in New Mexico, assassination might become a persistent feature of the public behavior of our people.

Positive Violence

POLICE VIOLENCE

The law enforcement system in colonial America was quite simple, consisting mainly of sheriffs for the counties and constables for the cities and towns. With the tremendous expansion of population and territory in the 19th century, the system took on much greater complexity. Added to the county sheriffs and local constables were municipal police systems, State police (including such special and elite forces as the Rangers of Texas[84] and Arizona), and Federal marshals and Treasury agents. The most important development of the century was the development of the modern urban police system in the midcentury years from 1844 to 1877. The new system was a direct response to the great urban riots of the 1830's, 1840's, and 1850's. The antiquated watch-and-ward system (daytime constables and nighttime watchmen) was simply inadequate to cope with the large-scale rioting and increasing urban disorder. The reform in the police system came first in New York, Philadelphia, Boston, and other cities which had acute problems of criminal violence and rioting.[85] Thus the riot era of the 1830–50's produced the present urban police system. Perhaps the riots of the 1960's will similarly spur the "professionalization" of the police—a major reform that is being widely called for at the present.

Scarcely less important than the development of the urban police system was the creation of the National Guard to replace the obsolete

State militia system that dated back to the 18th century. The rapid development of the National Guard system in the 1880's was largely a response to the great urban labor riots of 1877. The National Guard was established first and most rapidly in the leading industrial States of the North that were highly vulnerable to labor unrest: Massachusetts, Connecticut, New York, Pennsylvania, Ohio, and Illinois. By 1892, the system was complete throughout the Nation.[86] Officered primarily by business and professional men and sometimes the recipients of large subsidies from wealthy industrialists,[87] National Guard contingents were often called out to suppress labor violence from the late 19th century down to the time of World War II.

In the latter half of the 19th century there also grew up a sort of parapolice system with the founding of numerous private detective agencies (headed by the famed Pinkerton National Detective Agency)[88] and the burgeoning of thousands of local antihorsethief associations or detecting societies which often were authorized by State laws and invested with limited law enforcement powers.[89] After the Civil War, industrial corporations frequently set up their own police forces. Most notable in this category were the private coal and iron police which the State of Pennsylvania authorized to deal with labor unrest in mines and mills.[90] It was during the 19th century, as well, that the science of crime detection was inaugurated.[91]

Undue violence in the course of enforcing the law has long been a matter of concern. In an earlier generation the public worried about the employment of the "third degree" to obtain criminal confessions.[92] In our own time the concern is with "police brutality," chiefly against Negroes. Related to the use of violence by police in the prosecution of their regular duties has been the large measure of violence associated with the incarceration of the convicted in jails and prisons. For over a century and a half we have gone through bursts of prison reform only to have the system as a whole lapse back into (if indeed it ever really transcended) its normal characteristics of brutality and sadism. As time has passed many of the most well-meaning reforms (such as the early-19th-century system of solitary confinement) have proved to be ill-conceived.[93] Even as our knowledge and expertise have increased, prison reform has foundered again and again on the rock of inadequate financial support from an uncaring society.

REVOLUTIONARY VIOLENCE

Our nation was conceived and born in violence—in the violence of the Sons of Liberty and the patriots of the American port cities of the 1760's and 1770's. Such an event was the Boston Massacre of 1770 in which five defiant Americans were killed. British officers and troops had been goaded by patriotic roughnecks into perpetrating the so-called massacre. The whole episode stemmed naturally from the century-long heritage of organized mob violence in Boston. The same thing was true of the Boston Tea Party wherein the anciently organized South End Mob of Boston was enlisted in the tea-dumping work. During the long years of resistance to British policy in the 1760's and 1770's the North End and South End Mobs under the leadership of Samuel Swift and Ebenezer Mackintosh had been more or less at the beck and call of Samuel Adams, the mastermind of patriot agitation, and the middle-class patriots who made up the "Loyal Nine."[94]

With the decision in 1774 to resist the British by military means, the second round of Revolutionary violence began. The main goal of Revolutionary violence in the transitional period from 1774 to 1777 was to intimidate the Tories who existed in fairly large numbers in the seaport cities and hinterland. The countrywide Continental Association of 1774 was drawn up to cause an interruption of all trade between the Colonies and the mother country, but a related purpose was to ferret out Tories, expose them to public contumely and intimidation, and bring them to heel or to silence.[95] Where exposure in the newspapers was not enough, strong-arm tactics were used against the Tories. The old American custom of tarring and feathering was mainly a product of the patriotic campaign to root out Toryism.[96]

Aside from the regular clash of the Continental and British armies, the third and final phase of Revolutionary violence was the guerrilla strife that occurred all the way from the Hudson to the Savannah. Wherever strong British occupying forces were to be found—as in New York City, Philadelphia, and Charleston—in opposition to an American-dominated hinterland, the result was the polarization of the population and the outbreak of savage guerrilla strife, desperate hit-and-run forays, and the thrust and counter-thrust of pillage and mayhem. Thus the lower Hudson valley of New York was the theatre of rival bushwhacking parties of Whigs and Tories. The Hackensack Valley of North Jersey, opposite the British bastion on Manhattan Island, was a sort of no man's land across which bands of Whigs and Tories fought and ravaged.[97] South Jersey's bleak and trackless pine barrens furnished ideal cover for the "land pirates" of both Whig and Tory persuasion spewed up by the British and American competition for the allegiance of New Jersey and the Philadelphia area.[98]

South Carolina emerged as the great battlefield of the war after 1780. North Carolina and Georgia suffered at the same time from the scourge of guerrilla strife, but their casualties were light compared to the dreadful cut-and-thrust of the Whig and Tory forces in the Palmetto State where Andrew Pickens, Thomas Sumter, and Francis Marion led Whig partisan bands in their own particular sectors of the back country. Negro slaves were stolen back and forth, and baleful figures like the half-crazed Tory leader, Bloody Bill Cunningham, emerged from the shadows to wreak special brands of murder and massacre. Neither side showed the other any mercy. Prisoners were tortured and hanged.[99] Virginia felt the destruction of Benedict Arnold's vengeful campaign (1781) but experienced nothing like the suffering of South Carolina. Still it was characteristic of the rising passions of the time that strife among Whigs and Tories in Virginia's Piedmont, as noted earlier, gave rise to an early manifestation of lynch law.

Two things stand out about the Revolution. The first, of course, is that it was successful and immediately became enshrined in our tradition and history. The second is that the meanest and most squalid sort of violence was from the very beginning to the very last put to the service of Revolutionary ideals and objectives. The operational philosophy that the end justifies the means became the keynote of Revolutionary violence. Thus given sanctification by the Revolution, Americans have never been loathe to employ the most unremitting violence in the interest of any cause deemed to be a good one.

CIVIL WAR VIOLENCE

Violence was interwoven with the creation of the American nation. By the same token, it became the ineradicable handmaiden of its salvation in the era of Civil War and Reconstruction. The Civil War era was not only one of pervasive violence in its own right but had an almost incalculable effect on the following decades. The latter part of the 19th century was one of the most violent periods of American history—an era of Ku Kluxers, lynch mobs, White Caps, Bald Knobbers, night riders, feudists, and outlaws. The major part of this violence is traceable to the Civil War.

The years of prelude to the Civil War were years of mounting violence in both North and South. Feeling against the Fugitive Slave Law in the North gave rise to vigilance committees concerned with protecting runaway slaves and to increasingly fervent abolitionism. Below the Mason-Dixon Line abolitionists had long since ceased to exist in anything but the hallucinations of slaveholders and Southern nationalists. But from these delusions were formed vigilante movements to deal with the nonexistent abolitionists. Violence of the most tangible sort was far from absent. Bleeding Kansas was truly just that as marauding bands of slaveholder and antislaveholder sympathizers surged through the unhappy territory.

In the East, John Brown's raid on Harpers Ferry sent a tremor of fear through those who genuinely wished to forestall a bloody civil war. For the more sanguinary in the North, John Brown was an inspiration for holy war against slavery; to the warminded in the South the John Brown raid was seen as proof that the South could never rest easy in a Union that included free States and harbored abolitionists. The nation sensed that it was on the verge of a grand Armageddon.[100] The general nervousness came to a height in the South in the summer of 1860 as that section gloomily awaited the almost certain election of Lincoln. Forebodings never far from the surface suddenly blazed to the top in the Great Fear that swept across the South in the summer of 1860. From the Rio Grande to the Atlantic were exposed plot after plot by secret abolitionists and unionists for the raising up of slaves in bloody rebellion.[101] At this distance it seems that the fears of slave uprisings were groundless, but portions of the South were in the grips of a hysteria that was real enough. Vigilante groups and self-styled committees of safety blazed up.[102] The Great Fear of the South in the summer of 1860 seems to have been as baseless in fact as the remarkably similar Great Fear that swept the French peasantry in the first year of the French Revolution.[103] Both Great Fear and grande peur revealed the profound anxieties which lacerated the white Southerners and the French peasants in the summers of 1860 and 1789, respectively.

In symbolic terms, the Great Fear on the eve of the Civil War was altogether fitting as a prelude to the decade and more of violence and mischief that would follow. The struggle between the Northern and Southern armies still stands as the most massive military bloodletting in American history, but almost forgotten is the irregular underwar of violence and guerrilla strife that paralleled the regular military action. In numerous localities throughout the North, resistance to the military draft was continuous and violent. The apogee of resistance to the draft occurred with the massive riots of 1863 in New York City when the city was given over to three days of virtually uncontrolled rioting.[104] Related troubles occurred throughout the war years in southern Indiana, southern Illinois, and southern Iowa where widespread Copperhead feeling caused large-scale disaffection, antidraft riots, and guerrilla fighting between Union soldiers and Union deserters and other Copperhead sympathizers.[105] The guerrilla war that took place along the Kansas-Missouri border has seldom been equaled for unmitigated savagery. Jim Lane and his fearsome Kansas Jayhawkers traded brutal blows with the Confederate guerrillas of Missouri headed by the band of William Quantrell that included Frank and Jesse James and the Younger boys.[106] Kentucky, too, was the scene of frequent ambushes and affrays.[107]

The Confederate South was bedeviled by pockets of resistance to official policy. The mountain regions of north Arkansas, north Alabama, and eastern Tennessee had important centers of Unionist sentiment that never became reconciled to the war effort.[108] Even Mississippi contained one county (Jones) that was perforated with disloyalty to the Confederate cause[109]—as did Alabama (Winston). The frontier areas of northern and central Texas were liberally dotted with Unionist sympathizers and antislavery Germans. At best the German-Americans never gave more than grudging support to the War and sometimes resorted to sabotage. The result was brutal retaliation by the "heel-flies" (Confederate home guards) who were often quite careless of whom they injured.[110]

Perhaps no event in American history bred more violence than the Civil War. Racial strife and Ku Klux Klan activity became routine in the old Confederate states. Regulator troubles broke out in central Kentucky and the Blue Grass region. Outlaw and vigilante activity flamed in Texas, Kansas, and Missouri. Outbreaks of feuding scorched the southern Appalachians and Texas. As late as the closing years of the century white capping, bald knobbing, and night riding, while spurred by particular social and economic causes, remained as legacies of the violent emotions and methods fired by the Civil War.[111]

INDIAN WARS

Unquestionably the longest and most remorseless war in American history was the one between whites and Indians that began in Tidewater, Virginia, in 1607 and continued with only temporary truces for nearly 300 years down to the final massacre at Wounded Knee, South Dakota, in 1890. The implacable hostility that came to rule white-Indian relations was by no means inevitable. The small Indian population that existed in the continental United States allowed plenty of room for the expansion of white settlement. The economic resources of the white settlers were such that the Indians could have been easily and fairly reimbursed for the land needed for occupation by the whites. In fact, a model of peaceful white-Indian relations was developed in 17th-century New England by John Eliot, Roger Williams, and other Puritan statesmen. The same was true in 18th-century Pennsylvania where William Penn's humane and equitable policy toward the Indians brought that colony decades of white-Indian amity.[112] Racial prejudice and greed in the mass of New England whites finally reaped the whirlwind in King Philip's War of 1675–76, which shattered the peaceful New England model.[113] Much later the same sort of thing happened in Pennsylvania in 1763 when Pontiac's Rebellion (preceded by increasing tensions) ended the era of amicable white-Indian relations in the Keystone colony.

Other Indian wars proliferated during the 17th and 18th centuries, nor did the pace of the conflict slacken in the 19th century. It is possible that no other factor has exercised a more brutalizing influence on the American character than the Indian wars. The struggles with the Indians have sometimes been represented as being "just" wars in the interest of promoting superior Western civilization at the expense of the crude stone-age culture of the Indians. The recent ethnohistorical approach to the interpretation of white-Indian relations has given us a more balanced understanding of the relative merits of white and Indian civilizations. The norms of Indian warfare were, however, at a more barbaric level than those of Western Europe. Among the Indians of Eastern America torture was an accepted and customary part of warmaking.[114] In their violent encounters with Indians, the white settlers brought themselves down to the barbaric level of Indian warfare. Scalping was adopted by white men,[115] and down to the very last battle at Wounded Knee lifting the hair of an Indian opponent was the usual practice among experienced white fighters. Broken treaties, unkept promises, and the slaughter of defenseless women and children all, along with the un-European atrocity of taking scalps, continued to characterize the white American's mode of dealing with the Indians. The effect on our national character has not been a healthy one; it has done much to shape our proclivity to violence.

VIGILANTE VIOLENCE

The first large-scale American vigilante movement (and probably the first of any size) occurred in the South Carolina back country in the late 1760's.[116] The phenomenon of vigilantism seems to be native to the American soil. The British Isles—especially Scotland and Ireland—were violent enough in the 17th and 18th centuries, but vigilantism was unknown in the British Isles; taking the law into one's own hands (the classic definition of vigilantism) was repugnant to ancient British legal tradition. Vigilantism arose as a response to a typical American problem: the absence of effective law and order in a frontier region. It was a problem that occurred again and again beyond the Appalachian Mountains. It stimulated the formation of hundreds of frontier vigilante movements.

The first phase of American vigilantism happened mainly before the Civil War and dealt largely with the threat of frontier horsethieves and counterfeiters. Virtually every State or territory west of the Appalachians possessed one or more well-organized, relentless vigilante movements. We have tended to think of the vigilante movement as being typical of the Western plains and mountains, but in actuality there was much vigilantism east of the Missouri and Mississippi Rivers. The main thrust of vigilantism was to reestablish in each newly settled frontier area the community structure of the old settled areas along with the values of property, law, and order. Vigilante movements were characteristically in the control of the frontier elite and represented their social values and preferences. This was true of the first vigilante movement in South Carolina, 1767–69 (who were known as "Regulators"—the original but now obsolete term for vigilantes), and it was also true of the greatest of all American vigilante movements, that of San Francisco in 1856. The San Francisco vigilance committee of 1856 was dominated lock, stock, and barrel by the leading merchants of the city who organized to stamp out alleged crime and political corruption.[117]

Although the typical vigilante movements were dominated by social conservatives who desired to establish order and stability in newly settled areas, there were disconcertingly numerous departures from the norm. Many vigilante movements led not to order but to increasing disorder and anarchy. In such cases vigilantism left things in a worse condition than had been true before. Frequently the strife between vigilantes and their opponents (exacerbated by individual, family, and political hatreds) became so bitter and untrammeled that order could be restored only by the Governor calling out the militia. Such was the case when the Bald Knobbers of the Missouri Ozarks rose in 1885–86 to curb the evils of theft, liquor, gambling, and prostitution in Taney and Christian Counties. Intervention by outside authorities was finally needed.[118]

The elite nature of 19th-century vigilantism is revealed by the prominent men who belonged to vigilante movements. Included in a "Who's Who of American Vigilantism" would be U.S. Senators and Congressmen, Governors, judges, wealthy capitalists, generals, lawyers, and even clergymen. Even Presidents of the United States have not been immune to the vigilante infection. While serving in the Presidency, Andrew Jackson once approved the resort of Iowa pioneers to vigilante methods pending the clarification of their territorial status.[119] As a young cattle rancher in North Dakota, Theodore Roosevelt begged to be admitted to a vigilante band that was being formed to deal with rustlers and horsethieves. The cattlemen rebuffed the impetuous young Harvard blueblood but went on with their vigilante movement.[120] Today among educated men of standing vigilantism is viewed with disapproval, but it was not always so in the 19th century. In those days leading men were often prominent members of vigilante movements and proud of it.

America changed from the basically rural nation it had been in the antebellum era to an urban, industrial nation after the Civil War. The institution of vigilantism changed to match the altering character of the nation. From a generally narrow concern with the classic frontier problems of horsethieves and counterfeiters, vigilantism broadened its scope to include a variety of targets connected with the tensions of the new America: Catholics, Jews, Negroes, immigrants, laboring men and labor leaders, political radicals, advocates of civil liberties, and nonconformists in general. Neovigilantism flourished as a symptom of the growing pains of post–Civil War industrial America but utterly failed as a solution to the complex social problems of the era.[121]

The post–Civil War era also saw the climax of two movements with strong affinities to vigilantism. One was the antihorsethief association movement which had its greatest growth in the rural Midwest and Southwest after the Civil War, although its roots were to be found in the northeastern United States as early as the 1790's. The antihorsethief society pattern involved State charter of local associations which were often vested with constabulary power. By 1900 the antihorsethief association movement numbered hundreds of thousands of members in its belt of greatest strength, which stretched from the Great Lakes to the Rio Grande. Forming a flexible and inexpensive (the members shared costs whenever they arose) supplement to immobile, expensive, and inefficient local law enforcement, the antihorsethief association afforded the farmer insurance against the threat of horse and other types of theft. With the rapid development of the automobile around the time of World War I the antihorsethief association movement lost its *raison d'etre*.[122]

Quite different in character was the White Cap[123] movement. White Caps first appeared in southern Indiana in 1888,[124] but in short order the phenomenon had spread to the four corners of the nation. The White Cap movement copied the vigilante movements of the late 18th and early 19th centuries in its preference for flogging as a mode of punishment. White Capping varied greatly from locality to locality and region to region. In North Texas the White Caps were anti-Negro;[125] in South Texas they were anti-Mexican;[126] and in northern New Mexico the White Caps were a movement of poor Mexican herders and ranchers against land-enclosing rich Mexicans and Americans.[127]

In general, however, White Capping was most prevalent as a sort of spontaneous movement for the moral regulation of the poor whites and ne'er-do-wells of the rural American countryside. Thus drunken, shiftless, and wife-beating whites who often abused their families were typical targets of White Cap violence.[128] Loose women frequently became the victims of White Caps.[129] Vigilantism going back to the South Carolina Regulators of 1767–69 had often been concerned with the moral regulation of incorrigible whites, and hence White Capping was in part a throwback to the early era of frontier vigilantism. At the same time, White Capping seems to have been an important link between the first and second Ku Klux Klans. White Cap methods in regard to punishment and costume seem to have been influenced by the first Klan, while White Cap attacks on immoral and shiftless whites foreshadowed the main thrust of the second Klan of the 1920's. Chronologically, the White Cap movement formed a neat link between the first and second Klans. White Capping began in the 1880's about two decades after the first Klan, and by the turn of the century it had become such a generic term for local American violence that Booth Tarkington made White Cap violence the pivot of his popular novel, *The Gentleman from Indiana* (1899).[130] At the time of World War I, White Capping was fading from view; shortly thereafter the second Ku Klux Klan rose to take its place.

AGRARIAN UPRISINGS

The tree of liberty from time immemorial in America has been nurtured by a series of movements in behalf of the ever-suffering farmer or yeoman. Often these movements—generally considered to be liberal in their political character—have been formed for the purposes of redressing the economic grievances of the farmer; at times they have been land reform movements. The dissident-farmer movements have been deemed among the most heroic of all American movements of political insurgence; they have been the especial favorites of historians who with love and sympathy have chronicled their ups and downs. There have been a host of these agrarian uprisings, and they have been equally prevalent in both the colonial and national periods of our history. The initial agrarian uprising was that behind Nathaniel Bacon in late-17th-century Virginia[131] followed by the New Jersey land rioters of the 18th century.[132] Similarly, in the 1760's were the Paxton Boys movement of Pennsylvania,[133] the North Carolina Regulators (not a vigilante movement but one for reform of local government),[134] and the New York antirent movement (which stretched on into the 19th century).[135] With the gaining of independence there appeared Shays' Rebellion in Massachusetts (1786–87),[136] the Whiskey Rebellion in western Pennsylvania (1794),[137] and Fries' Rebellion in eastern Pennsylvania (1798–99).[138] Farther west—in the Mississippi Valley before the Civil War—there appeared the Claim Clubs to defend the land occupancy of squatters.[139]

After the Civil War a plethora of economic problems for the farmer gave rise to the Grangers, the Greenbackers, the Farmers' Alliance (which originally began in central Texas as a quasi-vigilante movement),[140] and the Populist Party.[141] About the same time there appeared a land-reform movement in California against the monopoly landholding of the Southern Pacific Railroad,[142] and in New Mexico there appeared the previously mentioned White Cap movement of poor Mexicans against the land-enclosing tactics of well-to-do Mexicans and Americans. Western Kentucky and the Ohio-Mississippi Valley area, generally, were the scene of a tobacco farmers' cooperative movement in the early 1900's to end the control of the American Tobacco Co. and foreign companies over the marketing system.[143] Farmers became increasingly attracted to the Socialist Party, and the nonindustrial State of Oklahoma soon led the nation in Socialist Party members. Connected with the rise of socialism among Oklahoma farmers was the appearance there during World War I of the Working Class Union which developed into a pacifist, antidraft movement of sharecroppers and small farmers.[144] In the upper Great Plains there rose in North Dakota in 1915 the radical Nonpartisan League which enacted many reforms in that State and inspired similar progressive farm movements in other States of the Northwest.[145] The farm bloc emerged in Congress in the 1920's to promote legislation for easing the agricultural depression. When conditions worsened in the 1930's, the Farmers' Holiday Association was formed in the Midwest to lead farmer strikes and boycotts against the economic system.[146] In our own 1960's the National Farmers' Organization has adopted similar tactics.

The insurgent farmer movements have thus formed one of the longest and most enduring chronicles in the history of American reform but one that has been blighted again and again with violence. Nathaniel Bacon's movement became a full-fledged rebellion that resulted in the burning of Jamestown. The New Jersey land rioters used violence to press their claims against the Jersey land companies. The New York antirent movement frequently used force against the dominant landlords. The North Carolina

Regulators rioted against the courthouse rings that ground them under the burden of heavy taxes and rapacious fees. The Paxton Boys of Pennsylvania followed their massacre of Indians with a march on Philadelphia. The followers of Daniel Shays in Massachusetts broke up court sessions in order to forestall land foreclosures. The farmers of Pennsylvania rose in rebellion against taxes on liquor and land in the Whiskey and Fries uprisings. The Western Claims Clubs (which, paradoxically, were sometimes dominated by land speculators pursuing their own interests) used intimidation to protect "squatters' rights." The land reform movement in California spawned a night-rider league in Tulare County, 1878–80, to resist railroad land agents. The tobacco farmer cooperative movement in Kentucky did not succeed in breaking monopoly domination of the marketing system until it utilized a "Night Rider" organization that raided several western Kentucky towns, destroyed tobacco warehouses, and abused non-cooperating farmers. The New Mexican White Caps employed a reign of terror to fight the land-enclosure movement. The Working Class Union of Oklahoma spawned the Green Corn Rebellion; the "rebels" contemplated only a peaceful march on Washington but did arm themselves and committed a few acts of violence before being rooted out of the hills and breaks along the South Canadian River by sheriffs and posses. The Farmers' Holiday Association dumped milk cans, blocked roads, and roughed up opponents. Farmer grievances have been serious. Repeatedly farmers used higher law—the need to right insufferable wrongs, the very justification of the American Revolution—to justify the use of violence in uprising after uprising.

LABOR VIOLENCE

The labor movement in American history has been bathed in the same sort of glorification that has anointed the agrarian uprisings. Most would agree that by raising the health and living standard of the working man the American labor movement has been a significant factor in advancing the social well-being of the nation. But the labor movement reveals the same mixture of glorious ends with inglorious means—violence—that has characterized the agrarian movement. (Ironically, the white "backlash" against black uprisings in the cities of today has been strongest in the rural countryside and the "blue collar" metropolitan wards, i.e., among the inheritors of the violent agrarian and labor movements.)

A rudimentary labor movement was to be found in the port cities of the colonial period. While there was no organization of laborers as such, sailors, longshoremen, and other workers of the maritime industry occasionally rioted—stirred up by impressment gangs and sporadic economic stringency.[147] The unskilled workers and skilled artisans who contributed the force to the violent Liberty Boy movement of the 1760's were made especially restless and turbulent by the economic depression that followed the end of the Great War for the Empire.[148]

It is with the coming of the Industrial Revolution to America in the 19th century that the labor movement really gets underway, particularly as a concomitant of the tremendous growth of American industry after the Civil War. Various labor organizations mushroomed: the Knights of Labor, American Railway Union, American Federation of Labor, Western Federation of Miners (WFM), and the Industrial Workers of the World (IWW). All made the strike a major weapon, and in case after case violence broke out in accompaniment of the strike. The blame was certainly not on the side of labor alone. The unyielding attitude of capitalists in regard to wages, hours, working conditions, and the desire to unionize led to the calling of strikes. Violent attempts of capital to suppress unions and break up strikes frequently incited the workers to violence. But laborers, too, were often more than ready to resort to violence, as many of the great upheavals after the Civil War indicate. The great railroad strike of 1877 triggered massive riots that in Pittsburgh reached the level of insurrection. About the same time the decade-long Molly Maguire[149] troubles in the hard coal field of eastern Pennsylvania came to a climax. The Molly Maguires were a secret organization of Irish miners who fought their employers with assassination and mayhem.[150] Such events as the Haymarket Riot in Chicago (1886),[151] the Homestead strike (1892),[152] the Coeur d'Alene, Idaho, silver mining troubles (1892ff.), and the 1910 dynamiting of the Los Angeles *Times* building (by the McNamara brothers of the supposedly conservative American Federation of Labor)[153] led Louis Adamic correctly to label the late-19th-early-20th-century period as the era of dynamite in American labor relations.

The Western mining State of Colorado affords a paradigm of the dynamite era of labor violence. From 1884 to 1914, Colorado had its own "Thirty Years War" of strikes and violence which typified the economic, class, and ethnic tensions of the period.[154] Colorado's 30-year period of acute labor violence came to a climax with what may have been the most violent upheaval in American labor history: the coal miners' strike against the Colorado Fuel & Iron Co., 1913–14. During the first 5 weeks of the strike (which took place in southern Colorado) there were 38 armed skirmishes in which 18 persons were killed. The final horror took place on April 20, 1914, at Ludlow, Colorado. A 15-hour battle between strikers and militiamen ended in the burning of the strikers' tent city during which 2 mothers and 11 children suffocated to death in the "Black Hole of Ludlow." Following this tragedy, maddened miners erupted in a 10-day rebellion which brought "anarchy and unrestrained class warfare" to a 250-mile area of southern Colorado before the entrance of Federal troops ended the violence.[155] The Ludlow conflict was in truth an actualization of the

apocalyptic visions of class warfare of Jack London (in *The Iron Heel*[156])
and other writers of the period.

The last great spasm of violence in the history of American labor
came in the 1930's with the sitdown strike movement which accompanied
the successful drive to unionize the automobile and other great mass-production industries.

Conclusion

What is to be made of this survey of violence in American history? The
first and most obvious conclusion is that there has been a huge amount of
it. It is not merely that violence has been mixed with the negative features
of our history such as criminal activity, lynch mobs, and family feuds. On
the contrary, violence has formed a seamless web with some of the noblest
and most constructive chapters of American history: the birth of the nation
(Revolutionary violence), the freeing of the slaves and the preservation of
the Union (Civil War violence), the occupation of the land (Indian wars),
the stabilization of frontier society (vigilante violence), the elevation of
the farmer and the laborer (agrarian and labor violence), and the preservation of law and order (police violence). The patriot, the humanitarian,
the nationalist, the pioneer, the landholder, the farmer, and the laborer
(and the capitalist) have used violence as the means to a higher end.

All too often unyielding and unsympathetic established political and
economic power has incited violence by its refusal to heed and redress just
grievances. Thus Governor Berkeley of Virginia ignored the pleas of Virginia planters and the result was Bacon's Rebellion. Thus the British government in 1774–76 remained adamant in the face of patriot pleas, and
the result was the American Revolution. Thus the tobacco trust scoffed at
the grievances of farmers, and the result was the Kentucky Night Rider
movement. Thus American capitalists ground workers into the dust, and
the result was the violent labor movement. The possessors of power and
wealth have been prone to refuse to share their attributes until it has been
too late. Arrogance is indeed a quality that comes to unchecked power
more readily than sympathy and forbearance.

By the same token, one can argue that the aggrieved in American
history have been too quick to revolt, too hastily violent. We have resorted
so often to violence that we have long since become a "trigger happy" people. Violence is ostensibly rejected by us as a part of the American value
system, but so great has been our involvement with both negative and positive violence over the long sweep of our history that violence has truly become a part of our unacknowledged (or underground) value structure.

Two major problems remain if we as Americans are ever to break our
bondage to violence. One is the problem of self-knowledge: We must
recognize that, despite our pious official disclaimers, we have always oper-

ated with a heavy dependence upon violence in even our highest and most idealistic endeavors. We must take stock of what we have done rather than what we have said. When that is done, the realization that we have been an incorrigibly violent people is overwhelming. We must realize that violence has not been the action only of the roughnecks and racists among us but has been the tactic of the most upright and respected of our people. Having gained this self-knowledge, the next problem becomes the ridding of violence, once and for all, from the real (but unacknowledged) American value system. Only then will we begin to solve our social, economic, and political problems by social, economic, and political means rather than evading them by resort to the dangerous and degrading use of violence.

Notes

1. Eric J. Hobsbawm, *Social Bandits and Primitive Rebels* (Glencoe, Ill.: The Free Press, 1959).

2. William A. Settle, Jr., *Jesse James Was His Name or Fact and Fiction Concerning the Careers of the Notorious James Brothers of Missouri* (Columbia, Mo.: University of Missouri Press, 1966).

3. For the enormous literature on Billy the Kid, see Ramon F. Adams, *A Fitting Death for Billy the Kid* (Norman, Okla.: University of Oklahoma Press, 1960).

4. Paul I. Wellman, *A Dynasty of Western Outlaws* (New York: Doubleday, 1961), ch. 12. This provocative book traces a Southwestern criminal dynasty from William C. Quantrill and the Jameses to Pretty Boy Floyd.

5. John Toland, *The Dillinger Days* (New York: Random House, 1963).

6. Herbert Asbury, *The Gangs of New York: An Informal History of the Underworld* (New York and London: Alfred A. Knopf, 1928). A significant study of the general level of urban criminal violence is the paper in this volume by Roger Lane, "Urbanization and Criminal Violence in the Nineteenth Century: Massachusetts as a Test Case."

7. Leo Katcher, *The Big Bankroll: The Life and Times of Arnold Rothstein* (New York: Harper, 1959).

8. Fred J. Cook, *The Secret Rulers: Criminal Syndicates and How They Control the U.S.* (New York: Duell, Sloan & Pearce, 1966).

9. Estes Kefauver, *Crime in America*, Sidney Shalett, ed. (Garden City, N.Y.: Doubleday, 1961).

10. *The Challenge of Crime in a Free Society: A Report of the President's Commission on Law Enforcement and Administration of Justice* (Washington, D.C.: U.S. Government Printing Office, 1967), pp. 187–200.

11. Virgil C. Jones, *The Hatfields and the McCoys* (Chapel Hill, N.C.: University of North Carolina Press, 1948).

12. Meriel D. Harris, "Two Famous Kentucky Feuds and Their Causes" (unpublished M.A. thesis, University of Kentucky, 1940).

13. Rufus L. Gardner, *The Courthouse Tragedy, Hillsville, Va.* (Mt. Airy, N.C.: Rufus L. Gardner, 1962).

14. On "Devil Anse" Hatfield, see Jones, *Hatfields and McCoys*, pp. 2–3

and *passim*. On Judge James Hargis, see Harris, "Two Famous Kentucky Feuds," pp. 100, 104, and *passim*.

15. The major feuds of Texas are related by C[harles] L. Sonnichsen in two outstanding books: *I'll Die before I'll Run: The Story of the Great Feuds of Texas* (revised edition; New York: Devin-Adair, 1961), and *Ten Texas Feuds* (Albuquerque, N.Mex.: University of New Mexico Press, 1957).

16. Sonnichsen, *I'll Die before I'll Run*, pp. 35–115.

17. *Ibid.*, pp. 125–149, 232–281, and 299–315.

18. One of the most spectacular of the family-factional feuds in New Mexico was the Lincoln County War, 1878ff., from which Billy the Kid emerged to fame. See Maurice G. Fulton, *History of the Lincoln County War*, Robert N. Mullin, ed. (Tucson, Ariz.: University of Arizona Press, 1968).

19. See the section in this paper on "Political Assassination."

20. Earle R. Forrest, *Arizona's Dark and Bloody Ground* (Caldwell, Idaho: Caxton Printers, 1936). Zane Grey, *To the Last Man* (New York and London: Harper, 1922).

21. Mitford M. Mathews, ed., *A Dictionary of Americanisms on Historical Principals* (one-volume edition, Chicago: University of Chicago Press, 1956), p. 1010.

22. Brown, *South Carolina Regulators,* pp. 38–39ff.

23. James E. Cutler, *Lynch-Law: An Investigation into the History of Lynching in the United States* (New York: Longmans, Green, 1905), pp. 24–31.

24. *Ibid.*, p. 177.

25. *Ibid.*

26. In addition to Cutler, *Lynch-Law,* see Walter White, *Rope & Faggot: A Biography of Judge Lynch* (New York and London: Alfred A. Knopf, 1929), and Arthur F. Raper, *The Tragedy of Lynching* (Chapel Hill, N.C.: University of North Carolina Press, 1938).

27. Cutler, *Lynch-Law,* pp. 180–181 and *passim*. A total of 3,337 Americans were lynched from 1882 to 1903. Of the victims, 1,169 were whites, 2,060 were Negroes, and 108 were of other races.

28. Winthrop D. Jordan, *White Over Black: American Attitudes Toward the Negro, 1550–1812* (Chapel Hill, N.C.: University of North Carolina Press, 1968), pp. 115–120. Jordan's massive study is essential for understanding the major cause of American racial violence; i.e., white prejudice against the Negro.

29. Herbert Aptheker, *American Negro Slave Revolts* (New York: Columbia University Press, 1943), pp. 219–227. Aptheker's book is the most complete treatment of the subject, although some scholars feel that he has exaggerated the degree of violent rebellion by slaves. An able recent treatment is M[artin] D. DeB. Kilson, "Towards Freedom: An Analysis of Slave Revolts in the United States," *Phylon,* vol. XXV (1964), pp. 175–187.

30. *Ibid.*

31. William S. Drewry, *The Southampton Insurrection* (Washington, D.C.: Neale Co., 1900). See also Herbert Aptheker, *Nat Turner's Slave Rebellion* (New York: Humanities Press, 1966), which reprints Turner's own "confession," pp. 127–151.

32. William Styron, *The Confessions of Nat Turner* (New York: Random

House, 1967). For a critique of Styron's novel, see John H. Clark, ed., *William Styron's Nat Turner: Ten Black Writers Respond* (Boston, Mass.: Beacon paperback, 1968).

33. Kenneth M. Stampp, *The Peculiar Institution: Slavery in the Ante-Bellum South* (New York: Alfred A. Knopf, 1956), ch. III. Two recent statements on what has become a very controversial subject are Eugene D. Genovese, "Rebelliousness and Docility in the Negro Slave: A Critique of the Elkins Thesis," *Civil War History*, vol. XIII (1967), pp. 293–314, and George M. Fredrickson and Christopher Lasch, "Resistance to Slavery," *ibid.*, pp. 315–329.

34. Stanley F. Horn, *Invisible Empire: The Story of the Ku Klux Klan, 1866–1871* (Boston, Mass.: Houghton Mifflin, 1939).

35. Two outstanding recent studies of the second Ku Klux Klan are David M. Chalmers, *Hooded Americanism: The First Century of the Ku Klux Klan, 1865–1965* (Garden City, N.Y.: Doubleday, 1965), and Charles C. Alexander, *The Ku Klux Klan in the Southwest* (Lexington, Ky.: University of Kentucky Press, 1965).

36. Ray A. Billington, *The Protestant Crusade, 1800–1860: A Study of the Origins of American Nativism* (New York: Macmillan, 1938).

37. See, for example, Robert E. Wynne, "Reaction to the Chinese in the Pacific Northwest and British Columbia: 1850 to 1910" (unpublished Ph.D. dissertation, University of Washington, 1964).

38. John E. Coxe, "The New Orleans Mafia Incident," *Louisiana Historical Quarterly*, vol. XX (1937), pp. 1067–1110, and John S. Kendall, "Who Killa De Chief," *ibid.*, vol. XXII (1939), pp. 492–530. The lynching of the Italians (which brought a threat of an Italo-American war) was the result of a vigilante action. Although there had been a recent criminal incident (the murder of the police chief) which to some seemed to justify vigilante action, the lynching was not merely a simple case of vigilante action. Ethnic prejudice against the Italians (who were allegedly members of a local Mafia organization) was crucial.

39. Donald L. Kinzer, *An Episode in Anti-Catholicism: The American Protective Association* (Seattle, Wash.: University of Washington Press, 1964).

40. See, for example, David Brody, *Steelworkers in America: The Nonunion Era* (Cambridge, Mass.: Harvard University Press, 1960).

41. Two important comparative studies of violence in 18th-century America and England are Lloyd I. Rudolph, "The Eighteenth Century Mob in America and Europe," *American Quarterly*, vol. XI (1959), pp. 447–469, and William Ander Smith, "Anglo-Colonial Society and the Mob, 1740–1775" (unpublished Ph.D. dissertation, Claremont Graduate School, 1965). Another important study is Pauline Maier, "Popular Uprisings and Civil Authority in Eighteenth-Century America," *William and Mary Quarterly*, 3d series (forthcoming).

42. Jesse Lemisch, "Jack Tar in the Streets: Merchant Seamen in the Politics of Revolutionary America," *William and Mary Quarterly*, 3d series, vol. XXV (1968), pp. 387–393.

43. See, for example, Richard Walsh, *Charleston's Sons of Liberty: A Study of the Artisans, 1763–1789* (Columbia, S.C.: University of South Carolina Press, 1959), pp. 3–55, and R. S. Longley, "Mob Activities in Revolutionary Massachusetts," *New England Quarterly*, vol. VI (1933), pp. 108–111.

44. Asbury, *The Gangs of New York,* pp. 1–45.

45. J[ohn] Thomas Scharf, *The Chronicles of Baltimore* . . . (Baltimore, Md.: Turnbull Bros., 1874), pp. 468–469, 476–479, 523, 528, 548–552, 555, 565, 570–574. The 12 riots were: (1) 1834—political riot, (2) 1835—bank riot, (3) 1847—firemen's riots, (4) 1848—election riot, (5) 1855—firemen's riot, (6) 1856—club riot, (7–8) 1856—two election riots, (9) 1857—labor riot, (10) 1858—anti-German riot, (11) 1858—election riot, and (12) 1859—election riot. In addition, Baltimore had three riots in 1861–62; they arose from Civil War tensions. *Ibid.,* pp. 588–594ff., 622–624, 627.

46. Ellis P. Oberholtzer, *Philadelphia: A History of the City* (4 vols., Philadelphia et al.: S. J. Clarke, 1912), vol. II, 283, 285–289, 291, 293–296. John Thomas Scharf and Thompson Westcott, *History of Philadelphia, 1609–1884* (3 vols., Philadelphia: L. H. Everts, 1884), vol. III, p. 2184. The 11 riots were: (1) 1834—anti-Negro riot, (2) 1834—election riot, (3) 1835—anti-Negro riot, (4) 1838—Penn Hall (antiabolitionist) riot, (5) 1838—anti-Negro riot, (6) 1840—antirailroad riot, (7) 1842—anti-Negro riot, (8) 1843—labor (weavers' strike) riot, (9) 1844—anti-Irish Catholic riot, May, (10) anti–Irish Catholic riot, July, (11) 1849—California House (election and anti-Negro) riot. Scharf and Westcott are the source for the 1840 antirailroad riot; Oberholtzer is the source for all the other riots. In addition, there were riots in 1828 (a weavers' riot involving Irish v. anti-Irish conflict) and 1871 (anti-Negro riot). Oberholtzer, *Philadelphia,* vol. II, p. 291. Joseph Jackson, *Encyclopedia of Philadelphia* (4 vols., Harrisburg, Pa.: National Historical Association, 1931–33), vol. I, p. 87. Sam Bass Warner, Jr., *The Private City: Philadelphia in Three Periods of Its Growth* (Philadelphia, Pa.: University of Pennsylvania Press, 1968), pp. 125–157, interprets the Philadelphia riots of the 1830's and 1840's as exemplifying "the interaction of most of the important elements of the big-city era: industrialization, immigration, mixed patterns of settlement, changing styles of leadership, weakness of municipal institutions, and shifting orientations of politics."

47. J[oel] T. Headley, *The Great Riots of New York, 1712 to 1783* . . . (New York: E. B. Trent, 1873), pp. 66–135. The eight riots were: (1) 1834—election riots, (2) 1834—antiabolitionist riots, (3) 1835—antiabolitionist riots, (4) 1835—labor (stone cutters') riot, (5) 1837—food (flour) riot, (6) 1849—Astor Place (theatrical factions) riots, (7) 1857—police (Mayor's police vs. Metropolitan police) riot, (8) 1857—Dead-Rabbits' riot (gang conflict). In addition to these riots and the great draft riots of 1863 there were two "Orange" riots (Irish Catholics vs. Irish Protestants) in 1870–71. On the Orange riots, see Headley, *Great Riots of New York,* ch. XXI.

48. Roger Lane, *Policing the City: Boston, 1822–1885* (Cambridge, Mass.: Harvard University Press, 1967), pp. 26–33. George A. Ketcham, "Municipal Police Reform: A Comparative Study of Law Enforcement in Cincinnati, Chicago, New Orleans, New York and St. Louis, 1844–1877" (unpublished Ph.D. Dissertation, University of Missouri, 1967), p. 54. The four riots were: (1) 1834—anti-Catholic (Charlestown convent burning) riot, (2) 1835—antiabolitionist ("Broadcloth Mob" assault on William Lloyd Garrison) riot, (3) 1837—Broad Street riot, (4) 1843—anti-Negro riot. Boston also had draft riots in 1861 and 1863. Lane, *Policing the City,* pp. 118–134.

49. Ketcham, "Municipal Police Reform," pp. 50, 53, 153. The four riots were: (1) 1836—pro-slavery riot in April, (2) 1836—pro-slavery riot in July, (3) 1842—bank riots, (4) 1853—Bedini (nativist vs. Catholic) riots.

50. Labor riots occurred in New York, 1835; Philadelphia, 1843; and Baltimore, 1857.

51. There were election riots in Baltimore in 1848, 1856 (2), 1858, and 1859, in Philadelphia, 1834, 1849, and in New York, 1834.

52. There were antiabolitionist riots in New York, 1834, 1835; Boston, 1835; Cincinnati, 1836; and Philadelphia, 1838.

53. Anti-Negro riots occurred in Philadelphia in 1834, 1835, 1838, 1842, and 1849, and in Boston in 1843. New York's great draft riots of 1863 featured much anti-Negro violence.

54. Anti-Catholic riots occurred in Philadelphia in 1844 (two) and in Boston in 1834. Anti-Catholic feeling was basic to Cincinnati's Bedini riot of 1853.

55. See, for example, Andrew H. Neilly, "The Violent Volunteers: A History of the Volunteer Fire Department of Philadelphia, 1736–1871" (unpublished Ph.D. dissertation, University of Pennsylvania, 1959).

56. On the events of 1877, see one of the most important works on the history of American violence: Robert V. Bruce, *1877: Year of Violence* (Indianapolis and New York: Bobbs-Merrill, 1959).

57. See the section below on "Police Violence."

58. See my paper . . . [in *Violence in America*] on "The American Vigilante Tradition."

59. The basic work on race riots in the first half of the 20th century is Allen D. Grimshaw, "A Study in Social Violence: Urban Race Riots in the United States (unpublished Ph.D. dissertation, University of Pennsylvania, 1959). A seminal treatment is Arthur I. Waskow, *From Race Riot to Sit-In, 1919 and the 1960's. A Study in the Connections between Conflict and Violence* (Garden City, N.Y.: Doubleday, 1966). Two important case studies are Elliot M. Rudwick, *Race Riot at East St. Louis: July 2, 1917* (Carbondale, Ill.: Southern Illinois University Press, 1964), and Robert Shogan and Tom Craig, *The Detroit Race Riot: A Study in Violence* (Philadelphia and New York: Chilton Books, 1964) which covers the 1943 riot.

60. Of the enormous literature on riots since 1964, the most important work is the monumental *Report of the National Advisory Commission on Civil Disorders* (New York: Bantam Books paperback; 1968). A useful brief survey is Joseph Boskin, "A History of Urban Conflicts in the Twentieth Century" in Audrey Rawitscher, comp., *Riots in the City: An Addendum to the McCone Commission Report* (Los Angeles, Calif.: National Association of Social Workers, Los Angeles Area Chapter, [1967]), pp. 1–24. See also the paper . . . [in *Violence in America*] by Elliot M. Rudwick and August Meier, "Black Violence in the Twentieth Century: A Study in Rhetoric and Retaliation."

61. Ralph Ellison, *Invisible Man* (New York: Random House, 1952), ch. 25.

62. Jack Altman and Marvin C. Ziporyn, *Born to Raise Hell* (New York: Grove Press, 1967).

63. *Time,* Aug. 12, 1966, p. 19ff. This was, apparently, the greatest single-

handed mass-murder in American history. The night before Whitman had killed his wife and his mother.

64. *New York Times,* Apr. 21, 1968, I, p. 1, c. 3–6ff.

65. Otto A. Rothert, *The Outlaws of Cave-In-Rock* (Cleveland, Ohio: Arthur H. Clark, 1924), pp. 55–156, 241–266. See also Coates, *Outlaw Years.*

66. John T. James, *The Benders of Kansas* (Wichita, Kans.: Kan-Okla Publishing Co., 1913).

67. Colin Wilson and Patricia Pitman, *Encyclopedia of Murder* (New York: G. P. Putnam's Sons, 1962), pp. 286–289.

68. In this direction a pioneering treatment is the paper . . . [in *Violence in America*] by Sheldon Hackney. Indispensable to any study of murder in American history is Thomas M. McDade, *The Annals of Murder: A Bibliography of Books and Pamphlets on American Murders from Colonial Times to 1900* (Norman, Okla.: University of Oklahoma Press [1961], whose 1,126 bibliographical entries are heavily annotated. A relevant literary study is David B. Davis, *Homicide in American Fiction, 1798–1860: A Study in Social Values* (Ithaca, N.Y.: Cornell University Press, 1957).

69. Charles E. Rosenberg, *The Trial of the Assassin Guiteau* (Chicago: University of Chicago Press, 1968).

70. Walter Channing, "The Mental Status of Czolgosz, the Assassin of President McKinley," *American Journal of Insanity,* vol. XLIX (1902–03), pp. 233–278.

71. *Report of the Warren Commission on the Assassination of President Kennedy* (New York: Bantam Books paperback, 1964), pp. 350–399, 596–659.

72. Two notable exceptions are, of course, the late Senators Huey P. Long and Robert F. Kennedy.

73. Luther M. Carlton, "The Assassination of John Walter Stephens," Historical Society of Trinity College [Duke University], *Historical Papers,* 2d series (1898), pp. 1–12. Albion W. Tourgée incorporated Stephens' assassination into his best-selling novel, *A Fool's Errand* (New York: Fords, Howard & Hulbert, 1879).

74. Daniel W. Crofts, "The Blair Bill and the Elections Bill: The Congressional Aftermath to Reconstruction" (unpublished Ph.D. dissertation, Yale University, 1968), pp. 244–245.

75. T. Harry Williams, "Louisiana Mystery—An Essay Review," *Louisiana History,* vol. VI (1965), pp. 287–291. Hermann B. Deutsch, *The Huey Long Murder Case* (Garden City, N.Y.: Doubleday, 1963). David Zinman, *The Day Huey Long Was Shot* (New York: Ivan Obolensky, 1963), holds that Long was accidentally shot by a stray bullet from a bodyguard.

76. Goebel's election as Governor was vociferously contested by Republicans who claimed that their candidate had really been elected.

77. Thomas D. Clark, "The People, William Goebel, and the Kentucky Railroads," *Journal of Southern History,* vol. V (1939), pp. 34–48.

78. Fountain and his young son disappeared and were never found. Contemporaries—and later historians—felt that Fountain had been assassinated.

79. Howard R. Lamar, *The Far Southwest, 1846–1912: A Territorial History* (New Haven, Conn.: Yale University Press, 1966), pp. 192–195.

80. In the 1890's, Fall was still a Democrat. He did not switch to the Republican Party until after the turn of the century. Today Fall is chiefly remembered for his connection with the unsavory Teapot Dome oil reserve affair as Harding's Secretary of the Interior.

81. Arrel M. Gibson in *The Life and Death of Colonel Albert Jennings Fountain* (Norman, Okla.: University of Oklahoma Press [1965]) has branded Fall as the leading plotter against Fountain. See also the milder but excellent treatment by C[harles] L. Sonnichsen in *Tularosas: Last of the Frontier West* (New York: Devin-Adair, 1960).

82. Two leading authorities attest assassination as political weapon in territorial New Mexico: Lamar, *Far Southwest*, pp. 192–195, and Warren A. Beck, *New Mexico: A History of Four Centuries* (Norman, Okla.: University of Oklahoma Press [1962]), p. 173.

83. See statements by Joseph Satten, Amitai Etzioni, and other social scientists reported in the *New York Times*, June 9, 1968, vol. I, p. 64, c. 1–3.

84. Walter Prescott Webb, *The Texas Rangers* (Boston, Mass.: Houghton Mifflin, 1935).

85. George A. Ketcham, "Municipal Police Reform: A Comparative Study of Law Enforcement in Cincinnati, Chicago, New Orleans, New York, and St. Louis, 1844–1877" (unpublished Ph.D. dissertation, University of Missouri, 1967). Roger Lane, *Policing the City: Boston, 1822–1855* (Cambridge, Mass.: Harvard University Press, 1967).

86. Martha Derthick, *The National Guard in Politics* (Cambridge, Mass.: Harvard University Press, 1965), pp. 16–17.

87. *Ibid.*

88. James D. Horan, *The Pinkertons: The Detective Dynasty That Made History* (New York: Crown, 1968).

89. See, for example, Anthony S. Nicolosi, "The Rise and Fall of the New Jersey Vigilant Societies," *New Jersey History*, vol. LXXXVI (1968), pp. 29–32, and Hugh C. Gresham, *The Story of Major David McKee, Founder of the Anti-Horse Thief Association* (Cheney, Kans.: Hugh C. Gresham, 1937). See also my brief account of the AHTA movement . . . [in *Violence in America*] in my paper, "The American Vigilante Tradition."

90. J[eremiah] P. Shalloo, *Private Police: With Special Reference to Pennsylvania* (Philadelphia: American Academy of Political and Social Science, 1933), pp. 58–134.

91. Jürgen Thorwald, *The Century of the Detective*, transl. Richard and Clara Winston (New York: Harcourt, Brace, 1965).

92. On the "third degree" problem, see the study by the Wickersham Commission: National Commission on Law Observance and Enforcement, *Report on Lawlessness in Law Enforcement* (Washington: U.S. Government Printing Office, 1931), pp. 13–261.

93. The huge literature on jails and prisons has been dominated by the work of criminologists, penologists, and sociologists; see, for example, Paul W. Tappan, *Crime, Justice and Correction* (New York: McGraw-Hill, 1960). Two older historical studies are Harry E. Barnes, *The Story of Punishment* (Boston: Stratford, 1930), and Blake McKelvey, *American Prisons* (Chicago Press, 1936). An able recent work is W. David Lewis, *From Newgate to Dannemora: The Rise of the Penitentiary, 1796–1848* (Ithaca, N.Y.: Cornell University Press, 1965).

94. G. P. Anderson, "Ebenezer Mackintosh: Stamp Act Rioter and Patriot," Colonial Society of Massachusetts, *Publications,* vol. XXVI (1924–26), pp. 15–64. On the background of Boston mob violence, see Smith, "Anglo-Colonial Society and the Mob," pp. 88–89, 108, 118, 157–159, 180–199, 208–222.

95. See, for example, Ivor Noël Hume, *1775: Another Part of the Field* (New York: Alfred A. Knopf, 1966), pp. 32–34, 125–130, 284–288.

96. Cutler, *Lynch-Law,* p. 61ff.

97. Adrian C. Leiby, *The Revolutionary War in the Hackensack Valley* (New Brunswick, N.J.: Rutgers University Press, 1962).

98. Miles R. Feinstein, "The Origins of the Pineys of New Jersey," (unpublished B.A. thesis, Rutgers University, 1963), pp. 56–73.

99. Edward B. McCrady, *The History of South Carolina in the Revolution, 1780–1783* (New York: Macmillan, 1902). See also Richard Maxwell Brown, "Back Country Violence (1760–85) and Its Significance for South Carolina History," in Robert M. Calhoon, ed., *Loyalists in the American Revolution: Central Participants or Marginal Victims?* (Holt, Rinehart & Winston, forthcoming).

100. See, for example, Francis Grierson, *Valley of the Shadows,* Bernard De Voto, ed. (New York: Harper Torchbooks paperback, 1966).

101. Allan Nevins, *The Emergence of Lincoln,* Vol. II, *Prologue to Civil War, 1859–1861* (New York: Charles Scribner's Sons, 1950), pp. 306–308.

102. See, for example, the hysteria which swept Texas in 1860 as described in Frank H. Smyrl, "Unionism, Abolitionism, and Vigilantism in Texas, 1856–1865" (unpublished M.A. thesis, University of Texas, 1961), pp. 49–74.

103. Crane Brinton, *A Decade of Revolution: 1789–1799* (New York: Harper Torchbooks paperback, 1963), pp. 35–37. The standard work on the subject is Georges Lefebvre, *La Grande Peur de 1789* (Paris: A. Colin, 1932).

104. James McCague, *The Second Rebellion: The Story of the New York City Draft Riots of 1863* (New York: Dial, 1968).

105. Frank L. Klement, *The Copperheads in the Middle West* (Chicago: University of Chicago Press, 1960).

106. Richard S. Brownless, *Gray Ghosts of the Confederacy: Guerrilla Warfare in the West, 1861–1865* (Baton Rouge, La.: Louisiana State University Press, 1958).

107. E[llis] Merton Coulter, *The Civil War and Readjustment in Kentucky* (Chapel Hill, N.C.: University of North Carolina Press, 1926).

108. Georgia Lee Tatum, *Disloyalty in the Confederacy* (Chapel Hill, N.C.: University of North Carolina Press, 1934), pp. 36–44, 54–72, 143–155.

109. This was Jones County. Tatum, *Disloyalty in the Confederacy,* pp. 97–98.

110. *Ibid.,* pp. 44–53. See also Smyrl, "Unionism, Abolitionism, and Vigilantism."

111. See the following sections of this paper on vigilante and agrarian violence.

112. Douglas E. Leach, *The Northern Colonial Frontier, 1607–1763* (New York et al.: Holt, Rinehart & Winston, [1966]). See also Alden T. Vaughan,

New England Frontier: Puritans and Indians, 1620–1675 (Boston and Toronto: Little, Brown [1965]).

113. Douglas E. Leach, *Flintlock and Tomahawk: New England in King Philip's War* (New York: W. W. Norton paperback, 1966).

114. Leach, *Northern Colonial Frontier*, pp. 12–13.

115. *Ibid.*, p. 112. William T. Hagan, *American Indians* (Chicago: University of Chicago Press, 1961), is a general history in which the major Indian wars are duly treated.

116. Brown, *South Carolina Regulators*. For a fuller treatment of vigilantism, see my paper . . . [in *Violence in America*] on "The American Vigilante Tradition." Vigilantism is also treated in the paper in this volume by Joe B. Frantz, "The Frontier Tradition: An Invitation to Violence."

117. Richard Maxwell Brown, "Pivot of American Vigilantism: The San Francisco Vigilance Committee of 1856" in John A. Carroll, ed., *Reflections of Western Historians* (Tucson, Ariz.: University of Arizona Press, 1969).

118. Lucile Morris, *Bald Knobbers* (Caldwell, Idaho: Caxton Printers, 1939).

119. Eliphalet Price, "The Trial and Execution of Patrick O'Conner," *Palimpsest,* vol. I (1920), pp. 86–97.

120. Granville Stuart, *Forty Years on the Frontier,* Paul C. Phillips, ed., (2 vols., Cleveland, Ohio: Arthur H. Clark, 1925), vol. II, pp. 196–197.

121. A well selected collection of documents that includes material on neo-vigilantism is John W. Caughey, ed., *Their Majesties the Mob* (Chicago: University of Chicago Press, 1960).

122. See the section on the antihorsethief association movement in "The American Vigilante Tradition."

123. White Caps: "A voluntary group formed ostensibly for punishing offenders not adequately dealt with by law." Mathews, *A Dictionary of Americanisms,* p. 1865.

124. White Capping seems to have begun in Crawford County, Ind., in 1888. Within the year it spread to Ohio. *Biographical and Historical Souvenir for the Counties of Clark, Crawford, Harrison, Floyd, Jefferson, Jennings, Scott and Washington: Indiana* (Chicago: John M. Graham & Co., 1889), p. 35. *Ohio State Journal* (Columbus), Nov. 26, 29, Dec. 1, 3, 5–7, 10, 12, 21, 1888.

125. Samuel L. Evans, "Texas Agriculture, 1880–1930" (unpublished Ph.D. dissertation, University of Texas, 1960), pp. 320–321. *Texas Farm and Ranch* (Dallas), Oct. 1, 8, 1898.

126. Sheriff A. M. Avant, Atascosa County, Sept. 20, 1898, to Governor C. A. Culberson in Letters to Governor C. A. Culberson (manuscripts in Texas State Archives, Austin).

127. "The 'White Caps,' 1890–1893" (file of manuscripts and clippings in the L. Bradford Prince papers in the New Mexico State Records Center, Santa Fe). See especially the August 12, 1890, memorandum of Governor Prince to John W. Noble, U.S. Secretary of the Interior.

128. For example, Robert E. Cunningham, *Trial by Mob* (Stillwater, Okla.: Redlands Press, 1957), pp. 12–13.

129. For example, E[thelred] W. Crozier, *The White-Caps: A History of the Organization in Sevier County* (Knoxville, Tenn.: Beam, Warters & Gaut, 1899), pp. 10–11, 87ff., 180ff.

130. Booth Tarkington, *The Gentleman from Indiana* (New York: Double-day & McClure, 1899).

131. Wilcomb E. Washburn, *The Governor and the Rebel: A History of Bacon's Rebellion in Virginia* (Chapel Hill, N.C.: University of North Carolina Press, 1957). Thomas J. Wertenbaker, *Torchbearer of the Revolution: The Story of Bacon's Rebellion and Its Leader* (Princeton, N.J.: Princeton University Press, 1940).

132. Gary S. Horowitz, "New Jersey Land Riots, 1745–1755" (unpublished Ph.D. dissertation, Ohio State University, 1966).

133. Brooke Hindle, "The March of the Paxton Boys," *William and Mary Quarterly*, 3d series, vol. III (1946), pp. 461–486.

134. John S. Bassett, "The Regulators of North Carolina (1765–1771)," American Historical Association, *Annual Report for the year 1894*, pp. 141–212. Marvin L. M. Kay, "The Institutional Background to the Regulation in Colonial North Carolina" (unpublished Ph.D. dissertation, University of Minnesota, 1962).

135. Irving Mark, *Agrarian Conflicts in Colonial New York, 1711–1775* (New York: Columbia University Press, 1940). David M. Ellis, *Landlords and Farmers in the Hudson-Mohawk Region, 1790–1850* (Ithaca, N.Y.: Cornell University Press, 1946). See also Sung Bok Kim, "The Manor of Cortlandt and Its Tenants: New York, 1697–1783" (unpublished Ph.D. dissertation, Michigan State University, 1966).

136. Marion L. Starkey, *A Little Rebellion* (New York: Alfred A. Knopf, 1955). Robert A. Feer, "Shays' Rebellion" (unpublished Ph.D. dissertation, Harvard University, 1958).

137. Leland D. Baldwin, *Whiskey Rebels* (Pittsburgh, Pa.: University of Pittsburgh Press, 1939).

138. William W. H. Davis, *The Fries Rebellion, 1798–1799* . . . (Doyles-town, Pa.: Doylestown Publishing Co., 1899).

139. Allan G. Bogue, "The Iowa Claim Clubs: Symbol and Substance," *Mississippi Valley Historical Review*, vol. XLV (1958), pp. 231–253.

140. Robert Lee Hunt, *A History of Farmer Movements in the Southwest: 1873–1925* (n.p., n.d.), pp. 28–29.

141. Although its interpretation has come under heavy attack in the last 15 years, the most complete account of the Populist movement remains John D. Hicks, *The Populist Revolt* (Minneapolis, Minn.: University of Minnesota Press, 1931).

142. James L. Brown, *The Mussel Slough Tragedy* (n.p., 1958), deals with the settlers' land league in the Hanford vicinity and its night riding activities which came to a climax in the Mussel Slough gun battle, an episode which Frank Norris used as the basis of his novel, *The Octopus: A Story of California* (New York: Doubleday, Page, 1901).

143. James O. Nall, *The Tobacco Night Riders of Kentucky and Tennessee, 1905–1909* (Louisville, Ky.: Standard Press, 1939). See also Robert Penn Warren's brilliant novel, *Night Rider* (Boston: Houghton Mifflin, 1939).

144. John Womack, Jr., "Oklahoma's Green Corn Rebellion" (unpublished A.B. thesis, Harvard College, 1959).

145. Robert L. Morlan, *Political Prairie Fire: The Nonpartisan League, 1915–1922* (Minneapolis, Minn.: University of Minnesota Press, 1955).

146. John L. Shover, *Cornbelt Rebellion: The Farmers' Holiday Association* (Urbana, Ill.: University of Illinois Press, 1965).

147. Lemisch, "Jack Tar in the Streets," pp. 381–400.

148. Smith, "Anglo-Colonial Society and the Mob," pp. 175–179.

149. "Molly Maguire" was an anti-British persona in Irish folklore whom the Irish miners of Pennsylvania adopted as a symbol of their resistance to the authority of the mine owners and bosses.

150. Wayne G. Broehl, Jr., *The Molly Maguires* (Cambridge, Mass.: Harvard University Press, 1964), is an outstanding study which treats in depth the sometimes present and usually overlooked European roots of American violence.

151. Henry David, *The History of the Haymarket Affair* (New York: Farrar & Rinehart, 1936).

152. Leon Wolff, *Lockout* . . . (New York: Harper & Row, 1965).

153. Louis Adamic, *Dynamite: The Story of Class Violence in America* (revised edition, New York: Viking, 1934), pp. 179–253. Another old but still useful work is Samuel Yellen, *American Labor Struggles* (New York: Harcourt, Brace, 1936). An excellent recent study is Graham Adams, Jr., *Age of Industrial Violence, 1910–1915: The Activities and Findings of the United States Commission on Industrial Relations* (New York: Columbia University Press, 1966). A searching study is the paper . . . [in *Violence in America*] by Philip Taft and Philip Ross, "American Labor Violence: Its Causes, Character, and Outcome."

154. George S. McGovern, "The Colorado Coal Strike, 1913–1914" (unpublished Ph.D. dissertation, Northwestern University, 1953), pp. 81–111.

155. *Ibid.*, pp. 151–307.

156. Jack London, *The Iron Heel* (New York: Macmillan, 1907).

A brief statement of the frequency and extent of violent crime in the United States as given in *The Report of the National Commission on the Causes and Prevention of Violence* shows that violence has increased markedly in the last ten years and places the United States in an uncomplimentary light when compared with other large nations. With due allowance for discrepancies, the figures establish beyond a doubt that there is an ugly problem that needs attention. *The Report* offers a profile of violent crime in the United States that is included in the following article.

Violent Crime

National Commission

When citizens express concern about high levels of violence in the United States, they have in mind a number of different types of events: homicides and assaults, rioting and looting, clashes between demonstrators and police, student seizures of university buildings, violence in the entertainment media, assassinations of national leaders. Foremost in their minds, no doubt, is what appears to be a rising tide of individual acts of violent crime, especially "crime in the streets."

Only a fraction of all crime is violent, of course. Major crimes of violence—homicide, rape, robbery, and assault—represent only 13 percent (or 588,000) of the Federal Bureau of Investigation's Index of reported serious crimes (about 4.5 million in 1968).[1] Moreover, deaths and personal injuries from violent crime cause only a small part of the pain and suffering which we experience: one is five times more likely to die in an auto accident than to be criminally slain, and one hundred times more likely to be injured in a home accident than in a serious assault.

But to suffer deliberate violence is different from experiencing an accident, illness or other misfortune. In violent crime man becomes a wolf to man, threatening or destroying the personal safety of his victim in a terrifying act. Violent crime (particularly street crime) engenders fear—the deep-seated fear of the hunted in the presence of the hunter. Today this fear is gnawing at the vitals of urban America.

In a recent national survey, half of the women and one-fifth of the men said they were afraid to walk outdoors at night, even near their homes. One-third of American householders keep guns in the hope that they will

From *To Establish Justice, To Insure Domestic Tranquility*, The Report of the National Commission on the Causes and Prevention of Violence. Washington, D.C., U.S. Government Printing Office, 1969. (An edited version of statement issued November 24, 1969.)

provide protection against intruders. In some urban neighborhoods, nearly one-third of the residents wish to move because of high rates of crime, and very large numbers have moved for that reason. In fear of crime, bus drivers in many cities do not carry change, cab drivers in some areas are in scarce supply, and some merchants are closing their businesses. Vigilante-like groups have sprung up in some areas.

Fear of crime is destroying some of the basic human freedoms which any society is supposed to safeguard—freedom of movement, freedom from harm, freedom from fear itself. Is there a basis for this fear? Is there an unprecedented increase in violent crime in this country? Who and where are most of the violent criminals and what makes them violent? What can we do to eliminate the causes of that violence?

Profile of Violent Crime

Between 1960 and 1968, the national rate of criminal homicide per 100,000 population increased 36 percent, the rate of forcible rape 65 percent, of aggravated assault 67 percent, and of robbery 119 percent. These figures are from the *Uniform Crime Reports* published by the Federal Bureau of Investigation. These Reports are the only national indicators we have of crime in America. But, as the FBI recognizes, they must be used with caution.

There is a large gap between the reported rates and the true rates. In 1967 the President's Commission on Law Enforcement and Administration of Justice stated that the true rate of total major violent crime was roughly twice as high as the reported rate.[2] This ratio has probably been a changing one. Decreasing public tolerance of crime is seemingly causing more crimes to be reported. Changes in police practices, such as better recording procedures and more intensive patrolling, are causing police statistics to dip deeper into the large well of unreported crime. Hence, some part of the increase in reported rates of violent crime is no doubt due to a fuller disclosure of the violent crimes actually committed.

Moreover, while current rates compare unfavorably, even alarmingly, with those of the 1950's, fragmentary information available indicates that at the beginning of this century there was an upsurge in violent crime which probably equaled today's levels. In 1916, the city of Memphis reported a homicide rate more than seven times its present rate. Studies in Boston, Chicago and New York during the years of the First World War and the 1920's showed violent crime rates considerably higher than those evident in the first published national crime statistics in 1933.

Despite all these factors, it is still clear that *significant and disturbing increases in the true rates of homicide and, especially, of assault and robbery have occurred over the last decade.* While the reported incidence of forcible rape has also increased, reporting difficulties associated with this crime are too great to permit any firm conclusion on the true rate of increase.

Violent crimes are not evenly distributed throughout the nation. Using new data from a Victim-Offender Survey conducted by our staff Task Force on Individual Acts of Violence, standard data from the FBI, and facts from other recent studies, we can sketch a more accurate profile of violent crime in the United States than has hitherto been possible. We note, however, that our information about crime is still unsatisfactory and that many critical details in the profile of violent crime remain obscure. Moreover, we strongly urge all who study this profile to keep two facts constantly in mind. First, violent crime is to be found in all regions of the country, and among all groups of the population—not just in the areas and groups of greatest concentration to which we draw attention. Second, despite heavy concentrations of crime in certain groups, the overwhelming majority of individuals in these groups are law-abiding citizens.

(1) *Violent crime in the United States is primarily a phenomenon of large cities. This is a fact of central importance.* The 26 cities with 500,000 or more residents and containing about 17 percent of our total population contribute about 45 percent of the total reported major violent crimes. Six cities with one million or more residents and having ten percent of our total population contribute 30 percent of the total reported major violent crimes.

Large cities uniformly have the highest reported violent crime levels per unit of population. Smaller cities, suburbs and rural areas have lower levels. The average rate of major violent offenses in cities of over 250,000 inhabitants is eleven times greater than in rural areas, eight times greater than in suburban areas, and five and one-half times greater than in cities with 50,000 to 100,000 inhabitants.[3]

For cities of all sizes, as well as for suburbs and rural areas, there has been a recent upward trend in violent crime; the increase in the city rate has been much more dramatic than that for the other areas and subdivisions.

The result in our larger cities is a growing risk of victimization: in Baltimore, the nation's leader in violent crime, the risk of being the victim of a reported violent crime is one in 49 per year. Thus, in the context of major violent crimes, the popular phrase "urban crisis" is pregnant with meaning.

(2) *Violent crime in the city is overwhelmingly committed by males.* Judgments about overall trends and levels of violent crime, and about variations in violent crime according to city size, can be based upon reported offense data. But conclusions about the sex, age, race and socioeconomic status of violent offenders can be based only on *arrest* data. Besides the gap previously mentioned between true offense rates and reported offense rates, we must now deal also with the even larger gap between *offenses reported* and *arrests made*. Accordingly, conclusions in these areas must be drawn with extreme care, especially since arrests, as distinguished from convictions, are made by policemen whose decisions in apprehending suspects thus determine the nature of arrest statistics.[4]

In spite of the possibly wide margins of error, however, one fact is clearly indisputable: violent crimes in urban areas are disproportionately caused by male offenders. To the extent that females are involved, they are more likely to commit the more "intimate" violent crimes like homicide than the "street crimes" like robbery. Thus, the 1968 reported male homicide rate was five times higher than the female rate; the robbery rate twenty times higher.

(3) *Violent crime in the city is concentrated especially among youths between the ages of fifteen and twenty-four*. Urban arrest rates for homicide are much higher among the 18–24 age group than among any other; for rape, robbery and aggravated assault, arrests in the 15–24 age group far outstrip those of any other group. Moreover, it is in these age groups that the greatest increases in all arrest rates have occurred. Surprisingly, however, there have also been dramatic and disturbing increases in arrest rates of the 10–14 age group for two categories—a 300 percent increase in assault between 1958 and 1967, and 200 percent in robbery in the same period.

(4) *Violent crime in the city is committed primarily by individuals at the lower end of the occupational scale*. Although there are no regularly collected national data on the socioeconomic status of violent offenders, local studies indicate that poor and uneducated individuals with few employment skills are much more likely to commit serious violence than persons higher on the socioeconomic ladder. A forthcoming University of Pennsylvania study of youthful male offenders in Philadelphia, for example, will show that boys from lower income areas in the city have delinquency rates for assaultive crimes nearly five times the rates of boys from higher income areas; delinquency rates for robbery are six times higher.[5] Other studies have found higher involvement in violence by persons at the lower end of the occupational scale. A succession of studies at the University of Pennsylvania, using Philadelphia police data, shows that persons ranging from skilled laborers to the unemployed constitute about 90–95 percent of the criminal homicide offenders, 90 percent of the rape offenders and 92–97 percent of the robbery offenders. A St. Louis study of aggravated assault found that blue collar workers predominate as offenders. The District of Columbia Crime Commission found more than 40 percent of the major violent crime offenders to be unemployed.

(5) *Violent crime in the cities stems disproportionately from the ghetto slum where most Negroes live*. Reported national urban arrest rates are much higher for Negroes than for whites in all four major violent crime categories, ranging from ten or eleven times higher for assault and rape to

sixteen or seventeen times higher for robbery and homicide.[6] As we shall show, these differences in urban violent crime rates are not, in fact, racial; they are primarily a result of conditions of life in the ghetto slum. The gap between Negro and white crime rates can be expected to close as the opportunity gap between Negro and white also closes—a development which has not yet occurred.

The large national urban arrest differentials between Negroes and whites are also found in the more intensive Philadelphia study previously cited. Of 10,000 boys born in 1945, some 50 percent of the three thousand non-whites had had at least one police contact by age 18, compared with 20 percent of the seven thousand whites. (A police contact means that the subject was taken into custody for an offense other than a traffic violation and a report recording his alleged offense was prepared and retained in police files.) The differences were most pronounced for the major violent offenses: of fourteen juveniles who had police contacts for homicide, all were non-whites; of 44 who had police contacts for rape, 86 percent were non-whites and fourteen percent whites; of 193 who had police contacts for robbery, 90 percent were non-whites and ten percent whites; and of 220 who had police contacts for aggravated assault, 82 percent were non-whites and eighteen percent whites. When the three sets of figures for rape, robbery and assault are related to the number of non-whites and whites, respectively, in the total group studied (3,000 vs. 7,000), the differences between the resulting ratios closely reflect the differentials in the national urban arrest rates of non-whites and whites in the 10–17 age group.

(6) *The victims of assaultive violence in the cities generally have the same characteristics as the offenders: victimization rates are generally highest for males, youths, poor persons, and blacks. Robbery victims, however, are very often older whites.* There is a widespread public misconception that most violent crime is committed by black offenders against white victims. This is not true. Our Task Force Victim-Offender Survey covering seventeen cities has confirmed other evidence that serious assaultive violence in the city—homicide, aggravated assault and rape—is predominantly between white offenders and white victims and black offenders and black victims. The majority of these crimes involves blacks attacking blacks, while most of the remainder involve whites victimizing whites. Indeed, our Survey found that 90 percent of urban homicide, aggravated assaults and rapes involve victims and offenders of the same race.

In two-thirds of homicides and aggravated assaults in the city, and in three-fifths of the rapes, the victim is a Negro. Rape victims tend strongly to be younger women; the victims of homicide and aggravated assault are usually young males but include a higher proportion of older persons. Nearly four-fifths of homicide victims and two-thirds of the assault victims are male. Generalizing from these data, we may say that the typical victim of a violent assaultive crime is a young Negro male, or in the case of rape, a young Negro woman.

Robbery, on the other hand, is the one major violent crime in the city with a high inter-racial component: although about 38 percent of robberies in the Survey involve Negro offenders and victims, 45 percent involve Negroes robbing whites—very often young black males robbing somewhat older white males. In three-fifths of all robberies the victim is white and nearly two-thirds of the time he or she is age 26 or over. Four-fifths of the time the victim is a man.

Data collected by the Crime Commission indicate that victimization rates for violent crimes are much higher in the lower-income groups. This is clearly true for robbery and rape, where persons with incomes under $6,000 were found to be victimized three to five times more often than persons with incomes over $6,000. The same relation held, but less strongly, for aggravated assault, while homicide victimization rates by income could not be computed under the investigative techniques used.

(7) *Unlike robbery, the other violent crimes of homicide, assault and rape tend to be acts of passion among intimates and acquaintances.* The Victim-Offender Survey shows that homicide and assault usually occur between relatives, friends or acquaintances (about two-thirds to three-fourths of the cases in which the relationship is known). They occur in the home or other indoor locations about 50–60 percent of the time. Rape is more likely to be perpetrated by a stranger (slightly over half of the cases), usually in the home or other indoor location (about two-thirds of the time). By contrast, robbery is usually committed outside (two-thirds of the cases) by a stranger (more than 80 percent of the cases).

The victim, the offender, or both are likely to have been drinking prior to homicide, assault, and rape, and the victim often provokes or otherwise helps precipitate the crime. The ostensible motives in homicide and assault are often relatively trivial, usually involving spontaneous altercations, family quarrels, jealous rages, and the like. The two crimes are similar; there is often no reason to believe that the person guilty of homicide sets out with any more intention to harm than the one who commits an aggravated assault. Except for the seriousness of the final outcomes, the major distinction is that homicides most often involve handguns while knives are most common in assault.[7]

(8) *By far the greatest proportion of all serious violence is committed by repeaters.* While the number of hard-core repeaters is small compared to the number of one-time offenders, the former group has a much higher rate of violence and inflicts considerably more serious injury. In the Philadelphia study, 627 of the 10,000 boys were chronic offenders, having five or more police contacts. Though they represented only six percent of the boys in the study, they accounted for 53 percent of the police contacts

for personal attacks—homicide, rape and assault—and 71 percent of the contacts for robberies.

Offenders arrested for major criminal violence generally have long criminal histories, but these careers are mainly filled with offenses other than the final serious acts. Generally, though there are many exceptions, the more serious the crime committed, the less chance it will be repeated.

(9) *Americans generally are no strangers to violent crime.* Although it is impossible to determine accurately how many Americans commit violent crimes each year,[8] the data that are available suggest that the number is substantial, ranging from perhaps 600,000 to 1,200,000—or somewhere between one in every 300 and one in every 150 persons. Undoubtedly, a far greater number commit a serious violent crime at some time in their lives. The Philadelphia study found that of about 10,000 boys 35 percent (3475) were taken into police custody for delinquency, and of the delinquents ten percent (363) were apprehended once or more for a major crime of violence before age eighteen.

A comparison of reported violent crime rates in this country with those in other modern, stable nations shows the United States to be the clear leader. Our homicide rate is more than twice that of our closest competitor, Finland, and from four to twelve times higher than the rates in a dozen other advanced countries including Japan, Canada, England and Norway. Similar patterns are found in the rates of other violent crimes: averages computed for the years 1963–1967 show the United States rape rate to be twelve times that of England and Wales and three times that of Canada; our robbery rate is nine times that of England and Wales and double that of Canada; our aggravated assault rate is double that of England and Wales and eighteen times that of Canada.

Notes

1. The FBI Index of Reported Crime classifies seven offenses as "serious crimes"—homicide, forcible rape, robbery, aggravated assault, burglary, larceny of more than $50 and auto theft. It classifies the first four—homicide, rape, robbery and assault—as "violent crimes" because they involve the doing or threatening of bodily injury.

2. Reasons for the gap include failure of citizens to report crimes because they believe police cannot be effective in solving them; others do not want to take the time to report, some do not know how to report, and others fear reprisals.

3. The direct correlation between city size and violent crime rates may not be as uniform in the south as in other regions. Available data indicate higher suburban violent crime rates relative to center city rates in the south, suggesting the possibility that smaller city rates may also be higher relative to larger city rates in the south (although direct evidence on this point is not presently available).

Also, it should be kept in mind that the relationships noted in the text are for cities within certain population ranges (*e.g.*, more than 250,000, 100,000–250,000, etc.), not for individual cities. Thus the five cities with the highest metropolitan violent crime rates in 1968—Baltimore, Newark, Washington, San Francisco and Detroit—had smaller populations than some very large cities with somewhat lower rates of violent crime.

4. According to the FBI Uniform Crime Reports, about half of all arrests for serious crimes result in pleas of guilty or convictions: in only 88 percent of all arrests does the prosecutor decide he has sufficient evidence to try the case, and of those cases that are prosecuted, only 62 percent result in a plea of guilty or a conviction, often for a lesser offense than the one originally charged. A wide margin of error thus exists between the making of an arrest and proof that the person arrested has committed an offense.

5. This is a study of 9945 males born in 1945 and who lived in Philadelphia at least from age 10 to 18. Of this group, 3475, or 35 percent, were taken into custody by the police for delinquent offenses other than traffic violations. Race, socioeconomic status and many other variables are analyzed in this study, supported by NIMH, to be published shortly by Thorsten Sellin and Marvin E. Wolfgang under the title, *Delinquency in a Birth Cohort.*

6. Because some police commonly associate violence with Negroes more than with whites, Negroes may be disproportionately arrested on suspicion, thus producing a higher reported Negro involvement in crime than is the true situation.

7. [In] Chapter 6, "Violence and Law Enforcement," [of the *Report*] this Commission indicates that gun attacks are fatal in one out of five cases, on the average; knife attacks are fatal in one out of twenty.

8. The FBI has reported that in 1968 588,000 violent crimes occurred. This is about 300 crimes of major violence per each 100,000 Americans. It is generally estimated that only about half of all violent crimes are reported; if this is true, the total number of violent crimes per year is in the range of 1,200,000 or 600 per 100,000 people. These are *offenses,* not *offenders.* Since violent crimes often involve several offenders committing a single crime—particularly among the large number of juvenile offenders—a fair guess might be that twice as many offenders (2,400,000) were involved. But some offenders account for more than one crime per year. If we assume the commission of two crimes per year per offender, the total number of offenders drops back to 1,200,000; if we assume the commission of four crimes per year per offender, the total number of offenders is 600,000. Thus the number of Americans who commit violent crimes each year appears to be somewhere between these figures—between one in every 150 and one in every 300 Americans. Since children under twelve and adults over 45 commit relatively few crimes, the rate for persons between 12 and 45 is even higher.

Ambiguity toward violence is attributable to the fact that one's response, or reaction, to a violent act is influenced by many factors such as who is committing
the violence and who is the victim. The purpose of the action may cause one to
condemn or justify. Ambivalence in an individual exists mostly because his
attitudes are determined by his perception of each situation, subject to the distortions caused by biases, fears, emotions, and inadequacies.

Response to Violence

W. Walter Menninger

Violence is a topic of common discussion and frequent concern these days.
People seem to be newly aware and increasingly anxious and fearful of it.
Despite the fact that violence has been with us through the ages, we react
as if it were a new phenomenon to be especially dreaded. And, while there
has been a good deal of study of violence, less attention has been paid to
the many responses it evokes.

One can catalog a wide range of such reactions—from programmed
investigations to passing emotions. Violence brought about the establishment of the National Commission on the Causes and Prevention of Violence,
which President Johnson announced less than 24 hours after the assassination of Sen. Robert Kennedy. It evokes indignation and disapproval from
some; it brings pleasure to others. More than 15,000 people recently turned
out to cheer a heavyweight boxing match in New York; the box office response to "Bonnie and Clyde" has been striking, and there is a large
segment of the population that gains the greatest of pleasure from hunting
and shooting.

Even such violence as has occurred in urban riots has seen a varying
pattern of responses. Reporters have observed the "carnival" atmosphere of
some of the participants in the riot. Other participants are angry. Still
others are fearful. Persons not directly involved in the riot area have nevertheless experienced considerable anxiety, and many have responded by
buying guns. Others have responded with vengeful words and feelings.

It is difficult to generalize about reactions to violence, in part because
the nature of violence itself is so broad. The Violence Commission has
taken the following definition for violence: The threat or use of force that
results, or is intended to result, in the injury of forcible restraint or intimidation of persons, or the destruction or forcible seizure of property.

One man's hurt may well be another man's pleasure, and the reactions

From "Response to Violence" by W. Walter Menninger. Reprinted by permission
of the author from the *Stanford Alumni Almanac.*

clearly range from pain and discomfort and anger and resentment to excitement and pleasure and exhilaration. This is because one's reaction to violence is a function of several factors: the subject or perpetrator of violence; the object or recipient of violence; the setting in which the violence occurs; the means by which it is expressed; the motivation and feelings expressed in the violence, and the purpose or objective of the violence.

If the perpetrator—either an individual or a group—is one we respect, we will generally take pleasure in identifying with the violence. We all respect the founders of our republic, the signers of the Declaration of Independence, and the many heroes who fought to establish our country. Yet one can hardly deny their actions involved both the threat and the use of force to achieve their goals in a violent manner.

More often, the perpetrator will be someone who is alien to us and who stands for something of which we disapprove and therefore is a threat. Our reaction is then clearly one of disapproval and rejection.

Likewise, if the target of violence—person or property—is someone or something close to us, we are likely to respond negatively; and even if the object is not preciously regarded, we may still respond angrily if it has a special meaning—such as to the burning of an American Flag, a symbol of freedom and identity. If the violence in some way threatens us or what we stand for, we will naturally react with anger and resentment.

However, if the object is related to someone or something bad, our reaction is to the contrary. Our satisfactions in wartime usually come from the victories we gain over others. These victories excite pleasure and evoke pride. And when adversity occurs to our "enemies," we are not unhappy.

The Setting of Violence

The setting of the violence is a subtle element. Obviously, reactions prompted by violence perpetrated in a football stadium or a hockey arena are far different from the reactions to violence which we see taking place in Saigon or Da Nang. Likewise, the violence in "Bonnie and Clyde" is different in the response it provoked from the violence of an armed robbery in real life. The reactions prompted by the deaths in automobile accidents are far different from the reactions to the deaths in Vietnam, despite the fact that more Americans are killed each year on the U.S. highways than have been in the entire Vietnam war.

We have many ways to express violent feelings, and not all are by violent means. Thus, the means of the expression of violence can also account for different responses. The direct personal attack by a gun (murder or assassination) prompts a different response from that of the slow and silent process of poisoning. Indeed, sometimes violence is perpetrated by commission of an act, and other times by an omission. Much of the reaction of the minorities is the result of public inaction, which is perceived by the minorities as destructive: Starvation, deprivation, or mis-education are as "violent" as any active assault on their integrity.

The emotions associated with violence are an important factor. The crowds at violent athletic contests seek emotional release. Many persons can openly acknowledge their elation or satisfaction from the overt release of aggressive feelings. We all generally identify with the "good guy" and are pleased when the "bad guy" gets it. We all laugh at the "sock-it-to-me." Yet there are limits, and when persons get too much pleasure from hurting others, we react to their sadistic outlook and are disapproving.

Other feelings are involved. Much violence stems from fear or panic, particularly when our security or our personal integrity is threatened. Violence also is prompted by, and can further prompt, rage and anger and resentment which stem from real or imagined hurts. Our reactions stem from the degree to which we sympathize with or are threatened by the violence of the perpetrator to the object of that violence.

The objective or purpose of violence is a final factor which affects our response to it. The violence may simply represent a retaliation—an eye for an eye—and we may fully approve of that. The death penalty is a retaliation, although we may give additional justifications for it. If the violence has as its objective the release for pent-up resentments which we also experience to some extent, we may well approve of it, or endorse it. If violence is the only way we can call attention to a cause which we feel is important and just, we have another basis for a positive response. "When in the course of human events . . . ," wrote Thomas Jefferson. Certainly, individuals or groups may feel that the social order is unresponsive to their concerns. Being frustrated in their attempts to be "heard," they may resort to violence. Obviously, if we are with them, we are pleased; if we are part of the institution that is being attacked, we will not be pleased.

As violence is generally the result of emotions, so our reactions are determined more by emotions than by reason. Man is called a "rational animal," yet as we look about us, we can't help but conclude otherwise. It seems much more appropriate to call us "emotional animals" who have a veneer of rationalization. Clearly the most powerful forces that motivate us are our emotions, which are not especially "rational."

Very often what really happens in our life isn't half so important as what we think and believe happens. We may get into a terrific argument with someone over a disputed event, and our reactions stem from what we believe we saw or felt to be so, not what actually happened. This is particularly true when we learn of events second-hand or third-hand.

Therefore, our reactions are not necessarily a function of the "truth" in reality, but the "truth" as we perceive it; and there are many inevitable distortions in our perception of the "truth." Our biases will affect our perceptions; and when we rely on the reports of others, we are subject to the added distortions of their prejudices.

The news media, sometimes conscientious but not always so, can likewise introduce significant distortions. Recently the Lemberg Center for the Study of Violence at Brandeis University reported that the news stories of a wave of planned guerrilla attacks on police last summer were "largely a myth of the news media."

Reactions to Violence

The intensity of reactions which we experience to violent events is in part the function of our fear and anxiety of the consequences of destruction. Equally significant, or more so, is our inner struggle against similar trends and drives which we do not admit to consciousness. Within us we have violent impulses which we must keep repressed in order to remain civilized. We all have violent feelings at one time or another, and we all have devices by which we keep ourselves "in line."

The idea that we might actually experience some pleasure from violence is most disconcerting to many people. Indeed, violence is so often equated with crime and destruction that to enjoy it would be equally sinful. Rather, violence is to be condemned. To do otherwise is to subject ourselves to the indictment of our own consciences, and to feel guilty for having pleasure from violence. Only under special circumstances, such as war or "games," can we escape the indictment of our conscience.

If some people express openly their destructive or aggressive impulses, others feel threatened when their capacity to control their similar feelings is jeopardized. Most people do have limits in their capacity to control impulsive behavior. The dissolution of these controls can be seen in children and it can be seen when a group turns into a mob. This is a potential within us all. For some, the threatened expression of a wish to be violent may be so intense that the individual must reinforce his controls with repressive measures. This is much like one might respond to a boiler with a dangerous head of steam—by simply applying more boiler plate.

Another reaction to violence is a scapegoating mechanism by which we displace our feelings and reactions from some frustrating objects in our lives on to another object which we can safely attack. We can shout loudly about riots or violence on campus; we may not find it so easy to protest the frustrations and hurts which we experience in our work or from our loved ones—much more significant as they are to us. In humans, anger is universal and it is prompted by a wide range of events. Our wish to express our anger may have to be satisfied with a scapegoat.

The actual reactions and responses to violence are tinged very much with our own emotional makeup. Some people simply tune out violence, much like a husband who is preoccupied with something else and who nods when his wife says something to him, but who doesn't really hear.

All too often, the first reaction, and sometimes the only reaction, is a resentful irritation at the disruption. There is the scapegoating, an attempt to blame others for provoking the problem, and often a denial of what may be real grievances. The extreme response is either repression—to put the lid firmly on any further behavior and "show 'em we won't put up with any nonsense." Or, an opposite response develops of giving in, feeling guilty and being permissive. If a boiler plate has a head of steam and is about to blow up, the immediate crisis may be resolved by quickly applying a stronger boiler plate, or by opening up all the stops to let off the steam. Neither of these extreme reactions is efficient over the long haul.

Our reactions and our responses are complex, and often irrational in some elements. To cope effectively with violence, therefore, we must begin to understand and have some sensitivity to what is behind our reaction. We need to begin with ourselves and recognize when our reaction is inappropriate or out of proportion to the stimulus and reality. If we can keep the problem in perspective, we will be in a position to deal with it more effectively and more appropriately. This may simply be a matter of stepping back and reassessing what is going on.

We will always have difficulty in dealing with violence because of our emotional reactions—of fear, anxiety, guilt—reactions which may reflect our discomfort that we, too, have not yet created the perfect world. Individually, we must acknowledge that the place to start is within ourselves, to be a little less self-righteous and so sure that we have all the answers. No matter how sophisticated or suave a manner we present to the world, we still have within us childish pressures and reactions.

Humility is vital, and we must accept that we can be wrong, without feeling we are worthless if we are exposed as being wrong. Ultimately, our reactions must not be to respond to violence with hate, but to realize that the hate in this world can only be neutralized effectively by love, by real concern for others, concern which each one of us personally seeks.

Surveys of public opinion about the effects of mass media violence can discover
no more than what the population thinks or feels about the matter, which may
or may not be what is really true. Experts disagree on the issue, but most authorities contend that television is a reinforcing agent, not a causal one. This
British author believes that studies of the effects of television violence, to be
meaningful, must take into account those forces in society that both produce
and require violence.

Television and Violence

James D. Halloran

If one is to judge from the results of inquiries, the evidence recorded by
committees such as the Pilkington, letters to the press, and the formation of
"protection" societies and organizations, many people are deeply concerned
about what they imagine to be the effects of the mass media in general, and
of television in particular. Most of the charges that are made have been
heard before in relation to comics, radio and cinema, and usually take the
form of unsubstantiated generalizations and condemnations which accuse
television of encouraging anti-social attitudes by offering undesirable models
for imitation, stimulating aggressive tendencies and in general of being a
major contributory factor in the development of delinquent and criminal
behaviour. Although the debate does not go on at a very high level it would
be wrong to dismiss this concern as coming entirely from cranks and over-
eager moralizers. Although a recent survey carried out in June 1964 by
Research Services Limited on behalf of the Independent Television Authority found little spontaneous criticism about violence in television programmes, in answer to more specific questions 34 per cent of those interviewed thought that the statement that there was too much violence on
television was "very true" and another 22 per cent thought that it was
"partly true."

The Pilkington Committee found that disquiet at the portrayal of
violence was expressed on three main grounds: namely, that small children
were disturbed and frightened by scenes of violence, that such scenes could
lead children to dangerous and even disastrous experiments, and that the
showing of violence encouraged anti-social, callous and vicious attitudes
and behaviour. Many of those giving evidence to the Committee felt that
there was too much violence on television, that constant repetition of violence was bound to be damaging, that violence was unnecessarily em-

From "Television and Violence" by James D. Halloran. Reprinted by permission of
the author from *The Twentieth Century*, winter, 1964–1965, pp. 61–72.

phasized and lingered over and that, quite often, it was used gratuitously—thrown in for kicks—without adding materially to plot or characterization. Moreover, the concern and disquiet are not confined to this country; the Hearings before the United States Senate Sub-Committee to Investigate Juvenile Delinquency, and reports from several European countries, record the same story.

But what does all this amount to? Neither the Pilkington Committee nor the Senate Sub-Committee used any sort of population-sampling techniques and even if they had been more refined in their methods they would still only have provided evidence of what a more representative sample of the population *thought* or *felt* about the effects of violence on television. Obviously, this is not the same thing as the actual, established effects. It should be remembered that even a complete consensus on this or any other problem need not mean that public opinion represents an accurate picture of what really takes place.

We need to ask then, whether or not there is any justification for this disquiet and concern, and for an answer to this question we might look to the experts, to those who have studied the problem within their own particular discipline. But this is where the trouble begins, for the poor layman will quickly find that the experts are not agreed, and that the available evidence, such as it is, points in both directions. As I hope to show later the situation, although confusing, is not quite so hopeless and unhelpful as it might appear to be at first glance. Still, it is not surprising that a bewildered public does not readily turn for help to experts who seem to be providing evidence in partial support of every view, who at times appear to be generating more heat than light in their own incomprehensible disputes, and who certainly do not provide definitive answers to what the public may consider to be urgent social questions.

Who are the experts and what do they have to say? It is not quite accurate to split them into two camps, with the cautious sociologist and social psychologists in one and the rather more critical psychiatrists in the other, for there are important exceptions on both sides. By and large, however, the evidence provided over the years by those in the former group suggests that it is wrong to blame television for outbreaks of violence and the alleged increase in crime and delinquency rates. Generally, social scientists refer to television as a reinforcing agent, rather than as a direct causal or creative factor in the formation of attitudes and behavior patterns. To take this line, however, is not to absolve television producers from their responsibility; for in any society there will be some tendencies which it will not be considered desirable to reinforce. To these social scientists television, like the other media, is seen as working in and through a variety of other social factors, such as relationships and experiences with parents, brothers, sisters, teachers, companions, etc. Consequently, even if a link could be established between certain viewing patterns and some form of "social damage" these social scientists would suggest that the roots of this damage would probably be found in home, school, neighbourhood or other social setting. Only in certain circumstances, as for example when attitudes in a certain area have not been formed or developed, is television seen as being a direct cause of some particular attitude or form of behaviour in that area.

However, not all sociologists would adopt this line. In this country Bryan Wilson, like many non-sociological critics, has suggested that the mass media over-dramatize and pay too much attention to violence, provide those with anti-social tendencies with vivid fantasies, stimulate and satisfy criminal, violent, sensational and salacious appetites, provide technical knowledge and the glamour of publicity, and help to produce an atmosphere of greater tolerance for many forms of deviant behaviour. Supporting evidence is not produced by Wilson and indeed this type of indictment is more characteristic of those psychiatrists, most of them American, who have been so outspoken in their condemnation of the heavy dosage of violence on the American small screen. Again, it can be unfair and misleading to generalize, and by no means all psychiatrists in the United States would wish to associate themselves with the formidable Dr. Fredric Wertham and his supporters in their frequent and vociferous condemnations. Yet, as far as the experts are concerned, the main attack on the television companies for their portrayal of violence has been mounted by the psychiatrists. What is more, it would appear that their attacks have been pressed home with some success, for judging from the preliminary reports received in this country the United States Senate Sub-Committee on Juvenile Delinquency, which received several submissions from Dr. Wertham, has stated that it has found that a relationship has been conclusively established between televised crime and violence on the one hand, and anti-social attitudes and behaviour among juvenile viewers on the other. At first glance (the full report is not available at the time of writing) it would appear that the Committee has been more impressed by the unequivocal evidence of such as Dr. Wertham than by the more cautious statements of the social scientists. Wertham himself has little sympathy with the methods and works of the social scientists and he considers that their "statistical-questionnaire-control group method" is quite unsuitable for the intricate problems involved in measuring the effects of violence on young people. In one of his submissions to the Senate Sub-Committee he gives considerable space to a destructive criticism of the work of such well-known authorities as Hilde Himmelweit, Wilbur Schramm and Joseph Klapper. According to Wertham the clinical method is the only one capable of dealing with the effects of mass media in a scientific way. The clinical method includes a study of the whole child, a diagnostic evaluation of his personality and emotional life, his thinking, his background, his real satisfactions and dissatisfactions, the application of psycho-diagnostic tests and—most important—a follow-up of his further development and response to guidance and therapy.

Wertham bases his statements of the effects of television violence on his clinical studies of over 200 unselected cases. He finds that the surfeit of brutality, violence and sadism has made a profound impression on young people who are becoming more and more "teledirected," more hostile, more callous, more insensitive. He claims that inhibitions are lowered, resistances removed and sadism perpetuated or aroused. The media have helped to create and foster the belief that brutality is an expedient regulator in all social relationships, says Wertham, and slowly but surely we are raising a generation of violence worshippers.

As a sociologist I do not feel that Wertham supports his case with valid or objectively measurable evidence. Needless to say, controls are not used and little attempt is made to assess the part played by other social factors. He works within his own highly subjective and selective framework and, to mention but one point, appears to take at face value many statements made by his subjects although it is surely possible that such statements as "I saw it on television" can often be the delinquent's own rationalization of his behaviour. In many ways it is unfortunate that Wertham and others go too far and over-state their position, for a more sober, more objective and better argued case against the excessive use of certain types of violence on the screen is gradually being built up by some of the social scientists whom Wertham apparently despises.

The cathartic or abreaction hypothesis has long been used by authors, producers and critics as a justification for the presentation of violence. It is frequently argued that the viewing of aggressive scenes brings about a reduction in the aggressive drives of the viewer, that children get rid of hostility feelings in an innocuous way by watching violent television programmes, and that such programmes provide a necessary social function by presenting young people with a harmless outlet for latent hostility and by enabling them to relieve their pent-up aggression. Aristotle, and to a lesser degree Freud, are used as authoritative backing for these claims and although it might be mentioned here that this demonstrates a fundamental misunderstanding of both the philosophy of Aristotle and the psychology of Freud this is hardly the point, for in this context a correct understanding of the work of these great men is not so important as the views which the defenders of violence attribute to them. The labels of authority and respectability are given to phoney arguments and help to get these arguments accepted.

I use the word phoney, for gradually it is becoming clear that the bulk of the social scientific evidence available does not lend support to the cathartic argument but indicates that television violence can instigate aggressive behaviour immediately following the viewing experience. Although an early experiment by Seymour Feshbach, an American psychologist, had given some support to the cathartic argument, the results of an experiment carried out in the mid-1950s by Eleanor Maccoby suggested that aggressive content could be learned and levels of aggression influenced by the viewing of violent scenes on television. Eleanor Maccoby questioned the validity of the discharge of aggression theory, as also did Leonard Berkowitz from the University of Wisconsin in his criticism of the interpretation of the results of the Feshbach experiment. In this experiment a group of students, previously angered, were divided into two sections; one section was shown a film of a boxing match and the other a more neutral film. After seeing the films all the students were tested and those who had seen the boxing match showed less hostility than the others. It could be that the anger of these students had been discharged vicariously as Feshbach suggested. But there are other possible explanations, and Berkowitz has suggested that the students could have inhibited their hostile reactions, because as a result of viewing the boxing film they had become uneasy about their own aggressive tendencies and had begun to think that their aggressive behaviour might be wrong.

Another experiment demonstrated that young children who had been exposed to a cartoon film with an aggressive theme played more aggressively with their toys than did other children who had seen a less aggressive film. Moreover, these findings on aggressive behaviour are not confined to children, for in another experiment some adult males who had seen a film which included a knife-fight displayed more severe punitive attitudes to their colleagues, soon after the viewing, than did some comparable adults who had seen a less violent film.

Within the last few years some most ingenious experiments have been carried out by Berkowitz and his colleagues, and by Albert Bandura and his colleagues at Stanford University. Bandura holds that film models are as effective as real life models in transmitting deviant patterns of behaviour and that some forms of deviant behaviour are "released" by children who have been exposed to film models who have displayed the deviant behaviour freely on the screen. In one experiment he established that children subjected to mild frustration tended to imitate the aggressive behaviour of an adult they had seen on the screen. Of course, most of these experiments are carried out in relatively artificial conditions and in some cases the experiment proves only that the aggressive children learned to take out their aggressions on the same target as used in the experiment. Whether they would generalize this tendency and act aggressively toward other persons or objects in real life would obviously depend on other external social factors which were not controlled in the experiments. Much more research is required before clear-cut general statements can be made, but it should be noted that television does provide a continually available source of experience which children may readily imitate.

Despite the experimental limitations, however, it now seems quite clear that the viewing of filmed and televised violence does not necessarily lead to a discharge of anger or aggression to the extent and degree that many of those on the production side would like us to believe. Fortified by these findings and by the general confirmatory results of his own ingeniously contrived experiments, Leonard Berkowitz argues that there is no such thing as free-floating aggressive energy which can be released by viewing violence or aggression, or, for that matter, by any other activity. A person may derive pleasure or satisfaction from the viewing experience, as he views actors doing things he would like to do but is normally prevented from doing, but this need not be accompanied by a discharge of hostility. The hostility will still persist to the extent that the frustrations and aggressive habits persist. In fact, even when the angered person carries out an act of overt aggression himself, it seems likely that unless he thinks that he is attacking the known source of the frustration, the hostility will not be reduced. According to this view effective catharsis occurs only when the angered person perceives that the source of his anger or frustration has been attacked and damaged.

But the lessons that can be drawn from these experiments may be taken a little further. Cinema and television productions depicting crime and violence are often defended on the grounds that there is a "good" ending and that it is made perfectly clear that "crime does not pay." In many of these productions justice is not only done, it is seen to be done, and the method invariably used in punishing the evil character, the villain, is to repay violence with violence! This may give the audience a degree of satisfaction, probably because people approve of hurting those who hurt others, but it could also have harmful consequences for, according to Berkowitz, when a villain is defeated aggressively the restraints of audience members may be weakened, a sort of permission or warrant is given, and angered members of the audience, primed for aggressive action, are more likely to attack those whom they perceive as "villains" in their own lives immediately following their viewing experience.

Of course, it must be emphasized that these points stem from laboratory experiments and they are not put forward here in an attempt to establish a general law on the direct causal link between televised violence and crime, and anti-social attitudes and behaviour. Although it will be seen that these give little comfort to those who regard fantasy-aggression as having socially beneficial results, it is still necessary for us to make a distinction between potential or readiness for aggression and actual overt aggressive behaviour in social situations. In real life, as distinct from experimental situations, other factors operate and many of these will serve as constraints. In all probability the aggressive reaction will not be an enduring one and will gradually disappear as the person moves into new situations and has new experiences. Moreover, people react differently to different people. An angered man will strike some people more readily than others and this selection of target is not just a function of size or apprehension about the ability to hit back, for it seems probable that we are more likely to be aggressive toward those whom we can associate either with the source of the provocation of our anger or frustration, with the aggressive film we have just seen or, not surprisingly, towards someone we just dislike.

This draws attention to the significance of the link-up between what people see on the screen and their own real worlds, for in addition to the importance of the association already mentioned it would appear that viewers' emotions are most affected by what they see on the screen when they are able to link the filmed events with their own lives and experiences. Where the programme is associated with the types of conflicts which a person is experiencing or where the identification has some connections with his social life, the person is more likely to carry the stimulation over into real life with an increase in the amount of directly expressed aggression.

Again it is necessary to draw attention to the very real limitations in the research from which these points are taken. Admittedly, much more research will be required from psychologists and sociologists before the gap between the experimental and the real-life situation is adequately bridged. But these experiments are important starting-points and maybe in years to come they will be regarded as the beginning of a vital breakthrough in mass-media research. We may not feel justified at this stage in accepting the direct link findings of the Senate Sub-Committee, still less may we feel able to join with Dr. Wertham and his associates, but I think we may accept with Berkowitz, Bandura and others that the heavy dosage of violence in the mass media, although not a major determinant of crime and delinquency, heightens the probability that someone in the audience will behave aggressively in a later situation. The catharsis fallacy is by no means the only one in this field of discussion. Statements from all sides, from producers, professional critics and over-enthusiastic moralizers, show that the whole debate on the effects of filmed and televised violence is riddled with misconceptions.

Professional critics, whatever their sect, with their penchant for loose, pretentious judgments write of the artistic handling of violence, the responsible treatment of violence controlled by first-hand observation, violent incidents made acceptable by being presented in context, by being deeply embedded in the master plan, by delicate treatment, by being digested into the body, and it would appear that in a "really good work" even gratuitous violence can be explained away as being in character. These critics may be right, these may be accurate accounts of their own reactions and of the reactions of the authors and producers. But can we leave it at that? Are there not numerous implied assumptions about how other people will react? The whole field of film and television criticism abounds with élitist evaluations and superimpositions. It is implied that if they (the critics) see it in a certain way then others will also see it in that way; that if the violence is cushioned and made acceptable to them and if this is what the producers intend then it will also be made acceptable to others. That individuals bring different needs and predispositions to the screen and that they perceive content selectively and subjectively is either not appreciated or ignored. One frequently gets the impression that many of the critics work on the assumption that basically we are all the same under the skin, and that we all see the world in the same way.

Producers, too, are not free from these misconceptions. Several studies in the United States have shown that what the producer intends to convey to his audience and what is actually conveyed or perceived can be two very different things. The possibility of the existence of a "hidden message" which obviously relates to perceptions, needs and dispositions of the viewers and may be much more important than the overt message, is often not taken into account. A recent investigation in this country into the response of children to television, conducted jointly by the University of Cambridge and A.B.C. Television, drew further attention to the gap which exists between intention and perception and provided the makers of the programme with "a humiliating, funny, illuminating and humble-making experience."

The world does not appear to children as it does to adults, consequently adults do not see the same thing in a television programme as children do. The adult watching fairy stories will not take the fictional characters seriously, the young child probably will, because he believes he is seeing real people. Children do not respond uniformly, some children may be frightened, others amused and others totally unimpressed by the same stimulus. Moreover, what frightens and disturbs an adult may not produce the same reaction from a child. For example, death on the screen will elicit quite different reactions from the adult and the child and, similarly, aggressive action is likely to evoke different responses.

In general, we would expect response differences between adults and children to be greater and more varied than those between different adults, but the differences between adults are quite marked and can be linked to social, political, religious, economic and educational factors as well as to general personality. Violence in the content of a Bible story or even in a Shakespearian play will draw less adverse criticism than in the content of a western or a detective thriller, yet the response could be the same. When people complain about violence on television they rarely illustrate their complaints with references to news reels, rocket trials, the explosion of hydrogen bombs, historical documentaries or war films. Yet it is possible that for some people these may, in the long run, produce more injurious reactions than westerns and detective thrillers. Several years ago Professor Grunhut, then Professor of Criminology at Oxford University, suggested that we ought not to be surprised if young people solve their problems in a violent way, for the nation has been solving its problems in this way for some considerable time. Television reminds us of this problem-solving ability and the methods employed, quite frequently.

An important point to make here is that the field of research must be widened so that the attitudes, reactions, needs, states of mind, perceptual patterns can be fully understood in relation to the many sociological factors (family experiences, education, social-economic position, religious and political affiliation, social class, etc.) that produce and require them.

It would be unfortunate if in making these remarks about different people seeing things in different ways and if in drawing the attention of readers to the gap that exists between the intention of producers and the perceptions of viewers I gave the impression that those who make the decisions at various stages and levels in the production process were irresponsible and cared nothing about the possible injurious effects of their work. Such is not the case. The B.B.C.'s programme policy governing violence produced in 1960 by the Controller of Television Programmes, Kenneth Adam, is indicative of the concern and care which is shown in these quarters, and although the independent companies were criticized on this score in the Pilkington Report it would be quite misleading to present the officials and producers of the companies as irresponsible people. In any case the I.T.A. now promises to play a more active role in this respect than it has done in the past.

But although concern and responsibility are important matters, they are not the main issue here. Even when these qualities are not in question, as in the case referred to above, it is still possible that the stereotyped misconceptions and fallacies which I have instanced and which abound in this field will persist and continue to play their part in determining what is presented on the screen, what is repeated, what is banned, what is praised and what is condemned.

Is there too much violence on television? Is it increasing? The U.S. Senate Sub-Committee says "yes" to both these questions as far as the U.S. is concerned. The position in the United States is, of course, quite different from our own and although my own impression is, that in so far as any satisfactory definition of violence can be agreed on, there is far more violence on the American screen than on the British screen, there are many people in this country, as we have seen, who feel that there is too much violence on our television also.

But can these questions really be answered? First of all we have to answer the question, What is violence? and this as I have tried to point out is no easy matter. I am not denying that a common denominator of acceptance could fairly easily be established and used as a basis for decision making, but it must be emphasized that the traditional methods of content analysis are inadequate. The established, conventional procedures are crude and limiting and a much more refined and sophisticated approach to content analysis will be necessary before any real progress is made. Analysis in terms of deaths, blood, weapons, number of incidents, or even in the more sophisticated categories of the professional critics will not do. If we wish to examine the content of television programmes which contain violence and aggression, in an attempt to assess the effects of these programmes, then the most relevant categories of analysis should stem from the perceptions of the viewer. This is not to say that there is no place for the professional, evaluative critics; they have their own disciplines and skills, and bring valuable insight to the problem. But it cannot be stressed too often, that if we wish to ascertain the effect of violence, then it is more important to know how people really react, than to know how a small group of people *think* they will react.

But why all this concern and apparent preoccupation with violence? There are many other aspects of life which do not seem to attract the same attention. Could it be, as Gerson Legman speculated in his book *Love and Death,* that this concern and preoccupation and this "fixation on violence and death in all our mass-produced fantasies is a substitution for a censored sexuality, or is, to a greater degree, intended to siphon off—into avenues of perversion opened up by the censorship of sex—the aggression felt by children and adults against the social and economic structure."

This may or may not be true, but the statement does contain an important pointer and that is, that violence on television cannot be studied in isolation. We need to look at the whole social and economic structure of society and examine the portrayal of violence and the concern and disquiet which this brings about in this wider setting. No state of mind, no perceptual patterns, no needs, no reactions, no effects, no criticisms and no condemnations can be fully understood unless these factors are related to those forces in society which both produce and require the violence. In a manner of speaking, society gets the violence it deserves or, perhaps more accurately, it produces the violence it needs.

The numerous riots that occurred in Europe prior to the French Revolution were directed at specific and immediate economic objectives, not at the overthrow of the social order. Then, during the French Revolution, under the leadership of political strategists, the mobs became the instrument for attaining long-term ideological ends. The riots that have recently been occurring in the United States are similar to those that preceded the French Revolution in 1789. The question is whether the riots will be molded by revolutionary leaders into a movement that may finalize in a civil war, or whether they will fade away.

When Does a Riot Become a Revolution?

J. H. Plumb

The senate house in flames; mobs roaring and rioting in the Forum, full of hate, hungry for blood—off they went looting and pillaging. Confronted by rival gangs, they fought and killed even in the Sacra Via itself, not once, but year after year as the Roman Republic crumbled. And the empire of Augustus only brought an uneasy peace. Social welfare, free food, and free fun kept the excesses down, but it required little—rumor, bribes, stirring oratory—to bring the mobs back into the streets.

When the capital of empire moved to the east, the mob was not lost. At Byzantium it rioted with equal violence, played on by oligarchs and factions in politics and religion. For centuries the mob rose and destroyed, tearing down buildings, pillaging, burning, and howling as it went.

In the summer of 1780, London erupted. By June 7, the city was a sea of flames; the prisons were broken open; the breweries were looted, and the gutters flowed with beer, Roman Catholic chapels and households were first desecrated, then wrecked, and finally burned. Among the rioters at least 285 were shot dead, 173 wounded, and 450 taken prisoner. These, the famous Gordon Riots, were unusual only in their extent. There had been wild rioting, burning, and looting in the 1760's and 70's; in 1733, 1736, and 1753 London had been at the mercy of mobs, as it had been time and time again during the previous century.

Not only in London but in towns throughout the kingdom generations of Englishmen had to learn to live with riots as they did with disease or death. It became a part of the nature of society. Nor was rioting an Englishman's vice; across the Channel they were just as violent. In the 1620's, 30's, and 40's France erupted in bloody riots that, in Normandy, finally turned into a peasants' war. For the rest of the century scarcely a year passed without mobs coming out in the streets of some provincial town or of Paris itself. They wreaked their vengeance on those whom they thought responsible for their misery.

The French Revolution changed the nature of European riots quite fundamentally. The mobs began to acquire more than a directing intelligence (they had rarely been without that) and to fall under the leadership of political strategists bent on using them for long-term ideological ends. Gradually the dispossessed and the frustrated acquired a deeper, a more ruthless, sense of identity, which encompassed violence, tragedy, pain, and even death for the sake of the future. And so the riot became an instrument of revolution. The European towns and countryside became even more violent in the nineteenth century; and England did, too—at least until 1850.

Things got better toward the end of the nineteenth century. Baron Haussmann drove his great boulevards through the riotous heart of Paris, providing excellent vistas for the rifle and, later, the machine gun and the tank. The weapons at the command of authority outdistanced the capacity of the mob to retaliate once the issue was joined. It was not until the 1920's and 30's that the riot was resuscitated by the paramilitary formation of the Fascists, the Nazis, and the Action Française on the one hand, and the Communist Party on the other. The military fanatics having been rushed, riots declined in Europe into protest that teetered along the border of violence but rarely broke into it.

Last spring Europe again burst into flames, with student riots from Colchester to Cracow. Although these riots were usually provoked by academic situations, they are being exploited by acute political leaders. The students have become a type of false proletariat (a California professor has written "a student is a nigger"), and they are exploited as such. Attempts have been made—and with some success this past spring in France —to harness student idealism to the political programs of the working class. These recent riots in Europe belong to the tradition of both radical socialism and anarchism, but they are different in dimension from most American student riots and totally different in kind from the Negro rioting that America is experiencing.

The American riot is, as it were, the grandchild of the classical riot, which was bigger, more incoherent, more desperate—a deeper convulsion in the very bowels of society—than the recent disturbances in Europe. The present American experience is, more precisely, akin to the riots of pre-revolutionary Europe, before the mobs became infiltrated with political agents and exploiters who turned the riot to social revolutionary ends. This stage may be beginning in America, however, and it could develop rapidly.

The classical riot was generally more than a sudden hysterical outburst of anguish and despair. While it lacked political leaders, it did not lack leadership. Usually there were journeymen, artisans, skilled craftsmen, modest yeomen farmers, who made up the hard core of the mob and led it to its targets. Their approach was often direct—to break open the granaries, to lower prices by threats of destruction, or to improve wages or even secure work.

But the root causes of most riots were economic and specific. They never aimed at overturning the structure of eighteenth-century society, any more than most rioting Negroes wished to overturn American capitalism and its social structure. The rioters were out to secure immediate benefits— economic, social, and local—not to start a revolution.

In England in the seventeenth century rioters tore down the hedges with which landowners had enclosed the peasants' common fields. In the eighteenth century they ripped up turnpike tollgates that taxed the movement of their goods. Riots worked more often than not. True, some rioters were caught, some hanged, some transported, some imprisoned: but the rioting mass escaped scot free, often with loot, and many times they were successful in winning their immediate, short-term aims.

So far the American urban riot is working in the same way as its historic counterparts. "A little early Easter shopping," said a Negro woman going off with a coat in the Washington looting that followed the murder of Martin Luther King. And apart from immediate gains there are practical and psychological gains, too.

The practical gain is quite simple. Large physical losses of property scare owners into action. An urgent sense that something positive must be done for Negroes immediately follows riot. It is a sobering fact that, as in the past so in the present, riots rarely fail; the rioters always win—not in the long term, of course, but in the short term.

The second gain is the release of social emotion. Before the nineteenth century the lower classes had little social hope. Societies, as far as they could see, never changed. There had been, and always would be, rich and poor. Riot, therefore, brought revenge as well as a windfall. Men burned their way across the countryside and into the cities in an orgiastic release of hatred and frustration.

To the overwhelming majority of Americans, black or white, rich or poor, a fundamental change in social structure is just as unthinkable as it was to eighteenth-century Englishmen. But as long as the conditions that lead to violence continue, the riot with its emotional release and its material windfalls and illusory social gains will go on and on, hot summer after hot summer, as it did for centuries in Europe.

In most countries of Europe riot eventually turned to revolution. In England, and England alone, riots faded into insignificance in the nineteenth century. France in 1789 led the way; it proved through the Reign of Terror that social change and political power could be achieved through mobs harnessed to a political ideology of social hope—a lesson never forgotten by the French or by the countries to which they exported their ideas. England nearly followed suit—right up to 1850, revolution was possible. Then Britain was saved by the enormous affluence of its industrial revolution in full spate—supported by a dependent and exploited empire—and by the creation of a pattern of social hope for all classes through universal elementary education and full political participation. There were other and more complex factors at work, but these were the primary ones.

America is, in a sense, entering a political phase curiously akin to that of Europe in the nineteenth century, a world of savage social conflict and possible revolutionary turmoil. Which way will riot develop? Will it be molded by revolutionary leaders into a revolutionary movement, dedicated to social change, and if need be to civil war? Or will the riots fade away, as they did in Britain, by the creation of true, not false, social hope and by full, not spurious, political participation? I am not suggesting that the British governing classes made that social hope easily realizable, or that full political participation quickly pried their hands from the wheels of government. Of course not. But classes, like individuals, leap at a glimmer of real hope.

The hope must be real. If time and time again it proves illusory, then the looting will stop, the rioters will become disciplined, ferocious, dedicated, willing to die by the tens of thousands so that they can kindle an unquestionable spark of hope in the hearts of their own people. They will start fighting not for the present but the future.

The long-range cause of rioting is said to be the community's inattention to value conflicts, and the immediate cause is the lack of proper social control. Riots go through definite stages of development. There are clear distinctions between riots, insurrection, revolution, and civil disobedience, but there are relationships as well. Violence is as indispensable in our system as are peaceful acts of civil disobedience, because violence is a last resort when all other avenues for change have been closed or are ineffective. The alternative is to discover promptly the causes of grievances and rectify injustices.

Rioting, Insurrection, and Civil Disobedience

Ralph W. Conant

Rioting is a spontaneous outburst of group violence characterized by excitement mixed with rage. The outburst is usually directed against alleged perpetrators of injustice or gross misusers of political power. The typical rioter has no premeditated purpose, plan or direction, although systematic looting, arson and attack on persons may occur once the riot is underway. Also, criminals and conspirators may expand their routine activities in the wake of the riot chaos. While it is quite clear that riots are unpremeditated outbursts, they are not as a rule senseless outbursts. The rage behind riots is a shared rage growing out of specific rage-inducing experiences. In the United States, the rage felt by Negroes (increasingly manifested in ghetto riots) is based on centuries of oppression, and in latter times on discriminatory practices that frustrate equal opportunity to social, economic and political goals. While all riots stem from conflicts in society similar to those that inspire civil disobedience, they ordinarily do not develop directly from specific acts of civil disobedience. Yet repeated failures of civil disobedience to achieve sought-after goals can and often do result in frustrations that provide fertile ground for the violent outbursts we call riots.

The factors universally associated with the occurrence and course of any riot are the following: (1) preconditions, (2) riot phases, and (3) social control. The discussion here is drawn from a review of the literature of collective behavior as well as on studies currently underway at the Lemberg Center for the Study of Violence at Brandeis University.

From "Rioting, Insurrection, and Civil Disobedience" by Ralph W. Conant, *American Scholar*, Summer, 1968. Copyright Ralph W. Conant. Reprinted by permission of the author.

I. The Preconditions of Riot: Value Conflicts

All riots stem from intense conflicts within the value systems that stabilize the social and political processes of a nation. The ghetto riot is a concrete case of a group attempt to restructure value conflicts and clarify social relationships in a short time by deviant means.

There are two classes of value conflicts, each of which gives rise to a different kind of struggle. The first calls for normative readjustment in which the dominant values of a society are being inequitably applied. In this case, the aggrieved groups protest, and if protest fails to attain readjustment, they riot.

The anti-draft rioter at the time of the Civil War was protesting the plight of the common man who could not, like his wealthier compatriots, buy his way out of the draft. American egalitarian values were not being applied across the board. The readjustment came only after the intensity of the riots stimulated public concern to force a change.

The contemporary ghetto riots grow out of the failure of the civil rights movement to achieve normative readjustment for black people through nonviolent protest. This failure has produced lines of cleavage which, if intensified, will result in the second type of value conflict, namely, value readjustment.

In this case, the dominant values of the society are brought under severe pressure for change. The social movement that organizes the activities of an aggrieved sector of the population having given up hope for benefiting from the going value system sets up a new configuration of values. The movement becomes revolutionary. When Americans gave up hope of benefiting from the English institutions of the monarchy and the colonial system, they set up their own egalitarian value system and staged a revolution.

Now, Black Power and Black Nationalist leaders are beginning to move in the direction of value readjustment. They are talking about organizing their people on the basis of separatist and collectivist values and they are moving away from the melting pot individualistic values of our country, which are not working for them.

THE HOSTILE BELIEF SYSTEM

An aggrieved population erupts into violence on the basis of preexisting hostile belief. During the anti-Catholic riots in the early part of the nineteenth century, the rioters really believed that the Pope, in Rome, was trying to take over the country. The anti-Negro rioters in Chicago and East St. Louis (and even in Detroit in 1943) really believed that Negroes were trying to appropriate their jobs and rape their women and kill their men.

Today, many rioters in black ghettos really believe in the malevolence of white society, its duplicity, and its basic commitment to oppressing Negroes. An important component of the hostile belief system is that the expected behavior of the identified adversary is seen as extraordinary—that is, beyond the pale of accepted norms. In the black ghettos, people are convinced, for example, that the police will behave toward them with extraordinary verbal incivility and physical brutality, far beyond any incivility and brutality displayed toward whites in similar circumstances.

The hostile belief system is connected, on the one hand, with the value conflict, and, on the other, with the incident that precipitates a riot. It embodies the value conflict, giving it form, substance and energy. It sets the stage for the precipitating incident which then becomes a concrete illustration of the beliefs. A police officer shooting and killing a young black suspected car thief (as in San Francisco in September, 1966), or beating and bloodying a black taxi driver (as in Newark in July, 1967), confirms and dramatizes the expectations incorporated into the hostile beliefs and triggers the uprising.

Hostile beliefs bear varying relations to "reality." Their systemization means that in some aspects they are incorrect exaggerations; in others, very close to the truth. In the 1830's, the Catholic Church wanted more power and influence locally, but it did not, consciously, want to take over the country. Today, large numbers of white people want to keep Negroes where they are by allowing them to advance only gradually. But they do not, at least consciously, want to oppress them.

RELATIVE DEPRIVATION

An important and almost universal causal factor in riots is a perception of real or imagined deprivation in relation to other groups in the society. As James R. Hundley has put it, the aggrieved see a gap between the conditions in which they find themselves and what could be achieved given a set of opportunities. Ghetto residents in the United States use middle-class suburban living as a comparative point, and they feel acutely deprived. The areas of relative deprivation for the black American are pervasively economic, political and social.

OBSTACLES TO CHANGE

Another universal causal factor behind riots is the lack of effective channels for bringing about change. Stanley Lieberson and Arnold Silverman, in their study of riots in United States cities between 1910 and 1961, note a correlation between cities in which riots have occurred and cities that elect officials at large rather than from wards. In this situation, Negroes are not likely to have adequate representation, if any. The result is that they feel deprived of a local political voice and are in fact deprived of a potential channel through which to air grievances. An aggrieved population with no access to grievance channels is bound to resort to rioting if one or more of their grievances become dramatized in a precipitating incident.

HOPE OF REWARD

While riot participants do not ordinarily think much in advance about the possible outcome of a riot, still those who participate harbor hopes, however vague, that extreme and violent behavior may bring about desired changes. Certainly the contagion effect had a significant role in the crescendo of ghetto riots in the United States during 1967. Part of the spirit was that things could not be made much worse by rioting, and riots might achieve unexpected concessions from influential whites. Any hard-pressed people are riot-prone and the more so if they see others like themselves making gains from rioting. What happens is spontaneous, but hope raises the combustion potential.

COMMUNICATION

Ease of communication among potential rioters is less a precondition of riot than a necessary condition to the spread of riot, once started. Riots tend to occur in cities during warm weather when people are likely to be congregated in the streets and disengaged from normal daily activities.

II. The Phases of a Riot

A riot is a dynamic process which goes through different stages of development. If the preconditions described above exist, if a value conflict intensifies, hostile beliefs flourish, an incident that exemplifies the hostile beliefs occurs, communications are inadequate and rum inflames feelings of resentment to a fever pitch, the process will get started. How far it will go depends upon a further process of interaction between the local authorities and an aroused community.

There are four stages within the riot process. Not all local civil disturbances go through all four stages; in fact, the majority do not reach stage three. It is still not certain at what point in the process it is appropriate to use the word "riot" to describe the event. In fact more information is needed about the process and better reporting of the phase structure itself.

PHASE I. THE PRECIPITATING INCIDENT

All riots begin with a precipitating event, which is usually a gesture, act or event by the adversary that is seen by the aggrieved community as concrete evidence of the injustice or relative deprivation that is the substance of the hostility and rage felt by the aggrieved. The incident is inflammatory because it is typical of the adversary's behavior toward the aggrieved and responsible for the conditions suffered by the aggrieved. The incident is also taken as an excuse for striking back with "justified" violence in behavior akin to rage. The event may be distorted by rumor and made to seem more inflammatory than it actually is. In communities where the level of grievances is high, a seemingly minor incident may set off a riot; conversely, when the grievance level is low, a more dramatic event may be required to touch off the trouble.

A significant aspect of the precipitating event, besides its inflammatory nature, is the fact that it draws together a large number of people. Hundley explains that some come out of curiosity; others because they have heard rumors about the precipitating event; still others because they happen to be in the vicinity. Some of the converging crowd are instigators or agitators who are attempting to get a riot started; others come to exploit the situation and use the crowd as a cover for deviant activities. Local officials, church and civic leaders come because they see it as their duty to try to control the violent outburst.

PHASE 2. CONFRONTATION

Following the instigating incident, the local population swarms to the scene. A process of "keynoting" begins to take place. Potential riot promoters begin to articulate the rage accumulating in the crowd and they vie with each other in suggesting violent courses of action. Others, frequently recognized ghetto leaders, suggest that the crowd disband to let tempers cool and to allow time for a more considered course of action. Law enforcement officers appear and try to disrupt the "keynoting" process by ordering and forcing the crowd to disperse. More often than not, their behavior, which will be discussed below, serves to elevate one or another hostile "keynoter" to a position of dominance, thus flipping the riot process into the next phase.

The outcome of phase 2 is clearly of crucial importance. The temper of the crowd may dissipate spontaneously, or escalate explosively. The response of civil authorities at this point is also crucial. If representatives of local authority appear, listen to complaints and suggest some responsive method for dealing with them, the agitation tends to subside: a "let's wait and see" attitude takes over. If they fail to show up and are represented only by the police, the level of agitation tends to rise.

How the news media handle phase 2 has a critical effect on the course of the riot. During the "sensationalizing" era of a few years ago in the United States, almost any street confrontation was likely to be reported as a "riot." In the current policy of "restraint," a street confrontation may not be reported at all. Neither policy is appropriate. A policy of "adequate communication" is needed. The grievances stemming from the precipitating incident and agitating the crowd should be identified. The response of local authorities should be described. The adversary relations and their possible resolutions, violent or nonviolent, should be laid out insofar as possible.

PHASE 3. ROMAN HOLIDAY

If hostile "keynoting" reaches a sufficient crescendo in urban ghetto riots, a quantum jump in the riot process occurs and the threshold of phase 3 is crossed. Usually the crowd leaves the scene of the street confrontation and reassembles elsewhere. Older persons drop out for the time being and young people take over the action. They display an angry intoxication indistinguishable from glee. They hurl rocks and bricks and bottles at white-owned stores and at cars containing whites or police, wildly cheering every "hit." They taunt law enforcement personnel, risk capture, and generally act out routine scenarios featuring the sortie, the ambush and the escape—the classic triad of violent action that they have seen whites go through endlessly on TV. They set the stage for looting, but are usually too involved in "the chase" and are too excited for systematic plunder. That action comes later in phase 3, when first younger, then older, caught up on the Roman Holiday, and angered by tales of police brutality toward the kids, join in the spirit of righting ancient wrongs.

Phase 3 has a game structure. It is like a sport somehow gone astray but still subject to correction. Partly this openness derives from the "King-for-a-Day" carnival climate. Partly it is based on the intense ambivalence of black people toward the white system and its symbolic representatives; its hated stores and their beloved contents, its despised police and their admired weaponry, its unregenerate bigots and its exemplary civil rights advocates, now increasingly under suspicion. Because of the ambivalence, action and motive are unstable. Middle-class or upwardly mobile Negroes become militants overnight. Youths on the rampage one day put on white hats and armbands to "cool the neighborhood" the next. It is because of the ambivalence felt by Negroes, not only toward whites but toward violence itself, that so few phase 3 disturbances pass over into phase 4.

PHASE 4. SIEGE

If a city's value conflict continues to be expressed by admonishment from local authorities and violent suppression of the Roman Holiday behavior in the ghetto, the riot process will be kicked over into phase 4. The adversary relations between ghetto dwellers and local and City Hall whites reach such a degree of polarization that no direct communications of any kind can be established. Communications, such as they are, consist of symbolic, warlike acts. State and federal military assistance is summoned for even more violent repression. A curfew is declared. The ghetto is subjected to a state of siege. Citizens can no longer move freely into and out of their neighborhoods. Forces within the ghetto, now increasingly composed of adults, throw fire bombs at white-owned establishments, and disrupt fire fighting. Snipers attack invading paramilitary forces. The siege runs its course, like a Greek tragedy, until both sides tire of this fruitless and devastating way of solving a conflict.

III. Social Control

Studies of past and present riots show that the collective hostility of a community breaks out as a result of inattention to the value conflict (the long-range causes) and as a result of failures in social control (immediate causation). These failures are of two sorts: under-control and over-control. In the condition of under-control, law-enforcement personnel are insufficiently active. Although the condition may be brought about in various ways, the effect is always the same. The dissident group, noting the weakness of the authorities, seizes the opportunity to express its hostility. The inactivity of the police functions as an invitation to act out long-suppressed feelings, free of the social consequences of illegal behavior.

In some communities, as in the 1967 Detroit riot, under-control during early phase 3 produces an efflorescence of looting and is then suddenly replaced with over-control. In other communities over-control is instituted early, during phase 2. Local and state police are rushed to the scene of the confrontation and begin to manhandle everyone in sight. Since the action is out of proportion to the event, it generates an intense reaction. If over-control is sufficiently repressive, as in the 1967 Milwaukee riot, where a 24-hour curfew was ordered early in phase 3 and the National Guard summoned, the disturbances are quieted. In Milwaukee, the ghetto was placed under a state of siege as the Roman Holiday was beginning to take hold in the community. No "catharsis" occurred and there was no improvement in ghetto–City Hall communications. The consequences of such premature repression cannot yet be discerned. Short of the use of overwhelming force, over-control usually leads to increased violence. The black people in the ghetto see the police as violent and strike back with increased intensity. Studies being conducted currently at the Lemberg Center show that in the majority of instances, police violence toward ghetto residents precedes and supersedes ghetto violence.

An adequate law-enforcement response requires an effective police presence when illegal activities, such as looting, take place. Arrests can and should be made, without cruelty. It is not necessary that all offenders be caught and arrested to show that authorities intend to maintain order. Crowds can be broken up or contained through a variety of techniques not based on clubbing or shooting. The avoidance of both under- and over-control is a matter of police training for riot control. This was the deliberate pattern of police response in several cities (notably Pittsburgh) to the riots following the assassination of Martin Luther King in April [1968].

Commenting on the interaction between a riot crowd and social control agencies, Hundley observes (1) that the presence of police tends to create an event, provide a focal point and draw people together for easy rumor transmittal; (2) that the result of too few police is uncontrolled deviant behavior; (3) that a legitimate police activity (from the standpoint of riot participants) will not escalate the incident, but even if the original police activity is seen as legitimate, policemen observed being rude, unfair or brutal at the scene may touch off a riot; (4) success of a police withdrawal during a riot depends upon officials contacting the legitimate leaders of the community and allowing them to exert social control; (5) when officials do not know the community leaders (or no effective ones are available), their withdrawal simply allows the instigators and exploiters to create or continue the riot; (6) the presence of police who do not exert control promotes the emergence of norms that encourage deviant activity.

Hundley adds these further observations on social control factors: (1) the sooner help comes from outside control agencies, the sooner the riot stops, although we think a riot can be stopped too soon, before catharsis or settlement of grievances can occur. Hundley's next point, however, takes this matter into account: (2) the sooner the larger community seeks out real ghetto leaders and satisfies their grievances, the sooner the riot stops. (3) The sooner the audience ceases watching the riot activity, the sooner the riot disappears. (4) The greater degree of "normalcy" maintained in the community during the riot, the more likely it is that the riot will remain small or cease.

IV. Civil Insurrection

When community grievances go unresolved for long periods of time and efforts at communication and/or negotiation seem unproductive or hopeless, despair in the aggrieved community may impel established, aspiring or self-appointed leaders to organize acts of rebellion against civil authorities. Such acts constitute insurrection and differ from riots in that exceptions are riots that are instigated by insurrectionists.

Although insurrection is deliberate rebellion, the aim of the insurrectionist, unlike that of the revolutionary, is to put down persons in power, to force abandonment of obnoxious policies or adoption of desirable ones. The insurrectionist is not out to overthrow the system. (The organizers of the Boston Tea Party were insurrectionists, they were not yet revolutionaries.) Like the civil disobedient (or the rioter), the insurrectionist will settle for some specific adjustment in the system, such as a change in political leadership, increased representation in the system, repeal of an objectionable law, or abandonment of an inequitable policy. The revolutionary has lost hope for any effective participation in the existing system (as had the American revolutionaries by 1776) and presses for a total overthrow.

Civil insurrection is in a stage of civil protest that develops from the same set of conditions that inspire acts of civil disobedience or riot. Riots do not turn into insurrection, although insurrectionists are often encouraged by riots to employ organized violence as a means to attain sought-after goals. The participants in acts of civil disobedience and riots are obviously seen by insurrectionists as potential participants in organized acts of violent protest. Indeed, the disobedients and the rioters may themselves be converted to insurrection tactics, not by existing insurrectionists, but by disillusionment and frustration in the other courses of action.

Civil disobedience and insurrection, both of which are deliberate acts, characteristically involve relatively few of the aggrieved population, because it is hard to get ordinary people to participate in planned disobedience of the law (and run the risk of punishment) or premeditated acts of violence (and run the double risk of physical harm and punishment). Also the various social control mechanisms, aside from the law-enforcement agencies, tend to keep most people from willful, premeditated violence and disobedience. Riots, on the other hand, may involve large numbers of people, many of whom are usually law-abiding, not because a riot is any more acceptable than insurrection or civil disobedience, but because these are irresistible elements of contagious emotion rooted in commonly shared and commonly repressed feelings of frustration and rage. These feelings of frustration and rage are linked to and grow out of hostile beliefs about the adversary, and in the early stages of a riot are inflamed by some incident that seems to be an example of the adversary's typical behavior. The incident becomes an excuse for an angry, concerted outburst, which can spread very rapidly in the aggrieved community and rationalize otherwise unacceptable acts. Law-abiding citizens who participate in a riot are not so easy to organize for insurrection. Persons who can be recruited for organized acts of violent protest are more likely to be those who have already become involved in some form of criminal activity as an individual, private (perhaps unconscious) protest against a hostile society. It may also be easier to organize insurrection in a community with an established tradition of either rioting or insurgency.

V. The Justification of Civil Protest

There is substantial agreement among legal and political thinkers that non-violent challenges to the policies and laws of civil authority are an indispensable mechanism of corrective change in a democratic society. Insofar as possible, procedures for challenge which may involve open and deliberate disobedience should be built into the laws and policies of the system, for such procedures give the system a quality of resilience and flexibility, the capacity to absorb constructive attack from within.

As George Lakay has pointed out, one great strength of democratic institutions is that they build a degree of conflict into the decision-making structure just so that conflicts can be resolved publicly and without violence. Adequately designed democratic institutions deliberately reflect shifting views and power relations of interest groups and the normal workings of compromise and settlement, and equilibrium is usually maintained. Civil disobedience, and other forms of civil protest, are resorted to when political adversaries exhaust means of compromise in the political arena. Then the less powerful of the adversaries is forced to carry his challenge into a legal procedure or to the public in a show of protest.

Agreement on a policy of deliberate tolerance of peaceful challenge does not imply automatic agreement on what conditions justify challenges that involve disobedience. Moreover, agreement on a policy of tolerance toward nonviolent civil disobedience bears no necessary relationship at all to the question of the justification of civil protest involving violence, as riots and insurrection always do.

Nonviolent civil disobedience is justified under the following circumstances:

1) When an oppressed group is deprived of lawful channels for remedying its condition; conversely, a resort to civil disobedience is never politically legitimate where methods of due process in both the legal and political systems are available as remedies.

2) As a means of resisting or refusing to participate in an obvious and intolerable evil perpetrated by civil authorities (for example, a policy of genocide or enslavement).

3) When government takes or condones actions that are inconsistent with values on which the society and the political system are built, and thus violates the basic assumptions on which the regime's legitimacy rests.

4) When it is certain that the law or policy in question violates the constitution of the regime and, therefore, would be ruled unconstitutional by proper authority if challenged.

5) When a change in law or policy is demanded by social or economic need in the community and the normal procedures of law and politics are inadequate, obstructed or held captive by antilegal forces.

6) When the actions of government have become so obnoxious to one's own personal ethics (value system) that one would feel hypocritical in submitting to a law that enforces these actions: for example, the Fugitive Slave Law.

It seems to me that a citizen is justified in originating or participating in an act of civil disobedience under any of these circumstances, and, as Herbert Kelman has argued, that an act of civil disobedience in such circumstances should be generally regarded as obligatory in terms of the highest principles of citizenship. This does not mean that acts of civil disobedience should be ignored by civil authorities; on the contrary, aside from the damage such a policy would do to effectiveness of the act of civil disobedience, it must be considered the obligation of the regime to punish a law breaker so long as the violated law is in force. As William Buckley has argued, it is the individual's right to refuse to go along with his community, but the community, not the individual, must specify the consequences. For the regime to act otherwise would be to concede the right of personal veto over every act of government. At the same time, a conscientious challenge to civil authority (with full expectation of punishment) aimed at repairing a serious flaw in the system of justice is a step every citizen should know how to decide to take.

WHEN IS CIVIL PROTEST INVOLVING VIOLENCE JUSTIFIED?

Americans like to think of themselves as a peace-loving people, yet violence is and always has been an important and sometimes indispensable instrument of social, economic and political change in our national history. We do not need to be reminded of the role it has played in United States foreign policy and in domestic relations.

The fact is that Americans are both peace-loving and willing to resort to violence when other avenues of goal achievement seem closed or ineffective. In our national history violence was the ultimate instrument in our conquest of the lands on the North American continent that now comprise the nation. Violence freed the American colonists from British rule and later insured freedom of the seas (1812–1815). Violence abolished slavery, established the bargaining rights of labor, twice put down threatening tyrannies in Europe and once in the Asian Pacific. In the present day, violence is the unintended instrument of black citizens to break through oppressive discrimination in housing, employment, education and political rights.

Americans have always taken the position that violence could be justified as an instrument of last resort in the achievement of critical national goals or in the face of external threat.

While it is true that we have always felt most comfortable about government-sponsored violence and especially violence in response to an external threat, we have often rationalized post factum the use of violence by aggrieved segments of the population when the cause was regarded as a just one in terms of our deeply held egalitarian values. The anti-draft riots during the Civil War are one example; labor strife that finally led to legitimizing workers' bargaining rights is another. Two or three generations from now, the ghetto riots (and even the spasmodic insurrection that is bound to follow) will be seen as having contributed to the perfection of our system of egalitarian values. Thus, I conclude that violence in the cause of hewing to our most cherished goals of freedom, justice and equal opportunity for all our citizens is and will remain as indispensable a corrective ingredient in our system as peaceful acts of civil disobedience. The sole qualification is that all other avenues of legitimate and peaceful change first be substantially closed, exhausted or ineffective.

When an aggrieved segment of the population finds it necessary to resist, riot, or commit deliberate acts of insurrection, the government must respond firmly to enforce the law, to protect people and property from the consequences of violence, but it must, with equal energy and dedication, seek out the causes of the outbursts and move speedily to rectify any injustices that are found at the root of the trouble.

A study of individuals who had demonstrated their propensity for violent behavior by committing acts for which they were tried, convicted, and committed to a state penal institution found that men engage in violence because they gain satisfaction from it and find it to be helpful in achieving their objectives. They do not respond to tougher penalties, public debates, police hardware, or generalized talk about violence in the press. The control of violence depends upon the removal of the incentives for it and the changing of the motives that produce it.

Violent Men

Hans Toch

The current concern with the problem of violence has increased the demand for explanations and practical suggestions. This climate calls for caution, because it makes us over-ready to supply simplistic formulas that imply easy remedy. On the other hand, we may be tempted to advance over-pessimistic appraisals that consign the problem to the realm of comforting unresolvability. The discussion of violence today contains both types of explanations and is suffused with suggestions that would solve nothing.

Explanations can become merely decorative and innocuous, as is the case with catalogues of correlates or causes. We are not helped when we learn that violence can be produced by biological, economic, demographic, cultural, and psychiatric factors. Such explanations are inadequate, because they have no consequences. In relation to a Violent Man, the import of diagnosis rests on whatever it implies for his fate, and for the fate of others in his life, such as prospective victims. When a person's violence is attributed to anomalous brain functioning, the implication is that a physician can implant electrodes deep into the man's cerebrum, and can convert him into a raging maniac or a semi-comatose vegetable at the click of a switch. To the extent to which our man—now irreparably emasculated—*might* have been psychologically treated or re-educated, his diagnosis as an organic patient is obviously wasteful.

This problem cautions us to the danger of premature classification and disposition. On the other hand, there is equal risk in yielding to the temptation of remaining expansively diffuse. Especially in times of crisis, problems can come to be perceived so broadly that they cannot be tackled, and discussion takes the permanent place of action.

Violent Men do not respond to saber-rattling. They are not affected by public debates, by increases in police hardware, by generalized talk of violence in the press. They are not stimulated or inhibited by the level of vio-

Reprinted from Hans Toch, *Violent Men* (Chicago: Aldine Publishing Company, 1969). Copyright © 1969 by Hans Toch.

lence on television, nor by disputes concerning the availability of weapons. To be sure, some isolated act of violence may be prevented because precedent doesn't furnish a model for it, or because a shotgun to execute it is not readily at hand. But ultimately, violence occurs because men find it satisfying and effective in achieving their ends. Violence can thus only be fought by removing the incentives for it, and by changing the motives that produce it. This requires close-quarter, face-to-face combat with real-life Violent Men.

Violence and the Criminal Justice System

It is often brought home to us that we must know something about the personalities of offenders before we process them. We cannot subject to routine booking an alcoholic or an addict deep in a dream world of his own making. We have discovered the risk of releasing into prison yards bands of predatory homosexuals and raving lunatics.

If the goal of criminal justice is to rehabilitate, the need to consider personality attributes becomes greater than if we are merely guided by concern for the smooth operation of our police stations, courts, prisons, and probation systems. Most correctional clients prove no major embarrassment, but by the same token they are neither helped nor changed. To accomplish the latter objective, one would have to have different facilities available for different kinds of offenders, and one would have to distribute inmates to such facilities on the basis of special knowledge about them. One would also have to treat people at such locations with the aid of more refined knowledge than is now displayed in institutional settings.

In the case of violent offenders, the need for information is greater than it is in other offender groups. On practical grounds, violent persons are extremely troublesome. Many of them resist smooth handling, and when released, they commit the kinds of crimes that reflect adversely on our correctional machinery. To keep our system functioning, it is essential, in the case of these men, to take rehabilitation seriously. And the regeneration of Violent Men is difficult without information about the nature of their violence and of its psychological meaning. Whereas burglars and sneak thieves can be treated without knowledge of their antisocial conduct, violence is a symptom of social maladjustment, and the nature of a man's violence relates importantly to the techniques we must use to discourage it.

One must know more about a Violent Man than the fact that he is violence-prone. If we only know this fact, we are reduced to labeling him, and to secreting him away for several decades. In prison, the Violent Man often becomes a custodial problem, and he may dispense his violence more lethally, if less visibly. He creates a need for physical settings of a kind long recognized as outmoded. He contaminates other inmates and staff by enmeshing them in his violent games. And he must eventually be discharged—

usually as a more bitter and dangerous man. If the Violent Man is a model prisoner, his first assault takes place after release into the street. In such a case, we have accomplished a successful act of storage and segregation. This result may be modest, but it is admittedly positive. The difficulty, of course, is that this result is unpredictable. As long as we only know that a man is violent, we have no way of sorting the nonviolent inmate from the pool of Violent Men.

But are Violent Men not deterred by prison? Nothing in our picture suggests that they would be. To the contrary, in fact: Violence feeds on low self-esteem and self-doubt, and prison un-humans and dehumanizes; violence rests on exploitation and exploitiveness, and prison is a power-centered jungle. It is true that we try to teach inmates that the use of force can only produce more difficulty for them, but we make this lesson far from convincing. If a man harms others in prison, where else can he go? What extremity of discouragement can we furnish him? Many of our own interviewees preceded their discussions of particularly vicious acts with the declaration, "What the hell, I had nothing to lose!" It is an ironic commentary that prison violence is concentrated in the maximum punishment units, where violent inmates are sent from the yard.

The deterrence argument for long sentences sometimes has it that Violent Men will harken to the fate of their imprisoned comrades. This assumption is implausible. For one, violence is private and personal. Violent Men form no community, have no affinity for each other, join no unions. Where they are members of gangs or neighborhood groups, their status and prestige tend to rest squarely on their known propensity to violence. This fact is not neutralized by imprisoning other members of the group. In fact, enhancing the risk of violence would no doubt function to increase its prestige value, and hence, the benefits derived from its exercise.

The chief reason for doubting the impact of deterrence on Violent Men, however, lies elsewhere. It rests on the fact that destructive behavior is the least loss-and-gain motivated conduct of all antisocial activity. The rewards and punishments of violence are measured in increments and decrements to the ego, rather than in terms of future well-being. The perspective of violence is short-term and impulsive, rather than calculated and future-oriented. The Violent Man measures his worth by the distorted criterion of his physical impact, rather than by his ability to pursue a life plan. He has no career to be threatened, no stake to be impaired by prospective imprisonment. Of course, he desires freedom, and he would rather be at large than in prison; but his violence is neither stimulated nor inhibited by such remote and general needs. It is curiously true that deterrence is potentially most effective with those who least require its impact—with rational, career-oriented, future-invested individuals of the kinds who populate the ranks of the nonviolent, law-abiding middle class.

Of course, there are purposes to institutionalization other than storage and deterrence. Ideally, a closed institution furnishes the possibility of carefully controlling a person's environment and of providing him with continuing support and sustenance. It also makes it possible to monitor the person's progress on a day-to-day basis, and to adjust for adverse changes if they occur. Here, it is obviously important to provide constructive support and positive programming. There are no advantages to settings with custodial orientations. To multiply such facilities under the headings of the War Against Violence is equivalent to fighting any other enemy through isolation and news management.

Identification and Classification of Violent Men

A Violent Man is a person who has a propensity to take actions that culminate in harm to another. Such a person can be validly and reliably identified only on the basis of his record of violent acts. By "record," I don't mean his police "rap sheet," nor his list of accumulated convictions. Such documents are fragmentary and incomplete and are confined to unrepresentative acts that have come to the attention of authorities. A man brought into court as a first offender may have initiated scores of violent incidents at home, in the school and in the streets; a repeat offender may have become, on one or another occasion, a victim of fortuitous circumstances.

On the other hand, many persons are currently classified as violent offenders who are not really violence-prone, in the sense of tending to inflict harm on others. For instance, the consummate robber is a professional who is usually skilled at avoiding the use of the weapons he may carry. Such a man must be separated—for purposes of treatment—from the unstable amateur, who may shoot, because of a propensity to be clumsy, boisterous, fearful, touchy, or sadistic. This type of person is a Violent Man, and he must be processed as such. For this purpose, he can be identified through systematic review of his past conduct.

Our law enforcement agencies and our courts must thus make it their business to secure data about their clients' involvements in violence—without regard to the severity or the legal significance of the incidents that are uncovered. This information can be obtained through sympathetic interviewing, through searches of school files, through field surveys and other fact-gathering techniques.

An exhaustive listing of violent incidents can identify a person as a Violent Man. When such an identification has been made, it becomes important to secure detailed information about incidents, so as to categorize the person in terms of the nature of his violence. It is this information which makes sensible disposition possible, provided, that is, that relevant treatment is available.

The Objectives in the War Against Violence

Violence is not an isolated phenomenon, socially or psychologically. "Subcultures of violence" have attributes other than violence-proneness; Violent Men are blessed and cursed with diverse qualities, many of which are unrelated to their destructive potential. To reduce violence it is not necessary to remake people, nor to remodel society. Our assignment is to rechannel or to redirect specific undesirable propensities, without prejudice to the integrity of the persons involved. A more wholesale approach would not only be wasteful but might magnify the very problem it seeks to eliminate. Violence feeds on low self-esteem, and it thrives on a sense of inadequacy. We would therefore have to make sure that we stress to Violent Men that they are not condemned as individuals or as classes of people, but that our concern about their destructive behavior is ultimately governed by our regard for their worth as human beings, as well as by our feelings for the victims of their acts. We must make certain that every Violent Man understands that he himself is the victim of violence—not only because society reacts against him, but because violence is self-defeating. The history of each violent person contains ample documentation to support this case.

Reducing violence among "subcultures of violence" is a difficult process, and our research contains little information relevant to the problem. When a group assumes that certain kinds of violence are appropriate and legitimate, it is obviously sterile to combat this assumption by arguing the case that violence is undesirable. Sermons and speeches that decry violence are viewed as ludicrous and insolent by violence-prone audiences. This is only in small part due to the fact that sermonizers and speech-makers belong to a society that itself sanctions violence (sometimes vis-à-vis the very persons who are told to decry it). The main reason for cynicism lies in the fact that anti-violence propaganda takes no account of problems and needs that seem to require violence in the eyes of its practitioners. Nor does anti-violence propaganda take cognizance of the need to provide substitute avenues for the achievement of group aspirations.

Frequently, society preaches nonviolence while simultaneously reinforcing conditions that make violence attractive to large segments of the population. Ideally, social reform would have to go hand-in-hand with campaigns against subcultural aggression. Wolfgang and Ferracuti have pointed out:

> To intervene socially means taking some kind of action designed to break into the information loop that links the subcultural representatives in a constant chain of reinforcement of the use of violence. Political, economic and other forms of social action sometimes buttress the subculture by forcing it to seek strength and solace within itself as a defense against the larger culture and

thereby more strongly establishes the subcultural value system.[1]

If the resources for direct attack on social problems are not available or not used, society is limited to the indirect strategy of rescuing members of violent subcultures from the common fate of their brethren, and of building them into subcultures that make violence unnecessary for survival. In the words of Wolfgang and Ferracuti, "The personality must undergo a process of weakening of the subcultural ties by means of one of a variety of techniques until allegiance is decreased and a new value system can be introduced."[2]

This process, as I have indicated, does not require complete transmutation of a person, nor does it necessitate complete divorce from his erstwhile companions. Rather, it presupposes some remedial action directed at group aims that are invoked to legitimize violence. At minimum, it involves furnishing substitute means (such as constructive social action, or new career lines) for the achievement of these same objectives.

Unfortunately, however, the task of regenerating Violent Men is far from confined to their integration into nonviolent subcultures. Violent Men have propensities for violence that are built into their personalities and modes of functioning, and the difficult task we ultimately must tackle is that of reshaping or redirecting such propensities. The remainder of this discussion will address itself to this problem.

Strategies for Change

In planning strategies designed to change Violent Men, a number of considerations must be kept in mind: 1. The violence-prone person invites violence-prone interactions with other people. These interactions follow a pattern, in that they arise under repeatedly occurring circumstances, and in that they serve equivalent ends. The object of change must be (a) to reduce the needs and incentives for such games, or (b) to furnish alternative expressions or courses of action.

2. Violence-prone games tend to be played by men who feel unsure of their status or identity, and by others whose orientation toward people tends to be egocentric or exploitative. Such basic conditions should be specifically attended to.

3. Simultaneously, the task of the changer must be to provide each violence-prone person with insight into his conduct, in the sense of making him able to diagnose his own motives. Such insight must be accompanied with retraining, in that the person must be taught to respond to similar situations in different ways. Retraining must be accompanied by rigorous and reliable tests. As long as alternative behavior patterns are not firmly established, the person remains violence-prone.

4. It makes no sense to approach all Violent Men with the same remedial program; by the same token, it is unnecessary to tailor-make efforts

at change individually. Violence-prone persons can be grouped in terms of the nature of their violence; persons who follow the same pattern of violence can be subjected to a common strategy of change.

5. Efforts applied to homogeneous groups of violent offenders are not only economical but may be expected to have enhanced impact, since group pressure can be mobilized on behalf of constructive change, so that "outsiders" are not viewed as primarily involved, and so that individuals can use each other to gauge their own condition and to measure progress.

6. On the other hand, violent games are interpersonal in character, and they can be best modified by involving in the change process not only the violent men themselves but also the partners of their games.

THE PROBLEM OF INTERVENTION

Two facts must be set against each other in considering the problem of rehabilitating Violent Men: 1. If one confines efforts to convicted violent offenders, only few acts of violence can be prevented, because most Violent Men are at large and are unknown to us. 2. The formal treatment of people who have not been convicted, and who merely have a "propensity" to violence, would be grossly unfair and would force unpleasantness on a substantial number of persons whose future violence is merely hypothetical. The first statement implies that we must make an effort to extend our attention beyond the ranks of those Violent Men sentenced to prison; the second premise excludes their institutionalization and raises questions about any programs involving involuntary processing, manipulation, or restraint.

It is obvious that we must take steps to improve our prediction methods, particularly with respect to young boys who will someday seriously aggress against others. But we cannot await the results of such studies, which are likely to consume many years. In the interim, we must explore retaining possibilities of a kind that would invite participation and would not violate the integrity of its subjects.

Consider the case of a mythical lad who delights in forcibly relieving his classmates of their lunches, setting animals afire, and otherwise showing his faith in a two-fisted approach to interpersonal relations. Currently, the boy's life may be studded with summonses to the principal's office, threats of reform school, and impending disciplinary dispositions that carry a heavy nuisance value.

But it might be possible to offer such an individual the alternative of joining extracurricularly an activity or club involving contemporaries who have shown themselves similarly troublesome. In this setting, group discussions of violence could occur, violence-related games could be played, skits or plays could be produced, and behavior patterns could be generated that could meet the boy's requirements for self-affirmation, without its destructive consequences.

The young man thus might be recruited into a career as a performer, or as a member of team sports activities, or as a teacher's aide. Such nonviolent involvements, when combined with self-analysis linking them to destructive motives, could be effective—especially at this early stage—in heading off the development of a Violent Man. And civil libertarian objections would not apply to this strategy as validly as to more formal therapeutic efforts.

In the case of adult offenders, in whom convictions require formal dispositions, limits must be set in terms of rehabilitative requirements. At first, indefinite sentences are probably required, but these obligate us to insure (a) that the time is in fact used, and (b) that release follows rehabilitation. As soon as experience accumulates, success rates must be translated into maximum terms and paroles. Moreover, confinement must always be viewed as a last resort. Combinations of imprisonment and furlough time can be introduced to prevent stagnation, to ameliorate pain, and to test level of rehabilitation in real life.[3] This is especially important for offenders such as Violent Men, whose contact with social reality is deficient.

BUILDING MATURE PERSONALITIES

Probably the hardest task we face in the rehabilitation of Violent Men is that of developing their interpersonal maturity, or—in psychoanalytic parlance—of building their ego. Some reshaping of personality undoubtedly would occur if we simply taught people to be consistently nonviolent. We have seen that the exercise of violence has a cumulative effect, so that the violence-prone personality becomes increasingly warped over time. It would stand to reason that the continued exercise of peaceful options—if we could teach it—could lead to a less immature outlook on life. Moreover, if we could resocialize violent offenders in groups, as an experiment in living with others, one would expect some carry-over in the shape of a less egocentric orientation.

But more direct effort must be expended on the task of converting Violent Men into men in fact, into persons whose chronological maturity is matched by more mature outlook and conduct. Achieving this transformation entails supplying self-esteem and self-assurance to fragile selves that are domineering, blustering, self-advertising, and afraid. It includes the development of concern and consideration among individuals whose outlook on humanity is self-centered and exploitive.

This task probably requires the participation of clinical professionals who stand in the forefront of their field as sensitive carpenters for brittle psychological structures. Authorities of the caliber of Redl, Wineman, and Bettelheim, who have demonstrated the ability to resocialize violent children,[4] should also be involved in the challenging task of restoring personalities at the height of their destructive careers. Institutional climates and routines can be designed to permit clinicians to provide support for immature egos and to build into their patients the controls they need for civilized dealings with others. This sort of climate must include continued monitoring of personal reactions, with interview sessions designed to give every patient insight into his strategies for self-preservation at the expense of others.

Group pressure and feedback can more than supplement professional skills in this area. Sociologists—and most notably G. H. Mead[5]—have shown that the self is primarily a social product. Interpersonal immaturity must be the result of deficiencies in the way other people have supported (and controlled) the growing person in his formative years. If the child is catered to or neglected, the resulting man will view other people as instruments rather than as life-partners; if the child is unrecognized and unloved, the man will be filled with self-doubt and will be firmly convinced of his inadequacy.

Deficits resulting from such deficient socialization should be redeemable through the restorative acts of people bent on rebuilding each other.[6] Groups of Violent Men, given the task of re-educating each other, should be able to function as a "therapeutic milieu." They could do this by reinforcing each other's strengths, by helping each other in joint activities, and by each analyzing the others' roles in the enterprises of their community.

The task can be facilitated by creating meaningful projects in which the men can jointly engage, in which they can demonstrate proficiency, and in which they can practice cooperation and interdependence. The role of each person in such teamwork could be reflected in results obvious to him, as well as in the expressed esteem of his team members and supervisors.

Additional benefits could arise if the work assignments provided skills with market value outside the institution. And it is desirable for the work to be such that the men can build on existing aptitudes and experiences. Although this shrinks the number of available possibilities, it means that rehabilitation can start at the apprenticeship stage.

THE CONTEXT FOR RETRAINING

Probably one of the most direct approaches to the task of retraining Violent Men is to undertake re-educational programs in the context of violence-centered research. There are several advantages to linking self-study with subject matter concern. For one, the focus remains on the relevant theme. If the program is intensive enough, each man can become violence-conscious, to the point of sleeping, eating, and living violence. A related advantage is that of promoting self-involvement. Most violence-prone persons are opposed to violence in other people. A campaign against violence could be attractive to them and could constitute an acceptable means of entry into self-change.

This transition is not only seductive, but logically plausible. The awareness of the Violent Man often is populated with specters of negative pressures. These comprise power-centered relationships, omnipresent threats and fears, threatening and destructive intentions in others. The Violent Man assumes the necessity or desirability of violence in the sort of life in which he sees himself enmeshed. Attention to violence can help to sort this subjective component from social reality and can focus attention on the man's own role and his own contribution.

Another related benefit is the fact that in a research effort, the person can perceive himself as an expert, as well as knowing himself the focus of inquiry. This role can give him pride, furnish him with elements of a new identity, and even provide him with a few marketable skills. It can also introduce new meaning, in the shape of end products that transcend the person's own resocialization. These end products, moreover, are badly needed: case materials on violence are sparse, and the nexus between social environments and individual reactions to them are not easily bridged. Research into violence carried out by persons with experience in the world of violence can shape such materials.

Finally, inquiry is a respectable prelude to change; the transition is natural and easy. The first step toward self-examination is self-knowledge, and self-knowledge is tied to more general knowledge, encompassing the place of one's conduct in its social context. When such information has been acquired, not in the passive stance of the classroom learner but in the role of the information-gatherer and analyst, the next step, of applying the knowledge and of operationalizing its implications, can be more readily faced.

Another possible framework for the resocialization of Violent Men is that of social service work or philanthropic activity. This type of enterprise might be especially helpful in the reorientation of bullies, exploiters, and other manipulative persons. It might help them make a transition from "doing to" to "doing for," without sacrifice of "doing." Self-centered orientations could be undermined, as the person learns to evaluate himself in terms of the quality of the services he renders.

It is obvious that in this as in other types of programs there exists some danger of co-optation. A power-centered view of social relations can be easily translated into social service, as patronage politics and some social work efforts demonstrate. This sort of tendency can be undermined, however, if client initiative and involvement are stressed. Psychodrama, role-playing, and other techniques can be used to insure that altruism does not become transmuted into a system for dispensing gratuities or for accumulating credit.

THE CREATION OF VIOLENT INCIDENTS

One of the difficulties in devising strategies for changing violence-prone persons, and in monitoring their change, is the problem of simulating relevant situations. Obviously, we cannot afford to place Violent Men into the testing grounds of real-life incidents. By the same token, there must be clear relevance and transferability in the trial situations that we are able to devise. These must be subjectively equivalent to temptations and threats, goadings and pressures encountered in the tavern, the back alley, the home, and the prison cell. The stimuli must be intense, realistic, and convincing. The person must become oblivious of the make-believe character of the situation and of its role as a measure of his rehabilitation.

Several techniques are available at this stage. One of these is psychodrama, with scenes drawn from violent incidents in the person's past, and from variations on these scenes. The person can replay his own role, both constructively and destructively, and also that of other participants in the same incidents. He can discuss the implications of his behavior, after he has experienced it from every vantage point. He can carry incidents back to various stages of their origin, and he can explore alternative courses of action and their consequences.

Tapes, kinescopes, and other mechanical aids can be used to keep reactions in awareness, and to focus on relevant aspects for discussion. Such records are also useful for gauging progress or lack of progress. The participation of other violence-prone group members can provide tools for comparative analysis of various kinds.

Counseling sessions can be tailored to create pressures that matter. These pressures can be intense, and they can be meaningful. Having lived and worked with other members of the group for a period of time, each man will regard the others as important to him, and he will have formed special relationships with some of them. Experiments carried out in such contexts can have qualities similar to incidents in the street.

Two types of test situations can be devised; one of these would revolve around working and living relationships, in which roles can be assigned (involving power relationships, conflicts of interest, and issues of prestige and reputation) that carry violence potential, whose consequences the group could evaluate. The type of stress situations used in OSS training during World War II contains models that could be adapted and used for this purpose.[7] Inquisitorial interviews and group problem solving ventures under frustrating conditions constitute examples of mock stress. Leadership and followership roles in these kinds of exercises can be interchanged, and each task can be followed by a review of interpersonal conflicts and their resolution.

Another promising type of test situation has been developed in self-help movements, such as Synanon.[8] Here groups convene in counseling sessions, and members subject each other to systematic cross-examination and prosecution. The substance of the person's defense against such tactics, and the nature of his reaction to attack can ultimately be subjected to constructive recapitulation. This second, reviewing phase (which is not prominently featured in the Synanon use of the technique) seems especially important, because it converts the interaction from one of unmitigated hostility to a constructive and didactic one.

GAMES AS VIOLENT INCIDENTS

In several experiments currently under way in various institutions for juvenile offenders, simple retraining procedures based on principles of learning theory are being tried. These involve rewards for desirable conduct, such as completed work assignments, and they stress systematic praise and other signs of approval. First results indicate that the rewarded conduct becomes established after a time and the young inmate no longer requires external rewards when learning has occurred.

With adults, candy and coins may be merely a source of amusement in an atmosphere of dead seriousness, but they may be effective if taken lightly. No man likes to be treated as a maze rat, but most of us like to gamble. This fact makes leisure time important, both as a period for light-hearted testing and as an occasion for playful training. All manner of games could be devised, for instance, to make violence tempting and to reward nonviolence.

In general, commercially marketed children's games tend to emphasize competitive, retaliatory, amassing and aggressive solutions, to a disquieting degree. Variations on some of these games could place the premium on more desirable conduct. The emphasis could be placed on negotiation, for instance, in situations in which warlike acts are standard options. Reality-testing could be encouraged in game form. Self-defenders could be involved in a game of danger, for instance, in which gains are accumulated by acting in defiance of potential threat and discovering that harm does not exist, or, to be more accurate, that it most often does not exist. Games for self-image promoters and reputation defenders could stress the definition of force as a manifestation of weakness. Self-image defenders could be rewarded for non-retaliatory conduct in the face of provocatory moves, in games combining "Dirty Dozens" with alternatives featuring nonviolent resistance.

Equity, justice, and fairness could be built into some games. In many current games, for example, the elimination of weak opponents is routinely rewarded. This condition could be reversed in games designed primarily for bullies. Players could be penalized whenever they moved aggressively against a position of weakness and could be rewarded for protecting a weak partner against a strong opponent.

The number of variations on socializing games is potentially large and only limited by the ingenuity of the designer. Commercial toy manufacturers should welcome the opportunity of becoming involved in the production of constructive games. However, there is no reason why Violent

Men themselves could not be involved in the creation and building of anti-violence games. If playing is psychologically involving, knowing the principle of the game should not impair its effectiveness.

Although procedures such as these may seem playful and irreverent, they can perform a critical role in re-education. Violent Men play violent games because their nonviolent repertoire is restricted. Even when a violent person is aware of what he does, he rarely knows what he could do instead. In fact, such a man frequently assumes that violence is the only means available to achieve his objectives. Changing his needs is not enough; we must help him arrive at the discovery of new strategies for satisfying needs. Playful simulation enters here, because it represents a painless way to help the player abandon reactions that invite defeat or harm in favor of more constructive ones. Games may succeed where real-life situations fail, because there is little at stake, and there is small risk in rehearsing unfamiliar and untried moves. Simultaneously, games are ideal shorthand representations of life. They bring to the fore rewards and punishment that every Violent Man has encountered, whenever he is not immersed in his subculture of violence. And unlike life, games offer no opportunity to miss the point.

THE INTERPERSONAL SETTING OF RETRAINING

One of the ironies about Violent Men that we have repeatedly pointed to is that they not only play violent games but involve others in the playing of these games. Rep defenders *do* succeed in making innocent targets "lose their cool" and explode with undignified rage; self-image promoters *do* obtain responses in their efforts to challenge others to personal duels;[9] violent persons communicate their fear and resentment to substantial numbers of people and can thus be instrumental in initiating large-scale disturbances, such as riots.

Frequently, social environments are set up unwittingly to make the destructive task of the Violent Man relatively easy. Total institutions, such as prisons, often provide ammunition for the rationale behind violence; standard administrative procedures, such as police practices, can meet the Violent Man more than half way in his efforts to create an arena for violence. Often, the role taken by persons representing the controlling authority may trigger the playing out of a game that ends in violence. This role, which emphasizes physical and social distance, minimal communication, and a we-versus-they attitude, makes it all too easy for the instigator of the game to ignore individual differences among persons in the controlling role, to view them in terms of preconceived stereotypes, and to justify his behavior in terms of the stereotype. We may recall one of our subjects, whose core concern was defending his reputation as a fearless leader. One cannot, of course, be seen as fearless unless there is an enemy, perceived by others as both threatening and powerful, to attack. This man's way of maintaining his reputation among the inmates is to challenge the staff periodically, in defense of his peers. Since challenge invites retaliation and punishment, his attacks on staff are a proof of his fearlessness and he is able to maintain an unchallenged leadership reputation among the other inmates. Staff reaction to his provocations does nothing to discourage the playing of this game. In fact, it only increases its usefulness to him and makes him ready to play it again when his reputation needs to be bolstered.

Other persons use violent behavior to manipulate the controlling authority in a specific way. In these cases authority's reaction, which focuses on the violent act itself and not on its antecedents in the instigator's current experience, is readily predicted. It is this reaction which is the goal of the violent act. For example, an exploitive inmate wants to get out of a situation in an institution in which his game of taking advantage of others has been just about played out. He attacks another inmate in a way that brings minimal risk of harm to himself through the encounter but that makes certain the authorities will be informed. He knows the custody staff games sufficiently well to predict that this incident will get him transferred to another institution. He is right.

For still other persons, the low probability of being apprehended for a given incident built into the control procedures itself becomes an instigating challenge to play out some forms of violence-prone games. These games merely move around the authorities. If the instigator does not want to get caught while engaging in violent or violence-prone behavior, he can be assured that the probability of his being detected is (and even more importantly, is perceived by his peers as being) very slight. In our prisons, control staff admit tacitly (and sometimes openly) that they are not able to enforce regulations and to guarantee the protection of potential inmate victims. What they are able to do is engage in crude detective and spying intrigues with little chance of success for any given incident. The probability of "beating" the staff at any given time is therefore very high. Thus, the looseness within the control procedures and the lack of opportunity offered inmates to prove themselves as men in any other way than "beating the system" provides a climate in which these inmates concerned with proving their manhood rise to the challenge of playing out a violence-involved game.

What these facts imply is that training for nonviolence must involve not only Violent Men but also the standard partners in their violence-prone interactions, including peers, love-partners, authorities, and officials. This extended definition of retraining has multiple benefits. Not only does it alert nonviolent persons to the violence-prone sequences in which they become enmeshed, but it also brings the partners of standard violence-prone interactions into new, more constructive relationships.

Thus, law enforcement officials could be trained as participants in groups with multi-violent offenders who have assaulted officers. Participants in such training sessions could move from known role-playing games to games that spontaneously developed out of these. This would lead, covertly or overtly, to the officials identifying their own game participation for analysis.

In establishing such self-study training, it might be advantageous to work initially with staff and with violent offenders in separate groups, then bring them together as soon as the groups were reasonably comfortable with the method and its content. Such a procedure for working with separate interest groups with the intent of ultimately bringing them together was developed in a community action project conducted by the Youth Studies Center at the University of Southern California.[10]

In any event, as training programs for violent offenders are set up—most probably in the shape of special centers in penal institutions—it is desirable to involve outside staff in them as participating observers. Career correctional staff are often suspicious of new programs that veer from a philosophy of punishment and control, that appear to coddle offenders, and that seem to give scant respect to their own experience and training. Staff experience is as important as offender experience in the design of research and development. If program development is likely to involve shifts in staff functions and roles—and it inevitably will—then it is important not only that staff be involved in shaping the direction of new programming but also that career development opportunities be opened for them as well as for the offender group.

The War Against Collective Violence

In our discussion of riots, it has been suggested that collective violence tends to arise as a reaction against unmet aspirations and consists of retaliation against the symbols of perceived unresponsiveness.

This fact does not invariably imply that we must deal with collective violence by meeting the aspirations of those involved. Some past race riots, for instance, were based on the desire to retain a monopoly on neighborhoods, jobs, and living accommodations. Lynching mobs have sought to retain a social system in which other persons would remain subservient, or (in the case of religiously motivated lynchings) in which one set of beliefs would be universally enforced.

Moreover, the rhetoric of a riot sometimes disguises needs of questionable legitimacy. Some middle-class student rioters, for instance, couch a hedonistic demand for total autonomy in language deploring every evil of twentieth century existence. In other situations, the roots of collective violence are irremediable. For example, a panic may stampede persons to death, where physical safety can in fact not be assured. In such instances, action must be confined to helping people address their tragic fate more constructively, if possible.

. . . [A]t the juncture of collective violence it is no longer possible to set the clock back to the initial steps of riot history, in which citizens approach authorities with requests or demands. The situation of rioting includes various results of frustrated aspirations, such as feelings of resentment, hopelessness, helplessness, low status, and lack of identity. To dispense jobs and other material rewards is relatively fruitless at this stage, because it leaves beneficiaries in the role of passive and insignificant recipients. It thus becomes essential to promote activities that permit maximum participation, increase status, and provide meaningful life goals.

Potential participants in collective violence must be taught to see other means of achieving their objectives, in the same sense in which this lesson must be conveyed to Violent Men. Like the latter, they can be enlisted in the fight against violence, and they can be taught that nonviolent resources are available that would result in more gain and less damage to self and others. This presupposes, of course, that nonviolent means are accessible. Once it becomes true that some group can legitimately maintain that "we now know that violence pays" (the words of a college editor) the basis for such an assertion must be removed. Violence cannot be remedied when there is in fact no other way to achieve dignity and status.

One area of collective violence which requires additional exploration is the role of key rioters. Not only must we abandon the illusion that riots are created by "agitators," but we must face the more positive fact that destructive influences are exerted among riot participants by groups and individuals within their ranks. Such centers of violence-proneness can be selected for special attention and can be converted or neutralized.

. . . [P]recipitating incidents are crucial in the genesis of riots—which implies that such incidents are logical targets for prophylactic intervention. For example, increased flexibility in police handling of street encounters in hostile settings is clearly in order. We know that the answer does not lie in rapid mobility for police egress and the availability of reinforcements; at such junctures, the violence potential of the sequence has often already reached a point of no return, and only the shape of destruction can be affected. The police must learn that "backing down" or "standing up for the law" are not meaningful concepts for the assessment of strategy in the early stages of games of collective violence.

Police Retraining

The police have crucial roles to play on both sides of the War against Violence. Most obviously, they are our assault force and our first line of defense against Violent Men; less visibly, the police become involved in violence-prone games, and sometimes actively contribute to bringing these to a head. Both roles are played in relation to individual and collective violence; both contributions are matters of prime concern to society and to the police themselves.

Our research indicates that the ranks of law enforcement contain their share of Violent Men. The personalities, outlooks, and actions of these officers are similar to those of the other men in our sample. They reflect the same fears and insecurities, the same fragile, self-centered perspectives. They display the same bluster and bluff, panic and punitiveness, rancor and revenge as do our other respondents. To be sure, the destructiveness of these officers is circumscribed by social pressure and administrative rules; but it is also protected by a code of mutual support and strong *esprit de corps*. And whereas much police violence springs out of adaptations to police work rather than out of problems of infancy, the result, in practice, is almost the same.

In addition to the dangers posed by Violent Men among police, a less dramatic but more pervasive source of difficulty is that of police partnership in the games played by civilian Violent Men. We have seen that in interpersonal situations, causation is often unrelated to motivation: a fair, impartial officer can become involved in violence by unknowingly playing a part in someone else's script—and he can do so frequently and reliably. Unexamined police procedures can contribute to the officer's fate. They can do so because their prescriptions can be predicted and manipulated by persons who have a stake in police brutality.

Some prevalent beliefs about the "police problem" are unrealistic, and they can lead to misplaced programmatic efforts. The most obvious such fallacy is the premise that the "problem" consists of personality disturbances among small groups of officers, who can be fired after psychiatric screening and psychological testing. A related fallacy is the supposition that the difficulty takes the form of anti-Negro sentiment and that the solution consists of "human relations" programs, including lectures on Negro history and urban problems, dialogues with black nationalists, social psychology courses, and the like.

It is doubtful whether Violent Men among police officers could be psychiatrically diagnosed as emotionally disturbed. Theirs is not a psychological condition; it is a specialized propensity—a gift for escalating interpersonal encounters into explosive situations. This sort of conduct can be reliably isolated only by on-the-spot observations of on-the-street interactions.

Such observations are best conducted during a man's probationary period. Every recruit's patterns of social behavior could be examined to assess the degree of his violence potential and the nature of his approach to others. The critical question is, what next? If the man proves tactless, or overaggressive, or oversensitive on his maiden patrols, do we screen him out of the force? If we have no facilities for remedial training, this may be our sole option. But it is certainly not a desirable course of action. For one, there is the matter of due process. We cannot demand of a man that he display sterling conduct in an area where he has not been advised what is expected of him. Moreover, since violence-proneness consists of habits and propensities, it cannot be treated as an indictment of a man's worth. On the other hand, the willingness to modify one's conduct is obviously meritorious. And if change occurs as a result, we know that we can count on a promising officer, as well as on a mature fellow citizen.

By contrast, we must consider the fate of persons whom we are tempted to negatively assess and dismiss. It is inconceivable that such a course of action should not damage a man's self-esteem—especially when we already have evidence of compensatory conduct. And a rejected police-man could carry a sufficient chip on his shoulder to prevent his becoming a constructively engaged member of society.

Whereas the conduct of Violent Men among the police is at least partly due to dispositions brought into law enforcement from civilian life, vio-lence-proneness in other officers is largely engendered by police organiza-tion and procedures, and by formal and informal indoctrination. Sometimes, omissions are critical. Steps or policies necessary for sound interpersonal relations may nowhere be spelled out. No one, for instance, may impress on the young officer the need to communicate to civilian spectators the im-port of his actions and the reasons for them. As a result, the officer may take the position that if he is asked to justify his conduct, he betrays his force unless he points to his badge in response. And he can someday pro-voke a riot by leaving in his wake an information vacuum in which rumors can circulate.

Ambiguity in the definition of police powers is a perpetual source of difficulty. Often, an officer discovers that he has much discretion, but he receives little guidance as to its exercise. He may be informed that he can use "reasonable" force, for instance, without being told what this means. To no one's surprise, violent incidents described in police reports often terminate in the use of "reasonable force." An analogous problem exists when officers are instructed to request identification from suspicious civil-ians, but are not advised as to the risks of such a request. As we have seen, much violence results from indiscriminate requests for identification and information.

Police training (both formal and informal) occurs in the shape of general principles, which are far from uniformly applicable in street situ-ations. And verbalizations about police work, of the kind to which every new officer is subjected, are frequently misleading. Experienced officers may impress on the young recruit the need for a uniformly firm approach, or of differential approaches to pre-categorized types of civilians. Universal apprehensiveness about certain types of assignments may be communicated to the young officer, and they may induce panic in many situations.

The young officer may be brought up with myths in lieu of facts and may acquire prejudices under the guise of inside dope. Thus equipped, he may embark on self-destructive patterns of conduct that become established and cumulative.

Police structure can be improved with new definitions of criteria of conduct and with realistic preparation for life on the beat. Ultimately, such information must be communicated through directives and in-service training. The form of in-service training is important. Lectures, seminars, and other passive learning experiences, when transferred to the human relations area, are generally not very effective. In fact, they may increase bitterness and prejudice. More intensive and personally involving methods, such as sensitivity training and community-police confrontations, have more chance of impact, but their diffuseness makes them wasteful as violence-prevention techniques.

Situations that produce violence can be directly addressed, and their resolution can be worked out and demonstrated. Both idiosyncratic and prevalent errors can be subjected to analysis, dramatization, and correction. Simultaneously, successes in explosive situations can serve as positive training materials. (Creative prevention should be routinely rewarded. For instance, if an officer recruits citizens to his side in a conflict situation, or befriends someone who approaches him belligerently, or disarms a man without force, his effectiveness deserves commendation.)

Police training for violence prevention must vary with the clientele. It must be intensive, and indefinite in duration, when the objective is to redeem Violent Men. It need include only two or three sensitization sessions when its aim is to alert the average officer to violent games he will encounter on the street.

In all police training programs, the within-rank group cohesiveness of police can be turned to advantage. To accomplish this end, training can rely on peer pressure, both inside and outside the classroom. Nonviolence must become fashionable, and it must be defined as policeman-like conduct. Men who have been trained can be converted into a cadre for training others. Such emphasis is especially important for the violence-prone officer, who would feel isolated and threatened if he were singled out for individual attention. In retraining violent officers, homogeneous groups could be formed, or the men could be experimentally integrated into mixed (predominantly nonviolence-prone) groups.

In retraining officers, the procedures to be followed could take the form we have outlined for Violent Men in general. For instance, it would be possible to set up research units to deal with the problem of assaults on police officers. In such units, perennially assaulted (and hence, violence-prone) officers would be the research staff. An introductory phase of statistical research and general investigation could be followed by more intensive, clinical work, comprising counseling groups, stress situations, and various forms of simulation. At first, the contribution of the officer to violent incidents could be explored; later alternative resolutions could be worked out and rehearsed. Real-life experiments could be conducted on the street. Tapes, kinescopes, and other mechanical aids could be used, if they prove profitable. In terms of end result, such retraining efforts could produce, as important contributions to police work, case materials and other training aids, administrative guidelines, and in-depth research data.

In a sense, the problem of retraining violent officers presents fewer practical and legal problems than does the rehabilitation of other Violent Men. The structure of the police is such that job assignments are rarely questioned. The problem of skepticism and suspicion is eliminated if the task becomes personally involving and meaningful. And in the research approach, a focus on police victimization would remove much potential threat. The discovery of police contributions to violence would be made by the officers, and this discovery would lead to a natural shift in project emphasis.

There are ethical implications, to be sure, in the fact that the engineers of such a retraining program would be aware of its ultimate purpose, while the officers may only dimly suspect it. But this difficulty is inherent in any act of seduction. The redeeming quality (in all such instances) lies in the fact that aims are eventually pooled, and that free consent is ultimately achieved.

The Police and Collective Violence

One area we know too little about is that of group violence by the police. No observer of urban tensions would dismiss the police as neutrals. Most officers delight in strong measures when dealing with rioters, and most tend to be unsympathetic to black aspirations. This latter attitude is hardly surprising, given the fact that the highest-ranking ghetto aspiration is that of relief from alleged repressive practices by the police. What most officers define as respect, most black militants regard as capitulation to illegitimate force. What blacks view as respect, the police perceive as insolence. In its extreme forms, law enforcement ideology incorporates Blue Power concepts that are fully the equivalent of the Black Power beliefs of militant Negroes. The police outlook, like that of the Negroes, is that of a minority. The police—like the Negroes—feel persecuted and abandoned; they, also, feel that they are afforded insufficient recognition. And since recognition for police-defined law and order is sparse in the Negro ghetto, the police feel offended. They react with bitterness and hate, narrowly suppressed in their daily activities, which on occasion explodes into overt violence.

During cold war periods that precede riots, police violence takes the form of harassment of ghetto militants and of retaliation against persons who show overt disrespect for police; most dramatically, the police tend to punish individuals who express their contempt physically.[11] When riots break out, police resentment takes the form of collective retaliation, frequently indiscriminate and blind. The police may thus arrest anyone within reach, and they may administer physical punishment in the process.

This observation suggests that monitoring and control procedures must be instituted during riots, to prevent the extension of riot motivation to police personnel. Officers must be clearly identified, so as to be subject to accountability for their acts. The discretion to arrest must be circumscribed, and procedures for handling suspects must be detailed. Most importantly, numerous observers, responsible to command personnel and immune to violence-proneness, must join the fighting force to insure that regulations are followed, both in letter and in spirit.

Training procedures in the pre-riot period, and retraining after the riot, must deal with the temptations of collective violence. Incidents of personalized warfare must be dealt with as the equivalents of individual violent incidents, which in essential respects is precisely what they are.

Implications of Our Research Strategy

. . . [O]urs was a unique venture. We approached Violent Men for candid accounts of violence and we did so with colleagues who could penetrate their strange world with ease and familiarity. Our nonprofessional associates were persons we could rely on and whom our subjects could trust. As a result, we secured new types of data, some of which we have presented here. Our experience is susceptible to duplication, not only in research but in operational settings such as probation offices, judges' chambers, and penal institutions. Naturally, it must be made clear that adverse decisions could not follow from interview results; this framework is necessary to maintain the trust of interviewers, as well as of respondents. Another requisite for success is that the professional's premises must be shared with his nonprofessional associates.

Kinsey and his collaborators, among others, have demonstrated that information about controversial areas of human experience can be readily obtained by middle-class interviewers. We could add a footnote asserting that similar results can be secured in various contexts with appropriate personnel. This conclusion is not limited to inmates and parolees; our police researchers were able to document serious problems in situations where the average outsider would be faced with assurances that the system was perfect.

To be sure, appropriate questions must be posed. The closer we stay to actual experience, the more uncontaminated the reports we can expect. Validity is assured if each respondent knows that we are trying to view his actions from his point of view. And the subject's own descriptions of conduct and perception can then be placed in context to arrive at more general characterizations of human personality.

The use of nonprofessional research personnel such as inmates offers new career possibilities for nonprofessionals, as well as advantages to the researcher. It has been argued that technological unemployment must be alleviated by expanding careers in the people-processing professions.[12] This imperative, as we see in the case of research, coincides with personnel needs in the field. For instance, when social scientists take increasing interest in social change, they must rely on linkage personnel to obtain meaningful information from the disadvantaged. And, clearly, penology stands in need of new approaches to persons who are currently stored in correctional institutions. Research participation can easily and cheaply serve rehabilitative goals. (The chances of recidivism among several of our associates was originally very high; instead, these persons today occupy responsible positions in the human services industry.)

Needless to say, the benefits of converting inmates into researchers are not automatic and free of risk. Like professional workers, nonprofessional participants in research must be selected with care. Unintelligent or completely illiterate persons are of limited use, as are social isolates. A cynical, exploitive, or immature outlook can create a poor prospect for programs that have the usual training resources. This is also true of rigidly held preconceptions, though to a lesser extent.

On the other hand, too close attention to selection criteria can produce a staff of quasi-professional nonprofessionals, who may be rejected by research subjects and even be considered a species of Uncle Tom. Not being trusted, they may have relatively limited useful knowledge or insight, contribute little, discover they are marginal members of the team, and develop poor motivation.

Even careful selection will not altogether eliminate these possibilities. The nonprofessional must get training that is not only directly related to research but also can provide him with incentives, support, and a meaningful self-concept. Some of this training may be of the sort routinely encountered in graduate schools; some may be more characteristic of social movements. The nonprofessional researcher must be, in a sense, a "convert." He must acquire a new role, a new set of values, and new models and friends while remaining in close touch with his old associates. The professional merely places others under the microscope; but the nonprofessional must convert his own life experiences into data. While the rest of us can view research as a job, the nonprofessional must see his involvement as a mission or a crusade—or he will have trouble playing the role.

A Final Word

Our view of violence is not fatalistic nor suffused with hope. It promises that Violent Men can be assessed and understood, and that they can, in time, be regenerated. And it assumes that the games played by Violent Men need not end in tragedy. By the same token, a certain amount of tragedy seems inevitable. If Violent Men come to light through violence, their classification and rehabilitation must always follow in the wake of some personal and social harm.

What of prevention? Ultimately, nonviolence presupposes opportunities shared by all and material progress matched by advances in interpersonal conduct. Our observations suggest the importance of civilized child-rearing, of education that stresses selflessness and self-confidence and that leads to positive communication. Our Violent Men, after all, are basically children who have learned to use force as a compensatory tool.

We presume that a nonviolent society has no room for agencies that profit from the exercise of destructiveness, nor for persons who direct its large-scale use. Men who press explosive buttons or who sign bloodthirsty orders are entrepreneurs of violence, and they set the stage for lone operators. The same holds for individuals who coldly plan for inconceivable contingencies, or who produce and disseminate means of destruction. When the roles exercised by such persons have been eliminated from the games societies play, we can attend to our Violent Men with a clearer conscience and a more unambiguous mandate.

Notes

1. M. Wolfgang and F. Ferracuti. *The Subculture of Violence: Toward an Integrated Theory of Criminology* (London: Tavistock, 1967), p. 299.

2. *Ibid.*, p. 309.

3. H. Toch. Prison inmates' reactions to furlough. *Journal of Research in Crime and Delinquency* (1967), 4:248–62.

4. F. Redl and D. Wineman. *Controls from Within: Techniques for the Treatment of the Aggressive Child* (New York: Free Press, 1952); B. Bettelheim. *Truants from Life: The Rehabilitation of Emotionally Disturbed Children* (New York: Free Press of Glencoe, 1955).

5. G. H. Mead. *Mind, Self, and Society: From the Standpoint of a Social Behaviorist* (Chicago: University of Chicago Press, 1935).

6. D. R. Cressey. Changing criminals: the application of the theory of differential association. *American Journal of Sociology* (1955), 61: 116–20; O. H. Mowrer. *The New Group Therapy* (Princeton, N.J.: Van Nostrand, 1964); H. Toch, *The Social Psychology of Social Movements* (Indianapolis: Bobbs-Merrill, 1965), chapter 4.

7. OSS Assessment Staff, *Assessment of Men* (New York: Rinehart, 1948).

8. L. Yablonsky. *The Tunnel Back: Synanon* (New York: Macmillan, 1965).

9. Thus teachers frequently become involved in violence-prone games with their students. See F. Wertham, The function of social definitions in the development of delinquent careers. President's Commission on Law Enforcement and Administration of Justice, Task Force Report: *Juvenile Delinquency and Youth Crime* (Washington, D.C.: Government Printing Office, 1967), pp. 155–170.

10. H. R. Sigurdson, D. G. Dodge, Annette Gromfin, and R. Sanfilippo. Community education for delinquency prevention: Santa Monica Community Study. In *Corrections in the Community: Alternatives to Incarceration*. California Board of Corrections Monograph No. 4 (Sacramento, 1964).

11. W. A. Westley. Violence and the Police. *American Journal of Sociology* (1953), 49:34–41.

12. A. Pearl, and Riessman. *New Careers for the Poor: The Non-Professional in Human Service* (New York: Free Press, 1965).

The Task Force Reports of the National Commission on the Causes and Prevention of Violence comprise fifteen volumes and are based on research by two hundred leading scholars and innumerable hearings and conferences. This extensive study is summarized in a final report. The Commission identifies causes of violence and expresses the conviction that most of the violence can be prevented. A summary of the recommendations made by the various Task Forces is given in this excerpt from the final report.

Recommendations for the Prevention of Violence

National Commission

The Commission recommends:

1. that "the time is upon us for a reordering of national priorities and for a greater investment of resources in the fulfillment of two basic purposes of our Constitution—to establish justice and to insure domestic tranquility."

2. that "when our participation in the Vietnam War is concluded, we recommend increasing annual general welfare expenditures by about 20 billion dollars (stated in 1968 dollars), partly by reducing military expenditures and partly by use of increased tax revenues resulting from the growth of the Gross National Product."

3. that "as the Gross National Product and tax revenues continue to rise, we should strive to keep military expenditures level (in constant dollars), while general welfare expenditures should continue to increase until essential social goals are achieved."

4. that, to aid in the reordering of national priorities, consideration should be given to establishing a counterpart of the Council of Economic Advisers to develop tools for measuring the comparative effectiveness of social programs, and to produce an "Annual Social Report," comparable to the present Annual Economic Report.

5. that "we double our national investment in the criminal justice process, that central offices of criminal justice be created at the metropolitan level, and that complementary private citizen groups be formed.". . .

6. that cities provide "increased day and night foot-patrols of slum ghetto areas by interracial police teams, in order to discourage street crime against both blacks and whites; improved street lighting to deprive crim-

From *To Establish Justice, To Insure Domestic Tranquility,* The Report of the National Commission on the Causes and Prevention of Violence. Washington, D.C., U.S. Government Printing Office, 1969.

inals of hiding places from which to ambush victims; increase in numbers and use of community neighborhood centers that provide activity so that city streets are not deserted in early evening hours."

7. that cities undertake "increased police-community relations activity in slum ghetto areas in order to secure greater understanding of ghetto residents by police, and of police by ghetto residents."

8. that there be "further experimentation with carefully controlled programs that provide low cost drugs such as methadone to addicts who register, so that addicts are not compelled to resort to robbery and burglary in order to meet the needs of their addiction; increased education about the dangers of addictives and other drugs in order to reduce their use."

9. that we devise means of "identification of specific violence-prone individuals for analysis and treatment in order to reduce the likelihood of repetition; provision of special schools for education of young people with violence-prone histories, special psychiatric services and employment programs for parolees and released offenders with a history of violent criminal acts."

10. that "concealable handguns, a common weapon used in violent crimes, must be brought under a system of restrictive licensing.". . .

11. that we "meet the 1968 Housing Act's goal of a decent home for every American within a decade."

12. that we "take more effective steps to realize the goal, first set in the Employment Act of 1946, of a useful job for all who are able to work."

13. that the Congress "act on current proposals that the federal government pay a basic income to those American families who cannot care for themselves."

14. that "a more sophisticated understanding and appreciation of the complexity of the urban social system is required—and this will in turn require the development of new, dependable and lasting partnerships between government, private industry, social and cultural associations and organized groups of affected citizens."

15. that "the President might profitably convene an Urban Convention of delegates from all the states and major cities, as well as the national government, to advise the nation on the steps that should be taken to increase urban efficiency and accountability through structural changes in local government."

16. that "a primary object of federal urban policy must be to restore the fiscal vitality of urban government, with the particular object of ensuring that local governments normally have enough resources on hand or available to make local initiative in public affairs a reality."

17. that "federal urban policy should seek to equalize the provision of public services as among different jurisdictions in metropolitan areas."

18. that the federal government "assert a specific interest in the movement of people, displaced by technology or driven by poverty, from rural

to urban areas, and also in the movement from densely populated central cities to suburban areas."

19. that the federal government must work with state governments to encourage a more progressive, responsible exercise of the state role in the management of urban affairs.

20. that the federal government should "sponsor and subsequently evaluate alternative—in a sense 'competing'—approaches to problems whose methods of solution are imperfectly understood, as is increasingly being done in the areas of medical and legal services for the poor and educational assistance for disadvantaged children."

21. that the federal government should "provide more and better information concerning urban affairs, and should sponsor extensive and sustained research into urban problems."

22. that the federal government discourage further "unrestrained technological exploitation of the resources of land, air and water" and take the lead in encouraging and acting consistently with "a new conservation ethic more appropriate to a crowded urban society."

23. that "those of us who find authoritarianism repugnant have a duty to speak out against all who destroy civil order. The time has come when the full weight of community opinion should be felt by those who break the peace or coerce through mob action."

24. that "when group violence occurs, it must be put down by lawful means, including the use of whatever force may be required. But when it occurs—better still, before it occurs—we must permit aggrieved groups to exercise their rights of protest and public presentation of grievances; we must have the perception to recognize injustices when they are called to our attention, and we must have the institutional flexibility to correct those injustices promptly."

25. that police departments throughout the nation "improve their preparations for anticipating, preventing and controlling group disorders, and to that end to study the approaches that have been employed successfully on the three most recent occasions in Washington and Chicago."

26. that "the President seek legislation that would confer jurisdiction upon the United States District Courts to grant injunctions, upon the request of the Attorney General or private persons, against the threatened or actual interference by any person, whether or not under cover of state or federal law, with the rights of individuals or groups to freedom of speech, freedom of the press, peaceful assembly and petition for redress of grievances."

27. that "private and governmental institutions encourage the development of competing news media and discourage increased concentration of control over existing media."

28. that "the members of the journalism profession continue to improve and re-evaluate their standards and practices, and to strengthen their

capacity for creative self-criticism, along the lines suggested in the staff report of our Media Task Force."

29. that there be a "selective expansion of the functions of the Secret Service to include protection of any federal officeholder or candidate who is deemed a temporary but serious assassination risk."

30. that state and local governments provide "improved protection of state and local officeholders and candidates, and strengthened ties between those holding this responsibility and the appropriate federal agencies."

31. that Congress enact legislation requiring the restrictive licensing of handguns. . . .

32. that the federal government encourage the "development and implementation of devices to detect concealed weapons and ammunition on persons entering public meeting places."

33. that the President (and presidential candidates) minimize the risk of assassination "by carefully choosing speaking opportunities, public appearances, his means of travel to engagements, and the extent to which he gives advance notice of his movements."

34. that the Congress enact "a law that would grant free television time to presidential candidates during the final weeks preceding the national election" in the interest of the safety of Presidents and presidential candidates.

35. that the news media clearly present the complexities of the institutions of government, fully and fairly report the issues these institutions face, and delve into the issues deserving governmental attention.

36. that the news media lessen the attention given to the personal lives of the President and his family and give greater attention to the working nature and limitations of the presidency.

37. that the nation's schools emphasize in American history and social studies the complexities and subtleties of the democratic process; shun the myths by which we have traditionally made supermen of Presidents, "founding fathers," and other prominent persons; and restore to history books a full and frank picture of violence and unrest in America's past, in the hope that children can be educated to repudiate violence and recognize its futility.

38. that "the Legal Services Program of the Office of Economic Opportunity, which already has won the strong support of the organized Bar and the enthusiasm of graduating law students across the country, should be continued and expanded."

39. that all states "should provide compensation to attorneys appointed to represent indigent criminal defendants in the state and local courts."

40. that the federal government and the states "should provide adequate compensation for lawyers who act in behalf of the poor in civil cases."

41. that the federal government "allocate seed money to a limited

number of state and local jurisdictions demonstrating an interest in establishing citizens' grievance agencies."

42. that there should be "extension and vigorous enforcement of the 1965 Voting Rights Act, and intensified efforts to persuade all qualified citizens to vote."

43. that "we should give concrete expression to our concern about crime by a solemn national commitment to double our investment in the administration of justice and the prevention of crime, as rapidly as such an investment can be wisely planned and utilized."

44. that "the Law Enforcement Assistance Administration and the state planning agencies created pursuant to the Omnibus Crime Control and Safe Streets Act take the lead in initiating plans for the creation and staffing of offices of criminal justice in the nation's major metropolitan areas."

45. that we should create and support, with private and public funding, "private citizens' organizations to work as counterparts of the proposed offices of criminal justice in every major city in the nation."

46. that "the President call upon leading private citizens to create a National Citizens Justice Center."

47. that the National Rifle Association and other private organizations devoted to hunting and sport shooting aid in undertaking a public education campaign to "stress the duties and responsibilities of firearms ownership so that a new awareness of the proper role of firearms in American life can prevail in the more than 30 million homes which possess firearms."

48. that because of the risks of firearms accidents, individual citizens "reflect carefully before deciding that loaded firearms are necessary or desirable for self-defense in their homes."

49. that "further research be undertaken on the relationships between firearms and violence and on the measures that can reduce firearms violence."

50. that "research should be intensified on devices to assist law enforcement personnel in detecting the presence of concealed firearms on the person."

51. that "the federal government should join with private industry to speed the development of an effective non-lethal weapon."

52. that federal legislation be enacted "to encourage the establishment of state licensing systems for handguns. The federal legislation would introduce a federal system of handgun licensing, applicable only to those states which within a four-year period fail to enact a state law that (1) establishes a standard for determining an individual's need for a handgun and for the licensing of an individual who shows such a need and (2) prohibits all others from possessing handguns or buying handgun ammunition."

53. that "a system of federal administrative or judicial review be established to assure that each state system is administered fairly and does

not discriminate on the basis of race, religion, national origin, or other unconstitutional grounds."

54. that federal legislation be enacted "to establish minimum standards for state regulation of long guns under which (1) an identification card would be required for long gun owners and purchasers of long gun ammunition (a system similar to that recommended by gun manufacturers) and (2) any person 18 and over would be entitled to such a card, except certain classes of criminals and adjudicated incompetents."

55. that "persons who transfer long guns be required to fill out a single card giving the serial number, type, make, and model of the weapon, the transferee's social security and firearms identification card numbers, the transferor's name and social security number, and the date of the transaction."

56. that "the Gun Control Act of 1968, which is intended to curtail the import of firearms unsuitable for sporting use, should be extended to prohibit domestic production and sale of 'junk guns.' "

57. that "a federal firearms information center should be established to accumulate and store information on firearms and owners received from state agencies; this information would be available to state and federal law enforcement agencies."

58. that "licensed gun dealers should be required by federal statute to adopt and maintain security procedures to minimize theft of firearms."

59. that "the broadcasting of children's cartoons containing serious, non-comic violence should be abandoned."

60. that "the amount of time devoted to the broadcast of crime, western and action-adventure programs containing violent episodes should be reduced."

61. that "more effective efforts should be made to alter the basic context in which violence is presented in television dramas."

62. that "the members of the television industry should become more actively and seriously involved in research on the effects of violent television programs, and their future policies, standards and practices with regard to entertainment programs should be more responsive to the best evidence provided by social scientists, psychologists, and communications researchers."

63. that "adequate and permanent financing, in the form of a dedicated tax, should be provided for the Corporation for Public Broadcasting so that it may develop the kind of educational, cultural, and dramatic programming not presently provided in sufficient measure by commercial broadcasting."

64. that "parents should make every effort to supervise their children's television viewing and to assert their basic responsibility for the moral development of their children."

65. that parents "should express to the networks and to the local stations both their disapproval of programs which they find objectionable and their support for programs they like. We believe that most families do not want large doses of violence on television, and thus we urge them to make the weight of their opinion felt."

66. that there be "an evaluation of the effectiveness of the new movie-rating system with an emphasis on the question of the validity of the ratings as they relate to violence and the enforcement of the admission standards regarding minors."

67. that in "the university community a consensus should be achieved among students, faculty and administration, and embodied in a code of conduct, concerning both the permissible methods of presenting ideas, proposals and grievances and the responses to be made to deviations from the agreed-upon standards."

68. that "universities should prepare and currently review contingency plans for dealing with campus disorders."

69. that procedures for campus governance and constructive reform should be developed especially by the faculties, to permit more rapid and effective decision-making.

70. that "faculty leaders and administrative officers need to make greater efforts to improve communications both on the campus and with alumni and the general public."

71. that the American people do not let their understandable resentment for the few students who foment and engage in campus disorders lead them to support legislation or executive action which would withhold financial aid from students or universities.

72. that the American people recognize that the campus is a mirror of the "yearnings and weaknesses of the wider society" and that their focus ought to be on "the unfinished task of striving toward the goals of human life that all of us share and that young people admire and respect."

73. that "the Constitution of the United States be amended to lower the voting age for all state and federal elections to eighteen."

74. that there be implementation of all of "President Nixon's proposals for reform of the draft system, which are similar to those recommended in 1967 by the Marshall Commission and by the Clark Panel."

75. that "renewed attention be given to the recommendations of the Marshall Commission for building a greater measure of due process into the exercise of draft board discretion."

76. That "in exercising his power to appoint the members of local draft boards, the President name at least one person under 30 years of age to each local board."

77. that the President "seek legislation to expand the opportunities for youth to engage in both full-time and part-time public service, by pro-

viding federal financial support to young people who wish to engage in voluntary, nonmilitary service to their communities and to the nation."

78. that "the President, the Congress, and the federal agencies that normally provide funding for youth programs—notably the Office of Economic Opportunity, the Department of Labor, and the Department of Health, Education, and Welfare—take the risks involved in support of additional innovative programs of opportunity for inner-city youth."

79. that "the National Institutes of Health, working with selected universities, greatly expand research on the physical and psychological effects of marijuana use."

80. that "federal and state laws make use and incidental possession of marijuana no more than a misdemeanor until more definitive information about marijuana is at hand and the Congress and state legislatures have had the opportunity to revise the permanent laws in light of this information."

81. that all our citizens, young and old, try to bridge the "generation gap" by observing the guidelines for understanding and communicating with one another. . . .

Abrahamsen, Davis. *Our Violent Society*. New York: Funk and Wagnalls, 1970.

Anderson, Walt. *The Age of Protest*. Pacific Palisades, California: Goodyear Publishing Co., 1969.

Arendt, Hannah. *On Violence*. New York: Harcourt, Brace & World, 1969.

Baker, Robert K., and Ball, Sandra J. *Mass Media and Violence*. Washington, D.C.: Government Printing Office, 1969.

Bieman, Henry. *Violence and Social Change*. Chicago: University of Chicago Press, 1968.

Demaris, Ovid. *America the Violent*. New York: Cowles Book Co., 1970.

Graham, Hugh Davis, and Gurr, Ted Robert. *Violence in America*, vols 1 and 2. Washington, D.C.: Government Printing Office, 1969.

Gurr, Ted Robert. *Why Men Rebel*. Princeton, N.J.: Princeton University Press, 1970.

Kirkham, James F., Levy, Sheldon G., and Crotty, William J. *Assassination and Political Violence*. Washington, D.C.: Government Printing Office, 1969.

Larsen, Otto N., ed. *Violence and the Mass Media*. New York: Harper and Row, 1968.

Mulvihill, Donald J., and Tumin, Melvin. *Crimes of Violence*. Washington, D.C.: Government Printing Office, 1969.

National Commission on the Causes and Prevention of Violence. *To Establish Justice, To Insure Domestic Tranquility*. Washington, D.C.: Government Printing Office, 1969.

Newton, George D., Jr. *Firearms and Violence in American Life*. Washington, D.C.: Government Printing Office, 1969.

"Patterns of Violence." *The Annals* of the American Academy of Political and Social Science. March, 1966.

Skolnick, Jerome. *The Politics of Protest: Violent Aspects of Protest and Confrontation*. Washington, D.C.: Government Printing Office, 1969.

Wolfgang, Marvin E., and Ferracuti, Franco. *The Subculture of Violence*. London: Tavistock Publications, 1967.

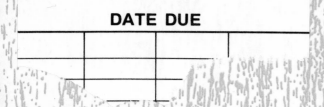

DATE DUE